Securing Livelihoods

Securing Livelihoods

Informal Economy Practices and Institutions

Edited by Isabelle Hillenkamp, Frédéric Lapeyre, and Andreia Lemaître

OXFORD
UNIVERSITY PRESS

OXFORD
UNIVERSITY PRESS

Great Clarendon Street, Oxford, OX2 6DP,
United Kingdom

Oxford University Press is a department of the University of Oxford.
It furthers the University's objective of excellence in research, scholarship, and education by publishing worldwide. Oxford is a registered trade mark of Oxford University Press in the UK and in certain other countries

First Edition published in 2013

Impression: 1

Published in the United States of America by Oxford University Press
198 Madison Avenue, New York, NY 10016, United States of America

British Library Cataloguing in Publication Data

Data available

Library of Congress Control Number: 2013941288

ISBN 978–0–19–968701–5

Printed and bound in Great Britain by
CPI Group (UK) Ltd, Croydon, CR0 4YY

Foreword

The great majority of the world's people derive their livelihood in the informal economy. Over the decades the informal economy has shown a remarkable resilience and vitality. Globalization has endowed it with new importance through outsourcing, and the euro crisis has enhanced its reach further in the European countries, especially in the southern zone. It is therefore of great importance to understand the socio-economic functioning of the informal economy. This book provides an original, insightful, and penetrating analysis of the working of the informal economy, with emphasis on issues of people's livelihood and security.

Based on thirteen case studies drawn from Latin America, Africa, and Asia, and reflecting a wide ecological, cultural, social, and economic diversity, the studies are united in their focus on how people struggle to eke out a livelihood and reduce their vulnerability. The studies break new ground in several domains. First, they are based on original data collected by the authors on the functioning of the informal economy, with the spotlight on the perceptions of the people operating in the economy. Second, the studies are embedded in a novel analytical framework inspired by the work of K. Polanyi. The key elements of this framework are reciprocity, redistribution, householding, and market. The studies analyse the behaviour of the popular participants in the informal economy, with an emphasis on how they perceive and pursue these objectives in different institutional settings.

Among the numerous novel insights and conclusions generated by the studies, we may highlight a few important findings. The principal objective pursued by most participants in the informal economy is livelihood security. Their work and lives are characterized by ubiquitous vulnerabilities and massive risks. It is understandable that in these circumstances they should pursue multiple strategies centring on enhancing livelihood security and reducing vulnerabilities. They pursue these objectives through strengthening social ties, cementing solidarity, constructing relations of reciprocity, promoting redistribution, and encouraging the sharing of resources.

The work in the informal economy is, however, more than a source of enhanced security and solidarity. Beyond that, it promotes participation and empowerment and citizenship. It may lead to collective action in the political domain to defend their interests and claim their entitlements. A few of the studies bring out some gender dimensions in the informal economy. Through working in their own cooperatives and organizations, women strive to attain greater flexibility in work to facilitate their child-rearing responsibilities. They acquire a greater sense of worth and dignity and are often able to enhance their status in the family.

The authors of the book, however, are careful not to romanticize the informal economy. They also point to the negative aspects of the struggle for livelihood in the informal economy, such as exploitation of the weaker elements, the marginalization of the vulnerable, reinforcing of gender disparities, and ruthless competition.

The informal economy is a work in progress. The situation is dynamic and constantly evolving. Participants in the informal economy have to constantly adapt to new crises—economic, political, and environmental—and to seize emerging opportunities. The editors and authors of the book have performed a valuable service in laying bare the social and economic dynamics of the working of the informal economy that provides livelihood and much more to billions of people around the world. They have also provided vital information to guide global and national policy to improve the well-being of those deriving their livelihood from the informal economy.

Dharam Ghai

Acknowledgements

This book is the outcome of an international conference on *Informal Economy, Vulnerabilities and Employment* organized by the Institute of Socioeconomics, University of Geneva, on 9–10 February 2012. We wish to thank, first of all, Professor Michel Oris, Sandra Constantin, and Nathalie Blanc from the Centre for the Interdisciplinary Study of Gerontology and Vulnerabilities of the University of Geneva (CIGEV) for their crucial roles in the launch, and scientific and administrative organization of the conference. We also gratefully acknowledge the participation, notably in the Scientific Committee and the moderation of the sessions, of researchers from the Swiss National Centre of Competence in Research 'LIVES—Overcoming Vulnerability: Life Course Perspectives', the Catholic University of Louvain (in particular the Interdisciplinary Research Centre on Work, State and Society and the Centre for Development Studies), the International Labour Organization, the European Social Network in Social Economy (EMES), Oxford University School of Interdisciplinary Area Studies, and the Graduate Institute of International and Development Studies (Geneva). In addition, the guest speakers, Professor Yves Flückiger, Vice-Rector of the University of Geneva, and Professor Barbara Harriss-White from the University of Oxford provided some valuable insights. Both the conference and the publication of this book would not have been possible without the financial support of the General Funds of the University of Geneva, the Swiss Academy of Humanities and Social Sciences, the Swiss Sociological Association and CIGEV. Their contributions are also gratefully acknowledged and appreciated. Acknowledgement and thanks are due to Praveen Bhalla for editing this book. Finally, we also thank two anonymous reviewers and the OUP commissioning editor for their helpful suggestions. The findings, interpretations, and conclusions of this book are entirely those of the authors, and do not necessarily represent the views of their respective institutions.

Contents

List of Boxes xi
List of Figures xiii
List of Tables xv
Notes on Contributors xvii

1. Introduction: Informal Economy, Vulnerabilities, and Popular Security-Enhancing Practices 1
Isabelle Hillenkamp, Frédéric Lapeyre, and Andreia Lemaître

Part I. A Plurality of Socio-Economic Logics: New Polanyian Approaches to Informality and Vulnerability

2. 'Popular Cooperatives' and Local Development in South-East Brazil: Towards Socio-Economic Pluralism 25
Andreia Lemaître

3. Solidarity and Protection in Bolivian Popular Economy 47
Isabelle Hillenkamp

4. Self-Managed Work, Social Protection, and Community Development: The Case of the UST Cooperative (Argentina) 64
Gonzalo Vázquez

5. An Analysis of the Socio-Economic Logics Underpinning Formal and Informal Strategies for Coping with Economic Hardships in South Kivu, Democratic Republic of the Congo 78
Maïté le Polain and Marthe Nyssens

Part II. The Role of Financial Practices and Institutions in Securing Livelihoods

6. Financial Practices as Adaptations to Increasing Vulnerability: The Dynamics of Solidarity and Protection in the Suburbs of Rosario, Argentina 99
Hadrien Saiag

7. Microcredit Policies in Brazil: An Analysis of Community Development Banks 115
Genauto Carvalho de França Filho, Ariádne Scalfoni Rigo, and Jeová Torres Silva Júnior

8. Demand for Microcredit, Informal Finance and Vulnerability in Rural Morocco 132
Solène Morvant-Roux, Isabelle Guérin, and Marc Roesch

9. Informal and Formal Microfinance in Urban Sub-Saharan African Markets: The Case of Micro-Entrepreneurs in Ouagadougou, Burkina Faso 147
Pierre-Germain Umuhire and Marthe Nyssens

10. Exploring the Black-Box of Economic Informality: Social Networks and Institutional Change among Micro and Small Enterprises in Nairobi, Kenya 167
Edoardo Totolo

Part III. Formalizing the Informal? A Critical Assessment

11. Determinants of Earnings in Informal Self-Employment: The Case of Ghana 191
James Heintz and Lynda Pickbourn

12. From the Street to the Store: The Formalization of Street Vendors in Quito, Ecuador 214
Sergio Ferragut and Georgina M. Gómez

13. Formalizing the Informal in Rwanda: From Artisanal to Modern Brick and Tile Ovens 235
An Ansoms and Jude Murison

14. Neoliberal Reforms, Regulatory Change, and the Informal Economy: The Case of Turkey from a Comparative Perspective 254
Basak Kus

Postface: Another Look at the Informal Sector, its Many Stakes and Challenges 274
Jean-Philippe Peemans

Index 293

List of Boxes

2.1 Multidimensional grid for the analysis of economic initiatives 28
3.1 Evolution of the criteria for measuring the informal economy in Bolivia 49
3.2 Evolution of social policies in Bolivia following the structural adjustment programme of 1985 52
9.1 Informal financial mechanisms used in the markets of Ouagadougou 152

List of Figures

2.1	External economic relations of politically driven popular cooperatives (average percentage share in total resources)	39
2.2	External economic relations of market-driven popular cooperatives (average percentage share in total resources)	42
9.1	Micro-entrepreneurs' enrolment rates with financial providers (per cent)	152
9.2	Micro-entrepreneurs' access to formal credit (per cent)	153
9.3	Use of both informal and formal finance (per cent)	153
9.4	Evolution in enrolment rates (per cent)	154
9.5	Purposes for using informal finance by micro-entrepreneurs (per cent)	160
9.6	Purposes for using informal finance by micro-entrepreneurs combining informal and formal (per cent)	161
9.7	Micro-entrepreneurs' use of formal credit (per cent)	162
9.8	Micro-entrepreneurs' use of informal financial resources (per cent)	163
10.1	Entrepreneurs' use of informal financial networks	178
10.2	Sources of start-up capital (per cent)	180
12.1	The formalization process	231
14.1	Informality in the Turkish economy (1980–95)	265
14.2	Economic informality in transition economies as a per cent of GDP	268

List of Tables

1.1	Polanyi's principles of economic integration as modalities of interdependence in production, financing, exchange or transfer, and consumption	5
1.2	From modernization theories to institutionalist approaches	8
2.1	Resources mix of the politically driven popular cooperatives, 2007 (percentage of total resources)	38
2.2	Resources mix of the market-driven popular cooperatives, 2007 (percentage of total resources)	41
2.3	Main results of the in-depth analysis of popular cooperatives: comparison of the two clusters	43
3.1	Indicators of vulnerability of the Bolivian informal economy	50
3.2	Summary of the vulnerabilities, protection practices, and principles of economic integration analysed in El Alto	60
8.1	Take-up rate variation across regions	136
8.2	Interviews: detailed sample	137
8.3	Branches included in the sample and take-up rates	137
8.4	Typology of visited branches according to eco-type systems	143
9.1	Summary statistics of the micro-entrepreneurs' characteristics	150
9.2	Description of the clusters	156
9.3	Marginal effects obtained from multinomial logit	157
9.4	An overview of the financial flows of the micro-entrepreneurs over the 12 months prior to the survey	159
10.1	Use of formal and informal financial instruments by households in three small urban centres (per cent)	174
10.2	Characteristics of the three research locations	177
10.3	Participation of men and women in different types of financial networks and average yearly contributions	180
10.4	Accounts and loans from commercial banks, by location	182
10.5	Accounts and loans from commercial banks, by gender	182
10.6	Use of MFI accounts and loans, by research location	183

11.1 Structure of employment in Ghana, 2005–6 (per cent) 195

11.2 Characteristics of operators of non-agricultural household enterprises (per cent) 195

11.3 Sources of start-up finance and sector of activity by enterprise, 2005–6 (per cent) 196

11.4 Median monthly earnings and assets of non-agricultural household enterprises, 2005–6 (thousands of cedis) 202

11.5 Definitions of independent variables used 204

11.6 Determinants of hourly earnings 206

11.7 Determinants of monthly income from non-agricultural household enterprises 208

11.8 Estimated coefficients and standard errors for the inverse Mills ratio, Heckman two-step selection models (standard errors in parentheses) 210

12.1 The dimensions of security and indicators used 218

12.2 Popular shopping centres in Quito after formalization (as of August 2009) 221

12.3 Analysis of dimensions of decent work before and after formalization 225

13.1 Comparative analysis of wage rates for different categories of labour in the brick and tile business 242

13.2 Roles of various socio-economic categories in the brick and tile business 247

14.1 Economic liberalization in transition economies (1989–97) 267

14.2 Legal effectiveness in transition economies 269

Notes on Contributors

An Ansoms is Assistant Professor of Development Studies at the Catholic University of Louvain, Belgium. She holds a PhD in Economics and is involved in research on poverty and inequality in the Great Lakes Region in Africa. She focuses particularly on the challenges to rural development and pro-poor growth in land-scarce (post-) conflict environments. Other areas of research interest include the problems related to large-scale land acquisitions and the causes and consequences of the recent food crises. Some of her more recent articles have been published in *Food Policy, European Journal of Development Research, African Affairs, African Studies Review, Journal of Modern African Studies*, and *Review of African Political Economy*. She co-edited a book entitled *Natural Resources and Local Livelihoods in the Great Lakes Region: A Political Economy Perspective*, published in 2011.

Genauto Carvalho de França Filho is a Professor in the PhD Program in Management and in the Master's Program in Development and Social Management, as well as Coordinator of the Technology Incubator in Economics Solidarity and Management of Territorial Development (ITES/UFBA) at the Universidade Federal da Bahia (UFBA), Brazil. After graduating in Business Administration from UFBA, he obtained a Master's degree in Business Administration from UFBA and a PhD in Sociology from Université de Paris VII. His work and research cover the fields of organizational studies and economic anthropology, with specific reference to the solidarity economy.

Sergio Ferragut has worked in the area of international development since 2000, when he began working at the United Nations. In 2006, he completed a Bachelor's degree at Hunter College (City University of New York), majoring in Political Science and Economics. In 2008, he moved to The Hague to pursue a Master's programme in Development Studies at the Institute of Social Studies, where his research focused on the role of local governments in leading and enabling processes of local development, the informal economy, and the use of sports programmes for peace and development. He recently completed a Certificate in Project Management at New York University.

Dharam Ghai was Director of the United Nations Research Institute for Social Development (UNRISD) from 1987 to 1997. Prior to that, he was Head of Research at the World Employment Programme of the International Labour Organization following his role as Director of the Institute for Development Studies at the University of Nairobi. He is an author/editor of several books and numerous articles on a wide range of development issues, particularly poverty, employment, rural development, and social dimensions of structural adjustment and environment. He is now a consultant based in Geneva.

Georgina M. Gómez is Lecturer in Institutions and Local Development at the Institute of Social Studies, The Hague, the Netherlands. She holds a PhD in Development Studies. Some of her more recent articles include 'What was the deal for the participants of the Argentine local currency systems?' published in *Environment & Planning*, and 'Selective spatial closure and local economic development: What do we learn from the Argentine local currency systems?' (co-authored with A. H. J. Helmsing) published in *World Development*. She has also written a book entitled *Argentina's Parallel Currency: The Economy of the Poor.*

Isabelle Guérin is a Research Fellow at the Institute of Research for Development, Paris I Sorbonne (Research Unit Development and Societies). Her research covers the political and moral economy of debt and finance, particularly in India and North and West Africa, with a specific focus on gender issues in debt and finance. Her most recent books include *Femmes, économie et développement* (co-edited with Madeleine Hersent and Laurent Fraisse) and *India's Unfree Workforce—Old and New Practices of Labour Bondage* (co-edited with Jan Breman and Aseem Prakash). Her work has also been published in the following journals: *World Development, Development and Change, Journal of International Development, Economic and Political Weekly*, and *Global Labour Journal*, as well as in various French journals on development studies.

James Heintz is Research Professor at the Political Economy Research Institute, University of Massachusetts, Amherst, US. He holds a PhD in Economics from the University of Massachusetts. His main recent published works include (with Imraan Valodia) the chapter, 'The informal self-employed in Africa' in *The Oxford Companion to the Economics of Africa* (forthcoming); the chapter, 'Employment, poverty, and inclusive development in Africa: Policy choices in the context of widespread informality' in *The Political Economy of Africa* (forthcoming); and 'Revisiting informal employment and segmentation in the South African labour market' (with Dorrit Posel), in the *South African Journal of Economics*, as well as the book, *An Employment-Targeted Economic Program for Kenya* (with Robert Pollin and Mwangi wa Githinji).

Isabelle Hillenkamp is Research Associate at the Institute of Socio-Economics (Department of Sociology), University of Geneva, attached to the Swiss National Centre of Competence in Research LIVES. Her research focuses on the informal and popular economy in Latin America, with particular interest in community and solidarity projects. Before joining the University of Geneva, she was a post-doctoral researcher at the University San Andres of La Paz (Bolivia) and the National Conservatory of Arts and Crafts (CNAM) in Paris. She holds a PhD in Development Studies from the Graduate Institute of International and Development Studies, Geneva.

Basak Kus is Assistant Professor at the Department of Sociology, Wesleyan University, US. Her research focuses on comparative political economy and the sociology of markets. Prior to that, Dr Kus worked as a post-doctoral researcher at Yale and Princeton Universities and then as a Lecturer in the School of Politics at University College Dublin. She holds a PhD in Sociology from the University of California at Berkeley. Her articles have been published in *Socio-Economic Review, International Journal of Comparative Sociology, International Sociology*, and *European Journal of Turkish Studies*.

Frédéric Lapeyre is informal economy team leader and Manager of the ILO Technical Cooperation Project 'Promoting Youth Employment in Katanga', International Labour Organization. He holds a PhD in Development Studies. Previously he was Professor at the Catholic University of Louvain, Belgium, Chairman of the Belgium Post-Graduate School for Development Studies, and Fulbright Post-doctoral Fellow at Brown University (Watson Institute for International Studies). His main recently published works include *The Contributions of the United Nations to Development Theory and Practices* (with R. Jolly, L. Emmerij, and D. Ghai); *Poverty and Exclusion in a Global World* (with A. Bhalla); 'Mondialisation, néo-modernisation et "devenirs": Un autre regard sur les pratiques populaires', in *La mondialisation contre le développement durable* (edited by G. Froger); *Growth, Employment and Decent Work in Namibia: A Situation Analysis* (with G. Kanyenze).

Andreia Lemaître is a socio-economist and Assistant Professor of Development Studies at the Catholic University of Louvain, Belgium. She holds a PhD in political and social sciences from that University and from the Conservatoire National des Arts et Métiers, France. She was also a Post-doctoral Fellow at the International Institute of Social Studies (ISS) of Erasmus University Rotterdam in The Hague. She is a member of the Centre for Development Studies (DVLP) and of the Interdisciplinary Research Centre on Work, State and Society (CIRTES). Her research focuses on popular and solidarity-based economy in the South, mainly in Latin America, and on substantive approaches to the economy. She teaches, notably, 'Development Theories', 'History and Streams of the Economic Thought', and 'Development Projects Management and Analysis'.

Maïté le Polain is an economist who graduated from the Catholic University of Louvain, Belgium. She worked for the Belgian Health Care Knowledge Centre (KCE) before joining various humanitarian and development organizations. In 2011, she worked as a researcher in South Kivu, Democratic Republic of the Congo, for the Catholic University of Louvain (UCL) in partnership with the University of Bukavu. She went back to Belgium in October 2012 and started a PhD in Development Studies at UCL.

Solène Morvant-Roux is Assistant Professor at the Department of Political Economy, University of Fribourg, Switzerland. She is also Associate Researcher at the Centre for European Research in Microfinance (CERMI). Her research interests range from financial inclusion in rural areas and debt as a social institution, to migration dynamics in Mexico and Morocco.

Jude Murison is a graduate of the Universities of York and Edinburgh, and holds a doctorate in Politics and International Studies from the University of Warwick. Her research focuses on human rights, forced migration, health and agricultural production, and on examining the interplay of national policies and laws, and how they are implemented on the ground. She is currently Senior Research Fellow at the Institute of Development Policy and Management (IOB), University of Antwerp, Belgium.

Marthe Nyssens is a socio-economist and Professor at the Catholic University of Louvain, Belgium, where she is also the coordinator of a research team on Third Sector and Social Policies at the Centre Interdisciplinaire de Recherches Travail-Etat-Société (CIRTES). Her work focuses on conceptual approaches to the Third Sector, both in developed and developing countries, as well as on the links between organizations and public policies in that sector. She teaches social policies and development theories at various non-profit organizations, and also conducts research and several studies for national, regional, and European government units. She is a member of the Board of Directors of the European Research Network, EMES, and the author of several journal articles and books, both in French and English.

Jean-Philippe Peemans is Ordinary Professor Emeritus, Catholic University of Louvain, Belgium, where he has been President of the Institute of Development Studies. His topics of teaching, research, and publications have been mainly in the fields of Development Theory and Policies, in Comparative Development History, and in African and Asian Studies. He is currently involved in an interdisciplinary research into the relations and interactions between the urban and rural popular actors in East and South East Asia.

Lynda Pickbourn is Assistant Professor of Economics at Keene State College in New Hampshire, US. Her research interests are in African economic development and feminist economics. Her current research examines the role of gendered social norms in shaping migration outcomes in rural households in northern Ghana. She is also interested in the determinants of employment and earnings in Ghana's informal economy. She graduated from the University of Ghana, and holds an MA and PhD from the University of Massachusetts, Amherst, US.

Marc Roesch is an agronomist with a PhD in Agro-Economics from the University of Montpellier (France). He has worked for more than twenty years in Africa and Asia. Since 1999 he has focused on the socio-economic aspects of finance for agriculture. His research is oriented towards microfinance in Africa, and in countries such as Morocco, Madagascar, and India. He spent three years (2005–8) in South India conducting research on the evolution of informal finance, indebtedness, poverty, and financial inclusion.

Hadrien Saiag studied economics, socioeconomics, and development studies at the University Paris-Dauphine and the Ecole des Hautes Etudes en Sciences Sociales (EHESS). He is currently Post-doctoral Fellow at the University of Pretoria (Human Economy program). He is the author of 'Les pratiques financières des milieux populaires de Rosario (Argentine) à l'aune du démantèlement du rapport salarial fordiste' (*Revue Française de Socio-Economie*, n°8), and a PhD dissertation (*Le* trueque *argentin au prisme de la dette: Une socioéconomie des pratiques monétaires et financières*). His current research is on financial practices of low-income households in Argentina and Cuba.

Ariádne Scalfoni Rigo is Professor at the Escola de Administração da Universidade Federal da Bahia (UFBA), Brazil. He is also a member of the Technology Incubator in Solidarity Economy and Management of Territorial Development (ITES/UFBA). He graduated in Cooperative Administration from the Universidade Federal de Viçosa, holds a Master's degree in Business Administration from the Universidade Federal de Pernambuco and is a doctoral student at the PhD Program in Management at Universidade Federal da Bahia (UFBA). His research and studies cover the areas of solidarity economy and finance, social currencies, and local development.

Jeová Torres Silva Júnior is Professor at the Universidade Federal do Ceará (Campus Cariri), Brazil. He graduated in Business Administration from the Universidade do Estado do Ceará (UECE), holds a Master's degree in Business Administration from Universidade Federal da Bahia (UFBA), and is a doctoral student in the PhD Program in Management at UFBA. He is coordinator of the research group, Interdisciplinary Laboratory of Studies in Social Management (LIEGS/UFC Cariri). His work and research cover the fields of social management, solidarity economy, and social organizations.

Edoardo Totolo is a PhD candidate in social sciences at the University of Trento, Italy, and a Research Associate at the Institute for Development Studies, University of Nairobi. He holds a Bachelor's degree in International Economics from the University of Verona, Italy, and a Master's degree in international development from the University of Amsterdam, the Netherlands. His current research focuses on private-sector development, entrepreneurship, and institutional change in informal markets in Kenya. He is currently based in Nairobi.

Pierre-Germain Umuhire is a PhD candidate in Economics at the Louvain School of Economics, Catholic University of Louvain, Belgium. He holds a Master's degree in International and Development Economics and a Research Master's degree in Economics from the Facultés Notre Dame de la Paix (FUNDP). His research interests include informal finance and microfinance in developing economies, particularly in sub-Saharan Africa.

Gonzalo Vázquez has been a Professor at Instituto del Conurbano (ICO), Universidad Nacional de General Sarmiento (UNGS), since 2001. He has also been Professor at Universidad Nacional de Luján (UNLU) since 2005, and Professor at Universidad Nacional de Moreno (UNM) since 2010. He holds a Master degree in Social Economy (MAES) from UNGS and a Bachelor's degree in Economics from Universidad de Buenos Aires (UBA), Argentina. His main research areas include urban economic systems, the popular economy, and the social and solidarity-based economy.

1

Introduction: Informal Economy, Vulnerabilities, and Popular Security-Enhancing Practices

Isabelle Hillenkamp, Frédéric Lapeyre, and Andreia Lemaître

The post-war modernization paradigm was a vast campaign which, by offering a single, straight path to development based on the experiences of developed countries (Rostow, 1960) and on the normative discourse on what should be a 'modern' man (Lerner, 1958), denied that people around the world could have different 'futures'. The symbolic violence of that paradigm, which dominated the development policy agenda on both sides during the Cold War, was to brush aside all the wealth and cultural diversity of societies and social practices. However, the 'universal' process of (neo)modernization has always 'leaked' from many spots, as an analysis of the processes of real development shows. It has been marked by a diversity of dynamics of social change resulting from the confrontation of the practices of popular actors in the informal economy and the modernizing offensives of the elites, which are endangering the structures of the everyday lives of the former (Peemans, 2002).

Contrary to the myths of convergence or the end of history associated with theories of modernization, popular practices in the informal economy are the most visible sign of spheres of autonomy which populations are managing to preserve or recreate for the management of resources, and for the organization of work, production methods, and lifestyles (Lapeyre, 2006; Sanyal, 2007). A radical new look at these 'forgotten actors' of modernization theories, that is, those who have long been regarded as non-actors in development, necessarily leads to a substantially different idea of the current debate on poverty reduction and the transition towards formality. Such a paradigm shift requires heterodox analytical frameworks to address the challenges of the informal economy for socio-economic development.

From this perspective, it is crucial to open the black box of the inner logic of the informal economy to better understand the functioning of its units, their modes of accumulation, and security-enhancing practices. While conventional approaches to the formal economy consider the market as the main matrix for economic actions (Nyssens, 2000), substantive approaches aim to study, without any a priori ranking, the various forms of coexisting economic logic within the informal economy and how they interact. In other words, informal economy actors are not only driven by cost and efficiency considerations, but also by other considerations such as risk minimization, livelihood security, and preservation of social ties, and their practices are the result of complex compromises between those different and sometimes competing considerations. Moreover, socio-economic practices within the informal economy interact with public policies and mainstream development strategies that have various impacts on communities' socio-economic environment.

1.1 From Modernization Theories to Institutionalist Approaches

Modernization theories have merely focused at length on the misery, impotence and, above all, the harm caused by tangential practices and stratagems within the informal economy, viewing them as marks of a traditional world that should disappear. Modernization theory assumes that 'traditional' or peasant societies do not change by themselves, that is, without external intervention to stamp its mark and sow and nurture the seeds of modernity. Supposedly, only this will lead—through appropriate structural policies—to the systemic transition from underdevelopment to development. Most of the abundant mainstream literature about the informal economy is based on the implicit assumption that development occurs through the growth of the formal, modern economy. The informal economy is viewed as an employment sector of last resort made up of pre-capitalist, informal production units that will disappear with the development process. Alternatively, it is seen to be the result of a massive opting out of rational firms and individuals from formal institutions on finding that the costs of those institutions outweigh the benefits (Perry et al., 2007). Thus the informal economy is seen as a consequence of the failure of modernization strategies.

However, when confronted with the current acute issues related to poverty reduction, the implementation of decent working conditions, and the creation of social protection mechanisms in developing countries, a growing body of literature highlights the necessity of taking into account the informal economy. In particular, it points to the logic underlying the functioning of that economy, its modes of accumulation, its ways of securing livelihoods, and how it interacts with public policies and the country programmes and projects of international organizations. Hart (1973, 2010), de Certeau (1984) and Braudel (1992) believe that it is a mistake to consign popular culture and practices to the past, to the countryside or to primitive peoples: they are part of the strength of contemporary economies and societies. They constitute what Balandier (2007 [1957]) called the 'constant inventiveness of daily life'—the tangible and intangible creation of what is needed to sustain it. They are the 'flesh and blood' of the informal economy and the world which stems from it. Therefore, in order to understand the informal economy it is necessary to take into account those 'forgotten actors' who live within the 'folds' of the modernization project.

From the perspective of the theories of modernization, the informal economy resembles a chaotic world that, literally, results from formlessness (Guha-Khasnobis et al., 2006). However, this apparent deficit applies only to the forms recognized by the State. Typically, with regard to the income-generating activities and microenterprises that constitute this 'sector', it signifies the lack of a legal form through, for example, registration in a trade record and with the tax authorities and social insurance schemes—a form which results from the rationalization process that has historically accompanied the constitution of the nation State (Hart, 1973). However, formalization does not erase the earlier norms, rules, and social forms, such as those inspired by the community, nor does it prevent the emergence of other, equally modern forms of social regulation, especially those adapted to the context of new urban neighbourhoods. These norms, rules, and social forms, which coexist, and in many cases compete, with those recognized by state bureaucracy, shape the practices of production, financing, exchange, and consumption of the popular actors that constitute the 'informal' economy. They provide a specific logic and a significant degree of stability and predictability.

In order to capture that logic, and, in particular, the ways in which popular actors secure their livelihoods, institutionalist approaches are needed that take into account the complex interactions between the economy, institutions, and social norms. Indeed, the second half of the 1990s saw a resurgence of institutionalist thinking in development economics as part of a new, post-adjustment paradigm (Hugon, 2008). It focuses primarily on arrangements that enable the functioning of markets, in particular for 'the poor'. These include individual arrangements, as expounded in contracts and property rights theories inspired by North (1990) and Williamson (1985), and collective arrangements through social networks in which 'real' markets are embedded—referring here to the 'reticular embeddedness' of the markets (Granovetter, 1985).

Yet these new approaches, while unravelling the logic of markets, do not fundamentally challenge the view that development will proceed through an extension of this sole principle. As a consequence, popular practices for ensuring livelihoods have been decisively set aside by mainstream analytical frameworks, relegating to the shadows an entire aspect of real development, but one which has never really ceased to haunt the thinking of (neo)modernizers (Jolly et al., 2004). What is needed is what Hart, Laville, and Cattani, in their proposal for a 'human economy', call a 'new "new institutional economics"' (Hart, Laville and Cattani, 2010: 7), of which Karl Polanyi can be considered a pioneer.

1.2 A Substantive Approach to the Economy: Polanyi's Intellectual Legacy

An analysis of the reality of popular practices and their evolution over a long period of time is crucial. It enables an understanding of the development demands of popular actors and illustrates the evolution of their individual and collective practices that are perpetually reinvented in order to ensure the material and spiritual security of their lives.[1]

The theoretical framework of the substantive economy proposed by Karl Polanyi (1957 [1944]) enables the further exploration of the logic of those actors by taking into account the existence of not one, but four principles of economic integration. The recognition of this plurality first draws attention to the multiplicity of existing resources in the informal economy: those originating from the market, but also from redistribution mechanisms at various levels and from relations of reciprocity as well as from households' resources. This recognition also leads to a reflection of the multiplicity of forms of exchange based on the principles of market, redistribution, reciprocity, and 'householding'.[2] More importantly, according to Polanyi, these principles of integration represent the fundamental logic that gives unity and stability to the economic process (Polanyi, 1957: 249). The principles underlie different types of resources and exchanges, but

[1] The anglophone world has only recently begun to recognize and employ this concept of 'popular'. Hull and James favour this term as a way to 'escape from such binaries and policy discourses [on the state and capitalist enterprise]...This recognizes the legacy, in South Africa, of earlier studies of popular culture which described a world of new identities and activities located in the city, where people had newly come into contact....What made this domain "popular" was its hybrid character, its inventiveness, and creativity, and the way it relied on particularly inventive "brokers"—even crooks and tricksters—for its operation' (Hull and James, 2012: 9–10).

[2] In Chapter 4 of *The Great Transformation*, Polanyi suggests three features of householding: 1) 'it consists of production for one's own use', according to Aristotle's distinction between production for use and production for gain; 2) 'its pattern is the closed group'; and 3) 'very different entities of the family or the settlement or the manor formed the *self-sufficient unit*' (Polanyi, 2001 [1944]: 55–6, our emphasis).

Table 1.1 Polanyi's principles of economic integration as modalities of interdependence in production, financing, exchange or transfer, and consumption

Principles of economic integration	Reciprocity	Redistribution	Householding	Market
Type of interdependence	Instituted complementarity	Instituted centrality	Varying (instituted complementarity or centrality or other)	Mechanical competition
Type of institutional structure	Horizontal (e.g. symmetric)	Vertical (e.g. hierarchical)	Domestic group, in some cases autarkic	Market system
Logic of action	Obligations among peers	Obligations in a (personal or functional) centralized system	Sharing production and work for satisfying the needs of the group	Bargaining in one's own interest

are not limited to the sphere of circulation alone: they include all spheres of activity that make up the economy in a substantive sense: circulation and exchanges or transfers, as well as production, financing, and consumption by which people sustain themselves. They represent ideal modalities of interdependence in these different spheres: interdependence resulting mechanically from price fluctuations in the case of the market; interdependence based on centralized systems in the case of redistribution; organized complementarity, for example based on a symmetric pattern, in the case of reciprocity; and lastly, interdependence within a group through sharing—usually a domestic group—in the case of householding (Hillenkamp and Servet, 2011) (see Table 1.1). The principles of economic integration therefore generate different types of institutional structures which can be combined in multiple configurations. They form a conceptual framework that takes into account the diversity of informal socio-economic practices of popular actors, without assuming them to be evolving towards a model of a 'modern' capitalist enterprise.

The Polanyian framework permits an analysis of the diverse ways in which popular actors protect themselves in the informal economy. In theories of modernization, protection is essentially addressed through capitalist accumulation. While these two approaches are not necessarily in conflict or contradictory, one cannot be substituted for the other. Recent literature has shown that few informal units aim at accumulation in the capitalist sense (Peemans, 2002). One central hypothesis of recent studies on the functioning of units in the informal economy is that informal socio-economic practices proceed from people's demands for security rather than for growth or capital accumulation per se.[3] A closer observation of the way popular actors secure their livelihoods shows multiple patterns of petty accumulation based on a diversity of resources and

[3] For a comparative analysis of the functioning of some sectors of the urban informal economy, see Lapeyre and Lemaître (2013).

types of interdependencies within families, communities, and professional, religious, and other types of groups. These interdependencies not only give structure to economic practices and regulate the accumulation process, they also create different forms of protection, depending on the types of relationships mobilized: protection based on solidarity and obligation among peers, according to the principles of reciprocity or householding, and vertical or hierarchical protection in the case of redistribution or other forms of householding.

Financial practices and institutions also play an important role in enhancing security of livelihoods and are particularly crucial for poor people. Poverty refers not only to low levels of income—the poverty line being less than US$1.25 a day, according to the World Bank (Ravallion et al., 2008)—but also to irregular income, particularly in the informal economy. Difficulties in coping with regular expenses and, a fortiori, with exceptional and unforeseen expenses—incurred, for example, by illness, accident, or death—are all the more important if people are poor. Confronted with these difficulties, the financial practices of the poor are often surprisingly complex. Through proactive financial management, they create real 'portfolios' of assets and liabilities that are essential in order to deal with their various expenditures (Collins et al., 2009).[4] For this, they resort to informal practices and institutions as well as to microfinance, and, in some cases, to the traditional formal banking sector.

Knowledge and debate on the contribution of financial practices and institutions for livelihood security of the poor have evolved considerably over the past thirty years. Field studies providing evidence that informal practices were not confined to loan sharks (Adams and Fitchett, 1992) contributed significantly to the recognition of other forms of financial practices. For example, rotating and non-rotating informal financial groups, informal credits without collateral, informal lenders, and pawnbrokers gradually gained the attention of researchers and policy-makers at the national and international levels. The 'invention' of microfinance dating back to the 1970s, which became increasingly popular in the 1990s and 2000s, partly shifted the terms of the debate. Microfinance was generally presented as 'good finance'. Through new techniques, such as group lending, it was supposed to offer an alternative access to financing denied by the traditional formal banking sector due to lack of collateral, information asymmetry, moral hazard, and adverse selection (Hulme and Mosley, 1996). According to this vision, it could gradually compensate for the deficiencies of this sector *and* replace informal finance, thereby offering the poor much-needed access to financial resources.

The assumption underlying this new form of modernization, according to which an initial injection of capital, in this case granted through productive

[4] We are grateful to Hadrian Saiag for drawing our attention to this publication and that of Adams and Fitchett (1992).

microcredit, would facilitate escaping the poverty trap, has not stood up to close scrutiny. In recent years, there has been increasing disappointment at the inability of microfinance to help reduce poverty (Diop et al., 2007; Banerjee et al., 2009; Bateman and Chang, 2009; Bédécarrats, Bastiaensen, and Doligez, 2011), and at the eruption of overindebtedness crises, as in Bolivia in 1999, Morocco, Nicaragua, and Bosnia Herzegovina in 2008, and Andhra Pradesh in 2010. These tragic events may have caused public opinion, policy-makers and managers of microfinance institutions to adopt a more realistic view of what it could accomplish. There is little evidence that microfinance has contributed significantly to poverty reduction or to risk reduction over the long term (Guérin, Morvant-Roux, and Servet, 2011), mainly because microfinance institutions have tended to give priority to managing their own credit risk over that of their members or clients (Hillenkamp, 2007). However, microfinance has been seen to contribute to financial inclusion by offering, not only credit, but also savings, insurance, and other specific services that enable people to manage their liquidity and secure their livelihoods.

It is therefore important to assess which tools are locally available and how they are appropriated by local actors. Furthermore, microfinance schemes must be examined in relation to the informal financial practices and institutions with which they interact locally (Morvant-Roux, 2006), and in the context of the social and cultural relations in which they are embedded (Servet, 2006). Thus, policy-makers need to carefully examine individual, family, and collective economic and financial mechanisms for securing livelihoods, as well as the mechanisms of reproduction and distribution of the surplus, in order to formulate appropriate poverty reduction strategies. Improving the working and living conditions of workers in the informal economy implies having a better understanding of the access to resources by units in the informal economy, taking into consideration the principles underlying the market, redistributive, reciprocity, and householding practices.

Table 1.2 illustrates the specificity of a Polanyian approach of the economy by comparing how standard approaches in economics—as the basis for modernization theories—and institutionalist approaches study: (i) the modes of economic coordination among individuals, (ii) the economic groups, understood as collective units of production of goods and services, and (iii) the relationship between the economic groups and their environment.[5] In standard economics approaches and their extensions, economic groups are analysed in terms of efficient solutions constrained by an environment viewed mainly in terms of the market, technology, and/or information. Socio-economic approaches, on the other hand, allow an understanding of economic groups in terms of social constructions and human choices that are not determined in

[5] For more details, see Lemaître (2009).

Table 1.2 From modernization theories to institutionalist approaches

	Standard approaches in economics		Institutionalist approaches		
	Neoclassical economics	Contract theories	Neo- institutional economics	Socio-economics	
				Reticular embeddedness	Polanyian framework
Coordination modes	The market is the first principle, and provides the matrix for economic actions The non-market principle is residual (mobilized in case of 'market failures') The non-monetary economy is hidden			Embedded market	Plural economy => market, redistribution, reciprocity and householding principles are analysed without any *a priori* hierarchy
Economic group	Black box – maximizing profit	Extension of the market	Efficient solution in case of market failures	Social construction	Social construction Integral view, plurality of actors and logic
Relationship of the economic group with its environment	It is mainly the environment that influences the economic group (contingency relationship) The environment is viewed mainly in market, technological or informational terms			There is interaction between the economic group and the environment Focuses on a market environment	Interaction between the economic group and the environment: just as the environment shapes the economic group, the economic group creates its own environment Focuses also on a non-market environment (political dimension of the economy)

Source: Lemaître (2009).

quite such mechanical terms by the environment. The relationship between an economic group and its environment is seen as an interaction: just as the environment shapes the economic group, the economic group is also able to generate changes in its environment. The Polanyian framework in socio-economic approaches enables a further broadening and deepening of our understanding of the economy. It goes beyond the market matrix of the reticular embeddedness approaches, which look only at market coordination mechanisms and market actors in a market environment, to analyse the plurality of an economy. Therefore it articulates a diversity of actors and socio-economic logic in both a market and a non-market environment.

The Polanyian approach to the economy has certain similarities with feminist approaches (Degavre and Lemaître, 2008). It goes beyond the conventional approaches that have a narrow market and monetary view of the economy in order to highlight and legitimize all forms of production and circulation of goods and services, that is, diverse economic means of securing livelihoods. In that sense, it sheds light on women's contributions to the economy, which tend to be neglected in the formal understanding of the economy. Whereas the roles of women, and in particular women in the popular or informal economy, in contributing to security of livelihoods and to the reproduction of life are neglected by modernization theories (Degavre, 2010), the Polanyian approach to the economy shows the importance of women in the informal economy. There, they play key roles in social protection, in general, and in economic solidarity initiatives, in particular (Guérin, Hersent, and Fraisse, 2011), based on diverse and complex relationships, which need to be carefully examined.

1.3 The Informal Economy: A Complex and Heterogeneous Reality

The literature has not yet reached a consensus on how to define 'economic informality'. Given the paucity of comparative and reliable statistical data on the informal economy, the available statistics must be treated only as a preliminary estimate of the extent and characteristics of that economy (ILO, 2002; Bacchetta et al., 2009; OECD, 2009).[6] According to data compiled by Bacchetta et al. (2009), informal employment accounts for a half to

[6] In June 2002, the International Labour Conference (ILC) adopted a resolution and conclusions concerning decent work and the informal economy, which provide a new framework for measurement. The conclusions define the informal economy broadly as referring to 'all economic activities by workers and economic units that are—in law or in practice—not covered or insufficiently covered by formal arrangements' (ILO, 2002). The broader term—informal economy rather than informal sector—takes account of the considerable diversity of workers and economic units in different sectors of the economy and across rural and urban contexts that are particularly vulnerable and insecure.

three-quarters of non-agricultural employment in developing countries. Its share in total employment is estimated to be 52 per cent in Latin America, 78 per cent in Asia, and 56 per cent in Africa (71 per cent in sub-Saharan Africa). Moreover, the level of informal employment in the *formal* sector is increasing in many countries (ILO, 2009). Another relevant aspect is the level of informal self-employment compared with informal wage employment. On average, across all developing countries, self-employment represents the greatest share of non-agricultural informal employment: 70 per cent in sub-Saharan Africa, 62 per cent in North Africa, 60 per cent in Latin America, and 59 per cent in Asia (ILO, 2009). In 2008, own-account and contributing family workers, mainly engaged in informal economic activities, accounted for about 80 per cent of the workforce in the least developed countries (LDCs) (UNCTAD, 2010: 36).

Beyond statistics, the heterogeneity of the informal economy needs to be analysed in terms of the specific processes that generate and/or maintain informality. It is important to distinguish between, on the one hand, recent informalization processes linked to trends in the global economy—particularly visible in South Asia where a significant proportion of the informal economy contributes to capital accumulation—and neoliberal policies, and, on the other hand, the resilience of the popular economy, which is still an important feature of everyday life for a large number of people. Moreover, deindustrialization and a shrinking public sector have pushed a large proportion of the few who had benefited from modernization towards the informal economy. In Africa, the implementation of structural adjustments programmes (SAPs) in the 1980s led to the rapid informalization of labour markets, yet prior to 1980, economic development did not result in the disappearance of the informal economy. Informal petty production for local markets coexisted with the formal economy. Indeed, the informal economy remained the main source of income and employment for most people in that region (ILO, 1972). An analysis of the evolution of the informal economy over a long period shows that dense and complex social ties in most developing countries have been able to preserve and reinvent themselves through associative and reciprocity mechanisms. When the debt crisis erupted in the 1980s, such mechanisms were able to provide income and employment for those who had been adversely affected by the SAPs. Examining the capacity for resilience of the informal economy leads to a new vision of its actors, their logic and practices, their demands, their coordination mechanisms, and their all-important social ties which enable them to continuously rebuild and preserve the community-based structures of their everyday lives.

Balandier (2007 [1957]: 2) suggests that modern-day Africa is constructed from what was left of its heritage and from its domestic adaptation of 'modernity'. It did not merely leave free rein to what could destroy it, or take sombre pleasure from a tragic and melancholic retreat to the margins of the modernization project. An examination of the special nature of the strategies of actors in the informal economy reveals a proliferation of artful transgressions that are the source of their resilience, which is difficult to grasp from a methodological point of view (de Sardan, 1995). The statistics give almost no clue to this stream of an ailing modernity, regulated, in principle, by the institutional frameworks that popular actors are steadily eroding and displacing. In the informal economy, there is no observable or readable system so cherished by the scientific literature. Rather there are fleeting, moving, disconcerting, and ambiguous realities that do not lend themselves to precise measurement, exact calculation, or strict logic. As de Certeau (1984: 118) stresses: 'Somewhere along the line in these practices, something always gets lost, something which cannot be said or "taught" but must be "practiced".'

Far from the vision of actors in the popular economy as reactionary and archaic, stubbornly resisting any move towards change, heterodox analytical frameworks emphasize their perpetually evolving strategies, characterized by a constant reinvention of their identity in the face of the strategies of dominance that seek to ensnare them. In Africa, it can be seen that the traditional system of distribution still functions, although it has changed greatly since solidarity based on family, lineage, or ethnicity has been in crisis, just as the State is in crisis, resulting in increasing insecurity. The decline of vertical redistribution in African society is partly offset by complex systems of horizontal solidarity within which the circulation of money and goods plays a crucial role through various mechanisms of reciprocity. The internationalization of support networks through migration also plays an ever-increasing role. This radical new look at the 'forgotten actors' of modernization and a better understanding of popular practices reveal the huge gulf between the development demands of the people in the informal economy (identified through the multitude of practices they have developed for securing their livelihoods) on the one hand, and the policy priorities of the elite to modernize the world on the other (Peemans, 2002: 247).

In Latin America, informality increased during the 'lost decade' of the 1980s and also during the 1990s (Perry et al., 2007). The proportion of self-employed or wage workers engaged in individual income-generating activities and microenterprises tended to increase, while new forms of informal employment in formal enterprises emerged, or at least became more visible (ILO, 2011). Moreover, in the context of the external public debt crisis of the 1980s and 1990s, doubts about the efficiency of modernization and the 'developmental State' model spread, making it increasingly difficult to categorize popular actors as a 'proletariat', a 'native population', or 'peasants', in the process of modernization. Since the late 1980s, sociologists and economists in the region (e.g. Razeto and Calcagni, 1989; Larrachea and

Nyssens, 1994; Sarria Icaza and Tiriba, 2006) have proposed the concept of a 'popular economy' (*economia popular*) to draw attention to the unique and long-lasting character of this economy, which constantly adapts to changing socio-economic conditions.

The introduction of this concept has had the dual effect of renewing the critical discussion on the internal structure of 'dependent' societies and drawing attention to the specific socio-economic logic of actors in the popular economy. On the one hand, the issue of the 'internal expression' of dependence within Latin America (Cardoso and Faletto, 1978 [1974]) has been revived through the diverse forms of labour control in structurally heterogeneous societies (Quijano, 1990), and through the subordination of the popular economy to national and international capital (Coraggio, 2006). On the other hand, the biological and cultural reproduction of life and the mobilization of labour and local resources based on a logic of shared 'funds' (Coraggio, 2006) have been recognized as the purpose and operating principles of this economy. In contrast to the logic of accumulation in capitalist firms, the basic units of the popular economy are the domestic institutions, and their dominant logic is the Polanyian principle of householding based on sharing, even though sharing may not necessarily be equitable. However, the valorization of labour and local resources is not driven exclusively by the logic of reproduction within domestic institutions: it is also based on market activities. The opposite principles of householding and market are therefore articulated in the popular economy according to specific configurations (Hillenkamp, 2012).

The concept of popular economy also raises the question of the organic nature of this heterogeneous sector, and, in particular, its contribution to a 'solidarity economy' (*economía solidaria*) oriented towards democratization of the economy (Razeto, 1984 and 1996; Larrachea and Nyssens, 1994; Guerra, 1999; Coraggio, 2002; Carvalho de França Filho, 2005; Sarria Icaza, 2006; Singer, 2006; Hillenkamp, 2009; Lemaître, 2009). While the popular economy encompasses diverse activities and organizations, ranging from mere subsistence strategies, to individual income-generating activities, micro and small family enterprises, unions of producers, associations, and groups of the solidarity economy, one main common issue remains the recognition and economic and political structuring of this economy. Solidarity initiatives could represent its 'most advanced pole' (Sarria Icaza and Tiriba, 2006: 265). These initiatives, which rely on a new application of the Polanyian principle of reciprocity in a context of democratic self-management, have become increasingly visible, and have organized themselves at the political level in several countries in the region, especially in Argentina, Brazil, Bolivia, and Ecuador. However, in Venezuela, where the solidarity economy is mainly driven by strong government policies, there exists the risk of resurgent political populism (Lemaître, Richer, and Carvalho de França Filho, 2011).

1.4 Globalization and the Informal Economy

Polanyi's principles of economic integration provide heuristic tools for an analysis of informal socio-economic practices and processes for securing livelihoods at the local level. They also enable an analysis of the multiplicity of possible relationships between the informal and the formal economy, particularly under the global capitalist mode of production. Strong empirical evidence based on the growth experience of many developing economies shows that sizeable informal economies can coexist and sustain themselves side-by-side with the expansion of the formal economy and good growth performance (Castells and Portes, 1989). In analysing the relationship between growth and informalization, Heintz and Pollin (2005) show that higher economic growth will reduce the rate at which informalization increases in developing countries, though it cannot on its own create an environment in which informalization actually declines. Their observation was based on an analysis of a sample of twenty countries for which there were adequate data on both informalization and per capita growth over a sufficiently long time period. Moreover, they found that increasing rates of informalization were consistent with positive average rates of economic growth (Heintz and Pollin, 2005).

Thus the informal economy should not be seen as a vestige of the past or as a sign of backwardness, as workers and producers in the informal economy are linked to the global economy. Outsourcing, piecework, and petty commodity production within family units remain important features of the reorganization of production at the global level (Quijano, 1971; Moser, 1978; Harriss-White, 2012). These linkages highlight the importance of better understanding: (i) the growing 'informality' of the global economy, especially as a result of the expansion of international financial flows and global production networks; and (ii) the main drivers of informal socio-economic practices (Chen, 2007; Carr and Chen, 2002). The informal economy is operating in an environment marked by complex formal and informal economic linkages, global economic cycles, and domestic macroeconomic frameworks which are affecting the functioning and level of vulnerability of units in the informal economy.

1.5 Towards a New Policy Agenda

The high level of vulnerabilities, multiple kinds of processes contributing to insecurity, and the constant reinvention of systems of protection and solidarity within the informal economy shape the accumulation process in a non-capitalist way. It is necessary to recognize the capacity of popular actors to perceive the world and development projects in terms of their cultural identity, their history, and the place where they live, and not as a universal matrix suggested by the dominant actors. Bottom-up approaches and innovative institutional frameworks for better responding to people's needs should be core components of the debate on formalization and poverty reduction. As underlined by Lautier (2004), it is only on the basis of such approaches that it will be possible to devise innovative and appropriate social protection systems. Bearing in mind the constituent elements of this development pattern, growth is no longer a *meta* objective, or even an indicator of success; rather, it is an outcome of choices, because, depending on the nature of the goods and services identified as essential by communities, and on their technological choices, there will be more or less growth.

Taking into account the practices of actors in the popular economy therefore means thinking about the inherent nature of alternative development patterns related to these 'lines of escape' that are often simple survival strategies. In themselves they can be factors of social breakdown and can lead to new forms of violence, as exemplified in the development of sectarian communities, aggressive ethnic movements, and sectarian fundamentalism. The 'futures' which emerge from the multitude of popular practices following the crisis of the legitimacy of a neo-modernization project unable to keep its promises to everyone, are not all components of a shared project for the sustainable improvement of the living conditions of a population in a given place. This observation should induce a shift from idealizing local popular initiatives to trying to understand which, among these many practices of resistance, survival, solidarity, and enhancing of living conditions, can lead to a reinvention of living and working together.

Several chapters of this book analyse the adaptive capacities of informal economy actors. They describe how people develop their own strategies to solve their problems through the use of interpersonal networks, associations, and other community-based arrangements. Moreover, they show that informal economy actors systematically reposition themselves vis-à-vis the State, markets, and international and national policies with the aim of enhancing their economic and social security, and they may do this either individually or collectively. The book emphasizes how adaptability of the informal economy can be influenced by such factors as the macroeconomic context, access to financial, technological, and information resources, infrastructure, social protection schemes, and the institutional environment within which adaptations occur. Case studies stress the need to reformulate questions relating to policy intervention based on a more thorough understanding of the perspective of informal economy actors.

Indeed, the idea that those actors have capabilities, and not just vulnerabilities, has received increasing recognition in policy-making during the past thirty years (Scott, 1985; Anderson and Woodrow, 1989/98; Cannon, 2008). This is at the heart of approaches which recognize that local social systems can, and do, self-organize, despite limitations and stress factors (Gunderson and Holling 2002; Berkes, Colding, and Folke, 2003). Families and communities have varying capacities to adapt in response to short-term and structural changes in living conditions (IPCC, 2007; Meagher, 2010; Trosper, 2003). In many different places, people have been rethinking local risk management strategies and how scarce or declining resources should be allocated using multidimensional and associative strategies.

Such a paradigm shift requires multi-scalar policy frameworks—that is, at micro, meso, and macro level—to better address the challenges to development confronting the informal economy. It necessitates the development of supporting institutions and policies that allow local communities to enhance their capabilities of securing and improving their livelihoods, especially by developing and protecting their economic and social rights (Lapeyre, 2013). This book shows the importance of exploring cross-scale influences on the informal economy in order to identify, formulate, and implement relevant policies and appropriate interventions aimed at: (i) strengthening adaptive capacities at local, regional, and national levels; (ii) reducing communities' vulnerability to shocks and threats; and (iii) securing and improving livelihoods (Walker et al., 2004).

In both urban and rural areas, informal economy actors are taking advantage of newly created polices that support community-based management initiatives (Amoukou and Wautelet, 2007; Marschke and Berkes, 2006). However, given the considerable diversity of practices and institutions in the informal economy, one-size-fits all policy responses are inappropriate; instead, a diverse and rich array of possible responses is likely to emerge (Chapple and Lester, 2010). This implies the need for giving more thought to how national policy-makers could encourage transformative development from below and thus foster synergies, modularity, and connection between the local, regional, and the national levels in ways that increase the various options for ensuring security of livelihoods rather than constraining them. If these changes are to occur and the scope for appropriate policy responses is to change, the actions and policies of a very large number of different agents of change have to be coordinated vertically and horizontally through appropriate institutional frameworks at different spatial levels (Hudson, 2010).

1.6 Securing Livelihoods in the Informal Economy: Practices and Institutions

The book's overall aim is to contribute to a broadening and deepening of our understanding of the logic and socio-economic practices of popular actors operating in the informal economy. It focuses on the vulnerabilities of these actors, resulting from high exposure to different risks combined with low social protection, and on the interactions between vulnerability and poverty. It considers security of livelihoods as the guiding principle for multiple practices in the informal economy. Thirteen studies, based on careful analyses of empirical data in different contexts in Africa, Latin America, and Asia, contribute to this multidisciplinary discussion.

The chapters in Part I adopt a substantive approach to the economy, understood as 'an instituted process of interaction between man and his environment, which results in a continuous supply of want satisfying material means' (Polanyi, 1957: 248). Drawing on Polanyi's legacy, Lemaître proposes a multidimensional framework to analyse economic initiatives, and applies it to capture the way different 'popular cooperatives' participate in local development in the Brazilian State of Rio de Janeiro. Her final discussion reflects on the heuristic value of the Polanyian framework as a basis for an in-depth analysis of the plurality of socio-economic logic in the informal popular economy. Following this approach, Hillenkamp looks specifically at the protective mechanisms adopted by actors in the popular economy. Those mechanisms are rooted in their practices of production, exchange, and financing in a context of the lack of, or insufficient, social protection by the State. Based on a field study in the city of El Alto (Bolivia), she critically reviews four types of practices that provide protection against specific vulnerabilities, and distinguishes between protection based on solidarity and protection based on hierarchy. Vásquez' analysis of the experience of a 'recovered enterprise' on the periphery of Buenos Aires (Argentina) continues this discussion. He shows how the workers of self-managed workers' enterprises not covered by the state's social security system have developed different strategies, not only to generate jobs and promote community development, but also to cope with vulnerability. Finally, Le Polain and Nyssens look at the socio-economic logic underpinning formal and informal strategies for coping with economic shocks. Based on an exploratory study of shocks and coping strategies in the province of South Kivu (Democratic Republic of the Congo), they show the plurality of the principles used, among which reciprocity and householding predominate.

Part II, while also focusing on the logic of popular actors based on socio-economic pluralism, turns specifically to an analysis of financial practices and their role in reducing vulnerabilities and enhancing security of livelihoods. Saiag's study of household budgets in the city of Rosario (Argentina) highlights the role of a range of informal financial practices for livelihood security based on domestic solidarity and protection mechanisms in the context of the dismantling of the Fordist-like welfare regime. Carvalho de França Filho, Scalfoni Rigo, and Torres Silva Junior look at the role of microfinance in Brazil by examining the government's microcredit policies and analysing the unique experience of community development banks. They highlight the differences between market-based microcredit and solidarity finance, and the potential role of the latter for overcoming some limitations of the former. The factors contributing to the demand for microcredit services in rural Morocco is the focus of a study by Morvant-Roux, Guérin, and Roesch. They show that informal financing mechanisms and social attitudes and norms that disapprove of debt account for the low demand and use of microcredit services. They find that the extent of vulnerability of households is a major determinant of the varying rates of participation in microcredit schemes across rural Morocco. Umuhire and Nyssens deepen the analysis of the coexistence of informal and formal microfinance through a survey of the use of these mechanisms by micro-entrepreneurs in Ouagadougou (Burkina Faso). They show that such mechanisms serve different purposes and are not easily substitutable. Finally, the chapter by Totolo takes a look at the formal and informal networks used by different groups of entrepreneurs in their market activities in Nairobi (Kenya). Starting from the literature on the role of social networks in shaping market structures, he shows that informal financial networks are important for highly informal firms, although not in their start-up phase.

Part three turns to an evaluation of the benefits of informality and formality from the point of view of the actors, and provides a critical evaluation of the transition to formality in different contexts. Departing from the standard neoclassical approach that focuses on human capital and unobserved individual productivity and motivation, Heintz and Pickbourn first show the role of factors operating at the household and institutional level, as well as gender differences, in determining the level of incomes in informal self-employment in Ghana. From this perspective, increasing the level of incomes requires educational reform—rather than simply more education—and improving access to credit and infrastructure, instead of simply more formalization. Ferragut and Gomez extend this analysis by assessing the gains of formalization in terms of decent work based on a case study of newly created shopping centres in Quito (Ecuador). They show that these centres, which aim to eradicate informal street selling, have produced mixed results: while labour, employment, and security of work have generally improved, the levels of sales and incomes as well as the representation of vendors through associations have tended to deteriorate. Ansoms and Murison, who assess the policy of formalization in Rwanda, acknowledge the accomplishments of the government in improving the business climate. However, they raise the question of the negative impact of formalization on employment creation and local livelihoods based on a case study of the brick and tile business in two rural settings. Finally, Kus examines the link between neoliberal reforms and the growth of the informal sector from a regulatory perspective. Based on a case study of

Turkey, she identifies two concurrent regulatory trends underpinning these reforms: deregulation and the declining quality of law enforcement in the economic sphere. She notes that private-sector growth and informalization have emerged as two concomitant outcomes of these trends.

In his postface, Jean-Philippe Peemans suggests that the insights provided by this book are a valuable contribution to the growing debate on informality, protection, and development.

References

Adams, D. and D. Fitchett (eds.) (1992). *Informal Finance in Low-Income Countries.* Boulder, CO: Westview Press.

Amoukou, I. and Wautelet, J. M. (eds.) (2007). *Croisement des Savoirs Villageois et Universitaires: Enjeux pour le développement.* Louvain-la-Neuve: Presse Universitaire de Louvain.

Anderson, M. B. and P. J. Woodrow (1989/1998). *Rising from the Ashes: Development Strategies in Times of Disaster.* Boulder, CO: Westview.

Bacchetta, M., E. Ernst, and J. P. Bustamante (2009). *Globalization and Informal Jobs in Developing Countries.* Geneva: International Labour Office and World Trade Organization.

Balandier, G. (2007 [1957]). *Afrique ambiguë.* Paris: Plon-Edition Poche.

Banerjee, A., E. Duflo, R. Glennersterx, and C. Kinnan (2009). 'The Miracle of Microfinance? Evidence from a Randomized Evaluation'. Massachusetts Institute of Technology, <http://economics.mit.edu/files/5993> (last accessed: 06.02.13).

Bateman, M. and H.-J. Chang (2009). Microfinance Illusion, mimeo, University of Juraj Dobrila Pula (Croatia) and University of Cambridge (UK).

Bédécarrats, F., J. Bastiaensen, and F. Doligez (2011). 'Nouvelles gauches et inclusion financière: La microfinance contestée en Bolivie, en Équateur et au Nicaragua'. *Critique Internationale,* 52: 129–53.

Berkes, F., J. Colding, and C. Folke (2003). *Navigating Social-Ecological Systems.* Cambridge: Cambridge University Press.

Braudel, F. (1992). *The Structures of Everyday Life: The Limits of the Possible (Reprint).* Berkeley, CA: University of California Press.

Cannon, T. (2008). 'Reducing People's Vulnerability to Natural Hazards: Communities and Resilience'. Research Paper No. 2008/34, Helsinki: UNU-WIDER..

Cardoso, F. and E. Faletto (1978 [1974]). *Dépendance et développement en Amérique latine.* Paris: Presses Universitaires de France.

Carr, M. and M. A. Chen (2002). 'Globalization and the Informal Economy: How Global Trade and Investment Impact on the Poor'. *ILO WP Series,* no 1, Geneva: International Labour Office..

Carvalho de França Filho, G. (2005). 'L'économie populaire et solidaire au Brésil', in J.-L. Laville (ed.), *Action Publique et Économie Solidaire: Une Perspective Internationale.* Ramonville-Saint-Agne: Erès: 75–90.

Castells, M. and A. Portes (1989). 'World Underneath: The Origins, Dynamics, and Effects of the Informal Economy', in A. Portes, M. Castells, and L. Benton (eds.), *The Informal Economy: Studies in Advanced and Less Developed Countries*. Baltimore, MD: Johns Hopkins University Press: 11–37.

Chapple, K. and T. W. Lester (2010). 'The Resilient Regional Labour Market: The US Case'. *Cambridge Journal of Regions, Economy and Society*, 3: 85–104.

Chen, A. M. (2007). 'Rethinking the Informal Economy: Linkages with the Formal Economy and the Formal Regulatory Environment'. *DESA Working Paper* no. 46, United Nations, New York.

Collins, D., J. Morduch, S. Rutherford and O. Ruthven (2009). *Portfolios of the Poor: How the World's Poor Live on $2 a Day*. Princeton, NJ and Oxford: Princeton University Press.

Coraggio, J. L. (2002). *'La propuesta de economía solidaria frente a la economía neoliberal, Foro Social Mundial, Conferencia sobre Economía Solidaria, Eje I La producción de riquezas y la reproducción social'*. São Paulo: Incubadora Tecnológica de Cooperativas Populares, University of São Paulo.

—— (2006). 'Économie du travail', in J.-L. Laville, and A. D. Cattani (eds.), *Dictionnaire de l'autre Economie*. Paris: Desclée de Brouwer: 313–25.

de Certeau, M. (1984). *The Practice of Everyday Life* (translated by Steven Rendall). Berkeley, CA: University of California Press.

Degavre, F. (2010). 'La pensée "Femmes et développement": Critique des fondements et pistes pour reconstruire un point de vue féministe croisé Nord/Sud', in I. Guérin, M. Hersent, and L. Fraisse (eds.), *Femmes, Economie et Développement: Entre Résistance et Justice Sociale*. Paris: Eres/IRD: 63–84.

—— and A. Lemaître (2008). 'Approches substantives de l'économie: Des outils pour l'étude des organisations d'économie sociale'. *Interventions Economiques*, December, 38: 1–16.

de Sardan, J.-P. (1995). *Anthropologie et développement: Eessai en Socio-anthropologie du Changement Social*. Paris: Karthala.

Diop, A., I. Hillenkamp, and J.-M. Servet (2007). 'Poverty versus inequality', in B. Balkenhol (ed.), *Microfinance and Public Policy: Outreach, Performance and Efficiency*. New York: Palgrave MacMillan: 27–46.

Granovetter, M. (1985). 'Economic Action and Social Structure: The Problem of Embeddedness'. *American Journal of Sociology*, 91(3): 481–510.

Guérin, I., M. Hersent, and L. Fraisse (eds.) (2011). *Femmes, économie et développement: Entre résistance et justice sociale*. Paris: Eres/IRD.

Guérin, I., S. Morvant-Roux, and J.-M. Servet (2011). 'Understanding the Diversity and Complexity of Demand for Microfinance Services: Lessons from Informal Finance', in Armendáriz B. and M. Labie (eds.), *The Handbook of Microfinance*, London and Singapore: World Scientific Publishing, 101–21.

Guerra, P. (1999). 'Análisis socioeconómico-solidario de las economías alternativas'. *Revista Iberoamericana de Autogestión y Acción Comunal*, 34: 59–74.

Guha-Khasnobis, B., R. Kanbur and E. Ostrom (eds.) (2006). *Linking the Formal and Informal Economy. Concepts and Policies*. Oxford and New York: Oxford University Press, WIDER Studies in Development Economics.

Gunderson, L. and C. S. Holling (2002). *Panarchy*. London: Island Press.

Harriss-White, B. (2012). 'Capitalism and the Common Man—A Way of Seeing the Informal Economy'. Paper presented to the International Conference on Informal Economy, Vulnerabilities and Employment at the Institute of Socioeconomics, University of Geneva, Geneva, 9–10 February.

Hart, K. (1973). 'Informal Income Opportunities and Urban Employment in Ghana'. *Journal of Modern African Studies*, 11: 61–89.

—— (2010). 'Informal Economy', in K. Hart, J.-L. Laville, and A. D. Cattani (eds.). *The Human Economy: A Citizen's Guide*, Cambridge: Polity Press.

—— J.-L. Laville, and A. D. Cattani (eds.) (2010). *The Human Economy: A Citizen's Guide*. Cambridge: Polity Press.

Heintz, J. and R. Pollin (2005). 'Informalization, Economic Growth, and the Challenge of Creating Viable Labor Standards in Developing Countries', in N. Kudva and L. Beneria (eds.), *Rethinking Informalization, Poverty, Precarious Jobs and Social Protection*. Ithaca, NY: Cornell University Open Access Repository: 44–66.

Hillenkamp, I. (2007). 'La microfinance au service d'une économie solidaire? Exemples boliviens', *Revue Autrepart*, 44: 91–104.

—— (2009). 'Formes d'intégration de l'économie dans les démocraties de marché: Une théorie substantive à partir de l'étude du mouvement d'économie solidaire dans la ville d'El Alto (Bolivie)'. PhD thesis in Development Studies, Graduate Institute of International and Development Studies, University of Geneva, Geneva.

—— (2012). 'Le principe polanyien de householding aujourd'hui: Discussion théorique et approche empirique de l'économie populaire'. Paper presented at the international seminar on The World Between Crisis and Change organized by the Karl Polanyi Institute of Political Economy and the EMES European Network, Conservatoire National des Arts et Métiers, Paris, 15–16 February.

Hillenkamp, I. and J.-M. Servet (2011). 'Reciprocity and householding: Two Polanyian tools for analyzing solidarity today'. Paper presented at the workshop, New Directions in Polanyian Scholarship, Centre for Citizenship, Globalization and Governance, School of Social Sciences, University of Southampton, Salisbury, 12–13 March.

Hudson, R. (2010). 'Resilient Regions in an Uncertain World: Wishful Thinking or a Practical Reality?' *Cambridge Journal of Regions, Economy and Society*, 3: 11–25.

Hugon, P. (2008). *L'économie du développement et la pensée francophone*. Paris, Éditions des Archives Contemporaines et Agence universitaire de la francophonie.

Hull, E. and D. James (2012), 'Introduction: Popular Economies in South Africa', *Africa*, 82(01): 1–19.

Hulme, D. and P. Mosley (1996). *Finance against Poverty*. London: Routledge.

ILO (1972). *Employment, Incomes and Equity: A Strategy for Increasing Productive Employment in Kenya*. Geneva.

—— (2002). *Women and Men in the Informal Economy: A Statistical Picture*. Geneva.

—— (2009). *The Informal Economy in Africa: Promoting Transition to Formality—Challenges and Strategies*. Geneva.

—— (2011). *Efficient Growth, Employment and Decent Work in Africa: Time for a New Vision*. Johannesburg.

IPCC (Intergovernmental Panel on Climate Change) (2007). *Climate Change 2007: Impacts, Adaptation and Vulnerability*. Contribution of Working Group II to the Intergovernmental Panel on Climate Change Fourth Assessment Report. Geneva.

Jolly, R., L. Emmerij, D. Ghai, and F. Lapeyre (2004). *The Contributions of the United Nations to Development Theory and Practice*. Bloomington: Indiana University Press.

Lapeyre, F. (2006). 'Mondialisation, néo-modernisation et "devenirs": Un autre regard sur les pratiques populaires', in G. Froger (ed.), *La Mondialisation Contre le Développement Durable?* Paris: PIE Peter Lang, Collection Ecopolis: 151–62.

—— (2013) 'Securing Livelihoods in Africa: Towards Multi-Scalar Policy Frameworks', *European Journal of Development Research*. Available online at <http://www.palgrave-journals.com/doifinder/10.1057/ejdr.2013.5> (accessed 14 June 2013).

—— and A. Lemaître (eds.) (2014). 'Politiques publiques et pratiques de l'économie informelle en Afrique subsaharienne', collection *'Espace-Afrique'*, Louvain-la-Neuve: Academia-L'Harmattan.

Larrachea, I. and M. Nyssens (1994). 'L'économie solidaire, un autre regard sur l'économie populaire au Chili', in J.-L. Laville (ed.), *L'économie Solidaire: Une Perspective Internationale*. Paris: Desclée de Brouwer: 177–222.

Lautier, B. (2004). *L'économie informelle dans le tiers monde*. Paris: La Découverte.

Lemaître, A. (2009). *Organisations d'économie sociale et solidaire: Lectures de réalités Nord et Sud à travers l'encastrement politique et une approche plurielle de l'économie*. Louvain-la-Neuve: Presses Universitaires de Louvain.

—— M. Richer, and G. Carvalho de França Filho (2011). 'L'économie solidaire face à l'Etat en Amérique Latine: Les dynamiques contrastées du Brésil et du Venezuela'. *Revue Tiers Monde. Etudes interdisciplinaires sur les questions de développement* (208), October–December: 159–75.

Lerner, D (1958). *The Passing of Traditional Society: Modernizing the Middle East*. Glencoe: Free Press.

Marschke, M. J. and F. Berkes (2006). 'Exploring Strategies that Build Livelihood Resilience: A Case from Cambodia'. *Ecology and Society*, 11(1), at: http://www.ecologyandsociety.org/vol11/iss1/art42/ (accessed 11 May 2013).

Meagher, K (2010). *Identity Economics: Social Networks and the Informal Economy in Nigeria*. Woodbridge: James Currey.

Morvant-Roux, S. (2006). 'Processus d'appropriation des processus de microfinance: Un exemple en milieu rural mexicain.' PhD thesis in Economic Sciences, University Lumière Lyon II.

Moser, C. O. N. (1978). 'Informal Sector or Petty Commodity Production: Dualism or Dependence in Urban Development?' *World Development*, 6: 1041–1064.

North, D. (1990). *Institutions, Institutional Change and Economic Performance*. Cambridge: Cambridge University Press.

Nyssens, M. (2000). 'Les approches économiques du tiers-secteur, apports et limites des analyses anglo-saxonnes d'inspiration néo-classique'. *Sociologie du travail*, 42: 551–565.

OECD (2009). *Is Informal Normal?*. Paris: OECD.

Peemans, J. Ph. (2002). *Le développement des peuples face à la modernisation du monde*. Paris: Academia/L'Harmattan.

Perry, E. G., W. F. Maloney, O. S. Arias, P. Fajnzylber, A. D. Mason, and J. Saavedra-Chanduvi (2007). *Informality: Exit and Exclusion*. Washington, DC: World Bank.

Polanyi, K. (1944). *The Great Transformation: The Political and Economic Origins of Our Time*. Boston, MA: Beacon Press.

Polanyi, K. (1957). 'The Economy as Instituted Process', in K. Polanyi, C. M. Arensberg, and H. W. Pearson (eds.), *Trade and Market in the Early Empires: Economies in History and Theory*. New York and London: The Free Press and Collier-Macmillan Limited: 243–70.

Quijano, A. (1971). *Polo marginal y mano de obra marginalizada*, Santiago, Chile: CEPAL.

—— (1990). 'La nueva heterogeneidad estructural de América Latina'. *Hueso Húmero*, 26: 8–33.

Ravallion, M., S. Chen, and P. Sangraula (2008). 'Dollar a Day Revisited'. World Bank Policy Research Working Paper 4620, Washington, DC: World Bank.

Razeto, L. (1984). *Economía de solidaridad y Mercado democrático*. Santiago, Chile: Programa de Economía del Trabajo.

—— (1996). *Los Caminos de la Economía de Solidaridad*. Buenos Aires: Lumen-Humanitas.

—— and R. Calcagni (1989). *Para un proyecto de desarrollo de un sector de economía popular de solidaridad y de trabajo*. Santiago, Chile: Programa de Economía del Trabajo and Fundación Trabajo Para Un Hermano.

Rostow, W. W. (1960). *The Stages of Economic Growth*. Cambridge and New York: Macmillan.

Sanyal, K. (2007). *Rethinking Capitalist Development: Primitive Accumulation, Governmentality and Post-Colonial Capitalism*. New Delhi: Routledge India.

Sarria Icaza, A. M. (2006). 'Les politiques publiques pour l'économie solidaire au Rio Grande do Sul (Brésil)', in C. Auroi, and I. del Castillo (eds.), *Économie solidaire et commerce équitable: Acteurs et actrices d'Europe et d'Amérique latine*. Geneva and Louvain-la-Neuve: IUED and Presses Universitaires de Louvain: 247–59.

—— and L. Tiriba (2006). 'Economie populaire', in J.-L. Laville and A. D. Cattani (eds.), *Dictionnaire de l'autre économie*. Paris: Gallimard: 259–68.

Scott, J. C. (1985) *Weapons of the Weak*. New Haven: Yale University Press.

Servet, J.-M. (2006). *Banquiers aux pieds nus: La microfinance*. Paris: Odile Jacob.

Singer, P. (2006). 'Économie solidaire (1)', in Laville, J.-L. and A. D. Cattani (eds.), *Dictionnaire de l'autre économie*. Paris: Gallimard: 290–302.

Trosper, R. L. (2003) 'Resilience in Pre-Contact Pacific Northwest Social Ecological Systems'. *Conservation Ecology* 7(3): 6. Available online at <http://www.consecol.org/vol7/iss3/art6/> (accessed 14 June 2013).

UNCTAD (2010). *The Least Developed Countries Report: Towards a New International Development Architecture for LDCs*. Geneva: United Nations.

Walker, B., C. S. Holling, S. R. Carpenter, and A. Kinzig (2004). 'Resilience, Adaptability and Transformability in Social-ecological Systems'. *Ecology and Society* 9(2), at <http://www.ecologyandsociety.org/vol9/iss2/art5/> (accessed 12 May 2013).

Williamson, O. (1985). *The Economic Institutions of Capitalism: Firms, Markets, Relational Contracting*. New York: MacMillan, Free Press.

Part I

A Plurality of Socio-Economic Logics: New Polanyian Approaches to Informality and Vulnerability

2

'Popular Cooperatives' and Local Development in South-East Brazil: Towards Socio-Economic Pluralism

Andreia Lemaître

2.1 Introduction

Recent research looking at the inner logics of the informal economy suggests that practices are driven more by people's need for security than for monetary growth or capital accumulation per se. In this context, this chapter presents a Polanyian framework for the analysis of economic activities, which enables a pluralistic and comprehensive conception of economic initiatives (Lemaître, 2009a; Lemaître and Helmsing, 2012). We apply this methodology to an in-depth analysis of a set of 'popular cooperatives' in the State of Rio de Janeiro (Brazil), to gain a better insight into their contributions to local development. We conclude with a discussion of how methodological pluralism in socio-economics enables a broader and deeper understanding of economy than that allowed by the merely formal meaning of the word.

2.2 A Polanyian Framework for the Analysis of Economic Activities

In this chapter, we build on a *substantive* understanding of the economy derived from Polanyi's (1944) intellectual legacy. Polanyi sought to reconceptualize the economy in a pluralistic sense, moving away from a focus on utility-maximizing behaviour in a context of scarcity of resources (Robbins, 1932). He believed that for understanding an economy it is necessary to study all phenomena related to interdependencies, both among human beings and between human beings and their natural environment. Thus the economy should be understood as *plural*, that is, as combining a variety of actors and logics in the development of a given territory (Laville, 2004). Indeed, Polanyi (1944) showed that societies embody a plurality of modes of exchange of goods and services and principles of economic integration—the market, redistribution, reciprocity, and householding[1]—in diverse ways in time and space.

Neoclassical and contractualist economics, as well as neo-institutional economics, believe instead in the primacy of the market economy; it constitutes the main matrix for economic activities (Nyssens, 2000; Eymard-Duvernay, 2004; Lemaître, 2009a; Lemaître, 2009b). The non-market (or redistributive) economy is acknowledged, but only in residual (supplementary) terms, that is, to allocate goods and/or services in case of 'market failures'. The existence of reciprocity and householding, happening mostly in the non-monetary economy, is ignored. The market is seen as a natural phenomenon with an implicit hierarchy of the principles of economic integration and of the economic actors (firstly private for-profit enterprises, followed by state-owned, and non-profit organizations). In contrast, Polanyi (1944) argued that every society combines, through time and according to political choices, the different economic principles: the market, redistribution, reciprocity, and householding. A Polanyian framework thus aims to analyse an economy without any *a priori hierarchy* (Laville, 1994), by examining the specificities of each of these principles and how they interact—including in terms of the complementarities or the tensions between each economic principle—in order to protect individuals and nature.

In relation to the productive organization, neoclassical economics provides few tools for an in-depth study of the production units. The enterprise is analysed in purely narrow, technical terms, its *raison d'être* being the maximization of profits. It is seen as a 'black box' that varies according to the production function; it formalizes the state of the technology at a given point in time, and consequently the relation between the inputs and the outputs (Lemaître, 2009a; Lemaître, 2009b). As for contract theories, in addition to the production costs, they also take into account transaction costs, and the transactional aspects are central to the analysis. According to Eymard-Duvernay (2004: 32), 'the concept of the firm as a production function is supplanted by the concept of the firm as a structure of coordination' of contracts. The firm exists by virtue of market imperfections arising from information problems, but it is presented in these theories as an extension of the market, in the sense that it is a 'legal fiction' (Jensen and Meckling, 1976). That is to say, it is an artificial legal construction to concentrate a whole lot of contractual relations similar to the market (Coriat and Weinstein, 1995; Petrella, 2003). Neo-institutional economics is a vast field of inquiry that

[1] For details of these modes, see the introduction to this book.

goes beyond a mere contractual approach and aims at the study of economic organizations as institutions to show their efficiency as governance structures. This constitutes considerable progress for the analysis of economic initiatives, since it becomes possible to study them in more depth, and in particular, to apprehend their diversity. But even in this approach, organizational forms—like other institutions—are explained in terms of market failures: they emerge when the market cannot allocate resources efficiently, that is, by minimizing costs. The standard neoclassical theory and its extensions (Favereau, 2006) thus adopt either a minimal vision of the enterprise (Eymard-Duvernay, 2004), or a vision in terms of an efficient solution, seeing it as maximizing efficiency (Granovetter, 2000). It leaves little place for the logics and values underlying economic initiatives being able to pursue a plurality of objectives (Lemaître, 2009a; Lemaître, 2009b).[2]

Polanyi (1944) understood the economy as an institutionalized political process. Beyond the simple question of rationality, this leads to including the notion of legitimacy in the analysis, and to viewing the production unit not only in terms of its organizational dimension, but also in its institutional context.

2.2.1 A Plural Conception of Economic Initiatives

The Polanyian substantive economic approach enables us to examine production units, not only with reference to their economic goal and their monetary and market resources, but also according to a pluralistic and comprehensive conception of these initiatives, grasping the broader potential logics that underlie these organizations.

Based on this approach, a multidimensional grid (see Box 2.1) can be used to analyse how economic initiatives combine different relationships among actors within their governance structures and their reliance on a specific combination of multiple monetary and non-monetary resources in order to pursue various objectives linked to local development.[3] The different dimensions of an organization can be analysed, including how multiple principles of exchange connect with the plurality of its objectives.

With regard to the *achievements* of the economic initiatives in terms of their potential contribution to local development, it is possible to distinguish between different and specific categories of organizational achievements (Evers, 2001). They can be *economic*, related to the (collective) entrepreneurial nature of the organization. The economic goal corresponds to the *activity of*

[2] For a deep development of the arguments of this paragraph and the previous one, see Lemaître (2009a) or Lemaître (2009b).

[3] These objectives can sometimes be in tension (Lemaître, 2009a).

Box 2.1 MULTIDIMENSIONAL GRID FOR THE ANALYSIS OF ECONOMIC INITIATIVES

1. What benefits are generated?

Achievements (in terms of contributions to local development)

- Economic dimension (production of private or collective goods and services and employment creation)
- Social dimension (community bonds, social cohesion, gender issues)
- Environmental dimension (preservation of the environment)
- Political dimension (citizenship, actions in the public sphere)

2. What are the relations among internal actors?

Governance structures

- Founding group
- Decision-making processes
- Revenue distribution and surplus allocation

3. What exchange principles are used?

External economic relations (monetary and non-monetary resources)

- The market (revenues from sales of goods and services; links to markets)
- Public redistribution (subsidies or public funds from international development cooperation; possible links to public policies)
- Voluntary redistribution (donations; possible links to international solidarity)
- Reciprocity (mutual aid; community embeddedness)
- Householding (self-provisioning; the group)

producing goods and/or services and the necessity of doing this in a financially sustainable way. Production can consist of private goods and services, but also collective ones, such as the provision of a social service to improve living conditions in deprived areas. The mechanisms of employment and revenue creation are also studied, from a quantitative as well as a qualitative perspective (with a focus on working conditions). The *social* dimension of the organization relates to such aspects as the creation of community bonds, the strengthening of social cohesion, identity issues, and the reduction of gender inequalities.

Environmental achievements refer to the organization's contribution to the *preservation of the environment*. This can be the generation of environmental benefits when producing environmentally beneficial goods and/or services (such as sorting and recycling or recuperating and revaluing waste). It can also be the internalization of environmental externalities in the production process, that is, production activities done in an environmentally sustainable way, such as the use of ecological inputs, or minimization of the environmental costs of production (Anastasiadis and Mayr, 2009).

Finally, the political (or civic) dimension of the economic initiative is linked to *citizenship construction processes*. It is related to norms, values, trust, and networks in which the economic initiative can be embedded and, more generally, to its ability to promote public action, that is, collective expression in the *public sphere* (Habermas, 1991).[4] Linked to this achievement are workers' empowerment issues and advocacy efforts in the (even incipient) public sphere for the common good, such as demands for the implementation of decent working conditions, fair trade rules, or an alternative development model. Indeed, economic initiatives can offer a social critique and play the role of political actors who defend causes in public debate and call for the development of public policies related to them (Lemaître, 2009a). They may therefore influence institutional frameworks and future public policies.

A second research axis relates to the analysis of the *governance structures* developed by economic initiatives, that is, the types of actors inside and the kinds of relationships among them. This adopts a diachronical perspective for studying the founding groups, that is, the social relationships underlying the initiative and that make possible the emergence of economic practices. This is followed by an analysis of the ownership of the economic initiative, which means, in a broad sense, (i) the aspects linked to the decision-making processes (issues of economic democracy), and (ii) the mechanisms of distribution of the revenue from the activity, and the allocation of its surplus (Hansmann, 1996). Recent literature shows that few popular economic units aim at accumulation in the capitalist sense. Rather, logics of familial solidarity or 'collective reproduction' prevail (Coraggio, 2005), where priority is given to increasing the revenue, but also to employment creation and improving the living conditions of relatives and other members of a given community. For these reasons, other logics than strict monetary accumulation may be pursued, which do not prevent economic initiatives from attempting to extract the highest margin from a transaction. This could then be used, for example,

[4] According to the Habermasian approach, the public sphere is the 'arena of discursive debates between equals, the definition of a consensus around a "common good"' (Pirotte, 2007: 58). It is 'a particular sphere where is played a process of argumentation and of deliberation mainly within a dense fabric of associations and institutions' (Pirotte, 2007: 55).

for 'extensive accumulation' (Lautier, 2004), where the surplus is reinvested in order to expand the activity and/or multiply the units.

Lastly, the monetary as well as the non-monetary resources used by economic initiatives are examined as indicators of their embeddedness in the different types of economy. Indeed, a Polanyian understanding of the economy permits a study of the production unit, not only in terms of its monetary resources—appearing in the profit and loss account of the most formalized organizations—but also in terms of its non-monetary resources (e.g. voluntary work, gifts of inputs or equipment, personnel allowances, and building allowances), which can be quite significant in popular production groups. For a substantive understanding of the economy it is also necessary to examine the dynamics of the non-monetary economy. In our analysis below, to better understand the access of economic initiatives to various resources, we accorded values to their non-monetary resources at their market price (i.e. at the price they would have paid if they had acquired the resource through the market, which would then constitute a cost for the organization). The sum of the monetary and the non-monetary resources of the economic initiative constitutes its total resource base. This allowed us to develop a more complete picture of the entire mix of *principles of economic integration* mobilized by the economic group to be able to develop its activities (Gardin, 2006). This methodology enables the mapping, in an innovative way, of the different *external economic relations* on which the production units rely.

Laville and Nyssens (2001), following Polanyi (1944), distinguish between various kinds of resources: *market resources*, stemming from the sales of goods and services, which provide information about the link(s) of the cooperative with the market(s); *resources emanating from reciprocity relations* embedded in local networks of solidarity and in social ties, and thus arising from community embeddedness; and *resources stemming from householding*, that is, from self-provisioning (from members of the organization and/or members of their household). There are also redistributive resources, that is, resources previously collected by a central entity which has responsibility for distributing them. This can be *public redistribution*, comprising grants given by the public sector—local, regional, national, or even international. Public redistribution also includes what we call 'delegated redistribution', that is, public funds from international development cooperation[5] targeted at production groups in the south, which are channelled through non-governmental organizations (NGOs), unions, or other local support structures. In the case of public funds managed by NGOs and others, public policies are involved.

[5] Here we mean bilateral cooperation; indeed, in our sample there was no case of multilateral cooperation.

However, when the support of local NGOs and others to production groups in 'developing countries' is financed by own funds of the NGOs or other civil society organizations from 'developed countries' (i.e. money from international civil society), we call it *voluntary redistribution*. Indeed, even if, in this case, the support is financed by private international solidarity—and it is collected on a voluntary basis—we include it in redistribution because it is not related to the symmetry characterizing what for Polanyi (1944) would be reciprocity resources embedded in mutual knowledge and social ties (Servet, 2007). Rather, it has more to do with the redistribution being centralized: the resources being collected by a central entity, which has the responsibility to allocate it according to some predetermined criteria.[6]

Based on a Polanyian framework, we then analyse economic initiatives, not only in terms of their economic dimension, but also in terms of their social, environmental, and political dimensions. This takes into account the way the initiatives' actors organize themselves and how revenue is allocated and distributed. In addition, we look at their mobilization of resources, but not only the monetary ones on which the conventional formalized economy is based, where the value of goods and services is measured by their price.

The next section applies these main elements of a Polanyian substantive methodology to the case study of popular cooperatives in the State of Rio de Janeiro in Brazil.

2.3 The Coexistence of Traditional and 'Popular' Cooperatives in Brazil

The cooperative movement in Brazil was started in the late nineteenth century by Europeans immigrants who founded cooperatives in accordance with the teachings of Charles Fourier (Schmidt and Perius, 2003). These were mainly consumer cooperatives in the urban areas and agricultural cooperatives in the countryside. Most of the consumer cooperatives disappeared following the expansion of supermarket chains. However, the number of agricultural cooperatives increased, and many of them turned into large agro-industrial businesses, mostly active in the monoculture production of crops for export. The first laws regulating cooperatives in Brazil were introduced by the populist government of Getúlio Vargas. In 1971, under the military dictatorship, the

[6] There is a debate in the literature on this question, as Polanyi did not foresee such hybrid cases of international exchange that combine redistribution and reciprocity aspects. We could also have considered this as 'international reciprocity', as a mix of altruism and self-interest for a better world; however, we decided it was better to differentiate these more anonymous international solidarity funds from the gift-giving practices that characterize the relationships of reciprocity found in the local community.

structure of the cooperative system in Brazil was defined in law 5764, which still regulates cooperatives today. It was also at this time that the Organization of Brazilian Cooperatives (OCB) was founded.

Alongside these traditional cooperatives, there is a series of initiatives aimed at meeting the subsistence and income generation needs of their members who are from the 'popular classes' and are excluded from the mainstream systems of employment, income distribution, and social protection. These collectives of workers, referred to as 'popular cooperatives', are mostly informal and active in very diverse fields of production, and focused on improving the living conditions of their members. In contrast to the traditional cooperatives, which gradually transformed into big private companies, the logic of accumulation of the 'popular cooperatives' is not a capitalist one, but rather one that seeks 'improvement of the conditions of reproduction of the lives of their members', both materially and symbolically (Coraggio, 2005: 261).

Economic practices whose purpose is not capitalist accumulation have existed in Brazil for a long time, developed by the large section of the population living on the margins of the formal economy. By developing mutual support and solidarity practices, they tried to cope with the lack of access to dignified living conditions. Such practices evolved particularly from the second half of the 1980s when, after the end of the military regime, there was a resurgence of social movements and social actions by the Church and NGOs. This period also saw a growth in the number of excluded people, mainly in the urban areas, as a result of the economic crisis that hit the Latin American economies in the 1980s—often referred to as the 'lost decade' (Carvalho de França Filho and Laville, 2004). Neoliberal policies and budgetary orthodoxy imposed by structural adjustment programmes (SAPs) worsened the traditional lack of public policies for tackling such problems.

Facing a huge social crisis, popular actors, and civil society groups that supported these actors (e.g. NGOs, social movements, churches), saw the need 'to develop concrete options—immediate, medium, and long-term economic alternatives—which would boost struggles, previously mainly centred on the conquest of the political sphere to transform unfair structures or require the elaboration of social policies. Many initiatives appeared, which constituted new spaces for discussion and social practice' (Sarria Icaza, 2006: 2). Many local projects were developed, including mainly grassroots cooperatives and community production groups.

As a result, two main types of cooperatives came to co-exist in Brazil: the traditional cooperatives and a more recent wave of 'popular cooperatives'. The latter tend to regard traditional cooperatives as conservative. In addition, they seek to differentiate themselves from 'pseudo-cooperatives' also called '*copergatas*', that is, enterprises which fail to comply with cooperative principles, but which are legally registered as cooperatives so that they can take on workers on a self-employed basis, without them being considered as employees. This enables these enterprises to bypass the constraints of labour laws relating to employees, thus jeopardizing the security of the worker status. The 1971 law regulating Brazilian cooperatives is considered as being adequate for large traditional cooperatives, but not for popular cooperatives, most of them remaining informal. The latter do not consider themselves as part of the OCB, feeling far away from this political actor, even though every legalized cooperative is obliged by law to be affiliated to the OCB.

2.4 In-Depth Analysis of Popular Cooperatives in the State of Rio de Janeiro

This section provides an analysis of how the practices of the 'popular cooperatives' contribute to local development. It presents the main results of research undertaken in 2008 based on a sample of popular cooperatives (n = 15) in the deprived and violent shanty town districts of the State of Rio de Janeiro in Brazil.[7] We collected detailed quantitative and qualitative data on these cooperatives, based on the methodology of the in-depth case studies. A large set of indicators was used for collecting the data to help determine whether the 'popular cooperatives' were fulfilling their objectives, how their governance structures developed, and what resources they had mobilized, in accordance with the different dimensions of our multidimensional grid derived from a Polanyian understanding of the economy presented above (see Box 2.1). We also reconstituted, from a diachronical perspective, the genesis and history of these economic initiatives. We then applied a cluster analysis to our sample based on this wide set of data.[8] This resulted in two clearly identifiable clusters of subgroups of 'popular cooperatives', which we called 'politically-driven' and 'market-driven' cooperatives. Their multidimensional features and their contribution to local development are discussed below.

2.4.1 Politically-Driven Popular Cooperatives

The first cluster is composed of seven 'popular cooperatives' which came into being after receiving training from one or several NGOs, sometimes in partnership with local public authorities. They are all strongly supported by one or several NGOs. Five of the seven participate in the solidarity economy

[7] For more details, see Lemaître (2009a).

[8] The cluster analysis is a statistical classification method which minimizes the distances between the data (in our case, related to the organizations) in order to classify them in different contrasted groups (in our case, of organizations) that can then be compared (Everitt et al., 2011).

movement, a social movement born from the World Social Forums since 2001. The movement champions a 'new' mode of production, consumption, and wealth distribution—an 'alternative model of development to capitalism'—through the promotion of values such as cooperation, solidarity, and self-management in economic practices.

Most of these cooperatives are informal and are engaged in the production of handicrafts: five of them produce recycled notebooks and cosmetics, or are engaged in food catering, fancywork, sewing, and tailoring. The other two are active in waste sorting and printing. There is not a steady demand for their products and they face serious problems of commercialization, notably because of a lack of fixed sales outlets for their products. Consequently, they generate very small and variable turnovers, which vary from 8,100 to 54,111 reals per annum.[9]

These cooperatives are small, ranging from four to sixteen members, and thus offer few opportunities for employment. They generate variable and low incomes, often supplementary for the workers. The average monthly income per worker is below the national minimum salary.[10] The workers in these cooperatives are all of African descent, with very low levels of education, and they live in the shanty towns and other very deprived and violent informal settlements. Most of them are women, aged over 40 years, and they are the most disadvantaged workers of the sample.

The working atmosphere is friendly and there are significant relationships among workers. While in the dual society of Brazil, members of the 'popular class' are highly stigmatized, but through their integration into the popular cooperative, they acquire dignity at work. Generally, all members consider the boosting of their self-esteem and *recognition* to be among the main benefits of the organization. As Honneth (1996) mentions, the possibility of a positive relation-to-self can only develop from social interaction from which the individual can draw forms of recognition necessary to his or her development. It is even more important when workers experience situations of social disrespect in other spheres of their social life that threaten to injure and ruin their identity and that play, according to the author, a role in the emergence of social conflicts.

In addition, the cooperatives enable the women to reconcile their private and professional lives. Indeed, the lack of formal childcare facilities and the short time their children spend at school make it difficult for these deprived women to get a job. But in these cooperatives, the work time is flexible and, if they have children, they can take their handicraft work home to do while looking after their children.

[9] The exchange rate as on 31 December 2008 was 1 Brazilian real = 0.31 euros or $0.43.
[10] The national minimum salary was 415 reals at the time of the inquiry.

The members of the cooperatives mentioned how important it is that the cooperative considers every worker as a complete human being and feels responsible for him or her. For example, the cooperative encourages workers to pursue studies for personal development, beyond what they need to function within the cooperative. Production activity is adapted to make this possible. For the politically-driven cooperatives, economic activity does not appear to be the primary objective: it is considered a means to empower workers (Charlier, 2006) and for them to get access to a citizenship role.

Indeed, the politically-driven cooperatives which participate in the solidarity economy social movement and/or in other movements (e.g. of women or of waste collectors) develop a strong political dimension. They all stated that they pursue a political objective, which they always place in first or second place ahead of the objectives of production and of employment creation and income generation. Most of these cooperatives consider the values of the workers as being more important than their technical skills. The political dimension is shared by all the workers of the (small) cooperative.

The workers interviewed mentioned that through the cooperative they had gradually realized their potential and that it enables them to become self-reliant. Beyond the professional training, they are also trained in citizenship, notably by NGOs, and they become aware of the reality of their economic, social, and political exclusion. They progressively consider themselves as citizens, as social actors with duties and with entitlements for which they begin to militate together. They see themselves as 'multiplier agents'—as having a mission to empower other people through encounters and exchanges. Such cooperatives often become the stimulator or the protagonist of some social cause concerning their community.

From a gender perspective, most women interviewed said that learning to speak in public and the awareness of their capabilities and entitlements had in turn influenced their family life. In particular, it affected how they positioned themselves vis-à-vis their husbands, with whom many previously had a submissive relationship.

Their links with NGOs and participation in social movements allow the members of the 'popular cooperatives' to develop contacts outside their own community, which, in Brazil, used to be segregated and characterized by violent private forms of power (drug traffic or private militias). These contacts provide them with democratic experiences that are rare in the other spheres of their daily life. The insertion into the popular cooperatives of this first cluster has enabled them to access the public sphere, and to exercise their rights as citizens, because 'it is in the public sphere that citizens have access to political information, that they can deliberate and form an opinion and that they can choose the individuals who will exercise political power. It is in the public sphere that the citizens feel not only recipients but also authors of this right' (Dacheux and Laville, 2003: 10). From a local development perspective, the politically-driven cooperatives participate in the creation of *local political control*, local control being the ability to create 'the lifestyle desired in the region' (Nelson, 1993: 28).

As Bebbington (2007) observes, some authors see chronic poverty as an economic problem of *lack of resources*, whereas others see it more as a problem of *lack of entitlements* which can only be solved with political change. In that sense, researchers on social movements stress that poverty reduction does not simply require 'good policy'. but also the empowerment and the mobilization of deprived people in order to enable them to influence and to hold accountable those who make the policies. For them, 'chronic poverty is an inherently political problem [...] Its persistence over time reflects its institutionalization within social and political norms and systems, its legitimation within political discourse and by political elites, and the failure of the poorest groups to gain political representation therein' (Hickey and Bracking, cited by Bebbington, 2007: 798). We will come back to this discussion in the conclusion.

With regard to the environmental objective, as noted earlier, two cooperatives of the first cluster produce ecological goods/services (as waste sorting). All of the cooperatives try to produce in an ecologically sustainable way, attaching great value to the preservation of the environment.

Concerning the decision-making processes, in this first cluster, three of the eight popular cooperatives (the smallest ones in the sample) practise self-management *stricto sensu*, being totally managed, with equal participation, by the workers. Each of the other five cooperatives has a 'leader', sometimes called 'self-managed popular leader', who was a militant before the creation of the cooperative, and who takes the main decisions. These leaders, when interviewed, said they considered themselves as necessary initially, but that their position should disappear with time, after the members of the cooperative had received appropriate self-management training. Indeed, these actors have developed a *processual* definition of self-management. They mentioned that it implies learning to carry a voice and learning the meaning of co-responsibility, but that this is difficult to implement, particularly in a dual society like Brazil's, where the workers are not accustomed to the horizontal relationships that self-management seeks to stimulate. In aspiring to achieve cultural changes, self-management is considered as 'the horizon of the practices'—as an ideal which can only be implemented very gradually, through education and training processes. For them, in practice, it is the path travelled that is important (Mothé, 1980), the progressive learning of other relationships.

In the politically-driven popular cooperatives, as well as in those of the second cluster of organizations (presented in the next section), the rules for the distribution of revenue do not vary much. In both cases, the revenue is distributed among the workers according to criteria linked to productivity (e.g. hours worked, conditions of the contract signed with the client, number of pieces produced, and skill levels). We did not observe much solidarity amongst workers with regard to revenue distribution in the cooperatives in the sample.

Table 2.1 shows the external economic relations of the politically-driven popular cooperatives. According to a substantive understanding of the economy, we made an inventory of all the resources mobilized—monetary and non-monetary—by every cooperative in 2007.[11] The non-monetary resources were valued at their market price (as mentioned earlier), in order to make visible, within the conventions of the formal economy, all the resources that the cooperative uses to pursue its objectives. The sum of the monetary and the non-monetary resources constitutes the total resources of the cooperatives.

The resources from the *market* come from the sale of goods and/or services, and represent their gross revenue. The purchaser can be motivated either by pure market criteria (i.e. the quality–price ratio of the product) or by other considerations too, such as purchasing the product/service in order to support the cooperative, or other social, environmental or political criteria. In this case, the market relation is considered to be *embedded* in social criteria (Granovetter, 1985). The popular cooperatives of this first cluster have a low proportion of market resources (on average 43 per cent of their total resources), and these resources are in most cases embedded in social criteria. They have few *reciprocity* resources (e.g. local voluntary work and local gifts) when valued in monetary terms (on average 13 per cent of the total resources), and they do not have resources derived from *householding* relations (from self-provisioning).

[11] This was a particularly laborious exercise since there are a large range of monetary and non-monetary resources mobilized by the popular cooperatives annually. The *monetary resources* of the cooperative can be: (1.1) sales of goods and services (-> *market resources*), (1.2) subsidies (-> *redistributive resources*), (1.3) monetary donations from international cooperation agencies (-> *redistribution, delegated or voluntary*, according to how the NGO is financed), (1.4) monetary donations embedded in social ties (-> *reciprocity resources*), (1.5) monetary donations and contributions by the members and their households (-> *householding*), and (1.6) income from assets (-> *market resources*).

The *non-monetary resources* of the cooperative can be: (2.1) voluntary work embedded in social ties (-> *reciprocity resources*), (2.2) voluntary work by members of the workers' households (-> *householding*), and (2.3) non-monetary subsidies and aids. This last category includes personnel allowances (e.g. services and training by NGOs); capital allowances (space and equipment); donations in kind (e.g. space and equipment, raw material, free transportation) and benefits of low-interest loans (i.e. interest lower than the market interest rate). They can come (2.3.1) from public bodies (-> *redistributive resources*), (2.3.2) from international cooperation agencies (-> *redistribution, delegated or voluntary*, according to how the NGO is financed), (2.3.3) from local social ties (-> *reciprocity resources*), or (2.3.4) be given by the members and their households (-> *householding*).

Table 2.1 Resources mix of the politically driven popular cooperatives, 2007 (percentage of total resources)

	Politically-driven cooperatives							
	1	2	3	4	5	6	7	Average
External economic relations (%)								
Market exchange	**25**	**31**	**48**	**22**	**49**	**68**	**60**	**43**
Market relations motivated only by the ratio quality/price	7	0	7	22	5	14	21	11
Market relations motivated by social, environmental and/or political criteria	17	31	41	0	44	54	39	32
Public redistribution	**35**	**32**	**15**	**41**	**16**	**13**	**28**	**26**
International cooperation (delegated redistribution)	32	31	15	28	14	12	4	19
Brazilian public funds	3	1	0	13	3	1	24	7
National public funds	3	1	0	0	3	1	3	2
Local public agencies	0	0	0	13	0	0	20	5
Voluntary redistribution	**34**	**24**	**10**	**33**	**9**	**8**	**3**	**18**
Reciprocity	**6**	**13**	**27**	**4**	**25**	**10**	**9**	**13**
Householding	**0**	**0**	**0**	**0**	**0**	**0**	**0**	**0**

One important origin of the resources of these cooperatives is *redistribution* (on average, 26 per cent + 18 per cent = 44 per cent of the total resources). This concerns mainly delegated redistribution (19 per cent of total resources) or voluntary redistribution (18 per cent of total resources), which means funds reaching the popular cooperatives via the support given by NGOs. This support is almost always in kind, mostly in the form of training and other accompanying services.

Most authors situate popular cooperatives between 'the market and the gift' (Latouche, 1998), that is, between the market and local reciprocity. However, our study highlights the importance of the non-monetary resources emanating from international development cooperation. The average shares of the external economic relations of the first cluster of popular cooperatives can be represented as shown in Figure 2.1 below.

As already mentioned, the first cluster of popular cooperatives gained access to redistributive resources through NGOs (averaging 19 per cent + 18 per cent = 37 per cent of their total resources). NGOs also sustain the popular cooperatives by buying their products. Indeed, sales of goods and services to NGOs account for, on average, 33 per cent of the market resources of these politically-driven popular cooperatives. NGOs therefore play a major role in these popular cooperatives' acquirement of resources.

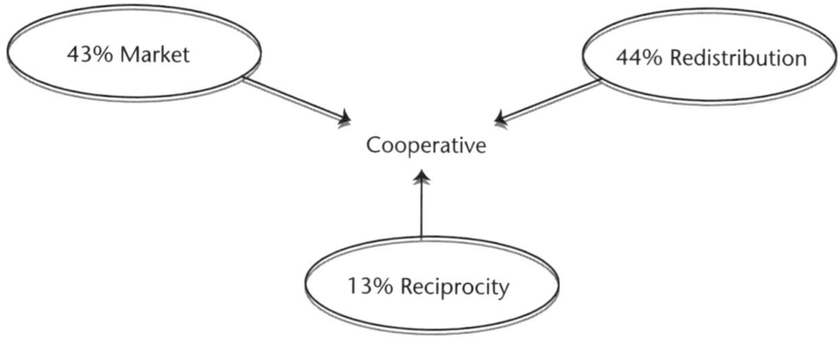

Figure 2.1 External economic relations of politically-driven popular cooperatives (average percentage share in total resources)

2.4.2 Market-Driven Popular Cooperatives

What we label market-driven cooperatives, constitute the second cluster in our sample, which consists of eight cooperatives. Their founding was more the result of the agency of the workers themselves than of support organizations, whereas the latter played a greater role in the founding of the politically-driven popular cooperatives. The market-driven popular cooperatives are more heterogeneous and much more independent of support organizations, and the latter are diverse, including universities and trade unions. Only three of these popular cooperatives are engaged in the solidarity economy movement, while the remaining five are not even actively involved in that or in other social movements.

The economic dimension is much stronger and central to these market-driven popular cooperatives than it is in the politically-driven popular cooperatives. Most of them are legally registered. They are active in diverse production domains: providing services to enterprises such as cleaning services, and working in the construction industry, the processing industry (screw manufacturing), computer services, nursing, and handicrafts (i.e. two cooperatives make clothes and handbags respectively). Generally, they have a stable customer base, which allows greater continuity in the flow of production. They generate higher and more stable turnovers, ranging from 117,000 to 1,250,000 reals annually.

These popular cooperatives are also bigger and create more jobs, ranging from 20 to 210 workers. They generate higher levels of more stable income. Their average monthly income per worker of 496 reals (which in two cases includes payment of the transportation costs) exceeds the national minimum wage. Although highly disadvantaged, their workers are slightly more qualified than those in the first cluster. There are more men who located between the 'popular class' and the proletarianized working class originated from the formal sector.

The working conditions guarantee dignity at work. Many workers mentioned that their current experiences at work differed very significantly from their previous ones. Those who had experienced work in the formal sector described their former working conditions as being particularly hard.

The group dynamics are much less significant in the cooperatives in this cluster than in the politically-driven ones. As these market-driven cooperatives are larger, the relationships between the workers are less strong and the atmosphere is less amicable. The production activity is more professionalized. The cooperatives are less flexible: there are schedules to meet and there are more formalized procedures. These cooperatives are also less open to external relations and do not appear so embedded in the local community as those in the first cluster.

The market-driven popular cooperatives have not developed a strong political dimension. Those that do not participate in any social movement stated that they do not have political objectives. The ones engaged in the solidarity economy movement stated that they do pursue a political goal, but only through members of their board of directors. It is a goal not subscribed to by all the workers, some of whom do not even know about the existence of such an objective. Only members of the board participate in the meetings of the social movement and do not necessarily provide feedback to the other workers.

The majority of the workers do not consider themselves as militants, and do not claim to subscribe to alternative economic values. Inside these cooperatives, there are few, if any, training schemes about citizenship and no dynamics to promote workers' access to the public sphere. The training provided to the workers is much more professionally oriented. It deals very rarely with questions of entitlements or global social issues. The focus of the cooperatives—including those engaged in the solidarity economy movement—is on employment and revenue creation for excluded people, a transformation of labour relationships including the implementation of decent working conditions, and respect for all human beings. In local development terms, market-driven cooperatives are more focused on achieving *local economic control*.

Compared with the politically-driven popular cooperatives, the market-driven ones do not pay much attention to the environmental dimension: none of them are active in the production of ecological goods and services, and only one pays attention to producing in an ecologically sustainable way.

Concerning the decision-making processes of these cooperatives, no one practises self-management, not even according to a processual understanding of it. Each of the cooperatives of this second cluster has a general assembly where the workers elect representatives to a board of directors—according to the rule of one vote per worker. This board has the responsibility for making day-to-day management decisions. Then, all these cooperatives follow the more traditional principles of cooperativism and of a workers' representative democracy.

It happens that the composition of the board of directors varies little or not at all in the history of the cooperative, because of a lack of involvement of the workers. Such involvement is not obvious to the workers, who are shaped by a history of proletarian working relationships. In such cases, training processes towards indirect economic democracy are developed, under the impetus of some leaders. Then, from observing the practices in the second cluster of cooperatives, they appeared to adopt, as in the first cluster, a *processual understanding of economic democracy*, in the sense that it is considered an ideal to be implemented very gradually through an education process (Mothé, 1980).

Table 2.2 presents the external economic relations of the market-driven popular cooperatives. These cooperatives are clearly market-driven, as evidenced by the high share of market revenues in their total resources (89 per cent on average). And in most cases these relations are motivated only by the

Table 2.2 Resources mix of the market-driven popular cooperatives, 2007 (percentage of total resources)

	Market-driven cooperatives								
	8	9	10	11	12	13	14	15	Average
External economic relations (%)									
Market exchange	**87**	**98**	**84**	**98**	**94**	**88**	**74**	**91**	**89**
Market relations motivated only by the ratio quality/price	52	98	67	98	66	0	74	90	68
Market relations motivated also by social, environmental and/or political criteria	35	0	17	0	28	88	1	1	21
Public redistribution	**5**	**0**	**1**	**2**	**0**	**0**	**20**	**0**	**4**
International cooperation (delegated redistribution)	4	0	0,5	0	0	0	5	0	1
Brazilian public funds	1	0	0,3	2	0	0	15	0	2
National public funds	0,4	0	0	0	0	0	0	0	0
Local public agencies	0,2	0	0,3	2	0	0	15	0	2
Voluntary redistribution	**3**	**1**	**0**	**0**	**1**	**0**	**6**	**0**	**1**
Reciprocity	**5**	**1**	**15**	**0**	**5**	**12**	**0**	**9**	**6**
Householding	**0**	**0**	**0**	**0**	**0**	**0**	**0**	**0**	**0**

price-quality ratio of the product (i.e. the customers are not motivated to buy from them based on social or political criteria).

Most of the cooperatives of this cluster develop few relationships of *reciprocity*. On average, only 6 per cent of their total resources come from reciprocity. Moreover, they do not engage in self-provisioning drawing on the *householding* principle.

Finally, and with the exception of one cooperative which is supported by the local public authority, these organizations have relatively few *redistributive* resources. None of the cooperatives of this second cluster benefit—or have ever benefited—much from international development cooperation, whether in the form of delegated or voluntary resources.

Figure 2.2 summarizes the degrees of contribution of the various external economic relations of these cooperatives.

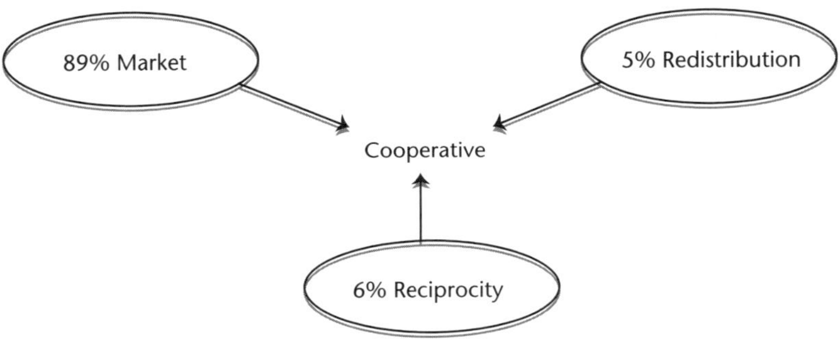

Figure 2.2 External economic relations of market-driven popular cooperatives (average percentage share in total resources)

The literature often relates cases of small cohesive self-managed popular cooperatives which progressively transformed, with time, into bigger cooperatives, that no longer practise self-management (Fortin, 1985). It is therefore interesting to notice that this was not the case in our sample. Indeed, from a historic point of view, the first cluster of cooperatives did not give birth to the second, and neither is the second cluster the future of the first. It is not a case of initially self-managed initiatives, sustained by international development cooperation, gradually growing, professionalizing, strengthening economically, and transforming into bigger cooperatives less dependent on international cooperation. The two clusters are different, with different roots, active in different fields, with different organizational practices, and have not changed much over time.

Table 2.3 summarizes the results of our in-depth analysis of the sample of 'popular cooperatives' using the clustering method.

Table 2.3 Main results of the in-depth analysis of popular cooperatives: comparison of the two clusters

Initiatives	Politically-driven coops ($n = 7$)	Market-driven coops ($n = 8$)
Achievements	Economic activity as a means	Economic activity strong and central
	Small groups, flexible work	Bigger groups and professionalization
	Weak creation of work and fluctuating income	Better and stable work and income
	Mostly women	More men, slightly more qualified workers
	Empowerment processes and access of workers to the public sphere	Dignity at work but no empowerment processes for the workers
=> CONTRIBUTION TO LOCAL DEVELOPMENT	=> PROMOTING *LOCAL POLITICAL CONTROL*	=> PROMOTING *LOCAL ECONOMIC CONTROL*
Governance structures (Workers)	Self-management (*stricto sensu* or according to a processual definition)	Cooperativism, workers' representative democracy (*stricto sensu* or according to a processual definition)
External economic relations	Non-market organizations Importance of international development cooperation, through the crucial role played by supporting NGOs	Market-driven organizations Little support from public policies and from agencies

2.5 Towards a Methodological Pluralism for the Analysis of Economic Activities

In this chapter, we have presented the results of a research project on 'popular cooperatives' in Brazil, following a methodology of substantive economics based on Polanyi's (1944) intellectual legacy. The heuristic value of such an understanding of the economy is that it transcends the arbitrary separations in the social sciences in order to reconcile economics with sociology and political science. As opposed to what Polanyi (1944) called the *disembeddedness of the economy*, this suggests considering the economy as integrating social, environmental, and political dimensions. Beyond the narrow market and monetary view of the enterprise adopted in formal economic approaches, it considers, *without any a priori hierarchy*, the economic activities as plural, articulating a specific mix of actors, logics, and monetary as well as non-monetary resources. Indeed, the formal vision of the economy, which accords a value only to what has a price, fails to consider the importance of the production of goods and services in the non-monetary economy.

Two groups of cooperatives clearly emerged from the cluster analysis. From a local development point of view, we found that the cooperatives of the first cluster—mostly informal—participate in the construction of their territory by increasing local *political* control through the empowerment of workers and by promoting their access to the public domain. The cooperatives of the second cluster—mostly formal—participate in the construction of their territory by expanding local *economic* control with greater and more stable employment and income creation.

The research results show that in popular cooperatives in the State of Rio de Janeiro, there is a tension between the economic dimension and the political dimension of the initiatives. Indeed, at the level playing field of the current market regulations, market mechanisms do not internalize social and environmental dimensions. In this case, the cooperatives in the first cluster—comprising the most vulnerable workers of the sample—are fairly dependent on the resources provided by NGOs to support the additional costs of their involvement in the social, environmental, and political dimensions of the economy.

The substantive approach of the research makes it possible to recognize the plurality of the benefits cooperatives can generate in the reduction of vulnerabilities. It enables an analysis of their effectiveness not only (1) in reducing material vulnerability and securing employment (i.e. *the economic dimension of the reduction of the vulnerabilities*, in distributional terms), but also (2) in developing social networks and social cohesion (i.e. *the social dimension of the reduction of the vulnerabilities*, in relational and recognition terms) and (3) in the construction of the democratic process (i.e. *the political dimension of the reduction of the vulnerabilities*). This last aspect is related to the ability of workers to develop a voice, first, in the domain of work—through which they gain access to public life—and in the public sphere in general, in the making of societal choices—leading to the possibility for the deprived populations to produce and control their own history. Lastly, it also appears to take into account *the reduction of the vulnerability of the future generations* through the contribution to environmental issues.

We have to think about frameworks that have the ability to analyse the reduction of all these vulnerabilities as 'all these axes of injustice cross in a manner which affects the interests and the identities of each one' (Fraser, 2004: 157). None of these dimensions seems to be sufficient in itself, since the vulnerabilities are mixed, of an economic, social, or political nature, and tend to reinforce one another.

The concurrent pursuit of multiple objectives is not easy for popular cooperatives, and responding at the organizational level to economic, social, political, and environmental needs may involve tensions. This is why some authors stress that the sustainability of such initiatives relies on the broader conditions of their institutionalization, that is, on political recognition of the socio-economic pluralism (Fraisse, 2003; Lemaître, 2009a).

References

Anastasiadis, M. and A. Mayr (2008). 'Work Integration Socio-Economic ECO-Enterprises—Their Potentials and Requirements in Reaching Social, Ecological and Economical goals—Results from a Current Research-Project on ECO-WISEs in Austria'. *EMES Conferences Selected Papers Series*, B08-12.

Bebbington, A. (2007). 'Social Movements and the Politicization of Chronic Poverty'. *Development and Change*, 38(5): 793–818.

Carvalho de França Filho, G., and J.-L. Laville (2004). *Economia Solidária: Uma abordagem internacional*. Porto Alegre: Universidade Federal do Rio Grande do Sul Editora, Coleção Sociedade e Solidariedade.

Charlier, S. (2006). 'L'empowerment des femmes dans les organisations de commerce équitable: Une proposition méthodologique', in C. Auroi and I. Yepez (eds.), *Economie solidaire et commerce équitable: Acteurs et actrices d'Europe et d'Amérique latine*. Geneva: Institut Universitaire d'Etudes du Développement, Presses Universitaires de Louvain: 87–109.

Coraggio, J. L. (2005). 'Economie du travail', in J.-L. Laville and A. D. Cattani (eds.), *Dictionnaire de l'autre économie*. Paris: Desclée de Brouwer: 261–70.

Coriat, B. and O. Weinstein (1995). *Les nouvelles theories de l'entreprise*. Paris: Livre de Poche, Collection Références.

Dacheux, E. and J.-L. Laville (2003). 'Introduction: Penser les interactions entre le politique et l'économique'. *Hermès, Economie solidaire et démocratie*, 36. Paris: CNRS éditions: 9–17.

Everitt, B. S. et al. (2011). *Cluster Analysis* (5th edition). Wiley Series in Probability and Statistics. Sussex: Wiley.

Evers, A. (2001). 'The Significance of Social Capital in the Multiple Goal and Resource Structure of Social Enterprises', in C. Borzaga and J. Defourny (eds.), *The Emergence of Social Enterprise*. London and New York: Routledge: 296–311.

Eymard-Duvernay, F. (2004). *Economie politique de l'entreprise*. Paris: La Découverte.

Favereau, O. (2006). 'Objets de gestion et objet de la théorie économique'. *Revue française de gestion*, 160: 67–79.

Fortin, A. (1985). 'Du collectif utopique à l'utopie collective'. *Anthropologie et Sociétés*, 9(1): 53–64.

Fraisse, L. (2003). 'Economie solidaire et démocratisation de l'économie'. *Hermès, Economie solidaire et démocratie*, 36. Paris: CNRS éditions: 137–45.

Fraser, N. (2004). 'Justice sociale, redistribution et reconnaissance'. *Revue du MAUSS*, *1*(23): 152–64.

Gardin, L. (2006). 'A Variety of Resource Mixes Inside Social Enterprises', in M. Nyssens (ed.), *Social Enterprises: Between Market, Public Policies and Community*. London and New York: Routledge: 111–36.

Granovetter, M. (1985). 'Economic Action and Social Structure: The Problem of Embeddedness'. *American Journal of Sociology*, 91(3): 481–510.

—— (2000). *Le marché autrement: Les réseaux dans l'économie*. Paris: Desclée de Brouwer, Sociologie économique.

Habermas, J. (1991). *The Structural Transformation of the Public Sphere: An Inquiry into a Category of Bourgeois Society.* Cambridge, MA: MIT Press.
Hansmann, H. (1996). *The Ownership of Enterprise.* Cambridge, MA: Harvard University Press.
Honneth, A. (1996). *The Struggle for Recognition: The Moral Grammar of Social Conflicts.* Cambridge, MA: Polity Press.
Jensen, M. C. and W. H. Meckling (1976). 'Theory of the Firm: Managerial Behavior, Agency Costs and Ownership Structure'. *Journal of Financial Economics,* 3, October: 305–60.
Latouche, S. (1998). *L'autre Afrique, entre don et marché.* Paris: Albin Michel.
Lautier, B. (2004). *L'économie informelle dans le tiers monde.* Paris: La Découverte.
Laville, J.-L. (1994) (dir.). *L'économie solidaire: Une perspective internationale.* Paris: Desclée de Brouwer.
—— (2004). 'Encastrement et nouvelle sociologie économique: De Granovetter à Polanyi et Mauss', in M. La Rosa and J.-L. Laville (eds.), *La sociologie économique européenne: Une rencontre franco-italienne, Sociologia del Lavoro, 93*: 11–25.
—— and M. Nyssens (2001). 'The Social Enterprise: Towards a Theoretical Socio-economic Approach', in C. Borzaga and J. Defourny (eds.), *The Emergence of Social Enterprise.* London and New York: Routledge: 312–32.
Lemaître, A. (2009a). *Organisations d'économie sociale et solidaire: Lectures de réalités Nord et Sud à travers l'encastrement politique et une approche plurielle de l'économie.* Louvain-la-Neuve: Presses Universitaires de Louvain.
—— (2009b). 'Des théories des organisations au concept d'encastrement', in J.-L. Laville and P. Glémain (eds.), *L'économie sociale et solidaire aux prises avec la gestion,* Paris: Desclée de Brouwer : 295–351.
Lemaître, A. and A. H. J. (Bert) Helmsing (2012). 'Solidarity Economy in Brazil: Movement, Discourse and Practice. Analysis through a Polanyian Understanding of the Economy'. *Journal of International Development,* 24, 745–62.
Mothé, D. (1980). *L'autogestion goutte à goutte.* Paris: Editions du Centurion.
Nelson, A.C. (1993). 'Theories of Regional Development', in R. D. Bingham et al. (eds.), *Theories of Local Economic Development.* London: Sage Publications: 27–57.
Nyssens, M. (2000). 'Les approches économiques du tiers-secteur, apports et limites des analyses anglo-saxonnes d'inspiration néo-classique'. *Sociologie du travail,* 42: 551–65.
Petrella, F. (2003). *Une analyse néo-institutionnaliste des structures de propriété 'multi-stakeholder': Une application aux organisations de développement local.* Louvain-la-Neuve: Presses Universitaires de Louvain.
Pirotte, G. (2007). *La notion de société civile.* Paris: La Découverte.
Polanyi, K. (1944). *The Great Transformation: The Political and Economic Origins of Our Time.* Boston, MA: Beacon Press.
Robbins, L. (1932). *An Essay on the Nature and Significance of Economic Science.* New York: New York University Press.
Sarria Icaza, A. M. (2006). 'Tercer Sector y Economía Solidaria en el Sur de Brasil: características y perspectivas'. *Red de Investigadores Latinoamericanos de Economía Social y Solidaria* (RILESS); available at <http://www.riless.org> (accessed 13 May 2013).
Schmidt, D. and V. Perius (2003). 'Cooperativismo e cooperativa', in A. D. Cattani, (ed.), *A Outra Economia.* Porto Alegre: Veraz Editores: 63–72.
Servet, J.-M. (2007). 'Le principe de réciprocité chez Karl Polanyi'. *Revue Tiers Monde, 190*: 255–73.

3

Solidarity and Protection in Bolivian Popular Economy

Isabelle Hillenkamp

3.1 Introduction

Over the past decade, there has been considerable convergence of the debates on informality, vulnerability, and social protection. The debate on informality, for example, no longer focuses exclusively on low productivity and tax evasion, but increasingly also on the lack of social protection (ILO, 2002 and 2011; Chen, 2005; Perry et al., 2007). The lack of income, health, and old-age security, in particular, is recognized as having negative impacts on both personal well-being and the economic performance of informal workers. Together with other risks, in particular commercial risks, inadequate regulations, exposure to macroeconomic shocks and corruption, this results in a high degree of vulnerability in the informal economy (Grimm, van der Hoeven, and Lay, 2011). It is also increasingly recognized that protection can be created within the informal economy, as demonstrated by a new branch in the literature on social policy and welfare regimes (Barrientos, 2004; Martínez Franzoni, 2008; Martínez et al., 2009). The capacity of workers in the informal economy to provide their own protection is based primarily on mechanisms of solidarity and personal protection grounded in local practices of production, exchange, and financing. So far, there has been little study of these mechanisms. To some extent, there has been a tendency to identify these mechanisms with 'abusive demands' by family or community members, that can result in 'forced redistribution' detrimental to business development. This negative interpretation might explain this lack of attention. But it may also be due to the epistemological and methodological difficulties of integrating solidarity and economic activities in a common analytical framework.

This chapter aims at helping to fill this gap by critically analysing the contribution of different types of informal economic practices to social protection using survey data from the city of El Alto (Bolivia) and local literature. It is based on an interpretation of Karl Polanyi's principles of economic integration (1944 [1983]) as modalities of interdependence in production, financing, circulation (or transfer), and consumption as observed in the Latin American approach of a 'popular economy' (as defined in section 3.3.1). Section 3.2 presents the relevant aspects of the current debate on the informal economy, vulnerability, and social protection, and the main characteristics of the Bolivian case. Section 3.3 describes the questions our research sought to address, the theoretical framework, and the case study. This provides the basis for our analysis of four types of socio-economic practices that seek to provide protection against certain vulnerabilities in the informal economy of El Alto in section 3.4. Section 3.5 concludes.

3.2 Informal Economy, Vulnerability, and Social Protection: Literature Review and the Bolivian Case

3.2.1 The New Debate on Informality

Conventional approaches to studies of the informal sector—be they dualistic, structuralist, or legalistic—usually assume strongly differentiated formal and informal labour markets, even though their interpretations of the origins of this segmentation, the relationships between the segments, and the public policies to be implemented differ significantly (Candia, 2003; Chen, 2005). Over the past decade, the debate has been evolving to increasingly reflect the inner dynamics and heterogeneity of the informal 'sector'. This heterogeneity derives from the following aspects:

- (i) The size of enterprises and the reasons for informality, which may be due to exclusion, or, on the contrary, to exit strategies to escape fiscal and social regulations (Perry et al., 2007).
- (ii) Productivity, distinguishing between a large segment of 'survivalists', a small group of top performers, and a substantial group of micro- and small enterprises with low levels of capital but high levels of return on the invested capital (Grimm, van der Hoeven, and Lay, 2011).
- (iii) Levels of income and employment status, ranging from employers, own-account operators, unpaid family workers, wage workers in informal enterprises, and industrial outworkers in formal enterprises (Chen, 2005).
- (iv) Degree of segmentation of the informal and formal labour markets. While in some countries, such as Argentina and Colombia, segmentation is indeed high, in others, such as the Dominican Republic,

significant rates of transition between the two labour markets can be observed (Perry et al., 2007).

As a consequence, the concept and measurement of the informal 'sector' have been reoriented in three main directions. First, the focus has moved from a simple observation of the characteristics of enterprises (formal or not) to the nature of employment relations—whether or not they are regulated and protected. The International Labour Organization (ILO), in particular, has reoriented its approach, from simply observing the 'dilemma of the informal sector' to the '[promotion of] decent work along the entire continuum from the informal to the formal end of the economy' (ILO, 2002: 4). Second, consequently, the informal 'sector' has given way to the broader concepts of *informal economy* and *informality*. Third, the criteria ascribed to the informal sector of non-compliance with regulatory frameworks and low productivity[1] have been extended to indicators of exclusion from state social protection (see Box 3.1).

Box 3.1 EVOLUTION OF THE CRITERIA FOR MEASURING THE INFORMAL ECONOMY IN BOLIVIA

Following the productivist definition, criteria for measuring the informal sector in Bolivia were initially based on a distinction between five segments of the urban labour market: domestic, family (own-account workers and unpaid family workers), semi-entrepreneur (workers in a private enterprise of no more than four people), entrepreneur (workers in a private enterprise of five people or more), and the state. The informal sector was defined as the sum of the semi-entrepreneur and family segments. Informality was further assumed to be characterized by low productivity.

In its special report on informality in urban labour markets in 2007, the Unit for the Analysis of Social and Economic Policies of Bolivia (*Unidad de Análisis de Políticas Sociales y Económicas,* UDAPE) introduced two new criteria: a legal one, based on tax contributions, and vulnerability, based on whether or not contributions were made to a pension scheme. Estimates for this third criterion are significantly higher than the first two (see Box table), drawing attention to the lack of state welfare benefits for a much larger proportion of workers than those working in small enterprises or not paying taxes.

Types of measure	Criteria	Informality as a percentage of working population (per cent), 2005
Productivity	Small size of the productive unit	59.31
Legal	No fiscal identification number	65.23
Vulnerability	No contribution to a pension scheme	78.64

Source: Author, based on UDAPE (2007).

[1] Recommended by the ILO at the 15th International Conference on Labour Statistics in 1993.

3.2.2 *Informality and Vulnerability*

The debates on informality are thus extending beyond the criteria of productivity and tax evasion to include also lack of social protection and vulnerability. In a broad sense, vulnerability can be defined as 'a state in which a deficit of resources or other adverse conditions affects the individual's capacity to cope with critical life events and processes and the ability to take advantage of opportunities'.[2] In this sense, informality and vulnerability, although not fully correlated, are linked in several respects. First, informality, understood literally as the absence of a formal structure and lack of consistency (Hart, 2010), and not just of appearance, is a cause of irregular sales and incomes. Second, informality tends to limit business opportunities, usually to the local level where micro and small informal enterprises can be recognized as reliable business partners. Third, informality deprives workers of long-term and short-term social insurance, while increasing the risk of occupational accidents and diseases due to poor working conditions. Lastly, informality generally reduces the monetary resources of individuals and families, as incomes in the informal economy are significantly lower than in the formal economy, except for a small group of top performers.

This relationship between informality and vulnerability clearly holds in the case of Bolivia, where the informal economy accounts for a considerable share of employment—the highest in South America—and is characterized by a high degree of fragmentation of entrepreneurship, and, particularly, by low incomes and low levels of education (see Table 3.1).

Table 3.1 Indicators of vulnerability of the Bolivian informal economy

Dimension	Indicator	Measure (per cent)	Year or period
Extent	Share of employment	67	2004
Growth	Growth of self-employed workers	+6.9	1990–2000
Fragmentation	Share of self-employed workers	81	2002
	Share of wage workers	19	
Low incomes	Ratio of average income in the informal sector to average income in the formal sector	38	2006
Low level of education	Share of informal workers with primary education	73.2	2006

Source: Author, based on Chen (2005); ILO Labour Statistics Database (2006); and UDAPE (2007 and 2010).

[2] Definition of the Swiss National Centre of Competence in Research 'Overcoming Vulnerability: Life course Perspectives', based on Oris and Ritschard (2004).

3.2.3 Informality, Vulnerability, and Social Protection

A second debate, on social policy and social protection, introduces new dimensions to the discussion on informality and vulnerability. Between the 1940s and 1980s, a 'Bismarckian' model prevailed in Latin America, according to which social rights would progressively expand from some 'nuclei' of wage workers in the public and private industrial sectors to successive 'crowns' of new protected workers. Clearly, access to this 'social citizenship' has remained limited in the whole region, as it has excluded urban informal workers and rural workers, and its coverage has varied greatly across the countries. Bolivia is one of the countries where it has been very limited, with health coverage for only 26.3 per cent of the total population and pension coverage for around 22 per cent of the economically active population in 1981–5 (Salazar, Jiménez, and Wanderley, 2009: 40–1).

In the 1980s, the Latin American external public debt crisis and the subsequent structural adjustment programmes profoundly challenged this model. As a result of declining employment in the public sector and in private industries, the nuclei of protected workers began to diminish rather than expand. New social assistance policies targeting 'the poor' were introduced, followed by new measures such as conditional and unconditional cash transfers. In the 2000s, the idea of a two-dimensional protection system, where the traditional coverage would be complemented by universal minimum guarantees began to gain ground in international organizations and national governments (Bayón, Roberts, and Saravi, 1998; Schteingart, 1999; Goirand, 2003, Barrientos, Gideon, and Molyneux, 2008; ILO, 2011).

Assessing these changes is complex. On the one hand, the reduction of the insurance scheme in favour of greater assistance has been criticized as a denial of social citizenship to the poor and as representing a form of depoliticization of the debate on redistribution. This criticism has been exacerbated by the fact that work force and resources of the poor have been used in so-called poverty reduction programmes (Dagnino, 2003; Goirand, 2003; Lautier, 2003). On the other hand, especially in countries like Bolivia where social insurance had so far been reserved for a few privileged segments of the population, the new assistance policies and the non-contributory transfers, particularly in the area of pensions, finally provided benefits to vulnerable populations (see Box 3.2). Moreover, and unexpectedly, these changes widened the extent of social protection and turned the attention of observers and policy-makers to the *informal* provision of welfare and protection (Bayón, Roberts, and Saravi, 1998).

This shift is reflected notably in the new literature on welfare regimes in Latin America (Huber, 2002; Martinez, Molyneux, and Sánchez-Ancochea, 2009; and Wanderley, 2009). Inspired by the pioneering work of Esping-Andersen (1990) on the forms of capitalism and welfare regimes in OECD countries, it

Box 3.2 EVOLUTION OF SOCIAL POLICIES IN BOLIVIA FOLLOWING THE STRUCTURAL ADJUSTMENT PROGRAMME OF 1985

In Bolivia, the welfare system experienced a significant setback with the structural adjustment programme of 1985: health coverage fell from 26.3 per cent of the total population in 1981–5 to 21.3 per cent in 1986–90. Meanwhile, as the average income fell by about 25 per cent in eight years (1981–9), new assistance programmes were introduced, notably a food-for-work programme and a Social Emergency Fund (created in 1987). However, their impact was limited in comparison with the needs. From the early 1990s onwards, social policies focused on mothers and children, leading, at the end of the decade, to new universal minimal benefits in maternal and infant care (SUMI) as well as elderly care. At the same time, pension insurance was privatized (in 1997), though its coverage did not increase. A non-contributory pension programme for all Bolivians over 65 years of age was created (BONOSOL), which was replaced by *Bono Dignidad* in 2008, with new conditions of access and a new funding model. Since 1997, the country has benefited from the Heavily Indebted Poor Countries (HIPC) Initiative of the World Bank and the International Monetary Fund (IMF), implemented through a series of measures, including employment programmes such as PLANE, PROPAIS, and, more recently, EDIMO.[3] The protection system is now much more diverse than it was thirty years ago, but it remains fragmentary and insufficient (Instituto Prisma, 2000; Farah, 2003; Salazar, Jiménez, and Wanderley, 2009; Wanderley, 2009; UDAPE, 2010).

broadens the perspective of social policy by drawing attention to its interaction with labour markets and families. New, Latin American specific typologies of these regimes point to the role of the informal economy and of households in providing protection. For example, Barrientos (2004) speaks of a 'liberal-informal' and 'hyphenated Latin-American welfare regime', relying on a mix of provisions through households, the market, and the state. Martinez Franzoni (2008) distinguishes between three groups of Latin American countries: (i) those following a '*productivist welfare regime*', as in Chile, where a large insertion of the population in the labour market acts as a direct protection against risk; (ii) those following a '*protectionist welfare regime*', as in Costa Rica, which relies on a significant redistribution of resources through public policies; and (iii) those following an '*informal-familialist regime*' exemplified notably by Bolivia, which, not being able to follow either of the above strategies, delegates much of the social protection to households, especially to the poorest.

[3] Respectively the *Plan Nacional de Empleo de Emergencia* (National Emergency Employment Plan), *Programa de Lucha contra la Pobreza y Apoyo a la Inversión Social* (Programme to Fight Poverty and Support Social Investment) and *Empleo Digno Intensivo de Mano de Obra* (Labor Intensive Decent Employment Programme) (author's translation from Spanish).

3.3 Theoretical Background and Research Design

3.3.1 Research Objectives and Theoretical Framework

The evolution of the debates on informality, vulnerability, and social protection, and growing evidence of the multiple sources of protection give rise to new questions. How is social protection being produced in the informal economy, especially in countries like Bolivia where an informal-familialist welfare regime prevails? On which types of social relations is such protection based? What kinds of vulnerability are the different protective mechanisms able to cope with? And how do these mechanisms interact with one another?

While comparative and statistical studies, especially those on welfare regimes, have proved useful for identifying these issues, they do not allow us to explore the complexity of the practices of protection in the informal economy. This objective calls for more localized studies and a shift from the classical approaches of the informal economy, focused on the nature of employment relations, on the conditions of transition to formality, and on the promotion of decent work, to studying the inner socio-economic logics of informal economy. In Latin America, such an approach has been introduced through the concept of 'popular economy',[4] which can be briefly defined as 'the diversity of economic activities and social practices developed by popular groups in order to ensure the satisfaction of their basic material and immaterial needs through the use of their own working force and available resources' (Sarria Icaza and Tiriba, 2006, author's translation from French). Combined with the principles of economic integration according to Karl Polanyi, understood as the modalities of interdependence of production, financing, circulation, or transfer, and consumption (as argued in the introduction to this book), this approach allows us to consider the various forms of protection rooted in the informal socio-economic practices of popular groups, but without idealizing them.

Various forms of protection arising from such interdependencies may be based on relationships of solidarity and obligation among peers, drawing on the principles of reciprocity or householding (e.g. between producers of the same cooperative, or *compadres* of an indigenous community); but they may also consist of centralized and often hierarchical relations, driven by the principle of redistribution or, again, householding (e.g. between the members of an indigenous community and their local authorities, or between the parents and children or husband and wife of a patriarchal family). However, while

[4] This concept has been used widely by Latin American sociologists and economists since the 1990s (Razeto, 1984; Razeto and Calcagni, 1989; Larraechea and Nyssens, 1994; Coraggio, 1995; Núñez, 1995; and Singer, 2000), but its use in the Anglophone world is more recent (see, for example, Hull and James, 2012).

reciprocity produces protection through solidarity between the members of a group, it may also lead to local exclusion, and hence to rising inequalities.

3.3.2 Case Study and Method

Our case study focuses on protection through practices of production, exchange, and financing in the popular economy of El Alto in Bolivia. This city of 1,000,000 inhabitants, located on the Altiplano above La Paz, grew from the rural migration of the last six decades. Almost three-quarters of its inhabitants identify themselves as part of the indigenous people of the Aymara. El Alto is also the poorest city in the country, with about two-thirds of its population living below the poverty line. Vulnerability in El Alto is due to three main factors: (i) rural migration in conditions of poverty; (2) a massive[5] insertion into the informal economy; and (iii) a lack of social policies and inadequate economic policies. In addition, El Alto is known for its strong unions, associations, and cooperatives of producers and vendors. Some of them belong to the Solidarity economy and fair trade Movement of Bolivia (*Movimiento de Economía solidaria y Comercio justo en Bolivia*) created in 2009.

The following is an analysis of four types of practices of production, exchange, and financing used by Aymara migrants in El Alto, based on urban-rural circuits, on family networks, and on 'solidarity economy organizations'.[6] Our aim is to illustrate some mechanisms of protection in the popular economy, and to demonstrate the utility of the Polanyian conceptual framework. The selected practices are significant in El Alto, but they do not constitute an exhaustive inventory; protection practices rooted in local churches, *fiestas*, or unions, to name just a few, are not taken into account here. Our analysis is based on both local literature (especially on small producers, social networks, and rural–urban linkages) and field data on solidarity economy organizations,[7] about which there is very limited literature.

[5] Amounting to 70 to 75 per cent of the working population, according to the productivist definition.

[6] As a first approximation, these organizations are groups of producers of the popular economy aiming, by various modes of collective action, at being inserted more favourably into the markets so as to increase and/or stabilize their incomes. For a more detailed characterization, see 3.4.3.

[7] An initial survey (2005–7) covered thirty organizations of solidarity economy; a second survey (2010–11) involved thirty women producers from eight organizations. Part 3.4.3 is based on the first survey, while parts 3.4.1, 3.4.2 and 3.4.4 are based on the second one. Both surveys were qualitative, aimed at understanding the inner logic of the socio-economic practices and situating them in their social, political, and macroeconomic contexts. In addition, our data are based on interviews with leaders of umbrella and support organizations, workers of microfinance institutions, political leaders, and researchers in Bolivia (Hillenkamp, 2009 and 2012).

3.4 Protection Practices in the Popular Economy of El Alto

3.4.1 New Family and Community Solidarity to Secure Food Supply

A first type of practice consists of compensating for weak and irregular cash incomes through small farming activities. This type of practice, long denounced by Karl Marx as a way of resorting to the 'natural' economy to reduce the cost of reproduction of the labour force, acquires a new meaning when considered in terms of protection. Different principles of economic integration can be distinguished between farming activities in urban plots and those in rural areas.

(I) FARMING ACTIVITIES IN URBAN PLOTS

The main type of habitation in El Alto consists of a few rooms built on a considerably larger plot of land. This leaves enough room for small, subsistence farming activities, especially in the outlying districts.[8] Residents raise small livestock, such as rabbits, sheep, or guinea pigs, or grow grains—typically quinoa—or vegetables for their own consumption.

The dominant principle of economic integration is householding: work and production are *shared* by the whole family or, less frequently, by part of the family living on the plot. This can be a nuclear family, or an extended family consisting of several generations and sometimes including lateral kin, especially young parents from the countryside. The strategy consists of partial autarky aimed at protecting part of the food consumption from market fluctuations. Protection is both direct, as food prices vary on local and international markets, and indirect, as incomes fluctuate as a result of changes in product and labour prices.

(II) FARMING ACTIVITIES IN RURAL COMMUNITIES

A large and stable proportion of about 30 per cent of the residents of El Alto maintain agricultural production in their rural community where they own land or livestock (typically sheep or camelids). This practice rests on two conditions. First, the city dwellers have to maintain tight social relations with their community, especially by participating in the local political system, by engaging in working groups, and by sponsoring social events and ritual celebrations. Second, they have to entrust part of the agricultural work to a member of their family living in the community, generally a brother or sister, as they cannot carry out the entire work themselves. They usually participate on an ad hoc basis, typically during seeding, harvesting, and food

[8] According to a recent survey of the Food and Agriculture Organization of the United Nations (FAO, 2011) in Latin America, urban agriculture is a significant and growing activity, including in El Alto.

processing, and give part of the production to the brother or sister or other family member(s) who helped them.

These practices rely on three different principles of economic integration and three different types of interdependencies: (i) reciprocity; (ii) redistribution, through the symbolic and material exchanges required to maintain one's membership in the community; and (iii) householding, with the member(s) of the family performing the agricultural work, as both labour and production are shared between the rural and urban part of this new family network. Far from diminishing community ties and nuclearization of the family, these interdependencies, based on new urban–rural complementarities (Albó, 2002; Antequera Durán, 2010), allow both parts to secure their livelihoods: they protect the urban dwellers' food supply from market fluctuations and they increase the rural dwellers' access to land and to urban products.

3.4.2 Domestic Solidarity for Market-Oriented Income-Generating Activities

A second type of practice in the popular economy of El Alto consists of mobilizing the variety of resources available within the family network to develop one or several market-oriented income-generating activities. These resources are varied, such as family know-how, for example in handicrafts, a room on the street to set up a small shop, a room or a place in the patio to accommodate a productive workshop, family networks to market a product, family savings to invest in a new activity, or an unused room of the house that can be used as collateral in a mortgage contract.

In all these practices, 'family' solidarity is mobilized to pool the resources needed for the development of one or more petty market activities. However, these solidarities should not be idealized. First, while in some cases these practices may represent a deliberate exit strategy from the formal economy, and may be valued by their proponents as a form of autonomous work (Rossel and Rojas, 2000; Wanderley, 2004), in the majority of cases, they are driven by exclusion from the formal economy, rooted in ethnic and gender discrimination (Rivera Cusicanqui, 1996; Salazar, Jiménez, and Wanderley, 2009) and poor formal education. In these cases, family solidarity appears to be a response to vulnerability arising from irregular and low incomes in the informal economy. It takes the form of a diversification of activities and the mutual sharing of risks and resources. Two principles of economic integration are mobilized in an asymmetric way: the market, which influences the type of production and the price levels, and householding, as an *instrument* of this production. Even though the role of family solidarity is positive at the local level, it raises the issue of social justice, because, on a structural level, it compensates for the lack of formal employment and provision of state welfare benefits.

Second, 'family' solidarity is not necessarily fair or efficient insofar as it relies on specific relations within family groups and networks. The concept of 'domesticity' helps explain this ambiguity. Etymologically, domesticity relates to life at home (*domus*), but also to servitude. The balance between these two conflicting aspects is shaped by historical social and economic conditions. In rural Aymara communities, relations between men and women are based on the principle of complementarity, and male and female roles are relatively undifferentiated at the household level (Harris, 2000; Farah and Salazar, 2007). With the migration to El Alto and insertion into the informal economy, gender roles tend to become differentiated and more hierarchical. First, the informal labour market is segmented according to gender, with a revenue gap of about 60 per cent.[9] Work in the domestic sphere then becomes increasingly separated from income-generating activities. It is considered inferior and falls essentially on women. In this context, domestic solidarity is far from being based on equal relationships within the family. Petty market activities of the different members of a family group are certainly interdependent, but the nature of the interdependence may take the form of domination and even exploitation, rather than support and fairness.

3.4.3 Solidarity Among Producers for Improving Their Position on Markets

A third type of practice has acquired some significance in the popular economy of El Alto: the creation of groups of producers claiming to practise a 'solidarity economy' (*economía solidaria*). Men or women producers with a similar activity, generally in the handicrafts sector (e.g. weavers, producers of musical instruments, tailors, carpenters, and goldsmiths) form an association, a cooperative or an informal group. Groups generally have at least an internal rule book and a legal status, and some are listed on the trade register and even in the fiscal system.[10] From the point of view of the producers, the group enables the production of larger and more regular quantities of products. This facilitates access to more demanding and lucrative markets such as 'fair trade' (*comercio justo*) markets, whether based on national or international certification through organizations such as Fairtrade Labelling Organizations International (FLO) or the International

[9] According to a survey by MECOVI (Programme for the Improvement of Surveys and the Measurement of Living Conditions in Latin America and the Caribbean) in 2001–2.
[10] In contrast, none of the groups interviewed was contributing to social security.

Fair Trade Association (IFAT), through non-governmental organizations (NGOs) involved in development cooperation, through direct orders, or through local stores. This marketing strategy requires a high level of coordination, which generally involves standardizing the products, sharing productive and financial resources, and searching for orders or retail outlets for the whole group. As for decision-making, solidarity economy groups are based on a model of democratic self-management through the election of an executive board based on a rotating system inspired from the community model, and debate among their members, generally through weekly meetings.

One principle of economic integration involved here is reciprocity. Based on the acceptance of horizontal interdependencies between producers, this principle is applied here in a very different context from that of rural communities. It aims primarily at reducing vulnerability resulting from the disadvantageous position of individual producers on the markets, due to their low level of production and limited radius of sale. However, this is not the only principle, even if it is certainly the most visible one, since it is cited frequently by producers. Another reason for producers to join a group is to collectively access training, funding, and support programmes, and, notably, to improve their access to markets.

Given the paucity and inadequacy of public policies for promoting small producers in Bolivia, such forms of support have been provided mostly by NGOs financed by international development agencies or by private foundations. These resources, although generally useful, and even indispensable for their beneficiaries, induce a vertical relationship that can generate dependence on the NGOs, in particular when the producers have to rely on only one or a few NGOs for such support. Far from idealizing public policies, which carry the specific risk of political 'clientelism', this type of support, based on generosity, is of a fundamentally different nature from that based on the right to public support. Protection, for instance by providing access to a fair trade market, induces a potential relationship of domination of the NGO which provides this access over the group of producers. Also within the group, a hierarchical structure tends to develop between some outstanding leaders able to 'capture funding' (*captar fondos*) and the other producers. The principle of redistribution thus has contradictory effects: on one hand, it strengthens the principle of reciprocity between producers by providing protection against vulnerabilities resulting from their disavantaged position on the markets; on the other hand, it induces a hierarchy within the group and a risk of dependence on the support organization, which contradicts the initial objective of solidarity among peers.

3.4.4 New Solidarity Among Women to Reconcile Their Productive and Reproductive Roles

Finally, solidarity economy groups may provide a specific means of solidarity for women. Since the 1980s, the number of such groups composed exclusively of women has increased significantly in El Alto and other Bolivian cities, contrasting with the former model of male-headed cooperatives and farmers' associations.[11] These new all-women urban groups reveal another ambiguous aspect of solidarity between producers. Starting from the rationale of women with different migration profiles and ages entering a group, two specific functions of the groups can be identified.

3.4.4.1 HELPING WOMEN TO FULFIL THEIR NEW PRODUCTIVE ROLE OF GENERATING A MONETARY INCOME

This function is essential, whether for married women whose income, arising from their participation in the group, is considered a 'supplement' to their husbands' (although this supplement might be considerable) or as the principal income for women heads of households.[12] This function also varies according to the professional aspirations of the women, which reflect their migration history and level of education. First generation migrants generally consider working as artisans in a group after having worked as domestic servants, street vendors, or home workers selling to a middleman. Second and third generation migrants, on the other hand, mostly aspire to 'professional' jobs, typically as secretary, nurse, or teacher, or to a better paid handicraft job that allows them to 'excel' (*superarse*). Groups can be a vehicle for these aspirations, insofar as they enable their members to perform more demanding activities (e.g. goldsmith), fund studies, supplement their income as professionals, or apply for professional jobs. They also give women access to training or enable them to become leaders.[13]

3.4.4.2 HELPING WOMEN RECONCILE THEIR PRODUCTIVE ROLE WITH THEIR DOMESTIC RESPONSIBILITIES

This second function of the women's groups, which is especially important for those with young children, is based on their ability to set their own organizational criteria within the production group. These include flexible work schedules adapted to those of their children's school, possibility to do part of their work at home or take their children to their workplace, and in some

[11] This was despite the fact that agricultural work usually involved the entire family.
[12] Which is the case for about one in six women in El Alto (Salazar, 2000).
[13] For an analysis of the contribution of solidarity economy groups to women's empowerment in Andean Bolivia, see Charlier (2006).

cases, receive specific support from the group, such as a small monetary compensation for maternity leave. It must be noted that these opportunities do not exist in all groups. It depends, in particular, on the share of work that can be performed at home, the technical characteristics of the activity, the cost of the equipment the women work with and the division of labour within the group.

While the self-organization of women in the popular economy deserves respect, it has its limits. The protection resulting from reciprocity among women is insufficient to cope with negative events of long duration, such as disease, or events affecting all women, such as the lack of old-age security. In addition, there is a particular risk that the existence of solidarity among poor women will provide an excuse for not expanding necessary social protection and failure to introduce important economic policies aimed at creating more employment.

3.5 Conclusions

Our analysis of four types of informal practices of production, exchange, and financing in El Alto (Bolivia), based on Karl Polanyi's principles of economic integration, demonstrates their contribution to social protection (see Table 3.2). Far from being obstacles to the economic performance of informal enterprises, these practices, based on the principles of reciprocity, redistribution, householding, and the market, provide different types

Table 3.2 Summary of the vulnerabilities, protection practices, and principles of economic integration analysed in El Alto

Dimensions or causes of vulnerability	Protection practices	Principles of economic integration
Fluctuation and/or insufficiency of cash income	Production of food for own consumption in urban plots, and, in rural areas, through new family and community links	Reciprocity, redistribution and householding
Exclusion from the formal labour market	Mobilization of the resources of the domestic group to develop petty market activities	Market and householding
• Disadvantageous position in goods markets • Lack of specific policies for economic development	Groups of solidarity economy	Reciprocity and redistribution
Contradictions between the productive and reproductive roles of women	Female groups of solidarity economy	Reciprocity and redistribution

of protection against specific vulnerabilities (see Table 3.2). Our analysis highlights this role, while drawing attention to the different types of interdependence underlying protection and their consequences for the status of individuals. While some practices that rely on the principles of reciprocity of householding are based on solidarity among peers, others, starting from the principle of redistribution or, again, householding, can lead to hierarchy, dependence, and even exploitation.

Lastly, our analysis also provides evidence of the limited protection available based on local resources in the informal popular economy and the complementary role of state welfare programmes (such as pensions and health insurance schemes for informal workers) and policies of economic promotion (in particular access to markets and financial schemes for organizations of producers). Showing the interaction between economic practices, protection, and solidarity thus points to the necessity of a much stronger integration of the fields of social protection and economic promotion through public policy.

References

Albó, X. (2002). *Pueblos indios en la política*. La Paz: Plural.

Antequera Durán, N (2010). 'Itinerarios urbanos: Continuidades y circuitos urbano-rurales como característica de las ciudades bolivianas'. *Seminario internacional, Ciudades en transformación: Modos de vida y territorialidades* ['International Seminar on Cities in transformation: Lifestyles and territoriality']. La Paz: CIDES-UMSA and LaSUR—EPFL.

Barrientos, A. (2004). 'Latin America: Towards a Liberal-Informal Welfare Regime', in I. Gough, G. Wood, A. Barrientos, P. Bevan, P. David, and G. Room (eds.), *Insecurity and Welfare Regimes in Asia, Africa and Latin America*. Cambridge: Cambridge University Press: 121–168.

——J. Gideon, and M. Molyneux (2008). 'New Developments in Latin America's Social Policy'. *Development and Change*, 39: 759–74.

Bayón, C., B. Roberts, and G. Saravi (1998). 'Ciudadanía social y sector informal en América Latina'. *Perfiles Latinoamericanos*, 13: 73–111.

Candia, J. M. (2003). 'Sector informal ¿treinta años de un debate bizantino?' *Nueva Sociedad*, 186: 36–45.

Charlier, S. (2006). 'L'économie solidaire au féminin: Quel apport spécifique pour l'empoderamiento des femmes? Une étude de cas dans les Andes boliviennes'. Doctoral thesis in social sciences. Catholic University of Louvain-la-Neuve.

Chen, M. A. (2005). 'Rethinking the Informal Economy: Linkages with the Formal Economy and the Formal Regulatory Environment'. *EGDI and WIDER Research Paper*, Helsinki: UNU-WIDER.

Coraggio, J. L. (1995). *Desarrollo humano, economia popular y educación*. Buenos Aires: Aique Grupo.

Dagnino, E. (2003). 'Citizenship in Latin America: An Introduction'. *Latin American Perspectives*, 2: 211–25.

Esping-Andersen, G. (1990). *The Three Worlds of Welfare Capitalism*. Cambridge, MA: Polity Press.

FAO (2011). 'Agricultura Urbana y periurbana en América Latina y El Caribe: Una realidad'. Available at <http://www.fao.org/fileadmin/templates/FCIT/PDF/Brochure_FAO_3.pdf> (accessed 02/12/2011).

Farah, I. (2003). 'Incorporación de la perspectiva de género en la Estrategia Boliviana de Reducción de la Pobreza', in S. Berger (ed.), *Inequidades, pobreza y mercado de trabajo: Bolivia y Perú*. Lima: International Labour Office.

—— and C. Salazar (2007). *La desigualdad entre mujeres*. La Paz: Universidad Mayor de San Andrés, Postgrado en Ciencias del Desarrollo.

Goirand, C. (2003). 'Citizenship and Poverty in Brazil'. *Latin American Perspectives, 2:* 18–40.

Grimm, M., R. van der Hoeven, and J. Lay (2011). 'Unlocking Potential: Tackling Economic, Institutional and Social Constraints of Informal Entrepreneurship in Sub-Saharan Africa: Main Findings and Policy Conclusions'. *Unlocking Potential of Informal Entrepreneurship: Project Papers*. The Hague: Institute of Social Studies.

Harris, O. (2000). *To Make the Earth Bear Fruit: Essays on Fertility, Work and Gender in Highland Bolivia*. London: Institute of Latin American Studies.

Hart, K. (2010). 'Informal Economy', in K. Hart, J.-L. Laville, and A. D. Cattani (eds.), *The Human Economy: A Citizen's Guide*. Cambridge: Polity Press, MA: 142–53.

Hillenkamp, I. (2009). 'Formes d'intégration de l'économie dans les démocraties de marché: Une théorie substantive à partir de l'étude du mouvement d'économie solidaire dans la ville d'El Alto (Bolivie)'. Doctoral thesis in development studies, Graduate Institute of International and Development Studies, University of Geneva, Geneva.

—— (2012). *La economía solidaria, ¿un camino de emancipación para las mujeres de la ciudad de El Alto?* El Alto, Bolivia: Centro de Promoción de la Mujer Gregoria Apaza.

Huber, E. (ed.) (2002). *Models of Capitalism: Lessons for Latin America*. University Park, PA: The Pensylvannia State University Press.

Hull, E. and D. James (eds.) (2012). *Popular Economies in South Africa,* special issue of *Africa* 82(01).

ILO (2002). *Travail Décent et Économie Informelle*. International Labour Conference 90th session, Report VI, Geneva: International Labour Office.

—— (2011). *Efficient Growth, Employment and Decent Work in Africa: Time for a New Vision*. Geneva: ILO, Employment Sector.

Instituto Prisma (2000). *Las políticas sobre la pobreza en Bolivia: Dimensiones políticas y resultados (1985–1999)*. La Paz: Plural.

Larraechea, I. and M. Nyssens (1994). 'L'économie solidaire: Un autre regard sur l'économie populaire au Chili', in J.-L. Laville (ed.), *L'économie Solidaire: Une Perspective Internationale*. Paris: Desclée de Brouwer: 177–222.

Lautier, B. (2003). 'Le léopard et la panthère écossaise: Mondialisation, éclatement spatial et fractionnement social dans les métropoles latino-américaines', in A. Osmont and C. Goldblum (eds.), *Villes et Citadins dans la Mondialisation*. Paris: Karthala: 51–89.

Martínez Franzoni, J. (2008). 'Welfare Regimes in Latin America: Capturing Constellations of Markets, Families, and Policies'. *Latin American Politics and Society*, 50: 67–100.

Martínez, J., M. Molyneux, and D. Sánchez-Ancochea (2009). 'Latin American Capitalism: Economic and Social Policy in Transition'. *Economy and Society*, 38: 1–16.

Núñez, O. (1995). *La economía popular, asociativa y autogestionaria*. Managua: Centro para la Promoción, la Investigación y el Desarrollo Rural Social.

Oris, M. and G. Ritschard (2004). 'La précarité: Etat absorbant ou accident de parcours?' In J.-P. Fragnière and M. Nanchen (eds.), *Entre science et action: La démographie au service de la cité. Mélanges en l'honneur de Herman–Michel Hagmann*. Lausanne: Réalités sociales: 115–26.

Perry, G., W. Maloney, O. Arias, P. Fajnzylber, A. Mason, and J. Saavedra-Chanduvi (2007). *Informality: Exit and Exclusion*. Washington, DC: World Bank.

Polanyi, K. (1983 [1944]). *La Grande Transformation: Aux Origines Politiques et Economiques de Notre Temps*. Paris: Gallimard.

Razeto, L. (1984). *Economía de solidaridad y Mercado democrático*. Santiago, Chile: Programa de Economía del Trabajo.

—— and R. Calcagni (1989). *Para un proyecto de desarrollo de un sector de economía popular de solidaridad y de trabajo*. Santiago, Chile: Programa de Economía del Trabajo and Fundación Trabajo Para Un Hermano.

Rivera Cusicanqui, S. (1996). *Bircholas. Trabajo de mujeres: explotación capitalista y opresión colonial entre las migrantes aymarás de La Paz y El Alto*. La Paz: Mama Huaco.

Rossel, P. and B. Rojas (2000). *Ser Productor en El Alto*. La Paz: CEDLA.

Salazar, C. (2000). *Pactos de Género e Intersubjetividad Familiar en Bolivia*. La Paz: United Nations Development Programme.

—— E. Jiménez, and F. Wanderley (2009). *Migración, cuidado y sostenibilidad de la vida*. La Paz: Plural.

Sarria Icaza, A. M. and L. Tiriba (2006). 'Économie populaire', in J.-L. Laville and A. D. Cattani (eds.), *Dictionnaire de l'autre économie*. Paris: Gallimard: 258–68.

Schteingart, M. (ed.) (1999). *Políticas sociales para los pobres en América Latina*. México: Miguel Angel Porrua.

Singer, P. (2000). 'Economía dos setores populares: Proposta e desafio', in G. Kraychete and L. B. Costa (eds.), *Economia dos setores populares: Entre a realidade e a utopia*. Brasil: Vozes.

UDAPE (2007). *Informe especial: La informalidad en el mercado laboral urbano 1996–2006*. La Paz, Bolivia: Unidad de Análisis de Políticas Sociales y Económicas.

—— (2010). *Políticas Macroeconómicas, Choques Externos y Protección Social en Bolivia*. La Paz, Bolivia: Unidad de Análisis de Políticas Sociales y Económicas.

Wanderley, F. (2004). 'Reciprocity without cooperation: Small producer networks and political identities in Bolivia'. PhD Dissertation, submitted in partial fulfilment of the requirements for the degree of Doctor in Philosophy, Columbia University.

—— (2009). *Crecimiento, empleo y bienestar social ¿Por qué Bolivia es tan desigual?*, La Paz: Plural.

4

Self-Managed Work, Social Protection, and Community Development: The Case of the UST Cooperative (Argentina)

Gonzalo Vázquez

4.1 Introduction

In order to study economic practices that move away from the ideal type of capitalist enterprise, a conceptual framework is needed that captures indications of alternative rationales, different from profit maximization and capital accumulation. For this reason we consider that the Polanyian framework of a substantive and plural economy (Polanyi, 1994; Coraggio, 2009a; Laville, 2010; see also the chapter by Lemaître in this book) is appropriate for the study of the economic experiences of self-managed workers.

Polanyi's view of a substantive economy establishes that there are several (plural) ways in which a society can organize (and, in fact organizes) its economy, and that in all known societies there are (at least) four economic principles: reciprocity, redistribution, householding, and exchange. Each of these principles is combined with certain institutional models: symmetry, centrality, autarky, and market respectively. The way in which these principles are applied is diverse and specific to each historical society, which institutionalizes them according to its prevailing social organization. There are also several ways in which these principles and institutions are combined in each society, some of them being more predominant and others subordinate or marginal, depending on the social organization (Polanyi, 1994).

The informal sector perspective (Tokman, 2001; Portes and Haller, 2004) usually analyses self-managed workers' economic initiatives as 'embryos' of capitalist enterprises, which, to survive and develop, should 'modernize' and evolve into 'normal' companies. The growth of enterprises through capital accumulation is the economic rationale underlying this viewpoint. Hence those who subscribe to this view interpret the behaviours and practices not guided by this logic as 'irrational'. In contrast, the substantive and plural economy perspective not only admits but also aims to understand other kinds of logic and economic principles underlying the practices of workers.

This chapter presents some analysis and thoughts based on a case study of the workers' cooperative, Union Solidaria de Trabajadores (UST), located on the periphery of Buenos Aires city, Argentina. The UST cooperative is a 'recovered enterprise' that resumed productive activities when the capitalist company where its members previously worked closed down. Over the years, it has gained rich experience in self-managed work and community development. During these years, it has been able to restore its jobs and has even generated new employment opportunities for the youth from the local community. It also offers several activities and social services for the development of its neighbourhood, which is its most innovative aspect and is, in fact, unique.[1]

However, despite its considerable achievements in realizing its productive and social goals, UST's workers are still in a relatively vulnerable position. This is because, as self-managed workers, they do not have social security protection similar to that of formal, salaried workers, since, historically, national regulations relating to social security have been designed only for salaried employees (Vázquez, 2011). This case study provides an example of the vulnerable situation of self-managed workers due to the inadequacy of legal and institutional frameworks that regulate them, despite their successful performance in production and income generation. Indeed, the International Labour Organization (ILO) has been calling for changes in state policies and regulations to guarantee 'decent work' for workers in cooperatives, on the basis that these organizations offer an important means to leave informality (ILO, 2002: 'Recommendation 193: concerning the promotion of cooperatives').

This study was developed in the context of a joint research project between the ILO and the European Research Network, EMES, entitled, 'Informal Economy, Vulnerabilities and Employment: Substantive Performance of the Informal Economy in Risk Management, Livelihood Securization and Employment Creation—Lessons for Facilitating Transition to Formality and Decent Work'.[2] In this project, the same conceptual framework and methodological approach, based on a substantive and plural economy perspective, have been applied to study cases from different countries. The specific

[1] For more details, see the cooperative website on Facebook: <http://www.facebook.com/pages/Cooperativa-UST/355704594931?fref=ts> (accessed 14 June 2013).

[2] For more details, see <http://www.emes.net> (accessed 14 June 2013).

case study examined here provides an analysis of the information obtained from semi-structured interviews conducted with various workers of the UST cooperative.[3]

Section 4.2 presents a brief description of the case study, with a focus on some aspects of the cooperative: its internal organization and governance structure and criteria for distribution of revenue. Section 4.3 analyses the restrictions imposed by political and institutional structures and the strategies of the cooperative to overcome these difficulties through networking and strong ties with its local community. In section 4.4, we reflect on the economic logic that guides the cooperative's decisions and actions, including an analysis from the substantive economy perspective (Polanyi, 1944; Laville, 2010). The final section, 4.5, provides an analysis of the sustainability of social and solidarity economy enterprises from a plural perspective (Coraggio, 2009b; Vázquez, 2010).

4.2 Key Aspects of the UST Cooperative's Experience

The UST cooperative was created in the context of a deep social and economic crisis in Argentina. In 2003, the biggest industrial group in the country (Techint) decided to close a company that employed 140 workers for collection, transfer, and disposal of solid waste generated in Buenos Aires city and its surrounding areas. Guided by their union leaders, forty workers decided to occupy the company site, and for several months they resisted the eviction orders and had to cope with a lack of income. They were supported by several families from the surrounding neighbourhood. As a collective strategy to keep their jobs, and based on other experiences from 'recovered enterprises' in Argentina, on 25 July 2003 they formed the Union Solidaria de Trabajadores (UST) workers' cooperative. Recovered enterprises are collective initiatives of workers who, facing the bankruptcy or closure of a capitalist-owned company and with few chances of finding jobs in the formal sector in the context of high unemployment, occupy the company premises and organize themselves as an associative and self-managed enterprise. Most recovered enterprises become workers' cooperatives. This new mode enables them to continue with the productive and commercial activity they were doing before.[4] Under this

[3] Our analysis is based on four in-depth interviews, three conducted by the author and María Victoria Deux Marzi (of which two took place between 2010 and 2011), and one by Valeria Costanzo in 2007. We also included in the analysis, records of two visits to the cooperative in 2009 and 2010 under previous academic activities, and a presentation made by representatives of the Cooperative to a post-graduate class on social economy (UNGS) in 2010.

[4] According to official data, in October 2010 there were 280 recovered enterprises in Argentina, involving a total of 16,400 workers (OSERA, 2010).

new legal form, this group of workers with experience in the area, offered their services to the state-owned company—*Coordinación Ecológica Área Metropolitana Sociedad del Estado* (CEAMSE)—responsible for waste disposal. After several months of struggle and conflict, in late 2003 CEAMSE signed an annual agreement with the cooperative to do maintenance tasks in the dump area after the closure of the dump. Since then, the cooperative has performed these tasks so successfully that CEAMSE has renewed its trust and increased its demand for their services, thereby guaranteeing UST's continuity and growth until the time of writing.

The main economic activities of the UST cooperative, which generate most of its income, are the sanitary service and the production and maintenance of green areas, for which it has specialized workers. However, in addition, it undertakes or participates in several projects and activities relating to community development in its neighbourhood, most of which are developed and implemented jointly with non-governmental organizations and state organisms (local, provincial, and national), as well as with local residents. The following are the main projects undertaken so far:

- The building of a recreation centre for several sports (football, gym, handball, and volleyball) and cultural activities (e.g. music, art, dance, and workshops), in which hundreds of children, adolescents, and adults from the neighbourhood participate.
- The building of a school for adults, at present attended by more than 100 participants at the primary and secondary levels.
- A community bank which offers microcredit mainly for women in the neighbourhood to enable them to operate small productive and commercial ventures.
- Recovery of abandoned tracts of land for an agroecological project to produce vegetables for the neighbourhood.
- Building and renovating houses for families suffering housing emergency in the neighbourhood.
- Education and employment of adolescents and adults in connection with public policies implemented in the territory.
- At present, a community health centre is being constructed, together with a community pharmacy and a market selling basic food requirements.

All these activities are deemed to cover the essential needs of the neighbourhood, where most workers from the cooperative live.

The cooperative is now composed of eighty-five workers, fifty-seven of whom are members and twenty-four are 'candidates for membership'. The latter is a first stage created by the organization to provide a testing period for potential members, when they need to show their commitment to the job and to the community projects promoted by the UST cooperative. In addition, nine technicians or specialists (e.g. engineers, lawyers, accountants) who work in the organization are not formally associated but provide services to the cooperative as professional freelancers, but they share the UST's ideology and usually participate (in discussions but without voting rights) in the members' assembly.

4.2.1 Organizational Structure of UST

The governing structure of the organization is based on the workers' cooperative statute. At the beginning they had no knowledge or training on how a cooperative works, but later, after some training, they were able to assume their role as cooperative members. Nevertheless, they always consider themselves mainly as workers who have organized themselves as self-employed in order to keep their jobs. The UST cooperative has an administrative council, which is chosen by the members' assembly. Most council members used to be part of the old trade union delegates' commission when they worked for the previous company. Some young workers who are deeply involved in the UST project have joined them. Since 2004, there has been some turnover in the management and in positions of responsibility, although the current president's leadership is very strong and for this reason it would be difficult to find a replacement.

The administrative council's leadership is an element to be considered in the case analysis since it has played a central role, and has achieved legitimacy throughout the process of recovery, growth, consolidation, and future plans of the cooperative. During their time as union leaders, before the cooperative was formed, the council members had defended the workers firmly, with coherence and honesty, even by suggesting alternative proposals in order to avoid the dismissal of the workers during the economic crisis. During the resistance and the company's recovery process, they refused to divide the collective, and were out of work for several months, during which time they had to be financially supported by their co-workers. Even when their employers offered them money and resources for personal benefit, they refused such bribes, ensuring that their co-workers were made aware of the situation. This strengthened their legitimacy and unity so that they were able to start the new self-managed organization and keep their jobs. Finally, they proved to be efficient administrators following the founding of the cooperative, and this gave them further legitimacy, especially since they were the ones who were responsible for the cooperative's sustainability and for improvements at work and in the lives of the workers of the UST. Additionally, the president of the cooperative has been a social activist in the neighbourhood for many years, which strengthens the organization's ties with the community and widens its recognition and legitimacy in the neighbourhood and in the cooperative.

The UST cooperative was able to plan a long-term project based on the development of a common vision among its members and its considerable political strength. The long-term project was a strategy proposed by the leaders and it was discussed in the first few assemblies. Initially the problem was the lack of machinery to enable them to produce without depending on third parties. For this reason they decided to save a significant amount of the available funds to be able to acquire new and better machinery with a greater production capacity. An important reason for this strategy was to prove to CEAMSE—the company to which they were offering their services– that they would be able to provide a competitive service. This strategy proved justified: they started with a one-year contract, which was renewed for another three years, and now they have a contract for five years, with changes in the amount (volume of work and higher rates) contracted every year. And there are prospects of contract renewals for several years to come. The purchase of their own machinery also allows them to diversify their clientele and the services they can offer in the market. Together with the strategy for acquisition of the means of production, UST has employed engineers and technicians trained for developing the work and transmitting their knowledge to the other employees. In addition, some of the members have studied business administration skills, and have linked with several universities to strengthen their economic management skills. It is important to bear in mind that in the past they were workers who carried out specific tasks under the orders of a boss; with the transformation of the company into a cooperative they had to assume responsibility for all the functions involved in running it, including its administrative, productive, and commercial organization.

As regards who is responsible for the decision-making process, that depends on the type of decision. Management decisions required to be taken on a daily basis are made by those responsible for each area, together with the management team. Strategic decisions are conceived by the administrative council and then proposed at the workers' assembly, where they are approved or rejected by majority vote. However, on several occasions they are decided based purely on consensus. This form of participation has resulted in a stronger long-term institutional project, since the general criteria are specified and decided by the assembly and this provides the framework for everyday decisions. An example of strategic decision-making by the assembly concerned how the surplus would be used. It was decided that 50 per cent would be earmarked for acquiring capital equipment to enable the cooperative to produce without depending on other enterprises, 25 per cent would be devoted to financing projects in the neighbourhood, and the remaining

25 per cent would be distributed among all workers, without distinguishing between leaders, members, and future members.

There had long been an internal dispute at UST over the distribution of resources. Some members of the cooperative suggested distributing a larger percentage to its members in order to provide higher incomes and increase consumption capacity, instead of assigning those resources to new means of production and to too many projects that benefit the community. They compared themselves with other workers who have higher salaries in similar companies. The leaders' response, supported by the assembly, was based on an alternative, long-term vision: 'We are a different type of organization, which works with a different logic. We started from scratch and we are growing, and besides, UST workers have very important non-monetary benefits, such as access to houses built or improved by the cooperative and at better prices than those of the market.'

Given the diversity of its objectives and social activities, the UST cooperative encountered several problems that required creativity and capacity for innovation. In addition to the conflict over how the surplus should be allotted, during recent years there has been growing dissatisfaction that all employees earn the same amount. This stems from large differences in terms of employees' degrees of commitment to the aims and social activities of the UST. In order to solve this problem, the cooperative has reformed the statutes, in order to state more clearly the community activities of the cooperative for meeting its social objectives. More recently, they have modified the internal regulations by designing a collective peer evaluation system which assesses the teamwork and social commitment of each worker more than his or her productive work. Based on the results of these collective assessments, in which the workers participate by grading their colleagues, a monetary award is given. This is considered a prize for the most committed, and at the same time serves as an incentive for those who just focus on complying with their individual tasks and do not collaborate in the community work.

4.3 Lack of Social Protection and the Cooperative's Different Coping Strategies

Both the market and the institutional and political context generate difficulties for the UST cooperative, which hinder its development possibilities and increase the vulnerability of its workers. On the one hand, its participation in the market requires it to develop the appropriate capacities and resources and a very high level of efficiency and quality in its production. Yet it is relatively weak compared with big capitalist companies that, for example, can access finance on better terms and reduce their operating costs by dismissing employees. On the other hand, the current institutional and political context in Argentina, as in most capitalist economies, does not help the setting up and consolidation of self-managed enterprises in most of the productive sectors. In particular, since the legal framework (laws and regulations) is based on the functioning and structure of capitalist companies and salaried work, cooperatives such as UST face bigger obstacles than a conventional company.

Examples of this are the current problems faced by UST's workers with regard to social security coverage,[5] which are analysed in this section. First, there is no separate tax category for self-employed workers. Normally, these workers are categorized as autonomous, individual, and independent. In Argentina, in order to have (only partial) access to social security, workers from cooperatives must enroll under the same category as small business owners[6] and pay income tax, even though their earnings just cover the basic needs of their family. For this reason, many self-managed workers who have low incomes prefer not to pay this tax, and consequently are not covered by the social security system. At the same time, they accumulate debts with the Treasury. Those who do manage to pay this tax only have access to small pensions and low-quality health coverage in comparison to those of salaried workers.[7] Regarding coverage for accidents and work-related illnesses, the law that regulates this type of insurance does not cover cooperatives and their workers, since it requires the existence of a dependent working relationship (between employer and employee), which does not apply to cooperatives. Finally, workers in self-managed businesses are not entitled to child benefits and to unemployment insurance, which are two important components of the social security system to which salary workers have access. Thus workers in self-managed businesses, in spite of paying the taxes required by law, lack access to two components of social security—pensions and health insurance. Moreover, they have no insurance coverage at all for work-related accidents and health risks, or for unemployment, and are not entitled to family benefits.

How has the UST workers' cooperative dealt with this problem? To reduce the degree of vulnerability from the lack of social protection of its members, it has developed three complementary strategies: (a) the collective use of resources of the cooperative; (b) organizing networking actions to promote

[5] In many other countries as well, workers in cooperatives face problems of access to social security. This is why the ILO and the International Cooperative Alliance (ICA) have been promoting 'decent work' in cooperatives worldwide (ILO, 2002).

[6] This category is known as Régimen Simplificado para Pequeños Contribuyentes, usually called 'monotributo', which establishes a payment system through which those enrolled pay both their taxes for the tax system (VAT and income tax) and their contributions to social security (pension and health care). On average, the cooperative workers surveyed are taxed at the rate of 400 Argentine pesos (i.e. $90) a month.

[7] Our observations concerning workers in cooperatives apply equally to all forms of independent workers, many of whom are owners of small, individual, or family businesses and do not earn enough income to meet their families' needs.

political and institutional changes; and (c) strengthening the link with the local community. These strategies are discussed below.

4.3.1 Collective Use of Resources to Compensate for the Lack of State Protection

In general, the UST cooperative tries to use its own resources to cover the cost of offering to its workers risk coverage similar to that guaranteed to formal salaried workers. First of all, it pays the corresponding tax for all its workers, making sure that none of them lose their coverage because of lack of payment. It then negotiates collective health coverage for the families of all the workers, which allows them to have better quality services than they would be able to access individually. It also takes out private insurance against accidents and work-related illnesses, although the coverage is not similar to that of the state system which, apart from paying to the injured, gives money to the company to cover the costs of hiring a replacement. Regarding family charges, the cooperative pays these out of its own funds, equivalent to the same amount per child that the state system provides. Finally, the minimum pension payments are complemented by an anticipated distribution of the social amounts to the workers who retire.

Overall, the UST cooperative administers its present resources taking into account the present and future risks that its workers and their families might face. For this, it applies foresight and relies on solidarity among the group of workers, since it uses collective funds to cover the additional costs incurred by individual needs or events. In some ways, therefore, the UST cooperative administers its own resources for its own workers and their families using similar criteria to those which govern the state social security system nationwide, thus trying to compensate for its relative exclusion from the state system of social security.

4.3.2 Organizing Networking Actions to Promote Political and Institutional Changes

Taking into account all the difficulties arising from the institutional context, the UST cooperative has adopted a strategy of forming networks and connections with many other social actors who support it in dealing with the State and even with market competition. As already mentioned, these political strategies are approved during workers' assemblies, and they are proposed as part of the long-term project of the organization. For example, the UST cooperative actively participates in several national and local social and solidarity networks[8] and cooperates with other recovered enterprises and with

[8] In Argentina, as in many other countries in Latin America and the world, broad social movements have emerged in recent years which promote policies and institutions aimed at strengthening alternative economic systems to capitalist ones. Formed from the conviction that 'another

self-managed workers in particular. After several meetings and specific collaboration and coordination of activities with other recovered enterprises, the UST promoted the creation of a National Association of Self Managed Workers (ANTA in Spanish) within the Argentine Workers Union (CTA in Spanish). In fact, the president of the UST cooperative was elected general secretary of that union, a position he currently holds. From this political place, the recognition of the category of self-managed workers as a subject of law is collectively required, since it is an emerging and socially necessary category of workers. In addition, the State's institutions are required to cover this category, modify the legal framework that regulates this type of work, and guarantee the same rights accorded to formal, salaried workers. In their own words:

> We were created out of necessity, from emergency, from the despair of losing our jobs and the only thing that opened the door to legality was to become a cooperative.... But now we need a legal framework that includes us all. We have been fighting several battles, managing, claiming, working to find legal and organizational tools... We are opening today a new path. It is logical that every construction of power takes time to grow and sometimes it is a slow development. We believe that... it is time for the institutionalization of a new social category: the self-managed worker.
>
> (CONTA, 2010: 3).

4.3.3 Strengthening Ties with the Community as a Way of Protection

Another strategy adopted by the UST cooperative to strengthen its relative position in the market and in the political and institutional field has been to deepen its ties with the local community. The initial reaction of the neighbours to its creation was not a positive one since the previous privately owned company (Techint) and the state company responsible for waste disposal (CEAMSE) had been reported to the authorities for causing environmental problems (soil, water, and air pollution) which directly damaged the surrounding neighbourhood. The UST's initial strategy was to work hard to change this negative image during the early stages of formation of the recovered enterprise by undertaking a vigorous cleaning-up operation. It also offered the local community part use of its workers' capabilities for developing diverse social services (e.g. sports, education, housing, health). Another way the UST benefits the neighbourhood is by giving preference to the local youth when hiring workers. At present

economy is possible', this political movement is the collective product of this alternative economy, usually called 'social and solidarity economy'. Within these social movements coexist intellectuals, academics, workers who are part of many initiatives, trade unions, federations of self-managed organizations, and even state officials and workers at various levels of government (for further details, see Vázquez, 2010).

80 per cent of the workers from UST live in the neighbourhood, which reinforces the reciprocal feeling of belonging between the cooperative and the community.

The UST cooperative appreciates the fact that during the recovery process of the enterprise, when the workers decided to occupy the land and resist eviction, they received support from people in the neighborhood who helped them in the fight to keep their jobs in a context of high unemployment and social crisis. Once established as a workers' cooperative, in every assembly a core principle was reaffirmed: the neighbourhood supported them when fighting for their work, now the UST cooperative had to give back to the neighbourhood through projects to improve the quality of life of the community. At the same time, this strategy guarantees continued support to the community, even in the event of possible future conflicts.

This strong bond with the community also helps gain local support when the UST has to face third parties: for example, both CEAMSE (the main client of UST services) and several state institutions at local, provincial, and national levels recognize the UST cooperative as an organization that generates important benefits for the community. This recognition strengthens its position in negotiations for obtaining support and resources. For example, CEAMSE improves its corporative image by hiring UST, and the local government implements territorial policies for supporting actions jointly with the cooperative, including offering resources to expand activities in the neighbourhood.

4.4 Substantive Economic Logic of the UST Cooperative

This section examines the economic logic underlying the functioning of the UST cooperative, taking into account the conceptual framework of a substantive and plural economy (Polanyi, 1994; Coraggio, 2009a; Laville, 2010; see also the chapter by Lemaître in this book). In particular, it is observed that a plurality of economic principles guides the actions and decisions of the cooperative.

First, it seems clear that this organization does not function on the basis of a logic of capital accumulation. It does not even try to maximize the workers' incomes, but guarantees work and a decent income for the largest possible number of workers. When facing the dilemma between increasing the workers' incomes or increasing the number of jobs, it chose the second option, giving priority to the young people from the local community. Another example of its non-capitalist logic is the time devoted to the provision of social services for the local community without any monetary returns for the organization. Summing up, it is not a capitalist economic rationale that predominates in the

UST cooperative, but rather a substantive economic logic that we characterize as 'reproductive rationality' (Hinkelammert and Mora Jiménez, 2009).

Second, the relationship between the UST cooperative and the local community is based on the economic principle of reciprocity: the workers received support from the local community during their fight for keeping their jobs and during the phase of recovery of the enterprise; in return, the workers' cooperative decided to use some of its resources to provide social services that aim at meeting local needs and improving the quality of life in the neighbourhood. Its contributions to the community strengthen the existing social relationship, the feeling of mutual belonging, the local identity, and the development of the area, and at the same time guarantee continuity of support for the cooperative from the local community in the event of possible situations of conflict in the future. Of course, reciprocity is evident, not only in the relationship with the local community, but also within the cooperative itself (for example, in their organization of the work, the decision-making process, and the distribution of collective resources), although there are sometimes material and ideological disputes among different groups of workers.

Third, the economic logic of the UST cooperative also observes the principle of redistribution: the collective work performed by all workers enables the production and sale of services in the market. From the resulting revenue, a basic income is distributed according to hours worked (and not according to the qualification or productivity of each worker); a small extra amount is given to workers who have received favourable assessments by their colleagues, and daily solidarity and commitment with the rest of the neighbourhood is also rewarded. Finally, several criteria and mechanisms have been created for the redistribution of funds (e.g. such as the number of children, specific problems, and work-related accidents), which are internal agreements within the workers' collective that replace or complement the deficient coverage of social security from the State for workers in self-managed businesses.

Fourth, the principle of householding is also applied in the administration of the resources of the UST cooperative. From the available working capacities, a significant proportion is assigned for the production of goods or services for consumption by the workers themselves and by the community. In other words, the logic of the organization is aimed neither at minimizing labour costs nor maximizing income per sale in order to produce the maximum surplus possible per person; instead, the aim is to maximize the number of jobs according to the income available,[9] assign the hours and work capacities in a way that

[9] The monthly revenue from UST, as opposed to that of most informal enterprises, is quite stable since most of it is based on contractual services in exchange for a fixed amount per month, which provides certainty of income flow and the possibility of earmarking specific resources for diverse objectives, whereas in a capitalist company the revenue would be treated as part of the profit.

guarantees provision of the main service, and then reassign resources and additional work capacity towards productive activities aimed at satisfying the needs of the whole group of workers and/or the local community (for example, in the construction or repair of housing, or community equipment such as a club, a school, or a health service). In this way, the workers' families as well as the neighbourhood have to spend less of their monetary income on the purchase of goods or services to meet those needs.

In summary, many actions and decisions of the UST cooperative, interpreted from a capitalist logic, would be characterized as irrational, but when analysed from a substantive economic perspective they are clearly understandable and express a different kind of logic or rationale. By adopting practices based on this substantive rationale, the organization has achieved significant levels of protection for its workers, especially when compared with the poor levels of coverage offered by the state social security system for self-managed workers.

4.5 Final Comments: Towards a Plural Sustainability Perspective

This case study confirms the need to adopt a new perspective on the sustainability of enterprises. Contrary to the currently predominant concept of sustainability, which emphasizes a microeconomic sustainability of individual businesses through integration in the market, we propose a perspective of plural sustainability of self-managed workers' enterprises through the recognition of a plurality of principles (reciprocity, redistribution, householding, and market exchange), as well as resources and institutional ways which contribute to the sustainability of these enterprises (Vázquez, 2010).

The resources and strategies adopted to make possible the sustainability of the UST cooperative include developing a reciprocal relationship of mutual support and collaboration with the local community; ensuring an income from the sale of services in the market; gaining the political strength to negotiate with the State and other social actors by means of participation in networks of other recovered enterprises and unions/associations of self-managed workers; and the social and political capital that emerges from a recognition of this organization as a key player in the development of the region.

In order to guarantee its long-term sustainability, the UST cooperative should continue to work in several areas, such as ongoing development of its workers' capacities to produce and compete in the market, influencing the national regulatory changes necessary to improve the social protection of self-managed workers, overcoming internal conflicts, and improving its self-management capacities. The eventual idea is to consolidate a plural sustainability for this type of organization, which is opening up non-capitalistic pathways towards the construction of another economy.

References

CONTA (Confederación Nacional de Trabajadores Autogestionados) (2010). 'Por una nueva institucionalidad: Reconocimiento del nuevo sujeto trabajador autogestionado'. Document for discussion, Florencio Varela.

Coraggio, J. L. (2009a). 'Polanyi y la Economía Social y Solidaria en América Latina', in J. L. Coraggio (ed.), *¿Qué es lo económico?* Buenos Aires: CICCUS.

—— (2009b). 'Sostenibilidad', in A. Cattani, J. L. Coraggio and J.L. Laville (eds.), *Diccionario de la otra economía*. Buenos Aires: UNGS-Altamira-Clacso.

Hinkelammert, F. and H. Mora Jiménez (2009). Economía, sociedad y vida humana. *Colección lecturas sobre Economía Social*. Buenos Aires: UNGS-Altamira.

ILO (2002). 'Promotion of Cooperatives Recommendation, 2002 (No. 193)'. Adoption: Geneva, 90th ILC session (20 Jun 2002). Available at <http://www.ilo.org/empent/units/cooperatives/lang--en/index.htm> (accessed 14 June 2013).

Laville, J. L. (2010). 'The Social and Solidarity Economy: A Theoretical and Plural Framework', in J. Defourny, L. Hulgård and V. Pestoff (eds.), *Social Enterprise, Social Entrepreneurship, Social Economy, Solidarity Economy: An EMES Reader on the 'SE Field'*. Roskilde: Roskilde University: 75–87.

OSERA (2010). 'Datos sobre la autogestión en la Argentina'. *Revista OSERA* no. 4; available at <http://webiigg.sociales.uba.ar/empresasrecuperadas/PDF/PDF_04/datosnacion4.pdf> (accessed 14 May 2013).

Polanyi, K. (1944). *The Great Transformation*. Boston, MA: Beacon Press.

Portes, A. and W. Haller (2004). 'La economía informal'. *Serie Políticas Sociales* no. 100, Santiago, Chile: CEPAL.

Tokman, V. (2001). *De la informalidad a la modernidad*. Santiago, Chile: ILO.

Vázquez, G. (2010). 'La sostenibilidad de los emprendimientos asociativos de trabajadores autogestionados: Perspectivas y aportes conceptuales desde América Latina'. Mg. thesis, Universidad Nacional de General Sarmiento (UNGS), Los Polvorines; available at<http://www.riless.org/en/component/virtualtecas/investigador/169> (accessed 14 May 2013).

—— (2011). 'Sobre los conceptos de trabajo asociativo y autogestionado, sus organizaciones y trabajadores', in C. Danani and S. Hintze (eds.), *Protecciones y desprotecciones: La seguridad social en la argentina 1990–2010*. Los Polvorines: UNGS.

5

An Analysis of the Socio-Economic Logics Underpinning Formal and Informal Strategies for Coping with Economic Hardships in South Kivu, Democratic Republic of the Congo

Maïté le Polain and Marthe Nyssens[1]

5.1 Introduction: Background and Research Objective

The inhabitants of South Kivu are vulnerable to poverty in the sense that they face high exposure to risks, shocks, and stress on a daily basis, and have difficulties in coping without damaging losses (Chambers, 1989). In the absence of public provision of safety nets and limited market-provided finance and insurance services, in times of economic hardship vulnerable households have to depend entirely on private individual and/or collective protection mechanisms.

Researchers have paid increasing attention to social protection mechanisms in low income settings and in particular to mechanisms devised by vulnerable households and communities aimed at dealing with the harmful consequences of a shock (for literature reviews, see Alderman and Paxson, 1992; Besley, 1995; Morduch, 1999, Fafchamps, 1999, Dercon, 2005; Cohen and Sebstad, 2005; Collins et al., 2009). Such studies have unveiled the existence of various mechanisms for coping with risks in rural and low-income

[1] With the collaboration of Guillaume Bidubula (Université Catholique de Bukavu) for the collection of empirical data. The research was conducted in partnership with a Belgian NGO, Louvain Coopération au Développement, within the framework of GRAP3A (Alimentation, Agriculture, Afrique) financed by the coopération universitaire belge (CUD).

settings as well as the potential and limits of strategies in terms of protection for the poor. Alderman and Paxson (1992) distinguish between risk management and risk-coping strategies. The former seek to mitigate potential risks (*ex ante* strategies), through income diversification for example, whilst the latter deal with the negative effects of shocks after they occur (*ex post* strategies). Mitigating and coping strategies in neighbouring contexts have been documented in the literature. For example, Cohen and Sebstad (2005) explored the impact of shocks on poor households in Kenya, the United Republic of Tanzania, and Uganda, and found that the poor have always used self-insurance mechanisms as a major way of coping with shock. Based on research in Ethiopia, Dercon (2005) reviewed the strategies used by households to avoid consumption shortfalls caused by risk.

The present chapter attempts to analyse the various forms of coping strategies, seen through the plurality of underpinning socio-economic logics. Following a substantive view of the economy that 'derives from man's dependence for his living upon nature and his fellows' (Polanyi, [1957], 1975: 243), Polanyi distinguishes between four forms of integration (market, redistribution, reciprocity, and householding, as noted in the introduction to this book), which are characterized by particular means of organization of production, financing, distribution, and consumption of wealth, and which in turn shape the social bonds and organization of society.

Polanyi stresses that 'in any case, forms of integration do not represent "stages" of development. No sequence in time is implied' (idem: 256). He adopts a non-evolutionary vision of these principles of economic integration, as all societies use a multiplicity of means for economic transactions (Servet, 2009). Moreover, in a given economic transaction, 'subordinate forms may be present alongside of the dominant one' (Polanyi, [1957], 1975: 256). These forms of integration are to be understood as 'ideal types', to quote Weber (1965), that is, abstract constructions that enable researchers to position a specific economic transaction relative to each 'ideal type'. The Polanyian view forms the basis for our analysis grid to highlight the socio-economic logics underpinning formal and informal coping strategies.

Beyond the goal of identifying the different principles prevailing in South Kivu, this chapter seeks to analyse the coexistence of several principles in a given practice or strategy to determine whether they are complementary or a source of tension. Polanyi highlights the fact that reciprocity can become more efficient if redistribution and market approaches are integrated as complementary logics: 'reciprocity as a form of integration gains greatly in power through its capacity of employing both redistribution and exchange as subordinate methods. Reciprocity may be attained through a sharing of the burden of labour according to definite rules of redistribution as when taking things "in turn". Similarly, reciprocity is sometimes attained through exchange at set equivalencies for the benefit of the partner who happens to be short of some kind of necessities—a fundamental institution in ancient Oriental societies. In non-market economies, these two forms of integration—reciprocity and redistribution—occur in effect usually together' (Polanyi, [1957], 1975: 253).

The chapter is organized as follows. Section 5.2 introduces the context and design of our exploratory research. Section 5.3 presents the main sources of economic hardships faced by respondents. Section 5.4 describes risk management and coping strategies used by households to alleviate financial pressure. We distinguish between individual strategies, and informal and formal group-based mechanisms. Section 5.5 highlights the socio-economic logics underpinning the diverse strategies before concluding.

5.2 The Context of the Study

Located in the Great Lakes region of Africa, South Kivu is a province of the Democratic Republic of Congo (hereinafter DR Congo) that borders Rwanda, Burundi, and Tanzania. Its population is estimated at over five million, more than half of whom are younger than fifteen years old.[2] Since 1996, the province has suffered two successive wars (in 1996–7 and 1998–2003) followed by chronic instability. Since then, active groups of rebels episodically create pockets of insecurity. This fragile situation is reflected in the number of internally displaced people, which was estimated in 2012 to be about 800,000 in South Kivu province alone.[3]

In 2011, DR Congo ranked last in the Human Development Index of the United Nations Development Programme (UNDP, 2011), and a national survey revealed that South Kivu was one of the eleven provinces with the lowest development indicators in the country: infant and child mortality rates are higher than the national mean (101 and 166 per 1,000, respectively, against a mean of 97 and 158 per 1,000 for the whole country), over one-fourth of the population under five years is underweight, and almost half of the women are illiterate (INS and UNICEF, 2011).

Decades of wars and conflicts have damaged the country's physical infrastructure (especially that facilitating communication), ruined the formal economy, and undermined the provision of public services, especially in the health and education sectors. DR Congo has a low annual gross domestic product (GDP) per capita, estimated at about $200.[4] Ironically, even though

[2] *Inspection provinciale de la santé* (IPS) estimates for 2011, which were obtained in September 2011.

[3] United Nations Office for the Coordination of Humanitarian Affairs (OCHA) estimates in March 2012 (see <www.rdc-humanitaire.net>, accessed 14 May 2013).

[4] World Bank estimate for the year 2010, in current US dollars (see <http://data.worldbank.org>, accessed 14 May 2013).

the country, and South Kivu in particular, is richly endowed with natural resources and valuable minerals (e.g. gold, coltan, cassiterite), precarious and informal income-generating activities are often the only sources of subsistence for the great majority of the population.

Our study is based on exploratory research conducted in the province of South Kivu in June 2011. We included in our sample an equal number of urban, semi-urban, and rural locations, assuming that coping strategies in these locations would differ. Areas that were insecure at the time of our survey or were inaccessible by road were not considered. The following six zones were selected: Uvira, Kalehe, Kiliba, Kalundu, Mushinga, and Bagira. Qualitative, face-to-face, semi-open interviews were conducted with sixty-nine respondents (with an almost equal number of men and women) with a view to discovering existing strategies for coping. Twelve focus groups were also conducted to uncover norms and beliefs that might influence the coping mechanisms. The main topics discussed were events that caused hardships, perception of risk, and strategies for coping.

5.3 Events Exerting Financial Pressure on the Household

Before enquiring about strategies for coping with economic hardships, respondents were asked to list events likely to exert intense financial pressure on the household. Previous studies have distinguished between 'emergencies' that include all sudden-onset occurrences that threaten life, health, or property; and 'life-cycle events' that include expenditures on childbirth, marriage, and education (Cohen and Sebstad, 2005; Collins et al., 2009). The events reported vary in terms of predictability, frequency, and financial pressure.

Serious injury/sickness appeared to be a frequent and unforeseeable cause of economic hardship reported by respondents. A member of the household who falls sick requires an immediate lump sum of cash to cover direct health care and transportation costs. Given the tight public budget, health care is largely financed by user fees. Thus, inpatient health-care costs can impose a heavy burden on the sick and their relatives. Many of the sick cannot afford hospital care and this has led many hospitals to resort to the dubious practice of detaining patients until their bills are paid. Besides direct costs, when the person falling ill happens to be one of the household's breadwinners, the lost income compounds the hardship. Respondents whose household member was hospitalized over a particular period had had to resort to more than one coping strategy to deal with the costs.

Faced with the unpredictable *death of a relative*, respondents incur expenses in meeting the immediate and unexpected costs of the funeral, including a coffin, which costs $20–40, and food for the mourners over a traditional period of three days. Again, there may be an indirect financial impact of deprivation of income if the deceased happens to have been an income earner.

Despite higher predictability, life-cycle events such as a *birth or wedding* also exert considerable financial pressure on households. Wedding costs are overwhelming since, in accordance with social norms, they are celebrated with hordes of guests, even among the poorest households. In addition to the ceremony, the traditional practice of giving a dowry to the bride's family of between one and ten cows (one cow costing $400–600, depending on the wealth of the groom's family) adds to the expenses incurred.

Payment of *school fees* was also frequently mentioned by parents as a source of financial stress. Due to the lack of public financing in the education sector, teachers' wages and the functioning of schools are supported entirely by the parents. This involves payments every three months of $5–15 per child in primary school and $30–60 per child in secondary school. If fees are not paid, children are temporarily sent home until payment is made. In large families, which are almost the norm in South Kivu—on average a woman has eight children during her lifetime (INS and UNICEF, 2011)—school fees are a burdensome and predictable expense.

Beyond the events involving the household, frequently cited threats to the household's financial conditions stem from an *economic downturn* and *political instability*. Macro-level shocks may be accompanied by increases in transportation costs and other inputs that are likely to lower the profitability of small businesses or inflate prices. Weak security due to political instability also increases the risk of being displaced or being a victim of robbery.

Adverse climatic conditions as well as *animal and plant diseases* are unpredictable and likely to shrink the revenues of households involved in farming or cattle-rearing activities. This is a type of income risk that is associated with the nature of household members' occupations.

5.4 Strategies for Coping with Hardship

To address the financial stress resulting from emergencies or life-cycle events discussed above, respondents make use of a wide variety of strategies. Based on the classification suggested by Alderman and Paxson (1992), on the one hand they can try to reduce the variability of income (risk management through income diversification); on the other hand they can cope with the risk through savings (self-insurance behaviour) or through risk-sharing among those outside the family. Because one strategy rarely provides the necessary sum of cash in a timely manner to thus fully protect the family against a shock, respondents acknowledged that they resorted to several means at the same time. Strategies vary in terms of the level of stress they impose on a household, as noted by Cohen and Sebstad (2005); low-stress solutions are thus preferred over last resort options that are often associated with harassment and higher stress.

5.4.1 *Individual Strategies: Self-Insurance and Income Diversification*

Individual strategies refer to actions that seek to reduce income variability through income diversification or smooth consumption through self-insurance. Self-insurance mainly refers to precautionary savings (Deaton, 1992; Dercon, 2002): 'to accumulate in good times to build up reserves for bad times' in the words of a respondent. This precautionary strategy was widespread in our sample and households drew on savings to alleviate financial pressure in lean times.

The dominant forms of savings in our sample are instructive. Lacking options to secure cash savings, the majority of respondents acknowledged reifying them. Savings are converted into productive assets such as livestock (poultry worth $5–10 each, goats worth $30–50 each, or cattle worth $400–600 each) and plots of land. In the words of a respondent in Uvira, 'having a goat is like having money in your pocket'. Added to this is the perceived advantage that such savings are inaccessible for immediate spending, thus reducing the temptation to spend. Reification of savings was found to be predominant among the rural poor, but, interestingly, it was also found to exist among urban interviewees who have access to microfinance institutions. Respondents from Uvira acknowledged possessing livestock or land plots in their native village, which are watched over by relatives, who in turn benefit from the by-products (milk or eggs) and the animals' offspring.

Few respondents admitted to saving in cash at home. A commonly cited reason was the fear of robbery and the difficulty of turning down relatives' demands for cash. This latter explanation was also given by Baland et al. (2011), who found loans from COOPEC in Cameroon that were fully collateralized by savings available on the borrower's savings account. They found that the rationale behind this was that by taking out a loan the borrower signals to his friends and relatives that he cannot respond to their demands and thus escapes such obligations.

Whilst savings are used to smooth consumption, diversification of income-generating activities was a common strategy among respondents to reduce income variability. As pointed out by Alderman and Paxson (1992), diversification smooths the flow of income by reducing the risk in the income-earning process. Faced with irregular, insecure, and low levels of income, the majority of respondents said they were occupied with more than one earning activity. They purposely sought multiple sources of cash flow. Examples from our sample include the woman who cultivated the family plot in the morning and sold cans of petrol in front of her house in the afternoon, or the teacher who also owned a small grocery store in front of his house. However Dercon (2005) highlights the limits of this strategy, as it usually implies the choice of low-risk and low-return activities.

As a very last resort, respondents acknowledged having to fall back on local moneylenders on the streets to ride out transitory economic hardships. As moneylenders are known for charging exorbitant interest rates and for harassment in case of default, this option was associated with high levels of stress by respondents.

5.4.2 Collective Informal Strategies

Clearly, mutual assistance operating among networks based on kin, community, neighbourhood, and workplace appeared as a great source for coping in lean times for all respondents. Although some respondents referred to it as *solidarité africaine* (African-style solidarity), mutual support within families and kinship groups is observed in many traditional rural communities around the globe (Townsend, 1994; Morduch, 1999). Mutual assistance implies that when a member faces hardship, other group members express sympathy towards the one in need through in-kind or cash donations.

It should be stressed that the concept of solidarity does not presuppose it being driven by generosity or by self-interest, nor indeed by any other moral value. The social norms governing this mutual assistance are so intrinsically embedded in the community that donations only partially rely on individual choices or decisions. Norms, even though informal, are well defined and collectively shared by all members of the network. Everyone more or less knows what he or she is expected to receive or to give according to social conventions. For example, as expressed by one respondent, 'for a sibling's wedding, one should donate a goat and packs of beer'. Informal mutual assistance also applies beyond that given to immediate relatives, although norms become less clear when there is only a distant relationship between the donor and the receiver.

At first sight the overwhelming cost of weddings hosted by the poor constitutes a puzzle. Commenting on high wedding costs found in Asia, especially in societies where dowry systems are added to the bill, Collins et al. (2009: 106) argue that the enormity of weddings in the financial lives of Indians mirrors an aspiration to improve the social-economic standing through a 'good marriage'. From our perspective, large hordes of guests also reflect a sophisticated risk-sharing strategy through which guests contribute to the costs of the weddings by giving substantial gifts. The number of guests thus mirrors the surface of the family host's social network on which they might later draw down in case of lean times.

Indeed, survey respondents also acknowledged making use of their network to seek credit. Depending on the amount of money needed and the relationship ties between lender and borrower, a zero or moderate interest rate will be charged. In a few cases, a third person known by the two parties may witness the transaction. Collins et al. (2009) draw a useful distinction between 'reciprocal' and 'obligatory' lending. In the first case, the lender can expect the borrower to reciprocate the favour and lend to him in return when the need arises. In contrast, under obligatory lending, the creditor is unlikely to become a future debtor. Rather, the loan is steered by the lender's sense of obligation to help out the person in need. Such informal loans can be re-scheduled or even cancelled, according to respondents.

As noted earlier, saving is a widespread precautionary strategy. Interestingly, a common form of this is the practice of collective savings known as *likirimba*, which is Swahili for a rotating savings and credit association (ROSCA). Similar to practices observed in Latin America, Asia and elsewhere in Africa (Lelart, 1995; Besley, 1995; Collins et al., 2009), *likirimba* involves a group of people who agree to contribute a fixed amount of money to a pot on a regular basis. At every meeting, the common pot is allocated to a different member on a rotating basis, so that at the end of the cycle each member has received one pot. Although the allocation of the pot usually follows a predefined order, a member in times of need can try to get priority in the payout order. Beyond the savings purpose, social cohesion within the group can generate additional aid transfers. Members of the group who gather on a regular basis may collectively decide to make a special contribution to assist a member in need.

A minority of respondents reported being members of mutual systems of solidarity (*Mutuelles de solidarité*—MUSO)[5] in order to cope with hardships. Inspired by traditional ROSCAs, mutual systems of solidarity are similar to *likirimba*, with the difference that they provide for savings accumulation, credit, and social insurance. In practice, a MUSO is organized around two boxes: a 'green box' for savings and a 'red box' for social insurance (and possibly a third 'blue box' for refinancing). According to well-defined rules of operation embodied in a constitution, each member of the union contributes two fixed sums of money at regular intervals—usually weekly or monthly—one to the savings and credit box and the other to the social insurance box. The MUSO is thus a tool that manages cash flows through self-organization of the members of a community based on democratic rules (Bidubula, 2011).

The group members collectively decide which shocks will be partially compensated by the social insurance (red box) at the time of constituting the

[5] Originating from Senegal and inspired by traditional forms of collective savings, MUSOs were introduced in South Kivu in 2002. In 2011, there were estimated to be over 1,000 in number, with approximately 16,000 members (Bidubula, 2011).

group. Interestingly, events insured are generally similar to those that trigger assistance provided by the network, that is, childbirth, wedding, funerals, and sickness. In South Kivu, the average sum contributed to the red insurance box is $0.80, but may rise to $5 in some groups (Bidubula, 2011). Beyond the compensation embodied in the constitution of the MUSO, respondents also recognized the possibility of collectively agreeing on additional special donations to the member in need. In the words of a respondent: 'In case of a birth delivery by one of our members, we usually add a *pagne* (a traditional length of fabric), a fistful of manioc meal and some dried fish.'

If a member needs a lump sum of cash, he or she can request a loan from the MUSO. Supplied with fixed and regular contributions, the 'green box' develops into a credit fund once it has accumulated sufficient resources. Loans are granted to members only and, unlike credit in microfinance institutions, are not conditional on the provision of collateral: interpersonal trust and the proximity of members suffice for granting the loan. The 'green box' shares similarities with accumulated saving and credit associations (ASCAs) or village savings and credit associations (VS&LA) found elsewhere in Africa (Collins et al., 2009). In 2010, the average amount lent annually was about $1,450, and on average each member benefited from a loan of about $58 over six months (Bidubula, 2011).

Rather than being charged an interest rate, the borrower reimburses the loan plus a fixed charge called PAF (participation aux frais—a contribution to costs) to the MUSO. Converted to monthly interest rates, PAF are exorbitant (from 3 to 10 per cent), but such informal loans are typically small and held for short periods, to deal with transitory lean times. This corroborates the conclusion of Collins et al. (2009: 135) that 'the interest rates may often be better understood as *fees* for a service than a *rate* for the use of money for a specific period'.

Despite the disadvantages mentioned, such as the high cost, waiting time, and the limited sum of money that can be borrowed, all the respondents agreed that the main advantages are flexibility and trusting relationships. In case of repayment problems, the member can always beg for the reimbursement to be re-scheduled.

Also noteworthy about these informal community-based groups is the development of collective income-generating activities. Monetary resources obtained through collective work, such as cultivating shared land, producing soap or constructing coffins, are then redistributed for the benefit of the members or deposited in either the insurance or credit box.

5.4.3 Collective Formal Mechanisms

A minority of respondents reported having voluntarily enrolled in community-based health insurance groups (*Mutuelles de santé*—MUSAs). To join such groups they had to pay a premium of $3–$6 per individual. However, the compulsory unit for enrolment is the household. After a three-month waiting period, subscribers are entitled to health care, provided they make a co-payment, fixed at 50 per cent for primary health care delivered by nurses or general practitioners and 20 per cent for secondary health care at hospital, whilst the health insurance group pays for the remainder. The group also negotiates contract rates with health-care providers.

Founded on the principles of risk-pooling and solidarity, community-based health insurance groups derive from private and collective initiatives that seek to improve the financial means to access health-care services. Fonteneau (2004) identifies five common principles of such initiatives: (1) social protection through risk-pooling; (2) community-based dynamics; (3) participative decision-making mechanisms and collective management; (4) voluntary affiliation; and (5) a non-profit objective. In South Kivu, community-based health insurance schemes were initiated in 1997. Despite a trend of increasing enrolments, the low net enrolment rates jeopardize their financial viability.[6]

Only a few respondents in our sample acknowledged using the services of savings and credit cooperatives (*Caisses d'action mutuelle d'épargne et de crédit*—COOPEC). COOPECs are formal microfinance institutions in which people can make savings deposits and are located in urban areas. There are no restrictions in access to them beyond the payment of a membership fee of $10–$25. However, some respondents from Uvira expressed suspicion about their governance practices. There are also some geographic and financial barriers. For instance, members can only apply for credit if they provide material guarantees, and in the event of default on repayments, the COOPEC confiscates the guarantees given as collateral. These seem to be the major reasons for the low membership of COOPECs.

5.5 Analysis through Polanyian Lenses

The various forms of risk management and coping strategies are evidence of the existence of diverse underlying socio-economic logics highlighted by Polanyi, which are discussed in this section.

5.5.1 Householding Principle: Putting Savings to Work

The principle of householding 'consists in production for one's own use. [...] Its pattern is the closed group. Whether the very different entities of the

[6] At the beginning of 2012, the number of subscribers was estimated to be over 100,000 in 21 different MUSAs (Source: *Cellule d'appui aux mutuelles de santé*, Bukavu).

family or the settlement or the manor formed the self-sufficient unit, the principle was invariably the same, namely, that of producing and storing for the satisfaction of the wants of the members of the group' (Polanyi, 1944: 53).

As emphasized earlier, individuals who have access to bank savings accounts in COOPEC save partly in the form of land and livestock in their home village. In-kind savings that are kept in the institutional unit (the family, the clan) are embedded in the householding principle. Not only land and livestock, but also their by-products (e.g. eggs and milk) and animals' offspring are seen as a means of protecting savings and contribute to satisfying the family's or clan's needs. The domestic unit is seen as a safe place to secure their savings, and allowing members in the villages the use of the by-products is considered to be a way to fulfil social obligations towards those members.

It has long been argued that diversification of income-generating activities is a way to reduce risk, but some income-generating activities can also be seen as a way to diversify production for one's own use. A share of production will serve the family's or clan's needs while the rest is for sale on the market. As highlighted by Hillenkamp in this book, production and consumption are closely interlinked under the householding logic, and they are shared within the whole family, even if this is partially based in rural areas and partially in urban settings.

5.5.2 The Key Role of Voluntary and Semi-Voluntary Reciprocity

Following Polanyi's analysis, we distinguish between semi-voluntary reciprocity within 'more permanent communities such as families, tribes or city states' and voluntary reciprocity within 'less permanent ones that may be comprised in, and subordinate to, the former'. In his words, 'kinship, neighbourhood, or totem belong to the more permanent and comprehensive groupings; within their compass voluntary and semi-voluntary associations of a military, vocational, religious or social character create situations in which, at least transitorily or in regard to a given locality or a typical situation, there would form symmetrical groupings the members of which practice some sort of mutuality' ([1957], 1975: 253).

5.5.2.1 SEMI-VOLUNTARY RECIPROCITY INHERITED FROM SOCIAL NORMS

On those occasions that are governed by social conventions, for example, births, weddings, and funerals, relatives, friends, and neighbours are expected to express their solidarity by donating in cash or in kind an amount that is considered socially acceptable. Enforcement of social obligations is accomplished by publicly announcing or recording each contribution in writing, thus facilitating the identification of individuals who fail to honour their social obligation.

Although the word 'solidarity' is often used to explain such donations, 'under a voluntary guise they are in essence strictly obligatory' to borrow Mauss's words (1923). Mauss insists, 'gifts' call for 'counter gifts'. Exchanges are based on the principle of a 'socially acceptable' counter gift, regulated by social norms, rather than perfect equality (Polanyi, [1957], 1975). As one survey respondent commented, 'It is not a gift, it is a debt.' This logic can even trap households in reciprocal relations. It can perversely lock people into patterns of counter-gift donations, to which they keep complying even during times of hardship and which may require them to cut down on some of their basic consumption requirements. However, despite continuous social pressures, this act is still one of individual liberty, as indicated by another respondent, 'It is not always easy to give, and not everybody will donate something.'

The need to comply with social norms clearly influences the decision as to which kind of crop to cultivate. For example, banana plantations are especially well developed, as they enable the production of traditional beer—a gift well appreciated for ceremonies. Forms of savings are also motivated by these insurance practices. Everybody shares a responsibility in insuring the members of their group. As an example, growers often save part of the crop, when possible, to comply with this obligation of semi-voluntary reciprocity.

5.5.2.2 VOLUNTARY RECIPROCITY: SELF-HELP GROUPS

Some people voluntarily choose to form or join informal self-help groups. This decision is often motivated by the perception, in the words of a respondent, of 'stronger, easier and faster solidarity' compared with semi-voluntary reciprocity. Even if these groups are still embedded in neighbourhood or clan ties, they result from individual decisions to join a specific group.

Reciprocity is the governing principle of the *likirimba* and the MUSO systems. Based on geographic proximity, affinity, and trust, members voluntarily choose to create, as highlighted by Servet (2007), 'interdependent and complementary relationships'. The members collectively and autonomously decide on: (1) the size of the group, (2) selection of the members, and (3) the level and frequency of contributions. *Likirimba* and MUSOs perform more than just an economic function: beyond savings, credit, and insurance, these groups crucially serve to create and maintain social cohesion. For example, one female respondent said that she and all the members of her group bought the same *pagne,* thereby reinforcing the identity of the group.

At the time of forming or joining a self-help group, the selection of trustworthy partners is essential. Since enforcement is guaranteed through social control, future partners should be people whose culture is shared and whose behaviour can be predicted (Collins et al., 2009: 53). This also means that groups are personalized and exclusive (Hoddinott et al., 2009). This was similarly found in our sample: transfers embedded in reciprocity appeared to be insulated, leaving the poorest households with poor social networks with a low capacity to deal with hardship.

Mutual ties uniting members lead to the flexible application of rules. For example, in a MUSO, when the red box is empty or no compensation is foreseen for an event that is causing hardship for one of the members, other members gather and collectively decide whether there is a need for solidarity. Similarly, when a member has a repayment problem, the group may decide to soften the loan conditions. Some groups have initiated collective income-generating activities with the benefits being redistributed or channelled to the red or green box. MUSOs are therefore not just a way to circulate money: they can also be a place where production activities are developed. Voluntary reciprocity strengthens social relationships and feelings of mutual belonging and local identity. Beyond providing a coping mechanism, this social role is of key importance in a population that has suffered two decades of wars and conflicts.

Can the fixed charge (*'participation aux frais'*) of a MUSO be considered a price? This is a tricky question. Members stress that this charge cannot be attributed to an anonymous price resulting from demand and supply equilibrium (Bidubula, 2011): it is more a way of socializing part of the benefits resulting from the members' economic activities. It is thus more the subjective meaning given by members themselves to the amount of money that can shed light on the nature of this fixed charge. The monetary contribution can also support reciprocity logics.

MUSOs are supervised by local NGOs, which also provide technical support, and the NGOs in turn are funded by international donors. However, our research revealed, in general, a bottom-up dynamic: first, people get together to develop self-help groups and only later do they seek technical support from an NGO. How can this logic, which links grassroots groups and NGOs, be explained in terms of Polanyi's framework? Based on Gardin (2006), it could be considered as 'unequal reciprocity', defined as solidarity between groups, one of which is unable to give back a counter-gift. This type of reciprocity occurs when a group or an organization (here the NGO) helps another group (here the MUSO) in order to satisfy the latter's social demands. However, symmetry between groups, which requires voluntary interdependence and complementarity and cements reciprocity (Servet, 2007), can be contested. Following Lemaître and Helmsing (2012), it would be more appropriate to describe the relationship between NGOs and MUSOs as being based on a redistributive logic, according to which international and local NGOs serve as intermediaries: they receive flows from civil society organizations and government agencies based in the North, which they redistribute to institutions in the South. Lemaître and Helmsing (2012) refer to this as 'voluntary redistribution'—voluntary because the money collected by civil society organizations is not from compulsory contributions, and redistribution because it is not based on symmetry characterizing the logic of reciprocity. 'The resources are collected by a central entity, which has the responsibility to allocate it according to some criteria' (Lemaître and Helmsing, 2012). This is a debate about the blurred frontiers between reciprocity and redistribution which has already been underlined by Mauss (1923) and Polanyi (1944, 1957). In some ways, it may be said that reciprocity, which is the guiding principle of a MUSO, is framed by redistribution logics.

5.5.3 The Redistribution Principle

Obligatory lending, when the creditor is unlikely to become the debtor in the future, is entrenched in the redistribution principle. Whereas reciprocity relies on a pattern of symmetry among the actors, redistribution presupposes the presence of an allocative centre. In contemporary societies, the state is the redistributive centre through the provisioning of public services. In South Kivu, characterized by the quasi absence of public services' provision, the centre can be personalized by the figure of a well-off merchant who stands above the rest of the community. His social prestige derives from his 'generosity', which attracts about him people seeking help. The sense of obligation and the desire to maintain social prestige steer the rich man's donations or obligatory lending. However, as stressed by Polanyi (1944), distribution may often cover up exploitation or political power games, since by the manner in which goods are redistributed, power can also be increased.

5.5.4 MUSAs and COOPECs: At the Crossroads of Reciprocity, Redistribution and Market, Complementarity, or Conflicting Logics?

MUSOs are self-help groups that are largely autonomous from the NGOs that offer them technical support and they are mainly based on the logic of reciprocity. MUSAs, on the other hand, are developed in a much more top-down manner. They have been, and still are, fostered by NGOs active in the health sector with a view to improving access of vulnerable populations to health care. With the withdrawal of the state and the lack of adequate health-care policies and services, international and national NGOs are trying to fill the gap. NGOs seek to develop MUSAs in a systematic way and on a large scale, since the rapid growth of the system is considered to be a key factor for the success of the strategy. It is well known that insurance is more effective when the risk is shared by a larger pool of insured people. Thus, isolated MUSAs are more vulnerable, and networking between them is a way to strengthen their viability. Moreover, if MUSAs are numerous and well organized, they are more visible and they have more power to negotiate with health-care providers. Given all these elements, MUSA could be considered as being embedded in a redistributive logic, which, nevertheless, is still voluntary, as the centre (the NGO) cannot force the population to enrol in this insurance system. The development of MUSAs is clearly driven by the social and political objectives of improving access to health care. For example, premiums are the same for all, and are not fixed according to the risk of the beneficiary as would be required by market logic.

However, ideally, MUSAs should rely on symmetry, implying voluntary interdependence and complementarity among their members. At least this is the spirit of the model (Fonteneau and Galand, 2006). However, if the movement is expanded too rapidly, it could weaken the self-help dynamics embedded in reciprocity. As underlined by Nyssens and Vermer (2012), a compromise needs to be found between the expansion and professionalization required to reach economic efficiency on the one hand and safeguarding a bottom-up approach to preserve their social efficiency on the other.

What about the underlying logics of COOPECs? Cooperative principles, such as voluntary participation, rules collectively decided by the members and the social objective of serving the interests of the members, ideally require symmetry, voluntary interdependence, and complementarity, which are fundamental to the logic of reciprocity. Like MUSOs and MUSAs, most COOPECs also receive technical support from NGOs. At first sight it would seem that reciprocity and redistribution are complementary logics in COOPECs and MUSAs: their organizational principles reflect mutualism, and the financial and technical support of NGOS reflects redistribution. However, our observations do not confirm this hypothesis. Interviews with members of both MUSAs and COOPECs show that they tend to follow market logic: membership fees are seen as prices, members consider themselves as clients, and the movement of goods and services (i.e. savings and credit products, insurance) is seen more as a form of market exchange than as part of an integrative system founded on reciprocity. Moreover, as redistributive resources coming from international cooperation are sometimes insufficient, some potential members are not admitted due to their lack of solvency: financial viability supplants the objective of serving the interests of the whole community. Indeed, COOPEC and MUSA members are often the richest among the poor, and underserved people are excluded as they cannot pay membership fees or lack the material guarantees required when applying for credit.

5.5.5 Market Strategies: A Logic of 'Customer Ties'

Polanyi (1944 and 1956) distinguishes between different types of market, namely long-distance trade and local markets. Following Servet (2009), we distinguish between 'marketplace' and 'customer ties'. According to Servet (2009: 82), 'the anonymity that prevails in the marketplace at one point in time is supposed to neutralize social identities and differences between actors'. In a logic based on customer ties, 'sellers discriminate between buyers in an attempt to generate loyalty and sustain the relationship' (idem: 83). Of course, the two logics can coexist, but at some point one prevails over the other. In the informal sector, the logic of customer ties is still prevalent, as observed on local informal markets in the region, which leads to the conclusion that it is very different from the logic of anonymity that characterizes the logic of the market. This observation recalls the distinction made by Braudel (1985) between capitalist markets and local markets. The local economy is the sphere of everyday economic life. Those active at this local level are peasants, craftsmen, and small sellers—whom Braudel refers to as 'les acteurs du bas' (actors from the bottom)—the cement of the society. Even the logic of small street moneylenders offering loans at huge interest rates and on which poor people fall back in time of need is entrenched in 'customer ties' rather than anonymity.

5.6 Conclusions

In South Kivu, conflicts and volatile security have resulted in the provision of poor public services. Faced with a high degree of uncertainty and risks, households protect themselves by relying on diverse private strategies, ranging from individual arrangements (precautionary savings and income diversification) to informal and formal group-based-mechanisms. All respondents combine more than one strategy to cope with lean times, since one mechanism rarely provides sufficient sums of cash in a timely manner. Shocks faced by people are often imperfectly handled and expose households at risk to increased vulnerability.

From our analysis of the forms of integration, reciprocity appears to be the dominant principle underpinning strategies for coping with economic hardships in South Kivu. It appears in two forms: semi-voluntary reciprocity drives mutual support occurring along the lines of family and kinship, whilst voluntary reciprocity underpins informal or formal group-based mechanisms. For many respondents, networks seem to be vital sources of assistance in times of misfortune. Group-based tools provide mutual insurance, mainly against idiosyncratic shocks such as illness, childbirth, weddings, and deaths, but leave households with weak responses when an entire community is confronted with a common shock such as political instability or an economic crisis.

The householding principle appears to drive some savings decisions. In-kind savings in the native village is a way for urban people to fulfil their obligation towards the members of their group. As stressed by Polanyi, the institutions in which reciprocity and householding are embedded not only have an economic function (such as production and exchange), they may also fulfil religious, social, or political roles. Economic activities are associated with a desire to establish a social bond between the partners and maintain social cohesion.

Within MUSA and COOPEC, reciprocity and redistribution logics do not appear to be complementary; rather they seem to compete with each other. In the absence of state intervention, redistribution implemented mainly through NGOs is perceived as an exogenous force. While these institutions are entrenched in symmetry, voluntary interdependence, and complementarity of their members (principles that are fundamental to the logic of reciprocity), they are often initiated in a top-down manner by NGOs, which weakens the self-help dynamics and interpersonal trust that characterize reciprocity. According to Fafchamps (2004), interpersonal trust arises from repeated interaction among people in the community and personal acquaintance. By the same token, redistribution and market mechanisms rely on institutional or generalized trust. However, decades of wars and conflicts have deeply weakened such generalized trust. The lack of generalized trust is an impediment to the good functioning of economic practices entrenched in these two logics.

References

Alderman, H., and C. H. Paxson (1992). 'Do the Poor Insure? A Synthesis of the Literature on Risk and Consumption in Developing Countries'. Policy Research Working Paper Series 1008, World Bank, Washington, DC.

Baland, J.-M., C. Guikinger, and C. Mali (2011). 'Pretending to Be Poor: Borrowing to Escape Forced Solidarity in Cameroon'. *Economic Development and Cultural Change,* 60(1): 1–16.

Besley, T. (1995). 'Non-Market Institutions for Credit and Risk Sharing in Low-Income countries'. *Journal of Economic Perspectives,* 9(3): 115–27.

Bidubula Juwa, G. (2011). 'Microfinance, micro-assurance et structuration du milieu pauvre: Etat des lieux des mutuelles de solidarité au Sud-Kivu'. Document GRAP 3A, RDC.

Braudel, F. (1985). *La dynamique du capitalisme.* Paris: Arthaud.

Chambers, R., (1989). 'Editorial Introduction: Vulnerability, Coping and Policy'. *IDS Bulletin,* 20(2): 1–7.

Cohen, M. and J. Sebstad, (2005). 'Reducing Vulnerability: The Demand for Microinsurance'. *Journal of International Development,* 17: 397–474.

Collins, D., J. Morduch, S. Rutherford, and O. Ruthven (2009). *Portfolios of the Poor: How the World's Poor Live on $2 a Day*. Princeton University Press: Princeton.

Deaton, A. (1992). 'Household Savings in LDCs: Credit Markets, Insurance and Welfare'. *Scandinavian Journal of Economics*, 94(2): 253–73.

Dercon, S. (2002). 'Income Risk, Coping Strategies and Safety Nets'. Discussion Paper no. 2002/22, World Institute for Development Economics Research (UNU-WIDER), Helsinki.

—— (2005). 'Risk, Insurance and Poverty: A Review', in S. Dercon (ed.), *Insurance Against Poverty*. Oxford: Oxford University Press: 9–38.

Fafchamps, M. (1999). 'Rural Poverty, Risk and Development'. FAO Economic and Social Development Paper, 144.

—— (2004). *Market Institutions in Sub-Saharan Africa: Theory and Evidence*. Cambridge, MA: MIT Press.

Fonteneau, B. (2004). 'Les défis des systèmes de micro-assurance santé en Afrique de l'Ouest: Cadre politique, environnement institutionnel, fonctionnement et viabilité'. KUL-HIVA, Vlaamse Interuniversitaire Raad/Direction Générale de la Coopération au Développement, Brussels.

Fonteneau, B. and B. Galland (2006). 'The Community-Based Model: Mutual Health Organizations in Africa', in Part 4, *Institutional Options*, in C. Churchill (ed.), *Protecting the Poor: A Microinsurance Compendium*. Geneva: ILO/Munich RE Foundation: 378–400.

Gardin, L. (2006). 'Réciprocité', in J.-L. Laville, and A. D. Cattani (eds.), *Dictionnaire de l'autre économie*. Paris: Gallimard: 514–22.

Hoddinott, J., S. Dercon, and P. Krishnan (2009). 'Networks and Informal Mutual Support in 15 Ethiopian Villages', in J. Kirsten, A. Dorward, C. Poulton, and N. Vink (eds.), *Institutional Economics: Perspectives on African Agricultural Development*. Baltimore: Johns Hopkins University Press.

INS (Institut national de la statistique) and UNICEF (Fonds des Nations Unies pour l'Enfance) (March 2011). 'Enquête par Grappes à Indicateurs Multiples en RDC, Rapport final'. *Kinshasa*.

Lelart, M. (1995). 'Tontines africaines et tontines asiatiques'. *Afrique Contemporaine*, 176(4): 75–86.

Lemaître, A., and B. Helmsing (2012). 'Solidarity Economy in Brazil: Movement, Discourse and Practice Analysis through a Polanyian Understanding of the Economy'. *Journal of International Development*, 24: 745–62.

Mauss, M. (1923). 'Essai sur le don', *l'Année Sociologique*, Nouvelle série, Volume I (1923–1924). *Fascicule* 1: 7–29.

Morduch, J. (1999). 'Between the State and the Market: Can informal Insurance Patch the Safety Net?'. *World Bank Research Observer*, 14(2): 187–207.

Nyssens, M. and M. C. Vermer (2012). 'La régulation des mutuelles de santé au Bénin', in F. Leloup, J. Brot, and H. Gérardin (eds.), *L'Etat, acteur de développement*. Paris: Karthala: 123–40.

Polanyi, K. (1944). *The Great Transformation*. Boston: Beacon Press.

—— (1957). 'The Economy as Instituted Process', in K. Polanyi, C. Arensberg, and H. Pearson (eds.) (1957). *Trade and Market in the Early Empires: Economies in History and Theory*. Glencoe: Free Press.

Servet, J.-M. (2007). 'Le principe de réciprocité chez Karl Polanyi: Contribution à une définition de l'économie solidaire'. *Revue Tiers Monde*, 190: 255–73.

—— 'Toward an Alternative Economy: Reconsidering the Market, Money and Value', in C. Hann and K. Hart (eds.), *Market and Society: The Great Transformation Today.* Cambridge: Cambridge University Press: 72–90.

Townsend R. (1994). 'Risk and Insurance in Village India'. *Econometrica*, 62(3): 539–91.

UNDP (2011). *Human Development Report 2011—Sustainability and Equity: A Better Future for All.* New York: United Nations Development Programme.

Weber, M. (1965). *Essais sur la théorie de la science (1904–1917)*, partial translation by Julien Freund. Paris: Plon.

Part II

The Role of Financial Practices and Institutions in Securing Livelihoods

6

Financial Practices as Adaptations to Increasing Vulnerability: The Dynamics of Solidarity and Protection in the Suburbs of Rosario, Argentina[1]

Hadrien Saiag

6.1 Introduction

This chapter aims to provide an understanding of the reconfiguration of protection mechanisms through a detailed analysis of low-income households' saving and indebtedness practices in Argentina. Financial practices are more than just technical solutions for smoothing individual consumption over time (Servet, 2006; Guérin, Morvant-Roux, and Servet, 2011; Guérin, 2006; Chamoux et al., 1994; Johnson, 2004): they involve a complex set of social relations specific to the household economy. These mechanisms act as a safety net, woven out of relationships of kinship. It is argued that the prominence of household solidarity today should be understood as a response to the weakening of employment-based solidarity and protection schemes, provoked by the dismantling of the Fordist-like wage-labour nexus. This argument is supported by an analysis of protection mechanisms found at both the level of households and wage-labour-related social protection institutions. In this respect, Karl Polanyi's (1944) distinction between four principles of economic integration (reciprocity,

[1] The author is grateful to Bonnie Brusky, Jean-Michel Servet, and Bruno Théret for their comments.

redistribution, householding, and the market) provides a useful analytical framework (Servet, 2007; Hillenkamp, 2009; Hillenkamp and Servet, 2011).

This chapter is based on research carried out from August to December 2009 among low-income households in the suburbs of Rosario.[2] The author observed the daily financial practices of eighteen households and conducted in-depth interviews with each of them to better understand the interdependencies among household members. The households' economic conditions varied (some were better off than others), but they shared two main characteristics: (i) the irregularity and low level of their income, resulting from informal economic activities; and (ii) their involvement in a Fordist-like wage-labour relationship[3] over the past twenty years. This characteristic, specific to Rosario, a highly industrialized economy until the 1990s, is important because it allows us to establish a hypothesis concerning the dynamics of household- and employment-based solidarity and protection mechanisms.

Section 6.2 argues that the dismantling of the Fordist-like wage-labour nexus and the related transformation of social protection schemes led to increasing difficulties for Rosario's low-income population to access money. Section 6.3 presents and contextualizes the wide diversity of households' saving and indebtedness practices aimed at preserving their access to means of settlement in case of need. Section 6.4 suggests that these practices reveal the prominence of household-level protection mechanisms. Finally, the conclusion proposes a hypothesis concerning the dynamics of employment- and household-based protection mechanisms as a result of the dismantling of the Fordist-like wage-labour nexus.

6.2 A Transformation of Social Protection due to the Dismantling of the Fordist-Like Wage-Labour Nexus

According to qualitative data obtained during the fieldwork (see also Sosa, 2007), until the beginning of the 1990s Rosario's northern and southern suburbs were highly industrialized. Prevailing norms of employment were similar to the Fordist-like wage-labour nexus found in most Western countries until the 1970s. That is, provided the hierarchical structures of (big) firms were not questioned, employment could be maintained until retirement. In the case of married couples, men were usually the sole breadwinners; wives stayed at home to manage the housework. However, the establishment of fixed parity between the Argentinean peso and the United States dollar in

[2] Rosario, located on the Parana River about 400 km north-east of Buenos Aires, is the third largest city in Argentina with almost 1,200,000 inhabitants in 2010.

[3] The Fordist-like wage-labour relationship is characterized by (i) employment stability, (ii) social protection related to the employment status, and (iii) a hierarchical organization of production.

1991, which led to an overvaluation of the peso, significantly altered this norm. This situation was problematic because at the same time Argentina had liberalized its trade regime. The peso could not be devalued, because trust was rooted in its fixed parity with the dollar (Roig, 2007). Therefore, given the fixed exchange rate and the overvaluation of the peso, the only way to enable domestic companies to remain competitive was to resort to deflation and a reduction in gross wages (Beccaria, Esquivel, and Maurizio, 2007; del Pont and Valle, 1998), while also introducing much greater flexibility in the labour market. During the 1990s, income inequality rose, and the number of workers without social security increased significantly.[4] These changes in Argentina's macroeconomic context strongly affected the previously highly industrialized suburbs of Rosario, resulting in massive deindustrialization and an increase in various forms of informal employment.

The consequence of this structural shift has been to relegate Rosario's working classes to the margin of Fordist-like wage-labour forms of employment. At a macro level, few, if any, efforts were made to redress this situation until the end of the convertibility regime in 2002, but since then public policy to stimulate employment has been pursued through macroeconomic measures: the peso's exchange rate with foreign currencies has been deliberately undervalued in order to improve the competitiveness of domestic products and support Argentina's partial reindustrialization (Giosa Zuazua, 2007). Admittedly, the proportion of non-registered wage earners (i.e. those not registered in the Argentinean social security system) decreased significantly from 2002 to 2007, from 42.5 per cent to 35 per cent of total wage earners (this proportion was approximately 34 per cent in October 1995), and has remained stable since the end of 2007. However, this sharp decrease is entirely due to the increase in the number of declared workers from 2002 to 2007: the absolute number of non-registered wage earners actually increased slightly from the third quarter of 2003 to the second quarter of 2010 (Damill, Frenkel, and Maurizio, 2011). Thus, macroeconomic policy has not yet been able to reduce informal forms of employment. Moreover, income inequalities between employment categories increased from 2001: only the private-sector's average wage recovered (in 2004) and then exceeded its October 2001 level. However, public-sector and non-registered private-sector real wages have remained stable since 2006—approximately 25 per cent below October 2001 levels.

Because Rosario's suburbs were highly industrialized, its working-class neighbourhoods have been directly affected by these macroeconomic

[4] It is difficult to quantify this phenomenon, as measurement methods are diverse and controversial. However, all the authors who have tackled this question contend that the labour market has become more precarious. See, for instance, Beccaria, Esquivel, and Maurizio (2007); Rofman and Lucchetti (2006); del Pont and Valle (1998); and Giosa Zuazúa (2007).

changes. Indeed, during the fieldwork, none of the interviewees was directly involved in a Fordist-like wage-labour relationship, despite having previously (in the past twenty years) held a job which offered stability, a regular salary, and social protection. Indeed, only the daughter of one interviewee and the father of another enjoyed a stable job, with a fixed salary and related social benefits (e.g. health coverage, unemployment benefits, and a pension scheme). Most of the interviewees' income derived from a combination of some kind of contingent labour (*changas*), self-employment (as clothes or food vendors, recyclers of urban waste, participation in second-hand markets), and social assistance subsidies.

The dismantling of the Fordist-like wage-labour nexus led to deep changes in low-income households' access to money. It deprived them of the protection and solidarity associated with the wage-labour employment and welfare state in two ways. First, access to money is much more uncertain and market-dependent in the 'new' forms of the informal economy than it was in the 'former' wage-labour nexus. In the latter, acceptance of hierarchical rules ensured relatively stable access to money, regardless of the short-term results of the firm (risk was absorbed by the owners of the means of production). In the 'new' forms of informal employment, low-income households are marginalized in terms of access to means of settlement: they depend on wage-labourers' expenditures, which in turn depend on those of the owners.[5] Indeed, in contemporary bank-issued money, owners of the means of production benefit from privileged access to means of settlement through productive credit, and wages are part of their expenditures. The income of informal workers, on the other hand, depends on wage earners' expenditures. Under this dynamic, the wage-labour nexus regulates the circulation rate of the means of settlement. In Rosario's suburbs, wage earners are usually paid either once (municipal employees) or twice a month (on the 5th and the 20th). Informal workers' incomes are highly dependent on these dates. And yet, neither informal income-generating activities nor household expenditures respect monthly or bi-monthly cycles. As a result, low-income households' access to money through their participation in informal forms of employment is highly precarious, and is not sufficient to meet their financial needs.

The dismantling of the Fordist-like wage-labour nexus has also threatened the linkages between employment relationships on the one hand, and solidarity and protection mechanisms, on the other, through changes to the social protection system.[6] Certainly, the Argentinean social protection system covers

[5] This is why Benetti and Cartelier (1980) qualified the relationship which binds and differentiates capitalists from wage earners as 'monetary dependence' (see also Orléan, 2008, and Cartelier, 2007).

[6] For a general theoretical analysis of national social protection systems, see Théret (2003).

a large segment of the population, as compared with other Latin American countries (Martinez-Franzoni, 2008). It is also quite old, as it was legally extended to the entire active population at the end of Perón's first presidency (1944–55). Until the mid-1990s, the system followed a Bismarckian model that combined protection by the state and employers (through tax transfers and employers' contributions, respectively) with wage earners' solidarity (through wage-earners' contributions). Part of the precautionary savings was pooled through the social protection system and has been centrally administrated since the 1968 pension reform (Goldberg and Lo Vuolo, 2006). This scheme was weakened with the growth of undeclared employment during the 1980s and 1990s: social benefits (e.g. pension, health care, and unemployment insurance) remained strongly tied to formal wage-labour employment until the end of the 1990s. The switch from a pay-as-you-go (public) pension scheme to a mix of pay-as-you-go and a defined contributory pension system (private) in 1994 deepened the schism between covered and uncovered populations by drastically reducing coverage for low-income groups (Rofman and Lucchetti, 2006; Mesa-Lago, 2002; Arza, 2008). The return to a pay-as-you-go public pension scheme in 2008 resulted in wider coverage, but long-term eligibility rules to contribution-based schemes did not change (Arza, 2009). In order to deal with the exclusion of informal workers from such social protection schemes, the Government of Argentina implemented a non-contributory assistance programme for vulnerable households (e.g. low-income, the elderly, mothers of seven or more children), based on a state (discriminatory) protection scheme (Barrientos, 2009). As a result, low-income households are excluded from wage-labour contributory social protection programmes and relegated to discriminatory poverty assistance schemes that provide poor benefits.

6.3 Reifying Savings, Keeping Debts Alive

The exclusion of Rosario's low-income population from the Fordist-like wage-labour nexus and institutionalized social protection schemes gave rise to increasing difficulties in accessing money. Therefore, the wide diversity of saving and indebtedness practices observed during the fieldwork should be viewed as strategies aimed at preserving households' access to the means of settlement in case of need. Those practices contradict the widespread view that poor households are unable to save because of their lack of monetary resources (see also Collins et al., 2009). Rather, because of a lack of monetary resources, households implement forms of 'financial self-discipline' (Guérin, 2006) aimed at preserving savings, and resist the temptation of spending them and remaining in debt. The practices are diverse, but they all seek to *separate* what can be spent from what cannot (Roig, 2010).

Most households are excluded from highly formalized financial institutions. The *Caja Nacional de Ahorro Postal* (National Postal Savings Bank)[7] closed in 1994, and has not been replaced by any other financial institution specifically devoted to poor households. In the rare cases that households do maintain a relationship with a bank, it is usually limited to the use of a debit card for withdrawal of social assistance subsidies, but not to holding savings in a bank account. Consumer credit supplied by non-banking financial institutions is the only highly formalized financial product widely used by low-income populations[8] (de Nigris, 2008: 31). Still, in our sample, more than half of the interviewees had no relationship with any formal financial institution at the time of our fieldwork.

Part of the population located in Rosario's northern suburbs has access to microfinance, provided by a local NGO, Poriajhú,[9] whose mission is the 'liberation of the poorest' through education.[10] It is the only organization proposing financial services that has established a long-term, trust-based relationship with low-income households. The lending methodology is based on joint liability groups of five borrowers. The loan amount ranges from 500 to 1,000 pesos (approximately 100 to 200 euros at the time of the fieldwork). Repayments are on a weekly basis, with an annual nominal interest rate of 6 per cent. Some borrowers invest the entire loan amount in inputs consumed on a weekly basis (such as sewing thread or foodstuffs), while others invest some in inputs and use the rest to acquire equipment for production purposes (e.g. hand mixer or sewing machine).

However, these microfinance services only represent a small share of low-income households' indebtedness and saving practices; indeed, most financial practices take place far from formal institutions. All the families interviewed testify to earmarking earnings to avoid the temptation of spending. For example, some of them put earnings from the first sales of each week into a separate box until the accumulated sum is sufficient to buy the inputs required for the next week's production. Only the earnings of the subsequent sales are included in the household's budget to cover daily expenses (Absi, 2007). This extremely common practice of saving in cash in order to

[7] This institution offered current accounts and savings account books (in which savings were marked by means of a stamp) from 1915 to 1994. This savings service was very popular amongst low-income populations until the inflation of the mid-1960s. Since its privatization in 1994 (Roig, 2010), it no longer offers any financial services to low-income populations.

[8] It is usually necessary to present a pay slip in order to have access to this kind of loan. However, it is very common for workers without any labour contract to borrow using the name of a relative or a neighbour who can supply a pay slip.

[9] Microcredit operations are funded by a government programme, *Bancito Popular de la Buena Fe* (Popular Bank of Good Faith).

[10] Poriajhú means literally 'the poor' in Guarani. For more details on the other activities carried out by Poriajhú and its microfinance activities, see Saiag (2011).

tackle cash-flow problems is specific to activities located at the margin of the wage-labour nexus.

Usually, cash savings do not involve large sums. Only those with relatively comfortable incomes are able to save substantially more than their weekly production needs. For larger sums, different practices of reification[11] of savings have been observed. Indeed, reification (through the accumulation of different kinds of materials) is a second way to avoid the temptation of spending by effectively rendering savings illiquid (Shipton, 1992; Roig, 2010; Servet, 1995): reified savings are relatively 'illiquid' because they are physically separated from monetary resources which might be spent for daily needs. For example, interviewees whose relatively capital-intensive income-generating activity (such as a home-based sewing shop) relies on considerable inputs (e.g. wool, sewing thread, or paint) systematically purchase more inputs than needed in the short term to make sure they will not spend savings on non-business items, as that would endanger the continuity of their activity.

A gradual acquisition of materials to improve housing conditions is also a common form of reifying savings—a practice observed among all the interviewees. They save 500 to 700 pesos in cash (through a system of separate boxes or envelopes), which they then spend on building materials (especially bricks and cement). Materials can also be obtained as payment for daily contingent labour (*changa*). Once the materials are in hand, construction gets under way. The male head of a household and his sons usually supply the labour, but neighbours might also help (against remuneration). The newly built rooms might be the beginnings of a house for a recently married son or daughter, a bedroom for the parents, a bathroom, a kitchen, a room from which to sell miscellaneous articles (e.g. clothes, food, or shoes), or a small sewing shop. This practice is a clear demonstration of how savings are made inaccessible to avoid the temptation of spending. The fieldwork revealed that no family ever resold bricks or cement in order to finance other spending.[12]

The acquisition of building materials should not be confused with another kind of reification of savings: the accumulation of recyclable goods, such as iron, zinc, copper, cardboard, plastic, or glass bottles. These materials can be obtained in different ways. For example, in the slums (*villa*), they may be salvaged by night from urban waste by men (and sometimes women and children), pejoratively called *cartoneros*, in reference to cardboard (*cartón*). Some of the materials are sold by weight at the end of the night, but others are

[11] The term 'reification' applied to savings is preferred to 'saving in kind', because the latter implies a dichotomous vision of the economy ('real' versus 'monetary' spheres), contrary to 'reification'. Both earmarking and reification practices allow households to access means of settlement in case of need (see also section 6.4).

[12] Alexandre Roig (2010) made the same observation during fieldwork carried out in the working-class suburbs of Buenos Aires.

physically taken apart and kept aside for sale later, to pay for an unexpected event (Roig, 2010). In addition, adults and children often salvage materials from the street, such as copper wire or a broken electronic item (e.g. fan or radio). These goods are stripped down and the parts that can be sold are stored in plastic barrels kept for this purpose. Lastly, some interviewees said they managed to obtain materials through work: for example, small shopkeepers break down cardboard packaging, and construction workers may reclaim used pipes (which often contain metal). Such objects are usually stored in front of the house (in Rosario's slums) or behind the house (in the adjacent low-income neighbourhoods). If necessary, they can be sold by weight to ambulatory buyers who park their trucks at night in Rosario's streets and buy recycled waste from the *cartoneros*. This form of saving is also very popular, even if it is usually associated with poverty (hence, slightly better off households in low-income neighbourhoods tend to do it more surreptitiously).

Some financial practices are a reminder that saving and borrowing often go hand in hand (see Shipton, 1992; Guérin, Morvant-Roux, and Servet, 2011). Every interviewee spoke of having recently borrowed or lent money to relatives.[13] Lending can involve members of the same or different generations. In the first case, it is common for family members who do not enjoy a stable income to save money by lending to relatives who are paid on a fixed-term basis. This constitutes a relatively safe form of saving, and enables the borrower to meet spending needs that arise before payday. When lending operations involve members of different generations, the creditors are almost always the elders, as discussed in the next section.

Other indebtedness practices involve parties outside the household. *Fiado* is one such practice (see also Roig, 2010 and Villarreal, 2000). The term comes from the verb *fiar*, or 'to trust', but it also refers to deferred payment for foodstuffs. Debts are usually counted in terms of commodities sold, and repaid in cash. To buy *a fiado* means to be restricted to buying from the shop that sells the *fiado*: it is usually not permitted to buy *a fiado* from different shops at the same time. All small shops (*almacen* or *granja*—but not supermarkets) as well as most street vendors offer this possibility to their clients, who reimburse their debt when they get paid. *Fiado* is among the most common sources of indebtedness among Rosario's low-income neighbours' residents.

Two other practices of indebtedness could be observed in our fieldwork, but they seemed to be much less common among the interviewees than *fiado*.[14] The first is supplier credit, which only applies to small shopkeepers (such as

[13] Lending among friends and neighbours is not unusual, but much less frequent than among relatives, and does not necessarily involve close relatives.

[14] Only one of the interviewees admitted using supplier credit frequently, and two had relatives who were involved in ROSCAs.

clothing vendors) who are already relatively well established and own or rent their commercial premises. Under this form of credit, a new order is delivered against the payment of the previous order (and not against the one being delivered)—a practice known as *boleta contra boleta*. Some local forms of rotating savings and credit associations (ROSCAs)[15] (*círculos de ahorro*) are also used to buy household goods. However, ROSCAs are not very common, since they are primarily used by the few remaining male wage earners employed in the major local industrial firms.

In the indebtedness practices described above, it is not always necessary for the debtor to repay in full in order to contract new debts. All that is necessary is to prove one's willingness to repay through regular payments (Villarreal, 2000). As a result, debt relationships tend to extend over long periods of time.

6.4 Some Household-Based Financial Practices

Understanding the mediating role of finance in a complex set of social relations calls for more than a mere inventory of saving and indebtedness practices: an in-depth analysis of each practice is also necessary.

Naturally, market relations are important: they tend to regulate the way low-income households access the means of settlement. For instance, in each interviewed household, at least one of its members was involved in the labour market. However, households' saving and indebtedness practices are not simply a by-product of market relationships. They reveal the specificities of a household's financial organization ('householding', in Polanyian terms), as compared with other Polanyian principles of economic integration (reciprocity and redistribution) (Hillenkamp, 2013; Hillenkamp and Servet, 2011). Indebtedness and saving practices reveal specific household-based protection mechanisms that are deeply embedded in relationships of kinship (the foundation of household solidarity). A careful analysis of these dimensions requires devoting specific attention to the ways savings are spent and debts incurred, and distinguishing between the different relationships to time induced by each practice (Bourdieu, 1963; Baumann, 1998; and Weber, 1996).

6.4.1 Protecting Households through Savings and Indebtedness

Households' financial practices, like savings and some indebtedness practices with people outside the family unit, serve to protect against specific risks.

[15] On ROSCAs, see for instance, Ardner and Burman (1996) and Bouman (1995).

The choice of saving through material support is not neutral. Admittedly, all savings are 'precautionary', since the lack of savings would expose households to high vulnerability. However, the fact that some savings are reified is indicative of the importance of protection mechanisms. Such an 'illiquidity preference' (Shipton, 1995) aims at preserving access to means of settlement in order to protect households against unforeseen financial needs. It is embedded in a linear, long-term, and uncertain relationship to time. Sources of such incertitude are diverse. Our fieldwork revealed that inflation was one of them, and the 6 per cent fixed annual interest on microcredit was a way to protect households against inflation, because the real interest rate turned negative with inflation. Moreover, long-term uncertainty is embedded in Argentina's recent financial history. Since the late 1980s, Argentina has suffered two major economic crises, the hyperinflation of the late 1980s and the end of the convertibility regime in 2001 and 2002, which have threatened a disintegration of the country's social fabric (Roig, 2007). Memories of these events are still fresh for most Argentineans, and many believe similar crises could recur.

However, even much less extraordinary events can jeopardize the precarious balance of household budgets, such as the loss of a source of income, illness, rupture with a family member, break-up of conjugal relations, or the death of a relative. All these are legitimate and recurrent reasons to liquidate savings (regardless its form), suspend debt repayments, sell household goods, or go into debt. Amassing construction materials follows a similar aim, since any other form of saving would expose households to the risk of liquidation, which would mean the project would have to be abandoned. Again, this form of saving specifically protects households from a highly uncertain future. Because nobody knows what will happen tomorrow, and because housing improvement is an imperious necessity, there is a need to protect housing projects from uncertainty related to the reduction of monetary resources.

Some saving and indebtedness practices also aim to protect households against the short-term cyclical expenditure needs specific to small-scale, non-wage labour income-generating activities. The aim of these practices is twofold: to protect household budgets from an irregular cash flow, and to ensure that the income-generating activity will not be jeopardized by the household's daily financial needs (for consumption). Indeed, households excluded from the formal wage-labour nexus must often cope with short-term consumption and income-generating activity cycles that are not necessarily synchronized. While the former usually has a daily cycle, the latter generally follows a weekly one (mainly because commercial activities are on a weekly basis) (Saiag, 2011: 307–11).

Hence, four of the practices presented in the previous section enable households to manage the lag between short-term cyclical financial needs and income. Savings in cash aim to tackle cash-flow problems, while supplier credit and microcredit create a separate short-term financial circuit for non-wage labour's income-generating activities, securing a specific weekly access to means of settlement. On the other hand, *fiado* and consumer credit allow household consumption to be relatively independent of short-term cyclical fluctuations of income. *Fiado*'s repayment terms are flexible, and can usually be repaid when the client receives some remuneration.

6.4.2 Kinship and Domestic Solidarity

Two key elements show how saving and indebtedness practices in kinship-based household safety nets provide protection.[16] Both these elements have a long-term and circular relationship with time (Shipton, 1995). The first one is life-cycle events (e.g. marriages, funerals, and birthdays), which are impossible to avoid, even if the timing of their occurrence is uncertain. Some entail considerable expense and must be financed through indebtedness (and/or liquidation of savings). For instance, in the event of marriage, in addition to the wedding ceremony, newlyweds are often expected to move out of the family home and build their own house, which requires buying a plot of land and building materials, and sometimes paying someone to help with construction. In order to cope with these expenses, money can usually be borrowed from someone in the extended family (for example, an uncle who has a successful small business). Parents, too, usually help the new couple, donating building materials and labour. The coming of age parties of 15-year-old girls (*fiesta de quince*) also involve considerable expenses (about 4,000 pesos, as revealed in the fieldwork), even if the amounts are substantially lower than for a marriage. These parties cannot be avoided because they are considered a rite of passage to adulthood.

Savings are also frequently used during these and other key events of social life. Some are usually more regular and less expensive than weddings and *fiestas de quince*. On the other hand, events such as the death of a relative can give rise to sudden and unexpected funeral expenses, which are met by selling stocks of copper, glass, or zinc. Illness can cause a similar depletion of savings by disrupting the household's productive organization (through a non-working family member, unexpected health-care costs or transportation to the hospital). Lastly, birthdays frequently give rise to considerable expenses, incurred out of pleasure, ostentation, or just the desire to socialize (termed '*consumation*' by Bataille, 1991 [1949]). For instance, it is quite usual

[16] The gender dimension of these practices is not addressed here for lack of space, but see Saiag (2011: 77–9 and 287–8), Zelizer (1994: chapter 2), and Guérin (2002) for an overview on the 'gender of money'.

in chronically indebted households for the husband to offer his wife a new pair of shoes which might cost almost half of the household's weekly income, or for a mother to give her young son expensive clothes, even while relying on government welfare programmes to meet daily food needs (Figueiro, 2009).

The second key element which demonstrates how households' financial practices are embedded within relationships of kinship is the common practice of lending and borrowing among members of the same household, especially when creditors and debtors belong to different generations. This practice does not necessarily finance life-cycle events, but it can relieve financial stress related to non-wage economic activities. Intra-household lending and borrowing is strongly codified by the indebtedness induced by kinship. Three points are worth highlighting in this connection. First, filial debts are asymmetrical. In all the interviewed households, it was considered inconceivable to refuse a loan to children if the parents could afford it. Cash, building materials, and labour are commonly lent in this way. Children do not have to repay the debts owed to their parents; on the contrary, parents have to repay their debts when they borrow money from their children (a daughter can be infinitely indebted to her mother, but the reverse is not true). Indeed, it is impossible to repay filial debts: it is only possible to pass them on to the next generation, when children become parents (Warnier, 2009). Second, financial solidarity between members of the same generation (e.g. brothers, sisters, and cousins) is a corollary of filial debt: it is usually taken for granted that a sibling will give financial help to another sibling in the event of illness, provided he or she can afford it. It is hard to refuse to lend to brothers and sisters, even when they became adults and their repayment capacity is uncertain. Third, marriage brings about a substantial change in the way filial debt occurs. Admittedly, it is not possible to repay debts incurred before marriage, but even after marriage parents find it hard to refuse to lend to the ascending generation, if parents can afford it. However, obligations towards the ascending generation are reduced after their marriage: once married, offspring are expected to repay any newly incurred debts owed to their parents.

Only an extreme event, such as death, can reverse the direction of filial debts, as pointed out by Raquel's painful experience. Our interview with her revealed a surprising gap between her income and her living conditions. Indeed, as a cleaning woman she is relatively well paid (compared with other interviewees), and she gains a substantial extra income from the sale of apple pies in a relatively well-off neighbourhood. In addition, the father of her child gives her 400 pesos every month to cover schooling expenses for the child. For many interviewees, this is an enviable situation. And yet, she and her child share a small 'house' with her parents in one of the slums located in Rosario's suburb. This paradox is the result of one major tragic event: one day, when she was a teenager, Raquel took her brother with her when she visited her boyfriend. Distracted, she turned her attention away from her brother and he drowned. The direction of the filiation debt was reversed: from then on, Raquel became indebted to her parents. Since life has no price, this debt cannot ever be repaid; it is only possible to honour it through regular payments (Théret, 2009). Thus, at the time of the fieldwork, Raquel was working hard to support her parents. From August 2009, she took charge of her ten nephews after their mother—her sister—died in a bus accident. As a result of the shock, her mother had to be sent to a public hospital. Raquel paid the expenses for her father to visit the hospital, and repaid her mothers' microcredit debt (and her own)—all this, despite having temporarily stopped the apple-pie business in order to visit her mother.

Saving and indebtedness practices simultaneously reflect alliance and filial-based, household level solidarity and household-based protection mechanisms. The two dimensions are interdependent: filial relationships may govern the use of savings, which in turn protect the household against specific risks (such as when a child gets ill and the household's reified savings are spent). Thus household financial organization provides household members with a safety net, which reduces the precariousness of their involvement in informal forms of employment.

6.5 Conclusions

This chapter suggests that there has been a reconfiguration of solidarity and protection mechanisms among Rosario's low-income households as a result of the dismantling of the Fordist-like wage-labour nexus and the growth of informal employment. Growing fluctuations in income and weakened solidarity and protection schemes for wage earners have led to a significant part of the burden of precautionary savings being transferred from social protection institutions to households. Today, financial practices of low-income populations in Rosario are characterized by the prominence of household-based safety nets. Admittedly, it is probable that the saving and indebtedness practices described in section 6.3 existed prior to the dismantling of the Fordist-like wage-labour nexus. What seems to be new, however, is their prominent role in households' protection mechanisms, as informal employment exposes households to new kinds of vulnerabilities. Moreover, solidarity among wage earners has been only partially replaced by state-sponsored poverty alleviation schemes.

However, this substitution of social protection schemes by household saving and indebtedness practices is still, at present, only a hypothesis based on exploratory research. It is necessary to probe the details of this reconfiguration in order to determine if there is in fact a link between the weakening of wage-labour solidarity and protection mechanisms, and the rise of households' saving and indebtedness practices. Further research is needed to deepen this analysis, through better knowledge of the dynamic dimensions of those practices. Such a research programme presents a methodological challenge: it is not easy to gain a historical perspective of households' financial practices, as revealed in our interviews when respondents were not able to give a particularly coherent account of them. Such a research programme should avoid making a simplistic opposition between market and protection. As shown by our fieldwork, the participation of Rosario's low-income neighbourhoods in the labour market through informal forms of employment led to a transformation of both their relationship with market transactions and modes of protection. Thus, a detailed analysis of ongoing processes of socio-economic change would need to address the question of the interdependencies of market and protection processes.

References

Absi, P. (2007). 'Il ne faut pas mélanger les fortunes: Travail, genre et revenus chez les commerçantes de Bolivie', in V. Hernandez, P. Ould-Ahmed, J. Papail, and P. Phélinas (eds.), *Turulences monétaires et sociales: L'Amérique latine dans une perspective comparée.* Paris: Editions L'Harmattan: 355–93.

Ardner, S. and S. Burman (1996). *Money-Go-Rounds: The Importance of ROSCAS for Women.* Oxford: Breg Publishers.

Arza, C. (2008). 'The Limits of Pension Privatization: Lessons from Argentine Experience'. *World Development,* 36(12): 2696–712.

—— (2009). 'Back to the State: Pension Fund Nationalization in Argentina'. *Documento de Trabajo,* 73: 1–41.

Barrientos, A. (2009). 'Labour Markets and the (Hyphenated) Welfare Regime in Latin America'. *Economy and Society,* 38(1): 87–108.

Bataille, G. (1991 [1949]). *The Accursed Share: An Essay on General Economy* [tran. from *La part maudite]*. New York: Zone Books.

Baumann, E. (1998). '"15%? Mais c'est trop cher!" Coût du crédit et représentation du temps en milieu populaire à Dakar', in J.-M. Servet and D. Vallat (eds.), *Rapport exclusion et liens financiers.* Paris: Economica: 35–41.

Beccaria, L.,V. Esquiveland, and R. Maurizio (2007). 'Crise et reprise: Les effets sur le marché du travail et sur la distribution du revenu', in V. Hernandez, P. Ould-Ahmed, J. Papail, and P. Phélinas (eds.), *Turbulences monétaires et sociales: L'Amérique latine dans une perspective comparée.* Paris: L'Harmattan: 173–208.

Benetti, C. and J. Cartelier (1980). *Marchands, salariat et capitalistes.* Paris: Maspero.

Bouman, F. J. A. (1995). 'Rotating and Accumulating Savings and Credit Associations: A Development Perspective'. *World Development,* 23(3): 371–84.

Bourdieu, P. (1963). 'La société traditionnelle: Attitude à l'égard du temps et conduite économique'. *Sociologie du Travail,* 1(1): 24–44.

Cartelier, J. (2007). 'The Hypostasis of Money: An Economic Point of View'. *Cambridge Journal of Economics*, 31(2): 217–33.

Chamoux, M. N., D. Dehouve, C. Gouy, and M. Pépin (eds.) (1994). *Prestar y pedir prestado: Relaciones sociales y crédito en el méxico de los siglos XVI al XX*. Mexico: Centre d'études méxicaines et centraméricaines [Centre for Mexican and Central American Studies].

Collins, D., J. Morduch, S. Rutherford, and O. Ruthven (2009). *Portfolios of the Poor: How the World's Poor Live on $2 a Day*. Princeton: Princeton University Press.

Damill, M., R. Frenkel, and R. Maurizio (2011). 'Macroeconomic Policy for Full and Productive Employment and Decent Work For All: An Analysis of the Argentine Experience'. *Employment Working Paper, n°109*. Geneva: ILO.

De Nigris, A. (2008). *La bancarización en Argentina*. Buenos Aires: CEPAL.

del Pont, M. M. and H. Valle (1998). 'Chômage et précarisation du travail en Argentine'. *Revue Tiers Monde*, 39(154): 451–8.

Figueiro, P. (2009). 'El gasto como simbolo: Notas en torno a la "utilidad" et "inutilidad" de las practicas de consumo'. Paper presented at the XXVII Congress of the Latin American Association of Sociology, Buenos Aires, 31 August 2009.

Giosa Zuazúa, N. (2007). 'L'emploi, intégrateur social dans l'Argentine de l'après-convertibilité?' *Revue Tiers Monde*, 189: 35–50.

Goldberg, L. and R. Lo Vuolo (2006). *Falsas promesas: Sistema de previsión social y régimen de acumulación*. Buenos Aires: Miño y Davila.

Guérin, I. (2006). 'Women and Money: Lessons from Senegal'. *Development and Change*, 37(3): 549–570.

—— S. Morvant-Roux, and J.-M Servet (2011). 'Understanding the Diversity and Complexity of Demand for Microfinance Services: Lessons from Informal Finance', in B. Armendáriz and M. Labie (eds.), *Handbook of Microfinance*. London: World Scientific Publishing: 101–22.

Hillenkamp, I. (2009). 'Formes d'intégration de l'économie dans les démocraties de marché: Une théorie substantive à partir de l'étude du mouvement d'économie solidaire dans la ville d'El Alto (Bolivie).' PhD thesis in Development Studies, University of Geneva/IHIED, Geneva.

—— (2013). 'Le principe de householding aujourd'hui: Discussion théorique et approche empirique par l'économie populaire', in I. Hillenkamp and J.-L. Laville (eds.), *Socioéconomie et démocratie: L'actualité de Karl Polanyi*. Toulouse: Erès: 215–39.

—— and J.-M. Servet (2011). 'Reciprocity and Householding: Two Polanyian Tools for Analyzing Solidarity Today'. Paper presented at the Workshop on New Directions in Polanyian Scholarship, Salisbury, 13 March 2011.

Johnson, S. (2004). 'Milking the Elephant: Financial Markets as Real Markets in Kenya'. *Development and Change*, 35(2): 247–74.

Martinez-Franzoni, J. (2008). 'Welfare Regimes in Latin America: Capturing Constellations of Markets, Families, and Policies'. *Latin American Politics and Society*, 50(2): 67–100.

Mesa-Lago, C. (2002). 'Myth and Reality of Pension Reform: The Latin American Evidence'. *World Development*, 30(8): 1309–21.

Orléan, A. (2008). 'Monnaie, séparation marchande et rapport salarial', in F. Lordon (ed.), *Conflits et pouvoirs dans les institutions du capitalisme*. Paris: Presses de la Fondation des Sciences Politiques: 55–87.

Polanyi, K. (1944). *The Great Transformation*. New York and Toronto: Farrar and Rinehart.

Rofman, R. and L. Lucchetti (2006). 'Pension Systems in Latin America: Concepts and Measurements of Coverage'. Social Protection Discussion Paper no. 0616, World Bank, Washington, DC.

Roig, A. (2007). 'La monnaie impossible: la convertibilité argentine de 1991'. PhD thesis in Economics, Ecole des Hautes Etudes en Sciences Sociales, Paris.

—— (2010). 'L'excédent négligé: Pratiques d'épargne et institutions financières dans les secteurs populaires argentins', in J. Marques-Pereira and R. Lo Vuolo (eds.), *Rapport final: Les conditions de la stabilité de la croissance, l'épargne et la distribution des revenus en Argentine*. Paris: Caisse des Dépôts et Consignations: 271–338.

Saiag, H. (2011). 'Le trueque argentin au prisme de la dette: Une socioéconomie des pratiques monétaires et financières'. PhD thesis in Economics, University of Paris-Dauphine, Paris.

Servet, J.-M. (ed.) (1995). *Epargne et liens sociaux: Etudes comparées d'informalités financières*. Paris: Association d'économie financière—Caisse des Dépôts et Consignations.

—— (2006). *Banquiers aux pieds nus: La microfinance*. Paris: Odile Jacob.

—— (2007). 'Le principe de réciprocité chez Karl Polanyi'. *Revue Tiers Monde*, 190: 255–73.

Shipton, P. (1992). 'The Rope and the Box: Group Savings in Gambia', in D. Adams and D. Fitchett (eds.), *Informal Finance in Low Income Countries*. Boulder, CO: Westview Press: 25–41.

—— (1995). 'How Gambians Save: Culture and Economic Strategy at an Ethnic Crossroads', in J. Guyer (ed.), *Money Matters: Instability, Values and Social Payments in the Modern History of West African Communities*. London: Currey/Heinemann: 245–76.

Sosa, R. (2007). 'El oncepto de trabajo en un cambio de época: Un estudio sobre la restauracion contemporanea del capital y los impactos objectivos y subjectifos en el mndo del trabajo en Argentina (1976-2006)'. PhD thesis in History, National University of Rosario, Rosario.

Théret, B. (2003). 'Responsabilité et solidarité: Une approche en termes de dette', in C. Bec and G. Procacci (eds.), *De la responsabilité solidaire. Mutations dans les politiques sociales d'aujourd'hui*. Paris: Editions Syllepse, pp. 51–67.

Théret, B. (2009). 'Monnaie et dettes de vie: A propos de quelques critiques adressées à La monnaie souveraine'. *L'Homme, Revue Française d'Anthropologie*,190: 153–80.

Villarreal, M. (2000). 'Deudas, drogas, fiado y prestado en las tiendas de abarrotes rurales'. *Desacatos*, 3: 69–88.

Warnier, J-P. (2009). 'Les politiques de la valeur'. *Sociétés Politiques Comparées*, 11: 1–67.

Weber, F. (1996). 'Réduire ses dépenses, ne pas compter son temps: Comment mesurer l'économie domestique?' *Genèses*, 25: 5–28.

Zelizer, V. (1994). *The Social Meaning of Money*. New York: Basic Books.

7

Microcredit Policies in Brazil: An Analysis of Community Development Banks

Genauto Carvalho de França Filho, Ariádne Scalfoni Rigo, and Jeová Torres Silva Júnior

7.1 Introduction

In recent decades, microfinance has been seen as an effective tool for poverty alleviation in Brazil and worldwide. The offer of credit to the poorest populations (especially those that operate in the informal labour market) is believed to be a possible way not only to reduce poverty, but to promote broader economic and social development. This chapter aims to offer a critical perspective on this belief. The success or failure of poverty reduction and development will be determined by the ways in which society is able to mobilize solidarity mechanisms according to various economic rationales in the management of microcredit.

This chapter is organized as follows. First, it analyses public policy relating to microcredit in Brazil with a view to showing both the merits and shortcomings of the conventional microcredit practices. The critical issue relates to the inability of public conventional microcredit programmes to effectively reach the lowest income segments of the population. Second, contrasting with this public policy, community development banks (CDBs) in Brazil are presented as a different means of delivering microcredit. Additionally, this chapter discusses the practical possibilities and limitations of CDBs as a new form of providing access to microcredit. With this approach we seek to comprehend the existing diversity of experiences in the world of microfinance. Thus we conclude that CDBs constitute a different form of microfinance, as they rely on mechanisms of a solidarity economy.

7.2 Microcredit Policies in Brazil and Their Limited Effectiveness in Poverty Reduction

Microcredit gained prominence worldwide after the 1997 Global Conference on Microcredit in Washington, which was attended by 2,900 people from 137 countries (Microcredit Summit, 1997). There was general agreement at this conference that microcredit would be a key tool for fighting poverty in the world (Carvalho et al., 2009; Costa, 2010). In Brazil, mainly since the 1990s, many 'promises' have been made through policies and programmes to support microcredit, involving a variety of public and private, as well as national and international institutions. Such policies and programmes have emphasized so-called production-oriented microcredit, which is designed for micro and small enterprises (both formal and informal) that are created and maintained by people with low incomes. In principle, production-oriented microcredit is not intended to finance consumption (Barone and Sader, 2008).

Since the 1990s, microfinance institutions have mushroomed in Brazil, following the stabilization of the Brazilian economy as a result of the Real Plan in 1994. They were largely the fruit of efforts of organized civil society and a number of municipal and state initiatives that provided funds through what were known as '*bancos do povo*', or 'people's banks' (Zouain and Barone 2007: 375). During the two terms of President Fernando Henrique Cardoso and another two terms of President Luíz Inácio Lula da Silva, the Brazilian federal government directly assumed the role of formulating and implementing public policies to provide low-income populations with access to productive credit (Zouain and Barone, 2007).

Under President Cardoso's administration (1995–2002), 'Microcredit was understood as a productive credit, capable of leveraging income' (Barone and Sader 2009: 1251). It was also believed that the benefits from microcredit would have a multiplier effect, and that this would encourage job creation and income generation. Accordingly, in 1996 the government created the Popular Productive Credit Programme (PCPP) and the Institutional Development Programme (IDP), both of which were designed by the National Bank for Economic and Social Development (BNDES) with a view to providing the means for the expansion of microfinance in Brazil. Since then, a legal and institutional framework that would support the government's actions has been considered necessary (Zouain and Barone, 2007).

Under President Luíz Inácio Lula da Silva (2003–6), both the concept of and access to microcredit, initiated by his predecessor, were expanded. The first step of the new government was 'bancarizar'—to integrate the lower strata of the population into the banking system and provide them with credit—not only for production, but also for consumption purposes. In this process, the public sector banks—Banco do Brasil and Caixa Econômica

Federal—developed as mechanisms to expand the government policy of access to microcredit (Barone and Sader, 2008). In addition, the public banks operated large networks of agencies for the transfer of money that were located in, for example, bakeries, pharmacies, and grocery stores (Barone and Sader, 2008).

Another measure included the creation of a microcredit package (*pacote de microcrédito*) in June 2003. It consisted of three pillars which provided a set of measures aimed at expanding the supply of financial services to low-income populations (Costa, 2010). The first pillar related to banking (*bancarização*): by simplifying the process of opening bank accounts it sought to provide widespread access to financial services, particularly to those segments of the population who until then had had no such access. As a result of this measure, the number of people with access to bank accounts in the country rose from 84 million in 2005 to 118 million in 2011 (IPEA, 2011). The second pillar consisted of stimulating the supply of credit through the compulsory collection of 2 per cent on deposits, which would be used to finance microcredit lines (regulated by Law 10735 of 11 September 2003). The third pillar sought to provide an incentive to form credit cooperatives. The idea was that such cooperatives would be set up in a set of institutions capable of serving low-income populations more easily than commercial banks. This more aggressive policy of increasing access to credit in Brazil was expected to have an impact, not only on the financial situations of the poorest families directly involved, but also on the national financial system and the economy as a whole (Costa, 2010).

For implementing this policy, the National Program of Oriented Productive Microcredit (PNMPO) was created through the enactment of Federal Law 11.110 of 25 April 2005. In addition, a set of resolutions and decrees was passed for implementation of the PNMPO. Resolution 3422 of 30/11/2006, of the National Monetary Council (CMN) regulates the use of the funds coming from the compulsory collection of 2 per cent of the deposits in the central bank, which are part of the funds allocated to the PNMPO. The latter's other source of funds comes from the Worker´s Support Fund (FAT),[1] the use of which was regulated by Resolution No. 511 of 18.10.2006. These two resolutions set the guidelines for implementing the policy with regard to the maximum monthly interest rate to be charged (up to 4 per cent, the maximum amount to be lent $10,000.00), the form of management, and the maximum credit opening fee (4 per cent of the value of the transaction) that could be charged.

[1] The FAT, a special fund linked to the Ministry of Labour and Employment (MTE) of the Brazilian federal government, is used to finance the unemployment benefits programme, and wage benefits and economic development programmes.

According to Braga (2011: 68), this programme had two basic objectives: 'To simulate income and job creation among micro-entrepreneurs, and to offer available resources for productive-oriented microcredit.' Its target audience was entrepreneurs with annual sales of up to 120,000 Brazilian reals (BR$) (about 50,000 euros). The programme brought about major institutional changes in the microfinance sector in Brazil (Barone and Sader, 2008). Coordinated and implemented by the Ministry of Labour and Employment (MTE), the PNMPO started to coordinate various organizations authorized to perform financial transactions, in addition to entities that only work with microcredit, such as civil society organizations of public interest (OSCIPs)[2] and micro-entrepreneur credit societies (SCMs).[3] By May 2007, the PNMPO had accredited a total of 231 institutions (Barone and Sader, 2008). The PNMPO served more as a liaison between institutions of production-oriented microcredit than as a regulator. Its purpose was more directly related to the promotion of microcredit and to the structuring of the microfinance sector in Brazil (Barone and Sader, 2008; Braga, 2011).

In the north-eastern region of Brazil, the programme 'CrediAmigo' of the Bank of Northeastern Brazil (Banco do Nordeste do Brasil—BNB)[4] deserves to be highlighted. Created in 1997, it has become the largest microfinance programme in the country and one of the largest in Latin America, both in terms of volume of resources and the number of clients (Zouain and Barone, 2007). In 2011 alone, CrediAmigo reported 1,970,043 operations that provided loans to small-scale businesses which totalled more than 1 billion euros. From 2002 to 2011, this type of credit extended by BNB has amounted to over 4 billion euros (BNB, 2011). According to Costa (2010) the CrediAmigo programme showed the importance of having a well-established physical infrastructure. Its success can be attributed to its good network of banking agencies in north-eastern Brazil.

In August 2011, the Brazilian federal government expanded and enhanced the PNMPO, renamed the Growth (Crescer) Plan, as part of the Brazil Without Poverty programme. The new programme aims to provide credit at lower interest rates to low-income individuals and micro-entrepreneurs, and is a major innovation in public intervention in the field of productive microcredit in Brazil. This is because by altering the PNMPO, the government gave the public banks (federal and state institutions) the task of

[2] OSCIPs (Civil Society Organizations of Public Interest) are non-profit organizations regulated by Law 9.790 of 23 March 1999 and Decree no.3.100 of 30 June 1999. They are engaged in providing credit with the objective of promoting social and economic development and reducing poverty, under the supervision of the Brazilian Ministry of Justice (Braga, 2011).

[3] The SCMs are for-profit organizations regulated by Law 10.194 of February 2001, and are supervised by the Brazilian central bank (Braga, 2011).

[4] This is a federal public development bank with activities in the north-eastern region of the country and the northern part of the states of Minas Gerais and Espírito Santo.

scaling up microcredit as a strategy for productive inclusion (REDE-BCDs, 2011). The federal banks are expected to convert their consumer credit portfolios into production-oriented credit portfolios, leading to an 87 per cent reduction of the annual interest rate to be charged on loans. The banks are expected to meet these goals by 2013, when the programme will be evaluated (SECOM, Secretary of Social Communication of the Presidency, 2011). Among the goals, the federal government aims for these banks' portfolios to serve 3.4 million clients by the end of 2013. Another goal in this context is for the loan portfolios of the four public-sector banks that participate in the programme to increase from the current BR$654.5 million up to BR$2.99 billion by the end of 2013 (Brazil, 2011). In 2011, the number of clients served was 734,200 (REDE-BCDs, 2011; SEBRAE, 2011). The Growth Plan sets the interest rates for microcredit at a maximum of 8 per cent per annum and the credit opening fee at 1 per cent (REDE-BCDs, 2011; SEBRAE, 2011). The resources for the loans come from the collection of 2 per cent of banks' deposits by the central bank (currently about BR$157 billion).The government is committed to providing up to BR$500 million annually (to compensate for the cost to the banks) in order to ensure they reduce interest rates and target the credit as required by the programme (Brazil, 2011).

7.2.1 Improvements and Shortcomings of the Microcredit Policies

Despite the enthusiasm for microcredit as a tool for poverty reduction, there is a debate about its efficacy in this respect. The question that arises is whether microcredit does in fact help decrease or eradicate poverty in the world, especially in developing countries (Carvalho et al., 2009). Despite the positive aspects and the notable expansion of access to credit in Brazil and abroad, some scholars believe the numbers are not sufficient to demonstrate the real impact of microcredit and its accessibility for the poorest sections of the population (Carvalho et al., 2009). Nichter, Goldmark, and Fiori (2002), for example, are sceptical about the adequacy of microcredit to generate income and to provide the individuals or families with enough resources to pull them out of poverty. And Carvalho et al. (2009: 7) argue: 'There is, in fact, a wide gap between the reality and the promise of microfinance. The promise of microcredit is irresistible—lift people out of poverty using their own energy and entrepreneurial potential. However, the impact of reducing poverty through microcredit remains elusive. Some empirical evidence . . . has found a low penetrating power of the vast majority of [microcredit] institutions in the poorest segments of the population.'

According to these authors, the providers of resources and aid agencies (national and international) have requested that microfinance institutions, mostly non-profit organizations, develop good economic and financial performance indicators. This is because they understand that good financial performance turns into effective social outcomes in combating poverty. But for these institutions, the question is how to achieve good economic and financial performance by offering credit to a target audience considered to be high risk. Carvalho et al. (2009) see a conflict between two main objectives pursued by microcredit organizations. On the one hand, they seek sustainability or financial autonomy, as expressed in their financial and economic objectives; and on the other hand, they need to reach the poorest segments of the population, which are supposed to be their target audience. The latter goal is the social objective, not only of microcredit organizations, but of any microcredit policy. 'The debate of sustainability vs. reaching/targeting the poorest is controversial and at its core lies the fundamental question, namely if and to what extent the very poor can actually benefit from microcredit programs and to what extent microfinance actually makes its promise and goals concrete' (Carvalho et al., 2009: 9).

Then there is the question of collateral, which has changed over time due to the pressures for financial efficiency from resource providers, both public and private. In general, the 'solidarity collateral' is the adopted practice in lending methodologies for microcredit. It consists of gathering three to five small-business owners with credit needs who trust each other to form a united group, which then collectively takes responsibility for the loans to each of the group's members (Carvalho et al., 2009:). However, by adopting lending criteria that are increasingly concerned with returns on investments and financial sustainability, non-profit organizations are adopting a utilitarian logic and parameters typical of private organizations based on the search for profit. 'This logic that is adopted by the microfinance sector tends to make it similar to the traditional financial sector, where market imperatives prevail' (Carvalho et al., 2009: 12).

Looking at what needs to be done with regard to microfinance in Brazil, and not only at what has been accomplished, it appears that the country's microcredit policies have yielded rather poor results so far. Zouain and Barone (2007) suggest that, judging by the effective supply and potential demand for microfinance in Brazil, the dissemination of microcredit to the potential client population has been rather low. This is confirmed by Braga (2011), who, in analysing the results of the PNMPO, shows that the penetration rate of production-oriented microcredit was only 8.55 per cent, for a population of 8.7 million, consisting primarily of self-employed workers (the core of the informal work force) whose primary job-related income does not exceed one minimum wage. Moreover, according to the author, the PNMPO has not reached the poorest workers, and if the analyses considered other audiences, for example unemployed individuals in search of employment, the penetration rate of microcredit would be even lower.

For the current government of President Dilma Rousseff, the main challenge continues to be employment generation and poverty reduction, which supposedly can be addressed with microcredit. According to Farranha (2005: 140), the PNMPO is poorly designed in that it does not allow for 'more direct integration of the program with low-income people'. Thus, the current methods used by microcredit initiatives are unlikely to help alleviate poverty in Brazil. Braga's research (2011) shows that the most recognized microcredit policies in the country are still failing to provide access to microcredit to a large segment of the population—the poorest of the poor. Even the microcredit programme of the BNB reached only 12.4 per cent of the potential beneficiaries/recipients of microcredit in 2009. One among the possible explanations for these shortcomings, relates to the problem of incompatibility of the criteria for granting credit to this population, whose low socio-economic level and predicament of social exclusion do not allow them to meet the stipulated criteria. Thus, even for public microcredit institutions, the cost of serving the poorest becomes very high, and requires the use of different, more appropriate methodologies for delivery.

7.3 Microcredit, Microfinance, and Solidarity Finance: Conceptual Differences and the Uniqueness of Community Development Banks

Microcredit is an instrument used to make small financial operations viable, which makes it different from practices such as solidarity finance that use microcredit under different conditions and for different purposes. Another substantial way in which it differs from solidarity finance is that it is based on market logic. These differences tend to be ignored by the conventional economic paradigm, which considers two supposedly common characteristics between these two forms of finance: a) they both deal with small financial operations, and b) they serve a low-income public, both of which therefore reflect a process of democratization of access to credit for populations excluded from the formal financial system. This kind of understanding (or interpretation), which prevails both in society at large and among policy-makers, hides the multifaceted nature of the universe of microfinance. Moreover, it shows a lack of a wider understanding of the real economy, usually limiting itself to the logic of the market and to market principles.

By adopting a wider approach to understanding economic data (França Filho, 2007), the distinction between the two forms of finance becomes clearer. The main difference resides in the 'place' that each of these practices occupies in the societal dynamic: whereas conventional microcredit represents a market niche within the formal financial system, there is no place for solidarity finance in the market economy. It is the product of society and, more specifically, it emerges from forms of collective self-organization formed by different populations and/or organized groups in their respective localities or communities in order to manage their own economic resources according to principles of solidarity, trust, and mutual aid. This chapter is thus part of a broader approach to the economy as proposal in Karl Polanyi's research programme, especially in 'The Great Transformation' and 'The Livelihood of Man'.

Various other differences ensue from this fundamental distinction: for example, the specific criteria used by conventional microcredit for extending credit results in a new kind of selectivity of its target public. Consequently, a large segment of that public, the 'extremely low-income' population, gets excluded for not being able to meet those market criteria. This also explains the high default rates of most of these programmes and/or practices. In other words, conventional microcredit is based on the criteria of expected returns on invested capital and seeks to continuously expand its operations. In solidarity finance, proximity of relationships is an important prerequisite in the credit-granting process. This is because values such as trust and solidarity hold a central position in this system, which turns out to be much more than a mere credit system. Indeed, solidarity finance is a system in which economic operations are subordinated to social relations, thus inverting the classic logic of the market. (França Filho, 2010). This is one of the reasons why the motto 'small is beautiful' prevails in a system of solidarity finance. In other words, solidarity finance follows a logic of socio-economic organization that is opposed to the idea of growth in terms of an increase in its scale of operations because this would defeat the very purpose of the system: to meet the needs and demands of people in a given geographical context—usually a small community or neighbourhood. This is why this form of finance constitutes a practice rooted in the local area or in the community, as the term 'proximity finance' suggests. An expansion of the system would necessarily compromise its ability to maintain the model in which social relationships based on trust and solidarity are its central criteria, and which derive from relationships stemming from proximity within communities. Growth would necessitate the establishment of impersonal relations between people so as to make the system functional, thus incurring estrangement in relationships. This would lead to another type of behaviour in which the priority stops being the human person or subject—as attested by institutions of the conventional economy.

In concrete terms, a look at the distinct forms of microcredit—microfinance and solidarity finance—in Brazil gives the following scenario. Besides microcredit provided by market/private organizations (private banks), government, or public institutions ('people's banks'), or even non-governmental or non-profit organizations within civil society (microcredit OSCIPs), and other kinds of organizations (e.g. credit unions), there are various other forms of popular and/or community organizations (such as revolving solidarity funds, community development banks (CDBs), time deposits, and collective investment groups) that increase the complexity of understanding what constitutes the world of microfinance (França Filho and Silva Jr, 2009). Such examples, combined with solidarity credit unions, constitute the field of so-called 'solidarity finance' in Brazil.

Solidarity finance is understood as a kind of microfinance system consisting of initiatives that promote the mobilization of local investment, the joint funding of consumption and production units, and the networks of social relations between individuals as a non-asset-based form of collateral and control (Abramovay and Junqueira, 2005). Solidarity finance organizations seek to achieve their economic sustainability while giving priority to their social goals, their constituents, and their territory. Common examples of solidarity financial services include credit for production and consumption, with guarantees based on relations of proximity, local credit cards, credit for urban and/or organic agriculture, solidarity exchange clubs, social currencies, and local saving accounts.

Fitting into this overall notion of solidarity finance, the community development bank (CDB) can be defined as an associative and community-based financial system aimed at generating employment and income in areas of socio-economically vulnerable populations, driven by the precepts of solidarity economics (REDE-BCDs, 2006; Silva Jr, 2006; Melo Neto and Magalhães, 2007; França Filho, 2007). Unlike conventional microcredit systems, which are geared to individuals or to individual organizations, CDBs are concerned with the locality to which they belong, be it a community, a neighbourhood, or a small town. CDBs seek to simultaneously invest in the territorial/local capacity of production, of generation of services, and of consumption. To this end, they fund and guide the construction of social and productive local service initiatives/projects, and promote local consumption. This is because, in addition to the supply of multipurpose microcredit according to credit lines defined by each CDB, the main goal and commitment is the building of local networks of solidarity finance through an amalgamation of producers, service providers, and local consumers (França Filho and Silva Jr, 2009).

The CDB's operations have four basic characteristics: (i) its resources are coordinated and managed by a community-based organization (generally a local community association); (ii) microcredit lines are provided for production and local consumption at fair interest rates with the purpose of generating income and work throughout the community; (iii) granting and collection of loans are based on neighbourhood relationships and solidarity, so that control is much more social than economic; and (iv) the creation of alternative instruments to stimulate domestic consumption (i.e. local credit cards and local complementary currencies[5]) are recognized by local producers, traders, and consumers as effective in boosting the local economy (REDE-BCDs, 2006).

Although there are some possibilities of institutional arrangements in the formation of a CDB, one of the conditions necessary for its creation relates to the mobilization of its endogenous area. In other words, the bank must be created as a result of an intrinsic desire of the community, even though external agents may contribute by motivating and mobilizing the community. The process of implementing a community development bank must begin with a genuine desire by the community for such an institution. In any case, some requirements must be met, such as financial capital for a credit fund; financial resources for paying the operating expenses of the bank; a community organization (e.g. association, board, or council) that can take over management of the bank; people trained for the roles of loan officer and credit manager; and support for the assimilation of the social innovation by the community. The aforementioned steps describe how a number of CDBs have been created through a process of institutional partnerships involving supportive organizations (e.g. university incubators and specialized NGOs in this field) and funding institutions (e.g. municipalities, state governments, government departments, and foundations).

Another unique aspect in the functioning of CDBs is that of assurance and control based on close relationships and mutual trust. In other words, a CDB considers the financial history of the borrower to be only one aspect to be considered alongside an assessment of his or her life in the community. The credit bank agents regard the network of neighbourhood relations as a valuable source of knowledge. In turn, the recovery of a claim involves a unique form of social control: residents of the area have the role of establishing mechanisms of peer pressure. According to Abramovay and Junqueira (2005), 'these mechanisms lower interest rates and default rates through monitoring "the invisible" in an effective way'. França Filho and Silva Jr (2009) state that the unique method of the credit operations of the CDB is through networks of 'prosumers'—*redes de 'pressumidores'*, so named because it involves the close association of producers and local consumers through the establishment of channels or specific circuits of trade and the terms on which it is done. The Brazilian Network of Community Development Banks (REDE-BCDs) developed this approach with the aim of strengthening local economies and reorganizing them to promote development based on the principles of solidarity economics.

[5] In the Latin American context, 'complementary currencies' or 'community currencies' are more commonly referred to as 'moedas sociais' in Brazil, or 'monedas sociales' in Spanish-speaking countries. They are a fact of life in the solidarity economy field.

7.3.1 Origins and Current Development of CDBs

In Brazil, the idea of CDBs was first conceived in 1998, with the aim of supporting a development project initiative of the residents of Conunto Palmeiris, a district of approximately 40,000 inhabitants situated on the outskirts of Fortaleza, capital of the north-eastern state of Ceará (França Filho and Silva Jr, 2006). The Residents' Association of Conjunto Palmeiras Banco Palmas founded the CDB of Conjunto Palmeiras, the goal of which was to create employment and generate income through the provision of various solidarity finance services to producers and consumers in the area (Silva Jr, 2004).

The Banco Palmas soon became well known because of its innovative practices that 'integrate into the same scenario of credit instruments, production, marketing and consumption, in order to stretch the supply chains providing the opportunity of work and income for its residents' (Melo Neto and Magalhães 2003). This public recognition has become the envy of other institutions that develop social innovation. In 2003, the Palmas Institute for Socio-Economic Development was founded with the aim of implementing the methodologies and social technology of solidarity economics in partnership with several other institutions, both in Brazil and abroad. The Palmas Institute for Socio-economic Development began to replicate the methodology of the first CDB in late 2004 in the PAR Bank in the municipality of Paracuru with ten activities (França Filho and Silva Jr, 2009). The following year, the Brazilian Government, led by the National Solidarity Economics Department within the Ministry of Labour and Employment (SENAES/MTE), invested in the project to support the establishment and consolidation of CDBs, in partnership with the Palmas Institute. This project demonstrated that the SENAES/MTE considered the CDB to be a catalyst for promoting area development activities, simultaneously engaging in production, marketing, financing, and civic education.

The federal project to support CDBs had an important effect on the expansion of these organizations as a kind of social innovation for the economic and social development of areas. The project served to deepen partnerships and catalyse efforts to increase the use of CDBs as part of a widespread policy of encouraging the creation of jobs and incomes for socially excluded populations. Indeed, since 2005, there have been a series of actions and partnerships between these organizations and federal, state, and municipal government agencies. The next step taken to strengthen the social management of CDBs was the creation of the Brazilian Network of CDBs. The Network aims to contribute to the exchange of experiences and knowledge and the coordination of resources and partnerships for the institutional development of all CDBs in the country (REDE-BCD, 2006).

The performance of the network in 2010 and 2011 has been largely marked by the implementation of the first national project by SENAES/MTE entitled, 'Action to promote solidarity finance based on community banks and solidarity funds', which shaped the first national policy for solidarity finance in Brazil. Despite the absence of revolving fund resources for the CDBs, the proposals of the national entity and its regional bodies provided for the creation of forty-three other CDBs and the consolidation of existing ones through the hiring of loan officers and technical advisors, training and capacity-building of local staff, purchasing equipment and institutional structuring, and connection of their regional networks. As the Brazilian Network of CDBs expanded, it gained valuable experience in 2011, with the deployment of the first CDBs under this national policy. The State Secretariat for Solidarity Economics created by the government of the State of Rio de Janeiro provided important support in creating the first CDBs in the state. By the end of 2011, there were sixty-seven CDBs deployed by the Brazilian Network of CDBs in different cities nationwide.

7.4 Conclusion: The Possibilities and Challenges for CDBs

In recent years, there have been many significant advances in Brazil to combat the poverty of communities operating in the informal economy. This is exemplified in the Dilma government's efforts through the Growth Plan (Programa Crescer). Building on what was started by President Lula da Silva is the stimulus given to the formalization of a considerable part of the informal economy through the creation of a new professional title called 'individual entrepreneur' (IE). This advance allowed for the facilitation of access to a formal framework of rights for a highly vulnerable category of workers, besides the stimulation of entrepreneurial activity of micro and small informal businesses that are characterized by the precariousness of working conditions.

However, it is important to assess the extent to which such policies have been victim of a typically 'economical' and fragmented concept of microcredit. If microcredit has given greater priority to economically successful entrepreneurs, would that not mean neglecting the philosophical approach of microcredit aimed at development of underprivileged areas, with its ability to link networks and local production chains based on a philosophy of 'associated entrepreneurship'?

Moreover, the policies promoting the expansion of microcredit in Brazil have one fundamental shortcoming, despite significant advances: so far they have not been able to reach those who really need such credit, namely the lowest income strata. Thus such policies have failed to fulfil their promise of poverty alleviation. Among the main reasons for this failure is the high cost of microcredit operations due to the high risk posed by people in the lower income strata because of their inability to provide collateral. This high cost can be explained by the inadequacy of the instruments deployed for dealing with people who are not subject to the formal control mechanisms. This lack of an appropriate method for providing microcredit for lower income clients is indicative of a deeper problem: the limitations of the very logic of capital accumulation. Until what point is it possible to use microcredit in an efficient way using conventional market mechanisms? The successes achieved by applying a different economic rationale, as evidenced by the practices of solidarity finance, seem to reveal the limits of the market paradigm.

Even very drastic solutions for greatly reducing the cost of operations for the borrower, as in the Growth Plan, need careful analysis. At least four aspects deserve to be highlighted in an analysis of the limitations and challenges of such a programme. The first has to do with the corporate culture of the banks issuing productive microcredit, as extending these kinds of loans conflicts with the rationale and aims of the traditional credit operators. Traditional banks (even the public ones) lack the competence for it. Indeed, public banks, organized as branches, are not accustomed to working in communities (endogenously), to dealing with small borrowers, or to providing favourable institutional conditions for the local economy and for productive inclusion. The big banks are set up to cater to the needs of a very different constituency than the poorest segments of the population. There is a very real possibility of resources being stranded in the 'heavy banking structure', without ever reaching their final destination. Therefore, relying solely on public-sector banks for promoting productive inclusion through a more ambitious microcredit programme is, at the very least, a risky bet.

A second challenge relates to the ability of public banks to reach popular economies. Achieving the goals set by the government requires hiring and training large numbers of people to work in communities to monitor microcredit operations and provide guidance to borrowers before extending microcredit. From the standpoint of the logic of CDBs, the problem is the concept of 'guidance', which at present is limited to the loan officer visiting clients' homes or enterprises to review their terms of payment, and to ask for payment when necessary. For the Brazilian Network of CDBs, appropriate 'guidance' for productive inclusion of the poor in microcredit also involves the dimensions of community and neighbourhood relationships, an understanding of the social and economic dynamics of the community, an effort to reorganize local production chains, consideration of collective strategies of production and marketing, the creation of alternative instruments for collecting, and finally, thought given to the creation of a local environment that will contribute to the success of the borrower of microcredit, that is, effective inclusion with the support of microcredit. It is only by becoming familiar with the slums or living among the poor that it is possible to understand just how difficult productive inclusion can be, given all the sociological aspects involved. In fact, according to CDB's personnel, there is no record of microcredit alone being able to lift a person out of extreme poverty, even with the help of a credit agent (or credit consultant). The idea that an individual can escape from conditions of extreme poverty seems to be based more on market ideology than on the reality of conditions in a community.

A third challenge relates to the criteria used to determine the achievement of the goals. The goal set by the government for the number of borrowers to be reached by the Growth Plan and by public banks, leads us to conclude that this requires a 'battalion of community agents' offering low interest rates and easy credit conditions, which any low-income person would find hard to turn down because it offers the possibility of having cash in hand. Thus, it is not difficult to imagine that the temptation of easy credit would be great and the result would meet the needs of public banks to achieve their objectives. However, such a situation, in the absence of sufficient supervision, could result in a large quantity of 'bad loans', which quickly exacerbate the conditions of poverty, deepening the debt burden of the poorest. Sometimes, in order to avoid increasing their debt to the banks, the poor will fail to pay for their basic requirements such as for water, electricity, medicines, and children's education. In this sense, for the Brazilian Network of CDBs, evaluating the success of a microcredit programme should take into account, along with the criteria relating to the volume of credit granted and the number of people reached, other criteria such as an increase in household income, job creation, an increase in local production and consumption, strengthening of local associations and productive chains, and strengthening of cultural identities and social bonds.

Finally, the fourth challenge relates to the absence of the logic of solidarity economics in the Growth programme. According to this logic, individuals cannot overcome poverty unless they are motivated by a great desire to overcome it. The experiences of CDBs have revealed that the success of their microcredit programmes in impoverished areas is partly due to the fact that they help people to find the means of collective forms of consumption, production, and marketing, to create local networks of '*prosumers*', where all, simultaneously, are producers, consumers, and actors of social transformation. Thus there seems to be an appreciable difference in the treatment of microcredit, depending on whether there is greater emphasis on the individual or the community. In the first case, there is a considerable risk of fragmentation and dispersion, and the ability to generate development may not be guaranteed. In the second case, the emphasis within the practice itself allows for the requalification of microcredit, enabling the organization of community development.

The analysis outlined above can lead us to conclude that the CDBs' policies and approach to microcredit have great potential to contribute to solving the shortcomings of traditional microcredit policies. However, the effective incorporation of these experiences for revising the design of a microcredit policy seems to require a twofold paradigm shift. It requires a shift in the economic paradigm, from a vision solely focused on market logic, to a vision that promotes a social economy approach based on solidarity finance. At the same time it calls for a shift in the political paradigm, from a vision centred on the management capacity of market players and on the ability of a sprawling developmental state to manage microcredit programmes, to a course of action focusing on institutional partnerships with public organizations and networks of solidarity finance with proven expertise in the field.

CDBs can be seen as potential actors for the effective delivery of microcredit. However a number of challenges prevent the strengthening of these practices in Brazil, due to the absence of a nurturing institutional environment to build on their experience. CDBs do not have their own regulatory framework. Strictly speaking, from a legal standpoint, they do not exist, which makes the possibilities of effective public policy support virtually impossible. Thus the support for CDBs comes from specific projects implemented by entities such as Banco Palmas Institute of Socio-Economic Development, NGOs, and university incubators. In most of these cases, the support involves partnerships with national, regional, and local governments, especially through SENAES/MTE and its project of support for solidarity finance. These actions enable the creation of new banks, but the replication or expansion of such experiences remains a major challenge. Added to this, are the effort and difficulty of strengthening the Brazilian Network of CDBs that does not yet have effective government support for its structure as a network. Such support is urgently needed before new CDBs can be created throughout Brazil, and without it there is a huge risk of trivializing these initiatives. The question that arises then is how CDBs can be multiplied and local demand for microcredit met through the existing structures without a fully established network structure. The CDB network is faced with a series of challenges relating to certification of new CDBs, training and qualification of the necessary staff, the development of new social technologies with a view to improving the dynamic management of microcredit in local communities, and monitoring and evaluating the performance of each CDB.

References

Abramovay, R. and R. G. P. Junqueira (2005). 'A sustentabilidade das microfinanças solidárias'. *Revista de Administração da USP-RAU*, 40(1): 19–33.

Barone, F. M. and E. Sader (2008). 'Acesso ao crédito no Brasil: Evolução e perspectiva'. *Revista de Administração Pública-RAP*, 42(6): 1249–67.

BNB (Banco do Nordeste do Brasil) (2011). 'CrediAmigo, Resultados', viewed 19 June 2012: <http://www.bnb.gov.br/content/aplicacao/Produtos_e_Servicos/Crediamigo/gerados/Resultados.asp>.

Braga, T. S. (2011). 'Programas públicos de microcrédito produtivo orientado: Uma avaliação da eficácia do Crediamigo para a inserção da população de baixa renda do setor informal no mercado de crédito'. PhD thesis, Universidade Federal da Bahia, Salvador.

Brazil (2006). Resolution no. 511, of 18 October 2006, viewed 21 December 2011, <http://portal.mte.gov.br>.

Carvalho, D. M., E. A. Araújo, G. T. Salazar, and R. N. Ferreira (2009). 'Ênfase dos programas de microcrédito em sustentabilidade e viabilidade financeira: Distanciamento do objetivo social de combate à pobreza?' *Proceedings of the Congresso da Sociedade Brasileira de Economia, Administração e Sociologia Rural*, Porto Alegre: SOBER.

Costa, F. N. (2010). 'Microcrédito no Brasil'. Discussion paper, Instituto de Economia da UNICAMP, Campinas.

Farranha, A. C. (2005). 'Olhares sobre a pobreza: Entre o global e o local, a experiência do microcrédito no município de Vitoria'. PhD thesis, Instituto de Filosofia e Ciências Humana da Universidade Estadual de Campinas, Campinas.

França Filho, G. C. (2007). 'Considerações sobre um marco teórico-analítico para a experiência dos Bancos Comunitários'. *Proceedings of the Encontro da Rede Brasileira de Bancos Comunitários*, Fortaleza: REDE-BCDs.

—— (2010). *Papel dos Bancos Comunitários de Desenvolvimento na visão da sua Rede*. Salvador: REDE-BCDs.

—— and J. T. Silva Júnior (2006). 'Uma dinâmica associativa emblemática no nordeste brasileiro', in G. C. França Filho et al. (eds.), *Ação Pública e economia solidária: Uma perspectiva internacional*. Porto Alegre and Salvador: Edufrgs-Edufba: 97–119.

—— (2009). 'Bancos Comunitários de Desenvolvimento', in A. D. Cattani et al. (eds.), *Dicionário Internacional da Outra Economia*. Coimbra: Almedina: 31–6.

Instituto de Pesquisa Econômica Aplicada (IPEA) (2011). *Bancos: Exclusão e serviços*. Brasília.

Melo Neto, J. J. and S. Magalhães (2003). *Bairros pobres, ricas soluções: Banco Palmas, ponto a ponto*. Fortaleza: Expressão Gráfica.

—— (2007). *Bancos Comunitários de Desenvolvimento, Uma rede sob o controle da comunidade*. Fortaleza: Publisher Arte Visual.

Microcredit Summit (1997). 'The Microcredit Summit Declaration and Plan of Action', viewed 15 December 2011, <http\\www.microcreditsummit.org>.

Nichter, S., L. Goldmark, and A. Fiori (2002). 'Entendendo as Microfinanças no Contexto Brasileiro'. BNDES, viewed 16 Decembre 2011, <http://www.bndes.gov.br/SiteBNDES/bndes/bndes_pt/Institucional/Publicacoes>.

REDE-BCDs (2006). 'Banco comunitário: Serviços solidários em rede', Fortaleza: Instituto Banco Palmas.

—— (2011). 'Carta Aberta: Considerações sobre o Programa Nacional de Microcrédito, Fortaleza: Instituto Banco Palmas.

SEBRAE (Serviço Brasileiro de Apoio a Micro e Pequenas Empresas) (2011). 'Crescer baixa juros do microcrédito para milhões de empreendedores', SEBRAE, viewed 21 December 2011,<http://www.sebrae.com.br/customizado/uasf/apresentacao_ministro_fazenda.pdf.

SECOM (Secretaria de Comunicação Social da Presidência da República) (2011). 'Lançamento do CRESCER—Programa Nacional de Microcrédito'. SECOM, http://www.brasil.gov.br/noticias/arquivos/2011/08/24/programa-crescer-pode-transformar-sonho-de-ter-renda-e-independencia-em-realidade-diz-dilma.

Silva Júnior, J. T. (2004). 'Gestão, fato associativo & economia solidária: A experiência da ASMOCONP/Banco Palmas'. PhD thesis, Unversidade Federal da Bahia, Salvador.

—— (2006). 'As experiências de bancos comunitários como ação de finanças solidárias para o desenvolvimento territorial'. *International Colloquium on Local Power*, Salvador, 11–13 December.

Zouain, D. and F. M. Barone (2007). 'Excertos sobre política pública de acesso ao crédito como ferramenta de combate à pobreza e inclusão social: O microcrédito na era FHC'. *Revista de Administração Pública-RAP*, 41(2): 369–80.

8

Demand for Microcredit, Informal Finance and Vulnerability in Rural Morocco[1]

Solène Morvant-Roux, Isabelle Guérin, and Marc Roesch

8.1 Introduction

Credit rationing has long been an implicit assumption in the microcredit industry (Stiglitz and Weiss, 1981). Up to the mid-2000s, those who promoted microcredit were not concerned with demand, as they believed that improved offers, a relaxation of collateral requirements, and a larger number of branch locations would inevitably meet unmet demand among the poor. They assumed that households facing some credit constraints would be willing to borrow money from any microcredit provider in order to make investments to start a new business, expand existing business activities, or increase spending in household assets, education, and/or health. Moreover, they argued that the need for individuals and households to cope with risk and vulnerability could affect their demand for financial services. Microfinance would thus automatically replace informal finance, considered by mainstream economics as a 'second best', and this relaxation of credit constraints would lead to a reduction of poverty and vulnerability of the targeted population.

Recent evidence, however, suggests that facilitating access to credit does not necessarily lead to user uptake, and that demand does not necessarily stem from the offer (Claessens, 2006). Some people or social groups may indeed choose not to use the offer of financial services (voluntary exclusion) or may encounter significant obstacles to accessing those services (involuntary

[1] The authors would like to thank Tanguy Bernard, Jocelyne Delarue, Zakia Lalaoui, and Jean-Michel Servet for stimulating discussions and inputs to the chapter. We also thank Al Amana's staff members for their support of the overall field research process. This work was supported by the French Agency for Development (Agence Française de Développement).

exclusion). There is now growing recognition that social, moral, cultural, and political criteria also influence credit demand and usage (Lont and Hospes, 2004; Guérin et al., 2011; Johnson, 2004; Shipton, 2007). Despite these recent advances in understanding, setting up a microcredit service is still too often viewed as a technical, rational, and linear process, as reflected in guidelines for credit officers, who are viewed as simply providing services for clients, considered to be passive consumers.

This chapter examines microcredit demand and use in rural Morocco as a case study of how households *appropriate* microcredit services. By this we mean not just how they use or reject such services, but how they assimilate them in relation to their own economic, social, and cultural context.

Rural Morocco provides an interesting case study of broad trends in the microfinance industry. There has been a massive, but patchy, growth in microcredit in Morocco since the mid-1990s. Indeed, the country has long been considered the flagship of microcredit in the Arab world, both in terms of the outreach of Moroccan microcredit associations and their 'good governance'. But the industry has been facing a serious loan delinquency crisis since 2008, the year in which the Fondation Banque Populaire took over one of the biggest microfinance providers, Zakoura (including its losses). Al Amana, another of the country's biggest microcredit providers and the focus of our study, has also been facing a loan delinquency crisis since 2008. Meanwhile, microcredit providers have been trying to expand their customer base in rural Morocco. Until the mid-2000s, there was a primarily urban market for microfinance, concentrated in Casablanca, Fez, and Marrakesh (PlaNet Finance, 2006). The biggest microcredit providers are now looking to redress this urban bias and the saturation of urban markets by targeting rural areas. Al Amana began to diversify its portfolio in 2006, but rural diversification has proved a major challenge.

A randomized control trial study done by the Abdul Latif Jameel Poverty Action Lab (J-PAL) has shown that, despite specific measures to enhance take-up rates, participation rates in the sample of overall branches have been quite low, though they have varied considerably among different villages (between 0 and 80 per cent). A quantitative analysis using a Proportional Hazard Model with three different components fails to capture the determinants of participation. First, variability seems strongly related to unobserved heterogeneity (the share of the variance related to unobserved heterogeneity is 82 per cent). Second, the model cannot explain the considerable differences among the villages (Duflo et al., 2008). The findings of the J-PAL study were the starting point for our research. However, the model used had limited predictive capacities and was only capable of marginally increasing the rate of participants in the sampled population compared with the population targeted by the microcredit scheme. The French Agency for Development, which commissioned our study, asked our team to qualitatively explain why the demand for microcredit in rural areas was low and varied. The aim was to capture unobservable characteristics at both individual and village/regional levels.

At the regional and village levels, varying agroecological conditions offer an obvious explanation. Al Amana microcredit is not tailored to addressing specific agricultural and rural constraints. Much like the microcredit industry worldwide, it is unable to adapt to seasonal constraints, low profitability in agriculture, and climate-related hazards (Morvant-Roux et al., 2010). Supply is best tailored to consumption needs and to the needs of regular income households in peri-urban villages, rather than to those facing uncertainty and unpredictability. Social and cultural factors and moral values also influence microcredit take-up rates.

At the household level, our application of institutional economics and economic anthropology (Bouman, 1994; Bouman and Hospes, 1994; Servet, 1995 and 2006) indicates that microcredit demand and use is influenced by debt-related norms: households' financial strategies highlight a low propensity to incur debt, and savings in kind are very important. Cultural and religious norms, including whether it is good or bad to incur debt, are an obvious explanation for the variations in demand. While credit rationing is a very common hypothesis in economic theory, economic anthropology shows that debt is embedded in social, cultural, and religious norms that influence the status of debt in everyday life. Debt may be considered by some as a normal feature of the human condition (Malamoud, 1980) and by others as something that should be avoided (Bourdieu, 1977). In rural Morocco, many rural households are reluctant to enter into debt, including informal debt. At times of financial difficulty, be it managing cash flow, financing investments or life-cycle-related events, households prefer to resort to savings in kind, as do people who own a small business. Low demand for microcredit therefore indicates a preference for saving. Moreover, all debts are not equally perceived (Shipton, 2007) by all, and it matters how real or potential clients perceive microcredit and the organization providing it (in this case, Al Amana). Key questions include where the money comes from, whether debt is perceived as good or bad, and if it is meant to be repaid or not. In that context, norms related to debt contribute to explaining the low level of demand for microcredit (assessed by take-up rates), whereas the diversity of take-up rates can be explained by differences in agroecological conditions and households' diversification strategies.

Section 8.1 of this chapter describes the research context and methodology. Section 8.2 details our main findings, and examines attitudes to debt and how it is interpreted. It explains that rural Moroccans are reluctant to take on debt and prefer to manage their cash flows by in-kind saving. Consequently, microcredit is used mainly for consumption needs and by households with a regular income. We then show how the varying microcredit take-up rates across regions can be attributed to agro-ecological disparities. Finally, some conclusions and major implications are drawn.

8.2 Context and Methodology

8.2.1 Microcredit in Morocco

In 2009, there were twelve microcredit institutions active in Morocco, with a combined portfolio of around 4.86 billion Moroccan dirhams (US$580 million) and over 950,000 active loans. Four organizations dominated the sector: Al Amana, Zakoura, Fondation pour le Développement Local et le Partenariat (FONDEP), and Fondation Banque Populaire pour le Microcrédit (FBPMC). In May 2009, the FBPMC merged with another major institution, the Zakoura Foundation, to become FBP Zakoura. These four leaders shared 97 per cent of the sector's loan portfolio by the end of 2009, and ranked among North Africa's biggest microcredit institutions. Al Amana accounted for 45 per cent of all the active loans issued. When it first began operations, this organization focused mainly on urban and peri-urban areas, but in 2005 it decided to expand into rural areas, creating new branches there. The expansion was swift: as early as 2007, rural areas accounted for 49 per cent of Al Amana's portfolio, which has since held stable (47 per cent in August 2010). Al Amana's strategy is for its operations to cover the whole of Morocco.

Al Amana offers solidarity group and individual loans. Solidarity group loans are provided for a three- to eighteen-month period, and their amounts can vary from 1,000 to 30,000 dirhams (US$120 to US$3,500). These are repayable in weekly, bimonthly, or monthly instalments, and amounted to 45 per cent of the loans Al Amana issued in 2010. Al Amana's individual loans are issued to clients who have previously borrowed as part of a solidarity group. These credits target investment in existing economic activities or housing, and are issued for six months to five years (or up to seven years for housing loans). Individual loan amounts vary from 1,000 to 50,000 dirhams, and account for 55 per cent of all loans. Al Amana does not provide savings services due to legislative restrictions.

8.2.2 Research Methodology

As mentioned earlier, our research used the results of a randomized trial evaluation as its starting point. Two striking findings emerged from that study: a low average take-up rate and significant disparities across and within regions (Crépon et al., 2011). Our research sought to better understand these findings.

Table 8.1 Take-up rate variation across regions

Take-up rates (wave 2, 37 branches, Dec. 2009)	% of branches (regions)
0 to 9%	47%
10 to 19%	19%
20 to 29%	19%
Over 30%	16%

Source: Al Amana and J-Pal follow up of take-up rates.

Table 8.1 shows the variations in the provision of loans by Al Amana's branches that reach several villages belonging to different municipalities but that exhibit common features in terms of socio-economic and agro-ecological context. Out of the regions covered by wave 2[2] in the J-PAL study (treatment groups) almost half (47 per cent) showed a participation rate of below 10 per cent, while 16 per cent showed a take-up rate of over 16 per cent. Measuring take-up was quite challenging, but the survey data indicated that total participation was 11 per cent, on average, and 13 per cent among the twenty-five households per village with the largest propensity to borrow (Crépon et al., 2011).

We found a variation of participation rates not just at the branch level, but also between villages that are reached by the same branches. At this level it is difficult to provide general figures, because the sub-samples of villages per branch vary from one to four or five villages. As noted in Duflo et al. (2008: 23) concerning the 'observable characteristics determining participation... There are also considerable differences among villages... Unfortunately we do not have enough villages here to try to disentangle the various possible effects.'

8.2.2.1 DATA COLLECTION AND SAMPLING

For our research project we used a qualitative approach, following specific criteria. Size and representativeness were of minimal importance for our sample, whereas diversity of situation and data saturation (when any additional interview doesn't bring new result) were much more important. The reliability and consistency of interpretation of our results were validated through contextualization (by information collection, learning about people's experiences, and analysis of events), and by cross-checking information sources. In qualitative analysis, data interpretations are validated by using

[2] J-PAL divided the regions where Al Amana planned to introduce its services into four zones where credit services developed progressively (called waves): wave 1, then wave 2, and so on. J-PAL's investigations followed this progressive set-up. To prevent hindering the development of the impact study, our study focused on the areas and branches covered by wave 2 of the J-PAL investigation. Wave 2 comprised 37 branches, most of which were opened in 2008.

different techniques, analysis levels, and, where possible, different researchers and informants in order to verify and cross-check information, and reveal significant and telling differences among the study sample.

The interviews were semi-directive, and followed outlines tailored to each category of actors to facilitate open and spontaneous discussion. In qualitative analysis, spontaneity is an essential element for ensuring interview quality, as the ultimate objective is to go beyond expected responses. Open-ended questions were used to encourage people to speak about events or subjects of importance to them. With both clients and non-clients of Al Amana, the approach used was to encourage them to narrate their life stories, in order to establish the main stages of interviewees' lives and the financial and economic implications. Table 8.2 gives a detailed sample of the interviews conducted.

8.2.2.2 SAMPLE

The team selected four study areas where the thirty-seven branches of the wave 2 sample operate (see footnote 2). We chose branches with a steadily increasing take-up rate, but which were also experiencing disparities in clients' borrowing rates between villages (*douars*), and on the request of Al Amana we also included a branch that was experiencing a high loan delinquency rate.

For each branch, our aim was to conduct interviews in villages where take-up rate profiles differed. The branches included in the sample and their profile in terms of take-up rate are described in Table 8.3.

Table 8.2 Interviews: detailed sample

Clients	36
Non-clients	23
Imams	6
Shop keepers	9
Credit officers	5
Total	79

Table 8.3 Branches included in the sample and take-up rates

Branch Name	Take-up rate (Dec. 2009)
CV Tighdouine	6%
MG My Abdellah Ben Driss	19.6%
AW Moulay Yacoub	27%
LJ Brachoua	1%

Source: Al Amana and J-Pal follow up of take-up rates.

8.3 Norms for Debt and Savings

Looking at how people perceive finance in their daily lives, whether in the context of credit, savings, or risk management, allows us to better understand how people appropriate financial services offered by outsiders, and in particular by microfinance institutions (Guérin et al., 2011). In the context of rural Morocco, a study of households' financial strategies indicates that there is a low propensity to take on debt, and that savings in kind are very important.

8.3.1 Low Propensity for Indebtedness

Various recent studies show that the analysis of informal finance can help to understand how people perceive microcredit (Collins et al., 2009; Guérin et al., 2012). In comparison to other rural contexts,[3] the informal credit offer in rural Morocco is rather low. According to J-PAL's data (Crépon et al., 2011: 8), before Al Amana reached the treatment villages there was little use of formal and informal credit. Only 26 per cent of households had some form of active loan and just 6 per cent of households used informal credit (grocers, neighbours, friends, etc.). These rates are much lower than those observed in other contexts (Collins et al., 2009; Guérin et al., 2012). This could lead to the conclusion, as did the J-PAL team, that households are highly credit constrained, and that there is strong potential for the development of microcredit (Crépon et al., 2011). But testimony from borrowers reveals that demand for credit is weak, simply because households are reluctant to borrow.

This reluctance appears to derive from local cultural and religious norms. Religion is often overlooked in development studies, although it clearly plays an important role (Deneulin and Rakodi, 2011). In Morocco, most people declare themselves to be practising Muslims. Therefore, in theory, the Islamic norm (*sharia*) which considers *riba* (i.e. interest) to be reprehensible and even illegal (*haram*) prevails. Its prohibitions apply to both creditors and debtors (Tripp, 2006). However, the testimonies of villagers—both potential microcredit clients and Imams—indicate that interest rates are not a particularly strong factor underlying the reticence to borrow. In order to conform to Islamic norms, Al Amana presents interest rates as an administrative fee or a payment for the credit agents' work, which most clients highlighted.[4] Some clients mentioned interest rates as posing a problem, but more in terms of

[3] See case studies in rural Mexico (Morvant, 2009; Villarreal, 2009), rural India, and rural Kenya (Johnson, 2004; Shipton, 2007).

[4] As stated by Ait Ali, a non-client in Izrafene (Zone 1, Branch CV), 'It is not *riba*, it is to pay the organization's fees.'

cost than their prohibition in Islam. Although the Islamic norm is acknowledged and is relatively clear, in most cases pragmatism and household need seem to prevail.

Beyond the issue of interest rates, there is a general reluctance to take on debt, regardless of the cost. Debt is often considered a disgrace and a question of 'pride' (*'makayr daouach'*). In Algeria in the 1950s, Pierre Bourdieu, investigating households' resistance to debt, observed that indebtedness implied that the head of a household had failed to meet his family's material needs (Bourdieu, 1977). Similar norms seem to prevail also in contemporary rural Morocco. Comments made during our interviews illustrate the negative moral connotations of debt: 'My pride will not allow me to go into debt,'[5] or as an elderly person whose son is an Al Amana client stated, 'If you were a man, you would not take out a loan.'[6] Another interviewee acknowledged having contracted a loan (farming credit) when he was young, but his children, who have a higher level of education, reacted to this negatively: 'When my sons learned that I had taken out a loan, they got angry and told me that if I needed money, all I had to do was ask them. They would have helped me.'[7] Another said, 'I want to be in charge of my life,'[8] which is also how other non-clients justify their position.[9]

Most shopkeepers we met were also reticent about debt, as the following examples illustrate. A shopkeeper who regularly gives credit to his clients, but does not borrow from his own suppliers as he is against taking on debt, stated: 'I need to feel free.'[10] Similar comments were made by another grocer, who is the biggest in a village of around 200 families, and who gradually set up his shop with the help of his father who has also worked as a shopkeeper for the past few decades. This grocer grants credit to most of his clients, but stated that he does not buy on credit from his suppliers because: 'I want to sleep soundly.'[11] A farmer and livestock seller looking to increase his number of calves but without taking on debt voiced a similar view: 'It would be a loss of freedom.'[12]

Islam's disapproval of charging interest is therefore not a major impediment to taking out a loan, but indebtedness in general is limited to matters

[5] Bricklayer/mason, Aitboujraf Douar, client, Zone 2, Branch MG.

[6] Farmer, Sidi Bengalssen Douar, client, Zone 3, LJ branch.

[7] Farmer, Tamrat Douar, client, Zone 2, AW Branch.

[8] Farmer, Sidi Bengalssen Douar, non-client, Zone 3, LJ Branch.

[9] This was analysed notably by sociologist Pierre Bourdieu during his investigations in mountain villages in Kabylie,Algeria (but also in the gatherings and slums around Algiers) in the 1950s (Bourdieu, 1977).

[10] Shopkeeper, Ait Abbas Douar, non-client, Zone 2, Branch MG.

[11] Grocer, Mchaa Krim Douar, non-client, Zone 2, Branch AW.

[12] Farmer and livestock seller, non-client, Ait Abbas Douar, Zone 2, Branch MG.

of survival and simple socio-economic reproduction. This conflicts with Al Amana's aim to provide microcredits for expanding economic activities.

8.3.2 The Importance of Savings in Kind

While households show a low propensity for indebtedness, the practice of saving is more widespread, particularly in terms of saving in kind.[13] There is considerable evidence of the prevalence of saving in kind among the poor, whether for the purpose of making ends meet, consuming or preparing important life-cycle events (ceremonies, social and religious rituals), and sometimes for investing in and managing non-agricultural economic activities (Collins et al., 2009; Guérin et al., 2011; Lont and Hospes, 2004; Shipton, 2007; Villareal, 2004).

In rural Morocco, savings in kind are used mainly to smooth over discrepancies between income and expenditure, and are topped up again as soon as resources permit. Informal credit is used only in case of necessity over a very short period of time. The most common forms of in-kind savings are sheep and cereals: families use one or both resources to juggle between their needs and market prices. Livestock and cereals are mobilized to meet unpredictable events, such as health problems, to prepare for annual religious festivals and life-cycle events, and to manage business cash flows. Indeed, the J-PAL study highlights the importance of such savings. According to their data, 50 per cent of households have sheep and/or goats, and 46 per cent have cattle that can be used in case of necessity. Thus about half of the households save in this way (Crépon et al., 2011).

The importance of savings in kind has strong implications for the demand for microcredit. Some households prefer to sell an animal rather than keep it and resort to debt. As one bricklayer put it, 'If you have a herd, you have no need to borrow.'[14] Other people juggle between livestock and credit. If they use credit to purchase an animal, this is often to maintain or restore the size of their savings in the form of herds. They decide whether to purchase livestock or other goods according to market prices and their needs. This is confirmed by the J-PAL study, which states: 'Microcredit serves, with agriculture, to generate supplementary income and, for livestock breeding, to constitute savings in kind' (Crépon et al., 2010: 19–20).

One such example is that of a regular client of Fondation Banque Populaire pour le Microcrédit who was interviewed. He had engaged in five loan transactions that were used mainly to renovate and extend his house, but if the

[13] In the areas studied, it seems that there are few Roscas (rotating savings and credit associations) which are more of an urban phenomenon in Morocco.

[14] Bricklayer/mason, Boulajrouf Douar (migrant), client, Zone 2, Branch MG.

loan came through at a time when he had no immediate needs, he would buy a sheep to sell it at a later date.

Microcredit can also prevent a reduction of capital, as explained by one interviewee: '*The others already have a herd so they take a loan to cover daily expenses... it comes to the same thing.*'[15] Livestock can also serve as a collateral for the loan and thus brings security for loan repayment. Both credit officers and clients view livestock as capital, with the potential to be used in the event of repayment difficulties. Clients are usually well aware that credit agents grant loans more readily to 'livestock businesses'. Owning a herd facilitates and justifies a demand for credit; animals are presented at inspections, but part or all of a loan is in fact often used for other purposes.[16]

It is worth pointing out that even shopkeepers sell their livestock rather than take out loans when buying goods to sell to villagers.

8.3.3 Widespread Use of Microcredit for Consumer Spending

Al Amana microcredit is in theory intended for 'productive' purposes, in order to generate direct income. Many microfinance institutions (MFIs) apply this rule with a view to encouraging their clients to initiate or expand income-generating activities in order to escape from poverty. Yet a number of recent studies show that in many regions of the world, microcredit is quite frequently used for activities that do not directly generate income (Collins et al., 2009).

According to Al Amana's figures (taken from forms filled out for its credit agents), 82.1 per cent of its microcredit was used to develop activities related to animal rearing, 15.1 per cent for shopkeeping and services, and 2.8 per cent for agriculture. Our own observations, alongside credit agents' testimonials in the zones studied, indicate that 60–80 per cent of loans are in fact devoted to consumer spending. It involves mostly everyday and home-related expenditures, including home improvements such as room or floor extension projects, home decorating, building a new house for newlyweds, and durable goods such as television sets, furniture, and mopeds. Between 10 and 30 per cent of loans are used for animal-rearing, while non-agricultural economic activities, such as small shopkeeping or offering services, make up at most 10 per cent. Such microcredit use places a considerable burden on those who draw on it: clients must have a regular, stable income in order to make repayments. However, as discussed below, this varies according to local contexts.

The loan officers interviewed during this study were perfectly aware of this situation. Most of them confirmed our estimated figures. Some try to monitor credit use and do not hesitate to ask neighbours questions. Others are

[15] Farmer-breeder, Ait Abass Douar, client, Zone 2, Branch MG.

[16] The J-PAL study introduced owning livestock in their model for loan forecasts.

not concerned about it, as their clients are well aware. For example, a client who has been loyal to Al Amana over several years regularly takes out a group loan (being unable to obtain an individual loan) for repairing or renovating his house. He always claims he is borrowing in order to rear animals, even though he has none, and the agent does not check if this is indeed the case. As stated by the client: 'They're perfectly aware it's for my house, but they don't say anything. I make my repayments, and they leave me alone.'[17] Another client mentioned that the agent 'took a quick look at the herd, which could have belonged to one of my neighbours'.[18]

This initial study allows us to better understand the profile of the current clientele: it is composed of households with relatively regular incomes who wish to make use of the loans for consumer spending, or for maintaining their livestock as savings, and, for a minority, for investing or taking advantage of market opportunities. This has several major implications at this preliminary stage. First, credit institutions' (or Al Amana's) loan conditions are poorly tailored to local needs and the rural context, which is a major cause of the low rates of borrowing. However, it is not the only reason why local populations generally do not seem particularly inclined to take on debt, preferring instead to save, especially in kind.

Another means of understanding the profile of the clientele is by analysing the use of loans. Insofar as most of the loans are used for consumer expenditure, participation is determined far less by the availability of economic opportunities than by households' capacity to have regular incomes that enable them to make repayments.

These initial general observations call for a further analysis of disparities in regional participation: such differences depend on type of income (non-agricultural regular income as opposed to income from agriculture and migration), consumer demand, the potential for expanding animal-rearing, and, to a certain extent, the existence of local economic opportunities.

8.4 Regional Disparities: The Role of Vulnerability Assessed by Regularity of Income

Using the criteria of agroecological landscape, livelihood opportunities and remoteness, we established three broad categories of area: (i) mountain areas, (ii) peri-urban areas, and (iii) extensive farming areas. These differences have a considerable impact on credit demand and on access to/use of Al Amana's microcredit services.

[17] Builder, Thratia douar, client, zone 2, branch AW.
[18] Farmer/animal-rearer, Ait Abbas douar, group credit, zone 2, branch MG.

Type 1 areas are mountainous regions with small agricultural plots that support subsistence agriculture. Local markets are extremely limited, incomes are low and irregular, and there are virtually no opportunities for non-farm work. Consequently, a large number of men migrate to the cities for work. From an economic perspective, households have neither the means nor the desire to borrow, as their needs are limited.

Type 2 'peri-urban' areas are where the village is close enough to a city, town, industrial, or artisanal area to permit daily commuting to and from the city for work. Such proximity to centres of activity provides opportunities to earn a regular wage income. In this type of area, demand for microcredit is higher, on average, both because households have higher and more regular earnings and because they have greater needs (daily consumption, housing, and for some, business investment). In our sample, the take-up reaches 19.6 per cent in the peri-urban area, and 27 per cent in the area combining peri-urban and extensive farming (see Table 8.4).

Type 3 areas cover fertile, relatively flat lands better suited to mechanized farming operations. Larger farms exist side by side with small, unsustainable farms. Households in these areas do need credit, but most require large amounts for agricultural use. Al Amana's loan conditions poorly match their needs, as its loans are too small, and regular instalments are demanded in the repayment schedule. As a result, participation rates in these areas on average are rather low (Table 8.4).

Each Al Amana branch in our study can be broadly situated within one of these area categories.

These differences by agroecological area considerably help to explain the variations in take-up across regions and branches (in line with Bouman, 1994). It should also be stressed that there is little overall potential for non-agricultural self-employment, despite disparities across areas. The potential is very weak in mountainous zones and large-scale farming zones, and somewhat greater in zones closer to centres of activity, notwithstanding competition from migration dynamics.

Table 8.4 Typology of visited branches according to eco-type systems

Branch	Eco type system	Take-up (Dec. 2009)	Portfolio at risk (30 days) 2010
CV Tighdouine	Type 1: Mountain area	6%	0.18%
MG My Abdellah Ben Driss	Type 2: Peri-urban area	19.6%	0.85%
AW Moulay Yacoub	Type 2 et 3: Peri-urban and extensive farming area	27%	37.4%
LJ Brachoua	Type 3: Extensive farming area	1%	22%

Source: Al Amana and J-Pal follow-up of take-up rates and and Al Amana's reporting of repayment defaults.

All things considered, animal-rearing seems to be the economic activity which Al Amana most frequently finances. The organization estimates that 82 per cent of its loans are allocated to activities related to animal-rearing. However, our observations and those of credit agents estimated this figure to be between 10 and 30 per cent. In reality, animal-rearing is stymied by various factors, although significant differences are observable across the zones. Three major factors limit the development potential of animal-rearing: scarcity of pastures and/or difficulty of access to them, shortage of winter fodder, and a lack of manpower. Here too, there are big differences across zones. In the mountainous zone, three types of limitations arise, while for the two other zones there are only one or two types of limitation. Moreover, families adopt a range of economic strategies for animal-rearing, which influence both its potential and development. Thus in mountainous zones, cattle are most commonly viewed as a form of saving, while in outer-urban and large-scale farming zones, farmers are driven more by profit-making motivations (as is confirmed by the data from J-PAL, 2008).

These agro-ecological differences greatly help to explain take-up heterogeneity across branches. Of course other factors, such as the perception of sanctions in case of default and the 'social life' of microcredit, namely, how local social actors, not least credit officers and local leaders, engage with microcredit, is also instrumental in shaping the demand for microcredit, and the ways it is used and appropriated (Morvant-Roux et al., forthcoming).

8.5 Conclusions

Our analysis sheds light on different factors behind microcredit take-up rates: social norms related to debt and resort to informal financing systems, agroecological conditions, and the vulnerability of households due mainly to irregular incomes.

From a theoretical perspective, our findings indicate that microcredit markets are not based on simple supply and demand factors, but rather, they emerge as a historically and socially produced, instituted process. Local perceptions of debt are fundamental to this process. In general, we found that there was a reluctance to take on debt, while savings in kind were a much more common and accepted cash-flow management strategy, including for small businesses. Understanding perceptions of specific forms of debt and of creditors (in this case the microcredit association of Al Amana) are also vitally important.

With regard to policy, our findings help to explain the challenges facing institutions that wish to offer access to microcredit in rural areas. Apart from our case study, the current repayment crisis in microfinance highlights the limitations of high levels of standardization and use of a one-size fits-all approach.

Microfinance institutions should adapt to local economic, social, and political contexts. This is not to argue that microfinance should tailor products to the requirements and characteristics of every kind of client. But our results highlight the fact that the success of a microcredit scheme partly depends on the local context in terms of labour markets, and, more broadly, of existing economic activities and opportunities for expanding those markets. Microfinance institutions need to better adapt their financial products to the differences across rural settings. Our study reveals that there is potential for developing loans for households in type 2 zones, and not for households in type 3 zones. For households living in mountainous regions, microfinance institutions could decide not to extend their activities to this type of area, or they could limit their offers of credit to housing expenses or investment in livestock as a way of helping to promote savings in kind in order to secure local livelihoods. Our study offers fresh evidence that not all the rural poor need microcredit. However, in a context of growing financialization of everyday life, including in remote areas of the developing world, the poor do need access to adequate financial services. To be effective and legitimate, such supply must be grounded both in people's financial needs and constraints, and in local economies (Shipton, 2010).

References

Bouman, F. J. A. (1994). 'Informal Rural Finance: An Aladdin's Lamp of Information', in F. J. A. Bouman and O. Hospes (eds.), *Financial Landscape Reconstructed: The Fine Art of Mapping Development.* Boulder, CO: Westview Press: 1–9.

—— and O. Hospes (1994). *Financial Landscape Reconstructed: The Fine Art of Mapping Development.* Boulder, CO: Westview Press.

Bourdieu, P. (1977). *Algérie 60: Structures Economiques et Structures Temporelles.* Paris: Les éditions de Minuit.

Claessens, S. (2006). 'Access to Financial Services: A Review of the Issues and Public Policy Objectives', *The World Bank Research Observer*, 21(2): 207–40.

Collins, D., J. Morduch, S., Rutherford, and O. Ruthven (2009). *Portfolios of the Poor: How the World's Poor Live on $2 a Day.* Princeton, NJ: Princeton University Press.

Crépon B., F. Devoto, E. Duflo, and W. Parienté (2010). 'Evaluation de l'impact du microcrédit en zone rurale au Maroc'. Paris, Agence Française de Développement, Available at <http://www.alamana.org.ma/Images/Microcredit_PresMaroc_122010_v3_FINALE.pdf> (accessed 4 February 2013).

—— (2011). 'Impact of Microcredit in Rural Areas of Morocco: Evidence from a Randomized Evaluation'. *Working paper,* J-Pal, 31 March. Available at <http://www.povertyactionlab.org/publication/impact-microcredit-rural-areas-morocco-evidence-randomized-evaluation> (accessed 4 February 2013).

Deneulin, S., and Rakodi, C. (2011). 'Revisiting Religion: Development Studies Thirty Years On'. *World Development*, 39(1): 45–54.

Duflo E., B. Crépon, W. Parienté, and F. Devoto (2008). 'Poverty, Access to Credit and the Determinants of Participation in a New Micro-credit Program in Rural Areas of Morocco'. *Série Analyse d'Impact Ex Post n°2*, Paris: Agence Française de Développement, October.

Guérin, I., S. Morvant-Roux, and J-M. Servet (2011). 'Understanding the Diversity and Complexity of Demand for Microfinance Services: Lessons from Informal Finance', in B. Armendariz and M. Labie (eds.), *Handbook of Microfinance*. London and Singapore: World Scientific Publishing and Imperial College Press: 101–22.

Guérin, I., M. Roesch, G. Venkatasubramanian, and B. D'Espallier (2012). 'Credit From Whom and For What? Diversity of Borrowing Sources and Uses in Rural South-India', *Journal of International Development*, 24: 122–37.

Johnson, S. (2004). 'Gender Norms in Financial Markets: Evidence from Kenya'. *World Development*, 32(8): 1355–74.

Lont, H., and O. Hospes (eds.) (2004). *Livelihood and Microfinance: Anthropological and Sociological Perspectives on Savings and Debt*, Delft: Eburon Academic Publishers.

Malamoud, C. (ed.) (1980). *La dette. Coll. Purushartha*, vol. 4. Paris: Éditions de l'École des hautes études en sciences sociales.

Morvant-Roux, S. (2009). 'Accès au microcrédit et continuité des dynamiques d'endettement au Mexique: Combiner anthropologie et économétrie'. *Revue Tiers Monde*, 197: 109–30.

—— I. Guérin, and J-M. Servet (2010). 'Politiques d'inclusion financière et financement de l'agriculture: Le cas de l'Inde et du Mexique'. *Mondes en Développement*, 151, 2010/3: 9–24.

Morvant-Roux, S., I. Guérin, M. Roesch, and J.-Y. Moisseron (forthcoming). 'Adding Value to Randomization with Qualitative Analysis: The Case of Microcredit in Rural Morocco'. *World Development*.

PlaNet Finance (2006). 'Étude sur les endettements croisés au Maroc'. PlaNet Finance.

Servet, J.-M. (ed.) (1995). *Épargne et liens sociaux: Études comparées d'informalités financières*. Paris: AEF/AUPELF-UREF.

—— (2006). *Banquiers aux Pieds Nus: La Microfinance*. Paris: Odile Jacob.

Shipton, P. (2007). *The Nature of Entrustment: Intimacy, Exchange and the Sacred in Africa*. New Haven: Yale University Press.

—— (2010). *Credit Between Cultures: Farmers, Financiers and Misunderstandings in Africa*. New Haven: Yale University Press.

Stiglitz, J. and A. Weiss (1981). 'Credit Rationing in Markets with Imperfect Information'. *American Economic Review*, 71(3): 393–410.

Tripp, C. (2006). *Islam and the Moral Economy: The Challenge of Capitalism*. Cambridge: Cambridge University Press.

Villarreal, M. (2004). 'Striving to Make Capital Do "Economic Things" for the Impoverished: On the Issue of Capitalization in Rural Microenterprises', in T. Kontinen (ed.), *Development Intervention: Actor and Activity Perspectives*. Helsinki: University of Helsinki: 67–81.

9

Informal and Formal Microfinance in Urban Sub-Saharan African Markets: The Case of Micro-Entrepreneurs in Ouagadougou, Burkina Faso

Pierre-Germain Umuhire and Marthe Nyssens

9.1 Introduction

In spite of the rise of a dynamic microfinance sector with the objective of redressing the problem of financial exclusion, informal financial mechanisms remain pervasive in developing countries (Emily, 2002; Collins, Morduch, Rutherford, and Ruthven, 2009). This seems puzzling, given that mainstream economics has long attributed the use of informal financial mechanisms to the lack of access to formal financial markets. Institutional microfinance has naturally been viewed as a potential substitute for informal finance. However, the persistence of informal finance even when microfinance is available, suggests that it is not being treated as a substitute.

Such an unexpected outcome, has led a number of scholars to investigate the reasons for the continued prevalence of informal financial mechanisms. There are two categories of reasons put forward in the literature. Some scholars view informal finance as a *solution of last resort* for individuals who lack access to formal financial (credit) markets. They draw their arguments essentially from the information asymmetry theory (Stiglitz and Weiss, 1981) and the financial repression theory (McKinnon,1973; Shaw, 1973). These theories show respectively how endogenous and exogenous market failures restrict access to credit markets, compelling some people to resort to informal finance. Information asymmetry refers to situations where lenders who cannot determine the risk profiles of their potential borrowers face two risks: the adverse selection risk and the moral hazard risk. The *adverse selection* risk refers to the ex-ante probability of selecting risky borrowers (i.e. borrowers with a relatively high probability of default) due to the presence of information asymmetries. The *moral hazard* risk refers to the ex-post risk of default, and arises from the difficulty of monitoring the borrower once the loan is granted. Due to these problems, lenders are likely to ration credit so as to avoid losing money in case of default. Thus, the individuals who are weeded out of the formal markets have no other option but to resort to informal finance (Hoff and Stiglitz, 1990; 1993). Moreover, the credit rationing resulting from information asymmetry is likely to be wealth biased (Boucher and Guirkinger, 2007). Indeed, one way of mitigating the problem arising from adverse selection and moral hazard is to offer collateralized loan contracts. However, this would mean that low-income borrowers without sufficient wealth to put up as collateral would not be offered any feasible loan contract. Similarly, lenders who are unable to determine the risk profiles of their potential borrowers tend to associate poverty with high risk and tend to offer loan contracts only to rich borrowers.

According to the financial repression theory, informal finance is believed to result from government intervention in financial markets through a set of regulations and restrictions which are prone to discourage savings while reducing the supply of credit by formal institutions.[1] Thus, some individuals are prevented from accessing formal credit, even though without these restrictions they would qualify for obtaining it. The resulting unsatisfied demand for loans is absorbed by the unorganized informal money market, which acts as a residual market allowing financial markets to clear (Van Wijnbergen, 1983).

Another set of theories suggests that the use of informal finance is a deliberate choice by individuals who are better off in informal finance than in formal finance. There are two theoretical arguments supporting this view: the argument in terms of transactions costs (Chung, 1995; Barham, Boucher, and Carter, 1996) and the argument in terms of contractual risks (Boucher and Guirkinger, 2007; Boucher, Carter, and Guirkinger, 2008; Guirkinger, 2008). The argument in terms of transactions costs posits that informal financial contracts are sometimes cheaper than formal financial contracts, or alternatively, that low-income individuals who require small transactions that are not profitable for formal institutions—due to the implied transactions costs—find it easier to resort to informal finance. The argument in terms of contractual risks emphasizes the risk for a borrower contracting a collateralized loan. As mentioned previously, collateral requirements aim at protecting

[1] Instruments of financial repression include policies such as ceilings on interest rates, high liquidity ratio requirements, high bank reserve requirements, capital controls, credit controls, and restrictions on market entry.

lenders against the risk of default. Unfortunately, they involve risks for the borrowers who are likely to lose ownership of part or all of their assets pledged as collateral in case of default. Comparing the formal and the informal credit markets, it appears that this risk is higher in formal markets than in informal markets (Boucher and Guirkinger, 2007).

The literature cited above provides an interesting basis for analysing the persistence of the demand for informal finance, and thereby the reasons for the coexistence of informal and formal finance. However, little is said about how informal and formal finance are used and combined by customers. Do they simply exist side by side, serving different types of customers? What about their substitutability? Are there people who use a combination of both types of finance? Moreover, the above literature focuses on the credit market but does not provide any insight into the savings behaviour of low-income individuals. We endeavour to help fill this gap through an empirical analysis of the financial behaviour of micro-entrepreneurs operating in Ouagadougou. Specifically, our analysis intends: (i) to assess the use of both informal and formal finance, (ii) to identify the financial mechanisms that are the most likely to be combined, (iii) to analyse the profile of micro-entrepreneurs who are most likely to combine the use of both informal and formal finance and, (iv) to check whether informal and formal finance are used for similar or different purposes. However, before dealing with these issues, we first briefly describe our empirical methodology as well as the characteristics of our sample.

9.2 Data and Empirical Methodology

The results discussed in this chapter were obtained from a survey of micro-entrepreneurs operating in three urban markets—the Nabi Yaar, the Rood Woko, and the Dasasgho markets—located in and around the centre of Ouagadougou, the capital of Burkina Faso. The survey was executed in two stages from mid-2009 to mid-2010. During the preliminary stage, conducted in 2009, a pilot survey was carried out on a small sample of thirty-two individuals using qualitative approaches that consisted of in-depth, face-to-face, semi-open interviews. The information collected during this phase was built up progressively until data saturation was reached.[2] Drawing from the information collected during the pilot survey, a comprehensive quantitative survey was designed and implemented in the first quarter of 2010. This survey involved structured, face-to-face interviews with a random sample of 398 micro-entrepreneurs. Note that our sampling unit, the micro-entrepreneur,

[2] 'Data saturation point' is reached when the interviews of extra respondents do not provide the researcher with any extra (new) information (Siniscalco and Auriat, 2005).

Table 9.1 Summary statistics of the micro-entrepreneurs' characteristics

Variables		N	Prop. (%)	Mean
Age of the respondent		396		38.64
				–12.63
Household size		392		7.75
				–5.08
Monthly income (in local currency: XOF)		386		167,375
				–197,528
Education of the respondent	None		41	
	Primary		28	
	Secondary		17	
	Koranic		14	
Gender	Woman		53	
	Man		47	
Type of activity	Local arts dealers		5	
	Vendors of shoes		6	
	Vendors of vegetables and food stuffs		10	
	Vendors of condiments		28	
	Vendors of clothes, cosmetics, and manufactured products		50	
Ethnicity	Mossi		84	
	Other		16	
Religion	Muslim		83	
	Catholic		15	
	Protestant		2	

Note: The abbreviations Prop and SE stand respectively for Proportion and Standard Error. Standard deviations from the mean are indicated between blankets.

is also our unit of analysis. Four enumerators were hired and trained to assist in implementing the survey. Finally, simple multivariate data-mining techniques, namely correspondence analysis and cluster analysis, were used to explore our dataset, while logit models were used to estimate the effects of micro-entrepreneurs' characteristics on their financial choices. The results discussed below are mainly based on these techniques. Table 9.1 presents a brief overview of the sample's characteristics.

It appears from the above table that the surveyed micro-entrepreneurs are not among the poorest. Their average monthly income of XOF 167,375 (or ≅ €255) is more than twice the average national household expenditure (XOF 72,198, or ≅ €110).[3] Moreover, the average micro-entrepreneur earns more than what is defined by the World Bank as the international poverty line of $1.25 a day

[3] XOF stands for West African CFA franc. The National Institute of Statistics (INSD, 2008) reports average annual household expenditures of about XOF 866,381 (which is approximately XOF 72,198 per month) for the year 2003, which is the latest year for which data were available. The exchange rate is XOF 655.9570 = €1. (For euro foreign exchange reference rates, see <http://www.ecb.int/stats/exchange/eurofxref/html/index.en.html>, accessed 18 May 2013.)

(Shaohua and Ravallion, 2010). Indeed, considering an average household size of 7.75 individuals, the average per capita daily income of a micro-entrepreneur's household is about XOF 720 (≅ PPP $3.4).[4] Nevertheless, it should be noted that there are income disparities between micro-entrepreneurs, as some of them have a monthly income that can be as low as 6,000 XOF (or ≅ €10). Moreover, men earn more than women, the average income differential being XOF 94,051 (or ≅ €143) with a median of XOF 79,200 (or≅ €121).

9.3 Enrolment in Informal and Formal Microfinance: Crowding out?

This section describes the financial landscape of the micro-entrepreneurs and evaluates the extent of their use of both informal and formal microfinance. It also seeks to determine whether or not there has been any crowding out of formal microfinance on informal finance. Before proceeding, let us note that the concept of informal finance is used here to indicate financial activities that take place outside the legal framework governing financial and microfinance markets.[5] Four informal and two formal financial mechanisms were identified during the survey. The informal mechanisms include Rotating Savings and Credit Associations (ROSCAs)—also referred to as *Pari*—money collectors locally known as *Cauri d'or*, loans between relatives and friends, and suppliers' credits (see Box 9.1). The formal financial mechanisms include ownership of cooperatives or bank accounts as well as formal microcredit.

It is important to note that some micro-entrepreneurs only resorted to financial mechanisms from time to time, and this sporadic use needs to be taken into account. Otherwise there is a risk of *underestimating the importance of financial participation.*[6] In order to stick to the reality, the survey sought to find out three different financial enrolment rates: (i) the *global enrolment rate,* which indicates the proportion of respondents who used the identified financial mechanism in the ten years prior to the survey; (ii) the *actual enrolment rate,* which reports the proportion of respondents who used the financial mechanism during the twelve months prior to the survey; and (iii) the *potential enrolment* rate, which accounts for the expected evolution in the use

[4] We used a purchasing power parity conversion rate of 214.405 for the year 2010 (<http://www.imf.org/external/pubs/ft/weo/2010/02/weodata/weorept.aspx?sy=2010&ey=2010&scsm=1&ssd=1&sort=country&ds=.&br=1&pr1.x=45&pr1.y=6&c=748&s=PPPEX&grp=0&a>, accessed 15 June 2013).

[5] This definition is in line with that of the International Labour Organization.

[6] Some financial mechanisms—such as ROSCAs—have a pre-defined life cycle, and it is quite possible to observe some time lag between two ROSCA cycles. In the same way, other informal sources such as supplier's credit can largely depend on other cyclical circumstances.

Box 9.1 INFORMAL FINANCIAL MECHANISMS USED IN THE MARKETS OF OUAGADOUGOU

Briefly, a *ROSCA* can be defined as a group of individuals who agree to meet on a regular basis and periodically convene to contribute a given sum of money to a common pot. The pot is allocated to one of them each time they meet on a rotational basis (Ardener, 1964; Baland and Siwan, 2002).

The Cauri d'or is an informal financial mechanism in which an individual called a 'tontinier' takes responsibility for collecting the savings of other people on a daily basis. At the end of thirty-one payments, the 'tontinier' refunds the equivalent of thirty days of payments and keeps a one-day payment for his or her remuneration. This amount is equivalent to a negative monthly interest rate of about 3.32 per cent. *Suppliers' credits* refer to deferred payments either between micro-entrepreneurs and their customers or between micro-entrepreneurs and their suppliers.

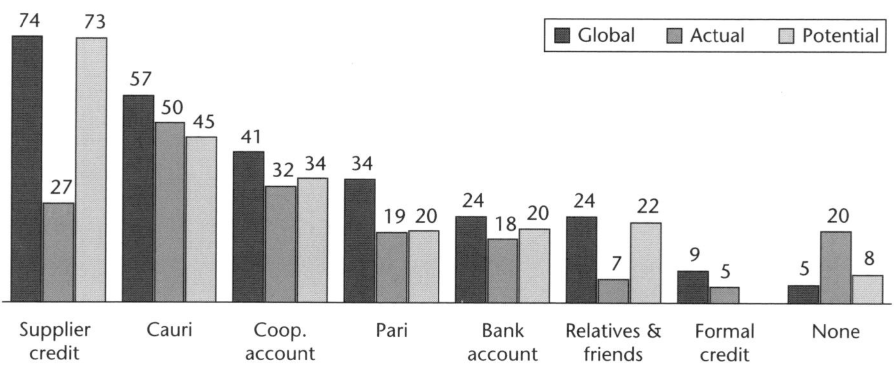

Figure 9.1 Micro-entrepreneurs' enrolment rates with financial providers (per cent)

of financial mechanisms by micro-entrepreneurs in the foreseeable future. To obtain this rate, micro-entrepreneurs were asked to indicate the financial practices they intended to be using in the next twelve months or so.

It appears from Figure 9.1 that a large majority of the surveyed micro-entrepreneurs resorted actively to financial markets. Only 5 per cent of them had never used any of the identified financial mechanisms for the previous ten years (actual: 20 per cent, potential: 8 per cent). However, access to formal credit was quite limited: only 9 per cent of the surveyed micro-entrepreneurs obtained formal credit during the previous ten years and only 5 per cent had an outstanding formal credit at the time of the survey (Figure 9.2).

Additionally, contrasting global enrolment rates in informal and formal financial markets, we observed that about 254 micro-entrepreneurs (54 per cent) had made use of some formal financial instrument, while 366 (92 per cent) had made use of some informal instrument. Therefore, it is evident

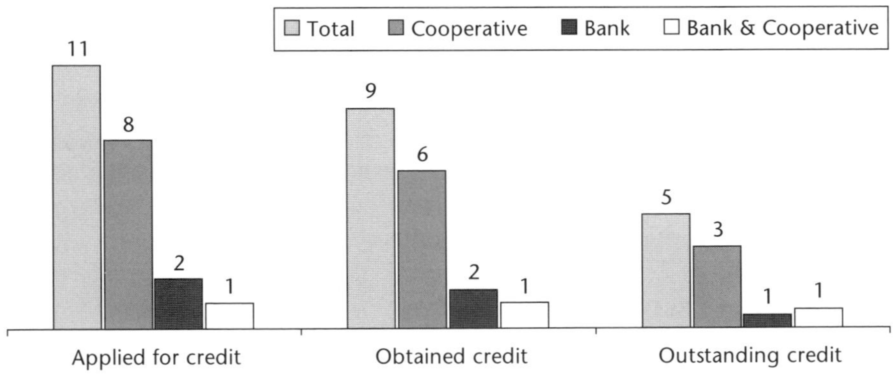

Figure 9.2 Micro-entrepreneurs' access to formal credit (per cent)

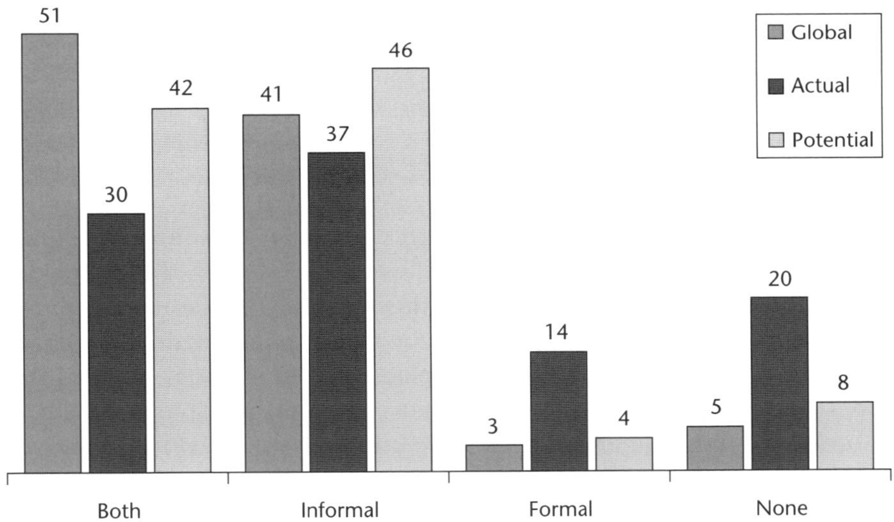

Figure 9.3 Use of both informal and formal finance (per cent)

that some micro-entrepreneurs (51 per cent) had been resorting to both types of financial markets, either simultaneously or successively (Figure 9.3). Restricting the time span to the twelve months prior to the survey period, this proportion falls to 30 per cent while it is expected to reach 42 per cent over the following twelve months.

Comparing the global and actual enrolment rates, it appears that about 21 per cent of micro-entrepreneurs who were using both informal and formal finance did not do so during the previous twelve months (51 per cent minus 30 per cent). It is interesting to check out what their financial choices were during that period. If they decided to resort exclusively to formal

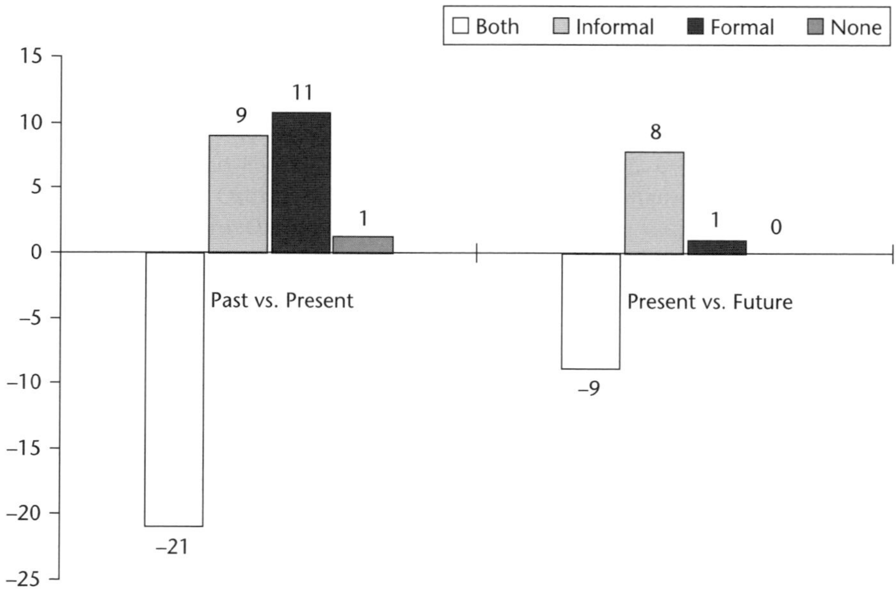

Figure 9.4 Evolution in enrolment rates (per cent)

microfinance, this would signal the presence of (some) crowding out of informal finance by formal microfinance. In the opposite case (i.e. they decided to resort exclusively to informal finance), this would signal the absence of any crowding out effect of informal finance by formal microfinance. The analysis of the changes in the actual versus global enrolment rates revealed that about 9 per cent of the micro-entrepreneurs who were previously using both informal and formal finance went back to informal finance, while 11 per cent decided to resort exclusively to formal microfinance (Figure 9.4).[7] The net level of crowding out is only 2 per cent. This finding suggests rather a limited substitution of informal finance by formal microfinance. Moreover, when micro-entrepreneurs were asked to reveal their future financial choices—as highlighted by the second part of Figure 9.4 (present vs. future)—the proportion of micro-entrepreneurs who said they were likely to shift from informal to formal microfinance fell to only 1 per cent. Therefore, assuming their expectations about their own future behaviour to be valid, we can confidently assert that the crowding out of informal finance by formal microfinance is likely to remain limited, at least in the foreseeable future.

[7] The 11 per cent of micro-entrepreneurs who moved from informal to formal microfinance were almost evenly split between banks and cooperatives: 5 per cent resorted exclusively to formal banks, while 4 per cent resorted exclusively to formal cooperatives, and the remaining 2 per cent used both banks and cooperatives.

9.4 How Micro-Entrepreneurs Combine Different Financial Mechanisms

In the section 9.3, it was shown that some micro-entrepreneurs combine both informal and formal finance. This section pushes the analysis further by explicitly examining how micro-entrepreneurs combine the six financial mechanisms identified during the survey. We use statistical techniques—namely correspondence and cluster analysis techniques—that allow the structure hidden within datasets to be analysed. While correspondence analysis is a data reduction technique that allows grouping correlated categories of variables (Benzecri, 1973; 1978; Lebart, Morineau, and Kenneth, 1984; Greenacre, 2007), cluster analysis allows observations to clusters to be assigned in such a way that two objects from the same cluster are more similar than two objects from different clusters (Řezanková, 2009).[8] In this study, we use the correspondence analysis output as the input for the cluster analysis. This is a useful method for obtaining refined clusters (Ciampi, Gonzalez, and Castejón, 2005). Eight clusters were identified. Each cluster displays a distinctive pattern of combining the financial sources. Table 9.2 provides a detailed description of each cluster.

Clusters 1 to 3 encompass micro-entrepreneurs who combine both informal and formal financial mechanisms. In absolute terms, the cooperative account is the formal financial mechanism that is most likely to be combined with the use of informal finance (clus2 and clus3). The next three clusters (clus4 to clus6) comprise micro-entrepreneurs who resort exclusively to informal finance while the last two clusters (clus7 and clus8) comprise respectively the micro-entrepreneurs who resorted exclusively to formal finance and the micro-entrepreneurs who did not resort to financial markets.

These results show that it is not unusual for micro-entrepreneurs to combine informal and formal financial mechanisms. However, a question remains unanswered: Who is combining both informal and formal microfinance? The next section analyses whether the combined use of informal and formal microfinance applies to a particular category of micro-entrepreneurs or whether it is a behavioural pattern common to the majority of them.

[8] Hierarchical clustering (ward's linkage) was applied to the coordinates of the correspondence analysis solution. The results of hierarchical clustering were further refined using k-means clustering.

Table 9.2 Description of the clusters

Clusters	Description	Freq	Per cent
Clus1	Micro-entrepreneurs who obtained a formal credit and yet resorted to informal finance; namely the supplier's credit (82%), the Cauri d'or (59%), the Pari (47%) and the loans between relatives and friends (18%).	34	9
Clus2	Micro-entrepreneurs owning a bank account and who are also likely to use informal finance such as supplier's credit (87%), the Cauri d'or (41%), the loans between relatives and friends (34%), the Pari (21%). Their probability of owning a cooperative account is estimated at 41%.	71	18
Clus3	Micro-entrepreneurs owning a cooperative account and who are likely to resort to informal finance such as supplier's credit (77%), the Cauri d'or (73%), the Pari (42%), the loans between relatives and friends (33%)	97	24
Clus4	Micro-entrepreneurs who used informal financial mechanisms except the supplier's credit: the Cauri d'or (89%), the Pari (33%), the loans between relatives and friends (3%).	36	9
Clus5	Micro-entrepreneurs who used exclusively informal financial mechanisms, except the loans from relatives/friends: the supplier's credit (100%), the Cauri d'or (55%), the Pari (32%).	96	24
Clus6	Micro-entrepreneurs who used exclusively informal financial mechanisms: the loans from relatives/friends (100%), the supplier's credit (100%), the Cauri (69%), and the Pari (47%).	32	8
Clus7	Micro-entrepreneurs who used only formal finance: the bank account (83%), the cooperative account (67%), and the formal credit (8%).	12	3
Clus8	Micro-entrepreneurs who did not use any financial mechanism.	20	5
	Total	398	100

Note: For each cluster, the probabilities for the micro-entrepreneur to resort to each financial mechanism are indicated between blankets.

9.5 Which Kinds of Micro-Entrepreneurs Are Using Both Informal and Formal Microfinancial Mechanisms?

In this section, we analyse the profiles of the micro-entrepreneurs to identify which kinds of micro-entrepreneurs are combining both informal and formal microfinance. This can be done in different ways (e.g. analysis of contingency tables, correspondence analysis, multivariate analysis of variance, discrete choice mode, etc.). We opted for the discrete choice models and used a multinomial logit model to estimate the probability of a micro-entrepreneur belonging to each of the eight clusters conditional on his/her demographic characteristics. The advantage of this statistical technique is that its results are easily interpretable. As it appears in the next table, Table 9.3, we found significant differences in the profiles of micro-entrepreneurs across the identified clusters.

Table 9.3 Marginal effects obtained from multinomial logit

	clus1	clus2	clus3	clus4	clus5	clus6	clus7	clus8
Income	2.09E–07[a]	5.28E–07[a]	–1.34E–07	–1.96E–07	–1.02E–07	–2.84E–07[b]	6.45E–10	–2.11E–08[a]
	(0.00E + 00)	(0.00E + 00)	(0.00E + 00)	(0.00E + 00)	(0.00E + 00)	(0.00E + 00)	(0.00E + 00)	(0.00E + 00)
Age	0.0043[a]	0.0026	–0.0053[b]	–0.0013	0.0002	–0.0005	1.8E–05[a]	4.13E–05
	(0.0012)	(0.0018)	(0.0024)	(0.0014)	(0.0025)	(0.0013)	(1.00E–05)	(0.0001)
Dependency ratio	–0.0001	0.0002	0.0001	0.0002	–0.0005	0.0001	1.91E–07	–5.03E–09
	(0.0002)	(0.0003)	(0.0004)	(0.0002)	(0.0004)	(0.0002)	(0.00E + 00)	(1.00E–05)
Formal education *(yes:1 no:0)*	0.1068[a]	0.0965[c]	–0.0621	–0.0237	0.1113[c]	–0.0062	0.0000	–2.90E–05
	(0.0404)	(0.0540)	(0.0618)	(0.0351)	(0.0605)	(0.0366)	(0.0002)	(0.0019)
Koranic education *(yes:1 no:0)*	–0.0390	0.1363	0.0316	–0.0001	–0.0975	–0.0452	–0.0068	–0.0027
	(0.0444)	(0.0888)	(0.0891)	(0.0002)	(0.0764)	(0.0363)	(0.0351)	(0.0019)
Gender *(man:1 woman:0)*	–0.0593[b]	0.1488[a]	0.0532	–0.0516	0.1181[b]	0.0268	0.0001	–0.0001
	(0.0301)	(0.0458)	(0.0572)	(0.0380)	(0.0596)	(0.0338)	(0.0002)	(0.0019)
Religion *(Christian:1 other:0)*	–0.0136	0.0420	–0.0382	0.0140	0.0232	–0.0245	–0.0022[b]	–0.0006
	(0.0318)	(0.0643)	(0.0741)	(0.0427)	(0.0705)	(0.0365)	(0.0011)	(0.0020)
Ethnicity *(mossi:1 other:0)*	–0.0063	–0.1864[a]	–0.0084	0.0906[a]	0.0594	0.0085	0.0024[b]	0.0403[b]
	(0.0325)	(0.0670)	(0.0748)	(0.0302)	(0.0693)	(0.0413)	(0.0011)	(0.0165)
marital status *(couple:1 single:0)*	0.0415	0.0156	–0.0106	–0.0200	0.0385	–0.0593	0.0002	–0.0059
	(0.0262)	(0.0477)	(0.0672)	(0.0381)	(0.0613)	(0.0466)	(0.0002)	(0.0038)

Note: Robust standard errors are reported. The superscripts a, b, and c indicate respectively significance levels of 0.01, 0.05, and 0.10.

Let us first consider the micro-entrepreneurs who used both informal and formal finance; that is, micro-entrepreneurs in the first three clusters. The probability of belonging to the *first cluster*—which is made up of micro-entrepreneurs who have obtained a formal credit and yet resorted to informal finance—is higher for *wealthier, older, educated (formal education), and female* micro-entrepreneurs. The probability of belonging to the *second cluster*—which is made up of micro-entrepreneurs who combine the use of a bank account with informal finance—is higher for *wealthier, educated (formal education), male, and non-mossi* micro-entrepreneurs.[9] Finally, the probability of belonging to the *third cluster*—which is made up of micro-entrepreneurs who combine the ownership of a cooperative account with informal finance—is higher for *younger* micro-entrepreneurs. Summing up, we note that the micro-entrepreneurs who combine both informal and formal finance have varying demographic profiles. Globally, two types of profiles can be highlighted: the micro-entrepreneurs who combine the ownership of a bank account and/or a formal credit with informal finance are *wealthier* and *more educated*, while those combining the ownership of a cooperative account with the use of informal finance (clus2) are likely to be *younger* and not necessarily *wealthy or educated*. Indeed, the probability of belonging to the second cluster is neither dependent on income nor on education level.

Three other points are worth noting with respect to the above results. First, they reveal that *wealthier and/or female* micro-entrepreneurs have a higher probability of belonging to the first cluster. Considering that this cluster is made up of micro-entrepreneurs who obtained a formal credit, we can infer that the wealthiest female micro-entrepreneurs have easier access to formal credit. It should be noted, however, that the positive correlation between income and access to formal credit cannot be considered, *ipso facto*, as a causal relationship whereby higher income necessarily enables easier access to formal credit. The causal relationship, if any, can be in the other direction as well, that is, access to formal credit can lead to higher earnings. The fact that women are more likely to obtain formal credit than men reveals a gender bias in microcredit programmes, which tend to focus more on female than on male micro-entrepreneurs. Second, the micro-entrepreneurs resorting exclusively to informal finance (clusters 4, 5, and 6) are globally more likely to be low-income earners and/or uneducated. Third, we observe a negative income effect on the probability of belonging to the eighth cluster which comprises micro-entrepreneurs without any financial activity. This reflects the preponderance of the poorest in this cluster.

[9] The fact that non-mossi micro-entrepreneurs are more likely to combine informal and formal finance constitutes quite probably a diversification strategy, as they cannot rely on a dense informal social network, unlike the mossi for whom Ouagadougou is at the centre of their native region.

9.6 Contrasting the Purposes of Using Informal and Formal Microfinance

Having described how micro-entrepreneurs combine the different financial mechanisms available to them in section 9.4, this section seeks to contrast the different uses of informal and formal microfinance. Table 9.4 provides an overview of the micro-entrepreneurs' financial transactions through the identified financial mechanisms during the twelve months prior to the survey period. Cash-out refers to deposits or loan granted by the micro-entrepreneurs through the financial mechanism, while cash-in refers to withdrawals or loan received by micro-entrepreneurs through the identified financial mechanism.

The remainder of this section seeks to determine how micro-entrepreneurs used the financial resources mobilized through the above financial mechanisms. First, we contrast the use of those mechanisms either for saving or for borrowing before analysing to what extent the financial resources mobilized by micro-entrepreneurs through the above financial mechanisms were used for commercial or non-commercial (private) purposes.

9.6.1 Borrowing vs. Saving

Determining whether the micro-entrepreneurs resorted to formal microfinance either for saving or borrowing is straightforward, given that a large majority of micro-entrepreneurs did not manage to obtain a formal credit. Recall that micro-entrepreneurs who obtained a formal credit represent 9 per cent of the entire sample. Considering only the micro-entrepreneurs who owned an account at a bank and/or cooperative (i.e. 254 micro-entrepreneurs), this proportion rises to 16 per cent. In other words, about *84 per cent* of

Table 9.4 An overview of the financial flows of the micro-entrepreneurs over the 12 months prior to the survey

Financial mechanism	N	Deposits/outgoing loans		Withdrawals/incoming loans	
		XOF	Euros	XOF	Euros
Cauri d'or	198	34,100,000	51,985	27,500,000	41,923
Relatives/friends	26	16,800,000	25,611	16,600,000	25,307
Pari (ROSCAs)	77	41,300,000	62,961	21,900,000	33,386
Suppliers' credit	108	23,000,000	35,063	26,500,000	40,399
Outstanding formal credit	23			27,200,000	41,466
Total		115,200,000	175,621	119,700,000	182,481

Note: The amount invested in ROSCA is normally equal to the amount received from it at the end of the life cycle of the ROSCA. The difference observed here comes from the fact that some ROSCAs to which the micro-entrepreneurs adhere had not come to the end of their life cycle.

micro-entrepreneurs who owned a formal account used it for saving purposes. Contrariwise, the analysis of the use of informal finance as a saving or a borrowing mechanism is trickier, as any micro-entrepreneur could easily combine the status of borrower, lender, and saver. For simplicity, we restrict the analysis to the twelve months prior to the survey period. About 264 micro-entrepreneurs had been using informal finance during this period. We first consider all the micro-entrepreneurs globally (Figure 9.5) before contrasting the eighth clusters identified earlier (Figure 9.6). Nonetheless, the results reported in the next figures do not include the use of ROSCAs. Indeed, it is the position of the micro-entrepreneur in the order of the allocation of the common pot that determines whether he/she used the ROSCA as a saving or a borrowing mechanism. Unfortunately, this information was difficult to obtain and, thus, no attempt was made to disentangle the effective use of ROSCAs as a borrowing or a saving mechanism.

It appears that micro-entrepreneurs used the informal finance—apart from ROSCAs–for saving and/or for both saving and borrowing. Only a very small number of micro-entrepreneurs resorted to informal finance exclusively for borrowing (Figure 9.5). The analysis of the purposes for using informal finance by micro-entrepreneurs resorting to both informal and formal finance confirms this pattern (Figure 9.6). It is particularly interesting to note that the micro-entrepreneurs used informal finance mainly for saving purposes. This finding is in line with a number of studies that highlight both the need and capacity of low-income individuals to save despite important revenue constraints (Hogarth and Anguelov, 2003; Gugerty, 2007). This aspect is often

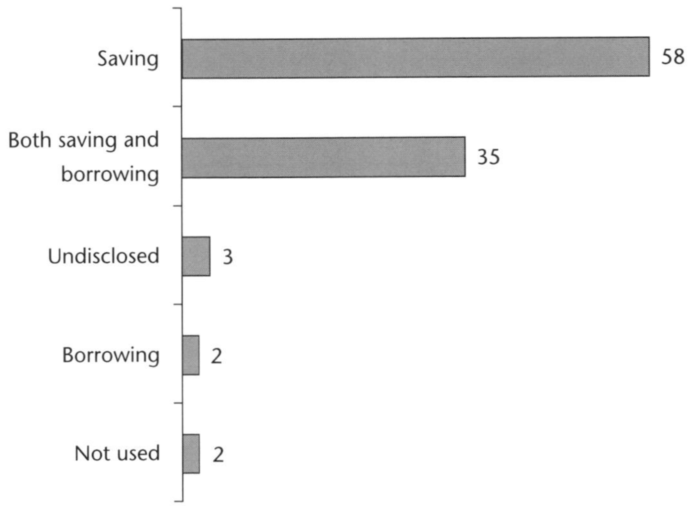

Figure 9.5 Purposes for using informal finance by micro-entrepreneurs (per cent)

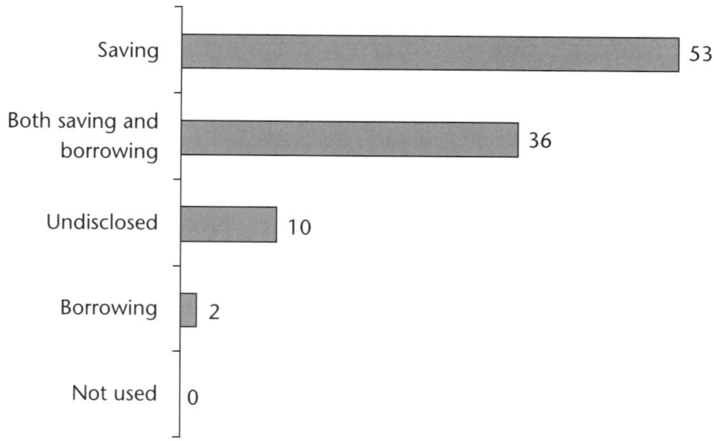

Figure 9.6 Purposes for using informal finance by micro-entrepreneurs combining informal and formal (per cent)

Note: In the above figures, the 'undisclosed' category refers to micro-entrepreneurs who did not disclose the reasons why they resorted to informal finance.

missed by financial providers in developing countries, who tend to emphasize the need of low-income individuals for credit while downplaying their capacity to save. Consequently, often, few savings options are offered to this income group (Karlan, 2010).

One might wonder why a micro-entrepreneur who owns a bank and/or a cooperative account would actually resort to informal saving mechanisms. At least three reasons explain this behaviour. First, the majority of micro-entrepreneurs (about 70 per cent) revealed that their choice was motivated by the need to take advantage of the disciplining mechanism offered by informal financial mechanisms. Indeed, as documented by Gugerty (2007), some informal financial mechanisms impose stringent saving discipline on individuals with time-inconsistent or hyperbolic preferences.[10] Another reason cited by a fair proportion of the micro-entrepreneurs (31 per cent) is that some informal financial mechanisms allow enhancing social ties. This finding is in line with a relatively new trend in economic literature which suggests that informal finance plays a role of social inclusion that cannot be provided by formal microfinance (Guérin, Morvant-Roux, and Servet, 2011). Finally, it was observed that even though only a small number of micro-entrepreneurs managed to obtain a loan from a formal source, a large majority of micro-entrepreneurs (68 per cent)

[10] Hyperbolic preferences refer to situations where preferences between two delayed rewards reverse in favour of the more proximate reward (Frederick, Loewenstein, and O'Donoghue, 2002). For instance, individuals with time-inconsistent preferences may declare that they prefer saving to spending their earnings, but once they have money they cannot refrain from spending it. Such individuals usually require an outside commitment mechanism.

declared they maintained a cooperative and/or bank account in the hope of securing formal credit in the future.

9.6.2 Commercial vs. Private Use

While examining how the financial resources mobilized through the different financial mechanisms were used by micro-entrepreneurs, we identified three categories of expenditures: (i) commercial expenditures, (ii) spending on equipment such as motorbikes and bicycles, and (iii) private expenditures. Since we could not obtain detailed information about the use of funds from bank and cooperative accounts, our analysis is restricted to the utilization of formal credit and of the resources mobilized through informal finance during the twelve months preceding the survey. The total credits secured by micro-entrepreneurs amounted to XOF 67,000,000 (≈ €102,141), of which XOF 27,000,000 (≈ €41,466) were still outstanding at the time of the survey. At the same time, the flow of financial resources from informal finance during that period amounted to XOF 92,425,500 (≈ €140,902).

Two major tendencies can be identified in the use of the financial resources mobilized through formal credit and informal financial mechanisms. On the one hand, the formal credit obtained by micro-entrepreneurs is mainly used for business activities and, to a lesser extent, for private non-commercial needs. A small proportion is used for the acquisition of equipment such as motorbikes and bicycles. We did not consider such equipment to be commercial expenditure, since they are also used for private purposes (Figure 9.7).

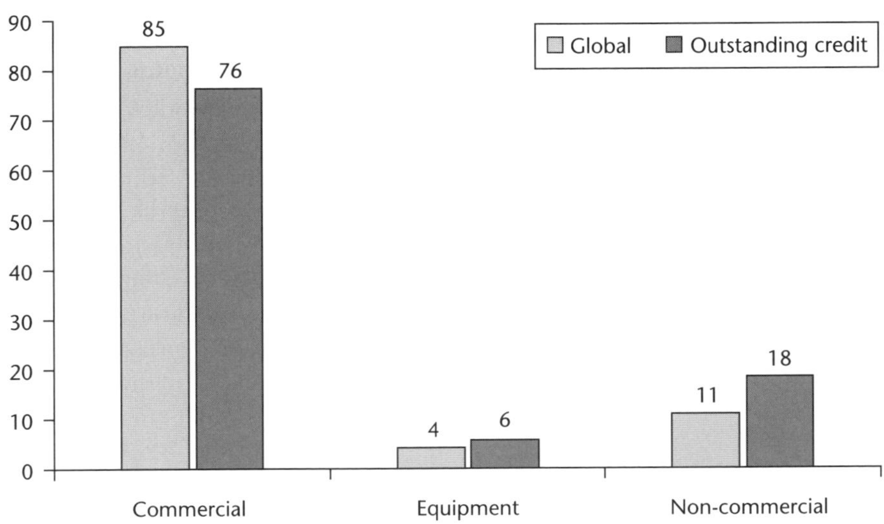

Figure 9.7 Micro-entrepreneurs' use of formal credit (per cent)

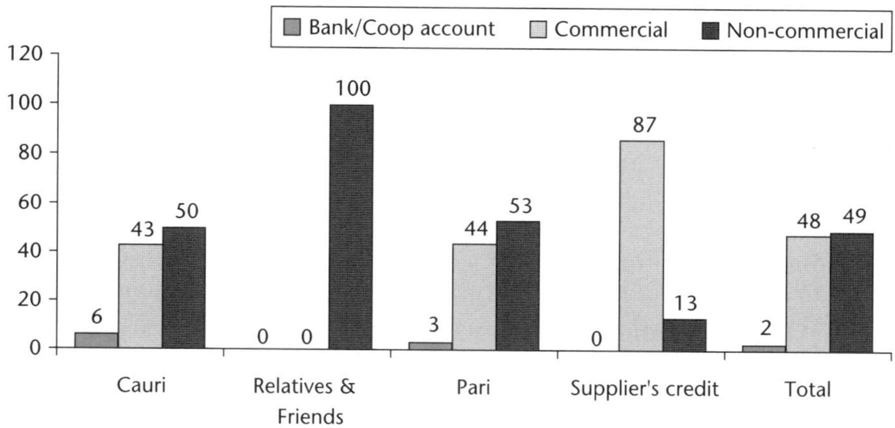

Figure 9.8 Micro-entrepreneurs' use of informal financial resources (per cent)

On the other hand, the resources mobilized through informal finance are almost evenly split between commercial and non-commercial purposes, as highlighted by the last two columns of Figure 9.8. Nevertheless, some informal financial mechanisms are almost exclusively used either for commercial purposes or for non-commercial purposes. For example, supplier's credit is almost entirely used for business purposes and loans from friends and relatives are used exclusively for private needs.

Finally, an extremely small proportion of informal financial resources—only 2 per cent—were directly deposited in formal bank or cooperatives accounts.[11] In other words, financial intermediation between informal and formal microfinance, whereby financial resources mobilized through informal financial channels are injected into formal (micro) finance was quite limited. However, it should be noted that that some scholars have observed the existence of financial *intermediation* between informal and formal finance whereby financial resources obtained through formal microfinance were on-lent or reallocated through informal financial channels (Morvant-Roux, 2009) or used to maintain *solvability in informal financial markets* (Guérin, Venkatasubramanian, and Héliès, 2009). Hence, these two findings suggest that financial resources mobilized through formal channels are likely to fuel informal financial mechanisms rather than the opposite.

[11] This refers to the amount of informal financial resources deposited directly in bank and/or cooperative accounts as soon as they are received. We did not consider deposits made after the money had been recycled for the micro-entrepreneurs' other activities.

9.7 Conclusions

In this chapter, it appeared that it is not unusual for micro-entrepreneurs operating in sub-Saharan African markets—the markets of Ouagadougou in this case study—to resort to both informal and formal microfinance. In particular, the use of cooperatives which are the emblematic microfinance institutions in Ouagadougou is often combined with the use of informal financial mechanisms. Our empirical evidence shows there is weak substitutability between informal and formal microfinance. Hence, the coexistence of informal and formal microfinance cannot be viewed just as a temporal or anecdotal phenomenon, but rather, as an important trend which is likely to persist over time. A direct policy implication of this finding is that microfinance institutions ought to take into account the *resilience* of informal finance and try to find out how their own products can be better harmonized with the pre-existing informal financial mechanisms.

The analysis of the socio-economic characteristics of micro-entrepreneurs revealed that wealthier and more educated micro-entrepreneurs were more likely to combine both informal and formal finance, while less wealthy micro-entrepreneurs mostly resorted to informal finance. However, it is important to note that the ownership of cooperative accounts does not seem to be affected by the wealth of the micro-entrepreneurs. This suggests that cooperatives are making efforts to be accessible to all income levels, even though the poorest micro-entrepreneurs remained totally excluded from both formal and informal financial markets.

It appeared also that the majority of micro-entrepreneurs used informal and formal microfinance mainly for saving purposes. Exclusive borrowing was quite rare. This clearly suggests that micro-entrepreneurs' saving capacity should not be downplayed. The *poor can and do save*. Thus, formal microfinancial providers would be well advised to design savings products adapted to the needs of these micro-entrepreneurs. Another striking finding is that most of the micro-entrepreneurs who saved through a bank and/or a cooperative account also kept savings in an informal finance institution. This shows that participation in informal finance is not necessarily triggered by the lack of access to the formal financial market. Rather, a significant number of micro-entrepreneurs reported resorting to informal finance in order to enhance their savings discipline and/or their social ties while maintaining a formal account in the hope of eventually securing a formal loan.

Finally, our survey revealed that the financial resources mobilized through formal credit were essentially used for commercial expenditures, while informal financial resources were used to meet both commercial and non-commercial needs—with the exception of suppliers' credit which was used exclusively for commercial purposes. This specialization reveals that formal credits available to micro-entrepreneurs are essentially business oriented.

References

Ardener, S. (1964). 'The Comparative Study of Rotating Credit Associations'. *Journal of the Royal Anthropological Institute of Great Britain And Ireland*, 94(2): 202–29.

Baland, J.-M. and A. Siwan (2002). 'The Economics of Roscas and Intrahousehold Allocation'. *Quarterly Journal of Economics*, 117(3): 983–95.

Barham, B., S. Boucher, and M. Carter (1996). 'Credit Constraints, Credit Unions, and Small Scale Producers in Guatemala'. *World Development*, 24(5): 792–805.

Benzecri, J. P. (1973). *L'Analyse des données: L'Analyses des correspondences*. Paris: Dunod.

—— (1978). 'Sur L'analyse des tableaux binaires associes à une correspondance multiple'. *Cahiers de l'Analyse Des Donnees*, 2: 55–71.

Boucher, S., M. Carter, and C. Guirkinger (2008). 'Risk Rationing and Wealth Effects in Credit Markets: Theory and Implications for Agricultural Development'. *American Journal of Agricultural Economics*, 90(2): 409–23.

Boucher, S. and C. Guirkinger (2007). 'Risk, Wealth, and Sectoral Choice in Rural Credit Markets'. *American Journal of Agricultural Economics*, 89(4), November: 991–1004.

Chung, I. (1995). 'Market Choice and Effective Demand for Credit: The Roles of Borrower Transaction Costs and Rationing Constraints'. *Journal of Economic Development*, 20(2): 23–44.

Ciampi, A., A. M. Gonzalez, and M. L. Castejón (2005). Correspondence Analysis and Two-Way Clustering'. *SORT*, 1: 27–42.

Collins, D., J. Morduch, S. Rutherford, and O. Ruthven (2009). *Portfolios of the Poor*. Princeton, NJ: Princeton University Press.

Emily, C.-W. (2002). 'Saving and Accumulation Strategies of Urban Market Women in Harare, Zimbabwe'. *Economic Development and Cultural Change*, 50(4), July: 979–1005.

Frederick, S., G. Loewenstein, and T. O'Donoghue (2002). 'Time Discounting and Time Preference: A Critical Review'. *Journal of Economic Literature*, 40(2): 351–401.

Greenacre, M. (2007). *Correspondence Analysis in Practice*. (Second edition). London: Chapman & Hall/CRC Press.

Guérin, I., R. Venkatasubramanian, and O. Héliès (2009). 'Microfinance, endettement et surendettement'. *Revue Tiers Monde*, 197: 131–46.

Guérin, I., S. Morvant-Roux, and J. M. Servet (2011). 'Understanding the Diversity and Complexity of Demand for Microfinance Services: Lessons from Informal Finance', in B. Armendáriz and M. Labie (eds.), *The Handbook of Microfinance*. Singapore: World Scientific Publishing Company: 101–22.

Gugerty, M. K. (2007). 'You Can't Save Alone: Commitment and Rotating Savings and Credit Associations in Kenya'. *Economic Development and Cultural Change*, 55(2), January: 251–82.

Guirkinger, C. (2008). 'Understanding the Coexistence of Formal and Informal Credit Markets in Piura, Peru'. *World Development*, 36(8): 1436–52.

Hoff, K. and J. Stiglitz (1990).'Imperfect Information and Rural Credit Markets: Puzzles and Policy Perspectives'. *World Bank Economic Review*, 5: 235–50.

—— (1993). 'A Theory of Imperfect Competition in Rural Credit Markets in Developing Countries: Towards a Theory of Segmented Credit Markets'. *IRIS Working Paper Series*, 58: 1–52.

Hogarth, M. J., and E. C. Anguelov (2003). 'Can the Poor Save?'. *Financial Counseling and Planning*, 14(1): 1–18.

INSD (2008). *Le Burkina en Chiffres*. Ouagadougou: Ministry Of Economy And Finance.

Karlan D. (2010). 'Helping the Poor Save More'. *Stanford Social Innovation Review, Winter*: 48–54.

Lebart, L., A. Morineau, and M. W. Kenneth (1984). *Multivariate Descriptive Statistical Analysis: Correspondence Analysis and Related Techniques for Large Matrices.* New York: John Wiley & Sons.

Mckinnon, R. I. (1973). *Money and Capital in Economic Development.* Washington, DC: Brookings Institution.

Morvant–Roux, S. (2009). 'Access to Microcredit and Continuity of Indebtedness Dynamics in Rural Mexico: Combining Anthropology with Econometrics'. *Rume Working Paper*, 3.

Řezanková, H. (2009). 'Cluster Analysis and Categorical Data'. *Statistica* 89: 216–32.

Shaohua, C., and M. Ravallion (2010). 'The Developing World is Poorer than We Thought, But No Less Successful in the Fight Against Poverty'. *The Quarterly Journal Of Economics*, 125(4), November: 1577–1625.

Shaw, E. (1973). *Financial Deepening in Economic Development.* New York: Oxford University Press.

Siniscalco, M. T. and N. Auriat, (2005). 'Questionnaire Design'. Module 8, *Quantitative Research Methods in Educational Planning.* IIEP Training Materials. Paris: International Institute For Educational Planning/UNESCO.

Stiglitz, J. and A. Weiss (1981). 'Credit Rationing in Markets with Imperfect Information'. *American Economic Review*, 71(3): 393–410.

Van Wijnbergen, S. (1983). 'Credit Policy, Inflation and Growth in a Financially Repressed Economy'. *Journal of Development Economics*, 13(1), August-October: 45–65.

10

Exploring the Black-Box of Economic Informality: Social Networks and Institutional Change among Micro and Small Enterprises in Nairobi, Kenya

Edoardo Totolo

10.1 Introduction

The need to understand how the informal sector works has become evident in development studies. Since the concept was introduced in the 1970s, several authors have focused on the heterogeneity of economic operators in this sector in terms of size, types of firms, and areas of operation (e.g. Chen, 2006; Carr and Chen, 2002); others have focused on the relationship of informal operators with the regulatory framework and the tax system, and the barriers to their formalization (e.g. De Soto, 1989, 2000; Feige, 1990; Loayza, 1994; Loayza et al, 2006; Djankov et al., 2002, Djankov et al., 2003; Kenyon, 2007; Dessy and Pallage, 2003). However, there is still little knowledge about the institutional dynamics of entrepreneurship occurring *within the boundaries of informality*. The informal enterprise is still treated as a black box: most practices and governance mechanisms that operate outside the framework of the State and in an informal context tend to be ignored.

There is no single, agreed definition of the informal sector, but it is generally understood to be the part of the economy that operates partly or completely outside the reach of official governance (Guha-Khasnobis et al., 2006). This definition, although analytically correct, has the shortcoming of stressing only the passive attribute of economic informality: indicating what the informal sector is not (Meagher, 2010). The view of informal firms as 'untaxed, unlicensed and unregulated' (Tripp, 2001: 2), or as activities 'unregulated by the institutions of society in a legal and social environment in which similar activities are regulated' (Castells and Portes, 1989: 12), associates informality with non-compliance with state requirements. This association, however, has caused a large strand of literature to implicitly or explicitly portray the informal sector as a confused environment, characterized by an absence of regulation, and to use terms such as 'unorganized sector' to define local economies (Guha-Khasnobis et al., 2006). Yet the informal sector now provides over 70 per cent of non-agricultural employment in sub-Saharan Africa (ILO, 2002). It has become clear that informal forms of governance and organization are central to local economies, as supplements or even as substitutes for formal institutions and regulations (Dixit, 2004; Guha-Khasnobis et al., 2006; Hart, 2006; Meagher, 2005, 2006, 2007, and 2010; Sindzingre, 2006; Portes, 1994).

Today, studies on the informal sector analyse it from a completely different angle based on new concepts, such as networks and institutions, emanating from different fields in the social science. As Meagher (2005: 217) notes: 'Many leading commentators on the informal economy have abandoned the informality paradigm in favour of a focus on the organizational role of social networks... Rather than representing economic informality in terms of an absence of regulation, social networks portray the informal economy as alternative forms of regulation operating outside the framework of the state.' The basic assumption of this new wave of research is that while formal enterprises can engage with the formal institutional context for sustaining their activity (for example, engaging with the local government for entering the market, with banks for credit, with legal courts for contract enforcement, and with public or private insurance in case of injury or sickness), most informal operators have to cope with partial or complete exclusion from these formal institutions. However, instead of being passive subjects of this exclusion, informal operators rely on a wide variety of institutions and organizational forms based on social ties such as kinship, friendship, ethnicity, or even location and sector, which replace or supplement formal regulatory and institutional structures.

In line with this new conceptualization of economic informality, the objective of this chapter is both theoretical and empirical. The first part reviews the recent theoretical efforts of economists and social scientists to study informal markets through the lenses of institutional economics and social network analysis. It discusses the numerous definitional challenges emerging from the literature and the attempts to apply these concepts in the context of developing countries, particularly countries in Africa. The second part discusses the preliminary findings of field research conducted in a low-income neighbourhood on the outskirts of Nairobi, Kenya. Compared with the theoretical chapter, the empirical section focuses specifically on the financial dimension of informality. It analyses the range of formal and informal financial instruments used by entrepreneurs to support their market activity. In particular, it assesses how these instruments change depending on gender and the degree of informality of firms.

10.2 Capturing the Inner Logic of Economic Informality: Towards a New Conceptual Framework

10.2.1 Institutions and Organizations, Formality and Informality

How does institutional economics contribute to our understanding of enterprise dynamics in the informal economy? Surprisingly, this question has seldom been discussed in the literature, and there is considerable need for improving the analysis of institutional arrangements in the informal economy. Institutional economics has sought mainly to understand the 'external relations' of informal firms with the formal sector and the formal regulatory environment (Feige, 1990), but it has seldom examined the micro level to understand how informal and semi-formal entrepreneurs actually manage their firms. In his study on market institutions in Africa, Fafchamps (2004: 4) made this point rather eloquently: 'We know little about how [African] markets operate in practice. Perhaps the best measure of this lack of knowledge is our propensity to call "informal" everything that is not of Western inspiration. The truth is that market activity is not without form; it is only without economic formalization.'

The best starting point is, arguably, the seminal work in institutional economics by North (1990, 2005), and in particular the two distinctions on which he has based his work. The first is between *formal* and *informal* institutions. He defines formal institutions as 'humanly devised constraints that shape human interactions' (North, 1990: 1) such as laws, regulations, and the formal legal systems. Informal institutions are characterized as 'extensions, elaborations, modifications of formal rules', 'socially sanctioned norms of behaviour', and 'internally enforced standards of conduct' (1990: 40). These can be norms, taboos, customs, and codes of conduct or other types of unwritten rules. According to North, both formal and informal institutions are used to reduce the uncertainty of human interactions. However, whereas formal institutions are 'designed' and enforced through the legal system, informal institutions tend to emerge spontaneously, to be unwritten and enforced through social sanctions. The second distinction at the core of North's analysis is between *institutions* and *organizations*. He argues that institutions can be considered the 'rules of the game', and should be distinguished from organizations that are the 'players of the game': 'Conceptually, what must be clearly differentiated are the rules from the players. The purpose of the rules is to define the way the game is played. But the objective of the team within that set of rules is to win the game' (1990: 5). He suggests that studying the 'players of the game' implies focusing on governance, internal structures, and conflicts within organizations, but he is interested in institutional change at the 'macro level', which can be studied only by analysing institutions, not organizations.[1]

However, this distinction is criticized by Hodgson (2006: 8), who interprets an organization, not as a different entity, but as a *special kind of institution* that has the additional features of (i) having specific criteria to establish who is a member and who is not, (ii) specifying the principles of sovereignty concerning who is in charge, and (iii) determining the responsibilities and tasks within the organization. In addition, Hodgson (2006) criticizes North's analysis of formal and informal institutions, and in particular the association of formality with *'legal'* and informality with *'illegal'*, which neglects the difference between rules *against the law* and rules that are simply *not expressed by the law*. He also questions the use of *'explicit'* versus *'tacit'*, and *'designed'* versus *'spontaneous'* as proxies for the formal/informal duality. He therefore reaches the conclusion that the term 'informal' in the context of institutional analysis 'should either be abandoned or used with extreme care: it may be best to use more precise terms, such as legal, non-legal, and explicit instead' (2006: 13).

Similary, Sindzingre (2006) argues that the array of notions gathered under the conceptual umbrella of informality is too diverse to be used in different contexts, and that it is more useful to focus on aspects such as the credibility and enforceability of institutions and contracts rather than on their formal or informal status. Furthermore, she stresses the importance of the cognitive foundation of institutions: 'State rules and institutions may be less credible in certain developing countries than local institutions (e.g. social insurance networks). When individuals are exposed to competing norms ("modern" and "traditional"), tradeoffs are determined more by the relevance and credibility of the norms, and hence by historical and cognitive path dependence' (Sindzingre, 2006: 67).

In the context of economic informality, the difference between 'social networks' and 'informal institutions' may be considered an informal parallel to the distinction between 'organizations' and 'institutions': the first focuses on the players and their interrelationships, and the second on the rules and functioning mechanisms of the 'game'. For example, with regard to rotating savings and credit associations (ROSCAs), discussed in greater detail in the second part of this chapter, the notion of social network refers to the social ties among members and whether they are based on ethnicity, family, friendship, or sector of operation. Institutions, on the other hand, refer to how these groups function: for example, whether they provide lump sums or loans, the rules for entry and exit from the groups, and their behaviour in case of

[1] This argument was exposed in personal correspondence with Geoffrey Hodgson, which was published in Hodgson (2006, appendix 1).

insolvency of the borrowers. However, at the higher level of abstraction, the question remains unsolved as to whether social networks can be considered synonymous with informal institutions or whether they are a special type or a separate conceptual entity from those institutions. Within the literature on the informal sector, this distinction is not developed. It seems that scholars with a sociological and anthropological background tend to favour the use of the term 'social network', whereas institutional and neoclassical economists appear to favour the term 'informal institutions'; but the two are not clearly distinguished and are often used interchangeably.

10.2.2 Social Networks: 'Infrastructures' for the Informal Economy

Despite some definitional challenges, over the past few years the concept of social network has been widely used in the literature on the informal sector, to the point of being portrayed as an alternative paradigm to that of economic informality in the analysis of local markets. According to this view, the State is only one of the 'candidates' in providing a framework of regulation and organization, whereas social networks, loosely defined as any kind of 'organizational ties', provide the basic institutional infrastructure for markets operating beyond the reach of the State.

One of the early advocates of this approach was Alejandro Portes (1994), who studied the dynamics of informal entrepreneurship among migrant communities in the United States and shed light on the incapacity of neoclassical economic theory to explain the nature of these markets. During the 1980s, and especially after studies by de Soto (1989), the informal sector was often considered to be an expression of the 'true market' free from government interference. In this context Portes (1994: 430) identified the 'first paradox' of the informal economy: 'the more [the informal sector] approaches the model of the true market, the more it is dependent on social ties for its effective functioning'. The idea is that, instead of being driven by pure market forces, higher degrees of informality, and the consequent greater detachment from formal institutions, result in a stronger dependence on social networks. This view led to different policy recommendations from those of neoclassical economists. Whereas de Soto (1989) proposed deregulation and a reduction of state presence in the economy, Portes (1994: 433) argued that 'capitalist markets are not spontaneous economic phenomena but deliberately structured and regulated institutions. The way to... avoid the chaos of the uncontrolled market is to implement detailed regulations and have them enforced by a competent bureaucracy immune to profit taking.'

Over the past few years, Meagher (2005, 2007, and 2010) has provided the most extensive account of the role of networks in African informal economies. She was the first to recognize a 'shift of paradigm' in the literature, from the concept of informality to one of social networks (Meagher, 2005). Her studies on shoe and garment clusters in Nigeria showed that in a context of widespread informality and state neglect, local cultural institutions substituted for formal institutions. They provided an organizational infrastructure for numerous aspects of the entrepreneurial activity, including entry into the market, training and skills development, distribution of goods, and access to labour and credit (Meagher, 2007 and 2010). Even more importantly, Meagher (2005) argued that, contrary to conventional assumptions about African economies, networks among entrepreneurs in Nigeria 'provided a basis for the development of market-oriented rather than redistributive institutions, ethnic integration rather than conflict, and organizational change rather than traditional immutability'. In her most recent work, Meagher (2010) identifies at least six types of networks that are relevant to entrepreneurial activities: entry networks, apprenticeship networks, production networks, subcontracting networks, supply networks, and marketing networks. She views them as playing a positive role in development, especially when considering their historical role in colonial and pre-colonial periods. However, IMF-led liberalization policies in the 1990s caused African countries to open up to Asian imports of manufactured goods, which put pressure on African clusters whose networks failed to promote innovation and economic growth.

10.2.3 Narrowing the Focus: Financial Dimension of Economic Informality in the Kenyan Context

Social networks and informal institutions shape the manner in which businesses function in a variety of ways. They play a key role in non-state forms of regulation and enforcement of contracts (Fafchamps, 2004; Harriss-White, 2010; Meagher, 2005, 2010; Roitman, 2005; Laurenço-Lindell, 2002); they contribute to entrepreneurs' welfare with mutual insurance and risk mitigation (Kinyanjui, 2010 and 2012; Gugerty, 2007; Johnson, 2004; Bhattamishra and Barrett, 2010; Barr, 1998); and they provide financial services in contexts of partial or complete exclusion from the formal banking system (Johnson, 2004; Collins et al., 2009). The remainder of this chapter focuses exclusively on the latter dimension.

The nature of financial landscapes in contexts of informality and marginalization is often assumed to be simple and of little interest to economists and social scientists. The tendency is to stress the issue as 'exclusion' from formal banks and welfare institutions rather than as alternative mechanisms used by entrepreneurs. However, recent research has provided a relevant contribution to this field. In particular, Collins et al. (2009) show that, contrary to popular belief, households living in extreme poverty in Bangladesh, India, and South Africa do not live 'hand to mouth'; rather, they tend to use a complex combination of financial instruments, relying on social networks and non-formal institutions to manage their resources. However Collins et al. focus on the household level—not on the enterprise level. Although their research shows interesting examples of the role of self-employment and small businesses in the economics of the household, the focus is not on the firm itself, and therefore lacks comprehensive analysis of non-formal institutions in enterprise financing, investment, and start-up capital, among other issues. Moreover, their sample is confined to the 'extremely poor', living on less than two dollars a day. Although poverty is widespread in low-income areas and markets, numerous owners of small and medium-sized enterprises (SMEs) are not necessarily trapped in extreme poverty, and therefore they are likely to use financial instruments offered by a combination of formal and informal providers.

The financial landscape is certainly very diversified in a low-income market like Kenya, where strong traditional institutions and social structures coexist with one of the most developed financial sectors in sub-Saharan Africa as well as with booming mobile banking technologies.[2] The reality revealed in recent literature is that, instead of *lacking* access to financial services, small businesses and households are able to *choose* among a plethora of (mostly unconventional) instruments, both formal and informal, market and non-market, according to their needs and opportunities. The term 'unbanked' is inappropriate for a dynamic economic environment like urban Kenya where most entrepreneurs use a combination of formal and informal financial institutions in different aspects of management of their business.

Previous studies conducted by Malkamäki et al. (2009), Johnson et al. (2012), Johnson (2004) and Atieno (2001) show that financial landscapes are extremely complex, and that households and firms use at least eight types of financial institutions and instruments. Formal financial providers include commercial banks, microfinance institutions (MFIs), and savings and credit cooperatives (SACCOs). The informal and semi-formal side of the financial landscape is more complex. It includes rotating savings and credit associations (ROSCAs), also known in Kenya as 'merry-go-rounds', and accumulating savings and credit associations (ASCAs). ROSCAs and ASCAs are similar types of organizations which are voluntary and independent, where members meet regularly (usually weekly or monthly) and put their savings in a common 'pot'. The main difference is that ROSCAs give out the contents of the pot immediately to one of the members on a rotating basis, whereas ASCAs do not give the funds immediately, but lend them to members and charge interest. The interest paid on loans accumulates in the group fund

[2] Over the past few years, a new mobile banking technology called M-PESA has begun to flourish throughout Kenya. For more information on the use of mobile banking in the Kenyan low-income markets, see Jack and Suri (2011).

and the dividends are distributed periodically to the members, usually at the end of the year (Malkamäki et al., 2009). The third type of financial institution/instrument is a *savings club,* where members contribute their savings for a predetermined period of time on a voluntary basis. These groups are often perceived as safer than saving at home and less expensive than opening a bank account. Another common type of financial network is a *welfare association,* which, unlike an ASCA and ROSCA, provides support only in cases of emergencies, usually for hospitalization or funerals. Some welfare associations also provide support for marriages and births, and are usually organized along family or ethnic lines. Finally, another common kind of network is the *investment club,* formed for the sole purpose of investing in profit-making activities or buying productive assets.

The empirical section of this chapter borrows largely from the classifications described above, except for two aspects. First, it does not include data on SACCOs, because they were not common in the area selected for the case study. Second, it adds a new typology of informal group called 'mixed financial networks' (MFNs), which are groups that combine the mechanisms of ASCAs, ROSCAs, and welfare associations. For example, a group collected a total of 12,000 Kenyan shillings (KSh) every month, of which 5,000 KSh were distributed immediately to one of the members on a rotation basis (as in ROSCAs), another 5,000 KSh were available to be taken on loan with interest (as in ASCAs) and 2,000 KSh were kept in a bank account and used only in case of emergencies (as in welfare associations).

A similar classification was used in a recent household survey conducted by Johnson et al. (2012) in three small towns in Kenya (Karatina, Nyamira, and Kitui). The sample of households selected in their study made relatively greater use of bank accounts (36 per cent), followed by welfare groups (34 per cent) and mixed financial networks (28 per cent), whereas there was a low participation in MFIs (only 5 per cent of the sample) (Table 10.1). This reveals

Table 10.1 Use of formal and informal financial instruments by households in three small urban centres (per cent)

	%
Banks	36
MFIs	5
SACCOs	23
Welfare groups	34
ROSCAs	24
ASCAs	15
Mixed financial networks	28

Source: Adapted from Johnson et al. (2012).

a low penetration of the microfinance industry in the selected locations. The survey also found that 23 per cent of the sample used only formal financial services, 25 per cent only informal ones, and approximately 27 per cent were excluded from both (Johnson et al., 2012: 9). It is important to note, however, that both the research context (small towns) and unit of analysis (households) differed from the ones employed in our study, which focused on entrepreneurs living and operating on the outskirts of Nairobi. However, the comparison helps to build a more thorough picture of the Kenyan financial landscape and helps assess the diverse financial needs of the Kenyan population.

10.3 The Financial Landscape of Small Enterprises in Nairobi: Results of the Empirical Investigation

10.3.1 Beyond the Informal–Formal Dichotomy: Identifying Degrees of Informality of Firms

The empirical analysis described in this section is based on 185 questionnaires and a series of qualitative interviews conducted with entrepreneurs and key informants in Kariobangi—a low-income neighbourhood about ten kilometres north-east of Nairobi—between August and December 2011. The area is characterized by a thriving semi-formal and informal economy, and a diverse population of micro- and small enterprises concentrated in a relatively small area. Three specific research areas were selected to ensure the sample was representative of the variety of businesses operating in the region. One is known as Kariobangi Light Industries, which is a manufacturing cluster with an estimated population of 300 enterprises (Sonobe et al., 2011) specializing in a variety of activities, including woodwork, metalwork, car repair, hardware retail, and paint manufacturing among others. The second research location is a tailoring cluster known as Kariobangi Market, which contains about 600 micro-enterprises involved in tailoring, dress-making, embroidery, and retail of tailoring products and equipment.[3] Finally, Korogocho Market is a street market specializing in the sale of vegetables and second-hand clothes. The sample was almost equally divided across the three research locations.[4]

[3] The area also has a considerable number of hairdressers and beauty salons serving mostly, but not only, the women working in the market. Some of these businesses were included in the sample.

[4] In the survey, sixty-six questionnaires were collected in Kariobangi Market, sixty-one in the Light Industries, and fifty-eight in Korogocho. Roughly two-thirds of respondents in Kariobangi Market and three-quarters in Korogocho were women. The sample in the Kariobangi Light Industries was almost exclusively composed of male respondents. Conversations with local authorities confirmed that these proportions were approximately in line with the wider populations of business owners in the areas, though there has been no official census.

The striking feature of Kariobangi is that, although the three productive areas are located in close proximity to one another, enterprises can easily be categorized into different degrees of informality, depending on the extent of their compliance with government regulations and their location of operation. The classification used in this study is based on whether entrepreneurs had (i) registered their business name with the Attorney General's office, (ii) obtained a single business permit from the city council, (iii) registered with the Kenya Revenue Authority for tax purposes, (iv) provided written contracts to their workers, and (v) operated from an authorized location or in a public space (e.g. on the side of the road). By taking this approach, we noticed that virtually all enterprises in Korogocho were completely informal: businesses did not comply with the licensing, registration, and tax requirements, and all of them operated in shacks on the side of the road. Businesses in the Kariobangi Market, on the other hand, complied with the licensing requirements and operated in spaces authorized by the city council. All entrepreneurs in the sample were required to obtain a special type of permit designed by the government for informal enterprises, which allows firms *not to* register their name at the Attorney General's office.[5] Finally, manufacturing firms in the Kariobangi Light Industries showed, on average, the highest degree of formality in the sample, as the majority of them complied with both the licensing and registration requirements, but only a few paid taxes or complied with labour laws.[6] The relevant characteristics of the sample are shown in Table 10.2.

This context provides an ideal setting for studying the diversity of institutional and social network dynamics among businesses with different degrees of informality. The case study also enables an understanding of whether the reality on the ground supports or contradicts the argument that social ties gain importance as businesses become more 'informal', as stated in the aforementioned 'first paradox' of the informal economy (Portes, 1994). The next section provides evidence of the differences between men and women and the instruments used in the start-up phase of the businesses.

[5] In order to obtain a business permit, firms are normally required to register their business name. For more information see Devas and Kelly (2001) and Abuodha and Bowles (2000).

[6] Compared with Korogocho and Kariobangi Markets, where the large majority of businesses were very similar in terms of regulatory compliance, among those in the Light Industries there was greater variability. Some businesses in the latter were almost 'completely formal', while others only complied with the licensing requirements. However, on average, the degree of compliance among businesses in the Light Industries tended to be higher than in the other two locations.

Table 10.2 Characteristics of the three research locations

Location	Degree of informality	Average no. of employees	Average age of entrepreneurs	Average years of education	% of women in the sample
Korogocho Market	High	0.3	41.1	7.8	61
Kariobangi Market	Intermediate	2.7	41.6	10.1	68
Kariobangi Light Industries	Low/ intermediate	4.1	42.3	11.2	12

Source: Author's fieldwork.

10.3.2 Use of Informal Financial Networks among Entrepreneurs in Kariobangi

Which financial instruments do entrepreneurs use in the management of their businesses? Are there differences between businesses with different degrees of informality? Does gender play a role? This section seeks to address these questions.

Capturing the 'inner logics' of economic informality implies asking several questions about the management of firms, including how entrepreneurs accumulate their start-up capital, and how they finance investments and manage cash flows. However, only some of these are addressed in this study. This section looks, in particular, at the different patterns of utilization of informal financial networks in the three research locations, depending on the degrees of informality of the firms.

Only 20 per cent of the sample in our research study did not belong to any financial group, whereas 80 per cent belonged to one or more groups (Figure 10.1),[7] which confirms the important role played by informal financial instruments in the local economy. However, the differences within the sample are noteworthy. Enterprises in Kariobangi Light Industries, which are characterized by lower degrees of informality, appeared to make the least use of informal financial institutions: over 34 per cent in our survey did not participate in any such institutions, whereas in Korogocho, where businesses are highly informal, the proportion was only 9 per cent. Respondents who did not participate in networks can be grouped into two types. First were the 'network sceptics' who tended to distrust groups because of the risk of fraudulent behaviour. Some also rejected groups because they considered them as being for women, stressing the gender connotation traditionally attributed to groups. Second, there were entrepreneurs who were simply constrained by a lack of resources, either because they were new in the market and still had

[7] This result is only moderately different from that of the Johnson et al. (2012) study. In that study, 27 per cent of the sample was observed as not belonging to any financial group.

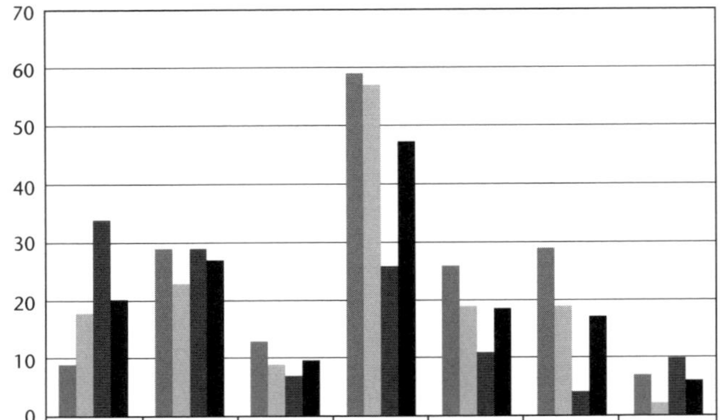

	No Group	Welfare Groups	Savings Clubs	ROSCAs	ASCAs	Mixed Financial Service	Investment Groups
Korogocho Market (%)	9	29	13	59	26	29	7
Kariobangi Market (%)	18	23	9	57	19	19	2
Kariobangi Light Industries (%)	34	29	7	26	11	4	10
Total (%)	20	27	10	47	19	17	6

Figure 10.1 Entrepreneurs' use of informal financial networks

low earnings, or because they were experiencing difficulties and were unable to pay the regular contributions to the groups.

Participation in savings clubs, ROSCAs, ASCAs, and MSNs follows a similar pattern: the higher the degree of informality, the higher the participation in these informal networks. In particular, the survey revealed a very high use of ROSCAs in Korogocho (59 per cent) and in Kariobangi Market (57 per cent)—more than double that of the Light Industries (26 per cent) (Figure 10.1). There was also a relatively high use of ASCAs and mixed financial services in Korogocho compared with the other two locations.

Entrepreneurs in the Light Industries appeared to have a preference for welfare groups (29 per cent), which can be categorized into two main types. The first resembles formal insurance products: contributions are made on a regular basis (usually monthly) to a trusted group representative, and the amount is kept in a shared bank account or by the group's treasurer. Members of the group can ask for money only in specific circumstances as specified in the group's constitution, usually for hospitalization or funerals, but smaller groups tend to be more flexible and will consider other emergencies as well. The second type of insurance group is both simpler and more common—a family network or a clan-based insurance group[8] which works on an irregular basis. When emergencies occur, entrepreneurs can rely on these networks for help (often with

[8] This terminology is borrowed from Johnson (2004).

the mediation of network elders), but the amounts received are uncertain and depend on the capacity of members to help during the specific period. In addition to welfare groups, entrepreneurs in the Light Industries reported having a relatively greater preference for investment clubs (10 per cent) compared with those in the other two locations. Investment clubs normally invest in land or other productive activities, while some are active also in the stock market.[9]

It is also relevant to look at how women and men differ in their utilization of financial instruments. Women were observed to make considerably greater use of networks such as ROSCAs, ASCAs, and mixed financial services (58, 23, and 24 per cent respectively), while men seemed to participate more in welfare groups, savings clubs, and investment clubs (29, 13, and 9 per cent respectively) (Table 10.3). In terms of annual contributions, ROSCAs collect the highest average amount of savings (over 54,000 KSh), followed by savings clubs (over 52,000 KSh), and mixed financial groups (over 30,000 KSh). Men pay larger sums to savings clubs, welfare groups, and investment clubs, whereas women pay more to ROSCAs, ASCAs, and mixed financial services.[10] These dynamics can arguably be explained by the traditional role of women and men in the management of household finances: women are generally responsible for the day-to-day expenses, and men for larger (but less frequent) expenses (Collins et al., 2009). Although there are enormous differences between groups, normally savings clubs and insurance groups distribute money less frequently but in larger amounts, whereas ASCAs and ROSCAs tend to distribute smaller sums more frequently.

The survey results seem to show that informal networks play a prominent role in supporting enterprises that are already in business. Are they equally important during the start-up phase and for the accumulation of initial capital? We asked entrepreneurs to indicate the main sources of funding during the initial phase of setting up their enterprise.[11] Figure 10.2 shows that informal networks play a relatively less important role than entrepreneur's own savings and loans from family or friends. Men reported relying more on their own savings (usually accumulated during previous jobs or from other businesses), and about a third of them said they had borrowed money from family or friends.[12] Women, on the other, hand reported making greater use of both informal networks and loans (or grants) from family or friends.

[9] In the period between 2006 and 2010 there were several highly oversubscribed initial public offerings (IPOs) at the Nairobi Stock Exchange (NSE), which also attracted sections of Kenya's low-income population. For a socio-economic analysis of this, see Yenkey (2010).

[10] The average values for some types of networks, such as savings and investment clubs, should be viewed with caution because they are based on relatively small samples (eleven for investment clubs and eighteen for savings clubs).

[11] Multiple answers were allowed.

[12] In many cases, the funds were received as grants rather than loans. When they were loans, creditors rarely charged interest.

Table 10.3 Participation of men and women in different types of financial networks and average yearly contributions

	Savings clubs	Welfare groups	ROSCAs	ASCAs	Mixed financial services	Investment clubs
Percentage of total sample participating in the network	10	27	47	19	19	6
Average yearly contribution (KSh)	52,548	11,341	54,459	27,691	30,803	19,019
Percentage of men participating in the network	13	29	35	14	13	9
Men's average yearly contribution (KSh)	58,732	14,360	43,791	25,356	30,128	19,444
Percentage of women participating in the network	8	25	58	23	24	4
Women's average yearly contribution (KSh)	42,500	8,552	60,896	29,113	31,164	15,200

Note: 100 KSh = 0.9 euro.
Source: Author's fieldwork.

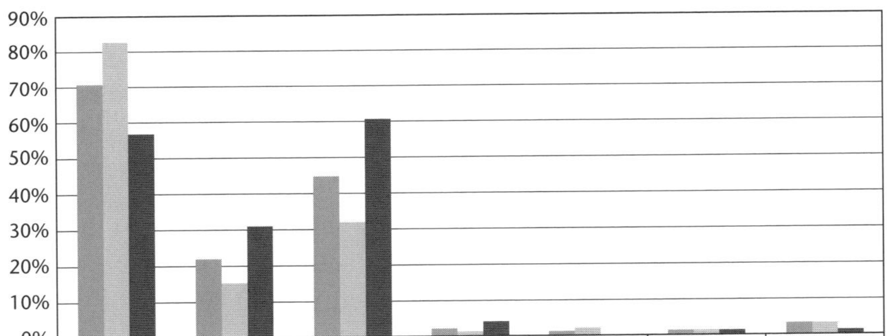

	Own Savings	Informal networks	Family/ friends	MFI	Commercial Bank	SACCOs	Inherited the Business
Total	71%	22%	45%	2%	1%	1%	3%
Men	83%	15%	32%	1%	2%	1%	3%
Women	57%	31%	61%	4%	0%	1%	1%

Figure 10.2 Sources of start-up capital (per cent)

10.3.3 Use of Formal Financial Services in Kariobangi: Banks and MFIs

The data show that the pattern of use of commercial banks is the opposite of the one described for informal networks. Banks are used more by businesses that are characterized by a higher degree of formality (i.e. Light Industries) than by informal businesses (i.e. Korogocho), and the more formal businesses have better access to bank credits. Nevertheless, contrary to popular assumption, bank accounts are surprisingly popular among both women and informal enterprises. The situation is different with regard to MFIs, where the extent of use depends more on gender than on the degree of informality.

Although more than forty commercial banks are licensed to operate in Kenya,[13] respondents in Kariobangi reported using only a few of them. Of the total respondents, 55 per cent with an active bank account reported using Equity Bank as their primary financial provider, 22 per cent used Cooperative Bank, 10 per cent Kenya Commercial Bank, and the remaining used either Family Bank, Barclays Bank, or Postbank. The high percentage of respondents with an active bank account reported in Table 10.4 is partly due to the success of Equity Bank over the past few years in targeting 'ordinary Kenyans' and extending its reach to low-income populations.

Of all the respondents, 77 per cent reported that they currently had access to an active bank account (though the proportion was considerably lower in the Korogocho area) and 14 per cent 'used to have' an account (27 in Korogocho) (Table 10.4). This usually refers to 'dormant' bank accounts that have not been used for more than twelve months. The proportion of respondents who obtained a loan from a commercial bank was relatively high as well: 8 per cent of all respondents reported currently having a loan (which they were still repaying at the time of the interview) and 10 per cent had taken a loan in the past.

In terms of gender differences, a larger percentage of women than men reported currently having access to a bank account (82 per cent of women compared with 79 per cent of men), and had access (either currently or in the past) to a business loan (21 per cent of women compared with 17 per cent) (Table 10.5). However, the size of loans was much higher for men. Bank loans received over the twelve months prior to the interview were twice as large for men as for women (over 208,000 KSh for men and only 83,000 KSh for women).[14]

[13] Central Bank of Kenya (2013).

[14] The result is also consistent for different time periods. Even though the proportions differ depending on the time frame under consideration, men received larger loans, on average. This was also the case in the two-year period, 2010–11, and if we were to consider all business loans ever received from respondents since they started their business.

Table 10.4 Accounts and loans from commercial banks, by location

	Account at a commercial bank (per cent)				Business loans from a commercial bank (per cent)			
	Korogocho	Kariobangi Market	Light Industries	Total	Korogocho	Kariobangi Market	Light Industries	Total
Currently have	57	90	84	77	2	10	12	8
Used to have	27	4	11	14	7	11	12	10
Never had	16	6	5	9	91	79	76	82
Total	100	100	100	100	100	100	100	100

Note: The table only indicates business loans, not loans for personal use (e.g. building a house, paying tuition fees) because the focus of this study is specifically on business dynamics.
Source: Author's fieldwork.

Table 10.5 Accounts and loans from commercial banks, by gender

	Account at a commercial bank (per cent)			Loan from a commercial bank (per cent)		
%	Men	Women	Total	Men	Women	Total
Currently have	79	82	81	7	10	8
Used to have	14	8	11	9	11	10
Never had	7	10	8	84	79	82
Total	100	100	100	100	100	100

Note: The table does not include loans received for personal use.
Source: Author's fieldwork.

The situation is different with regard to the use of MFIs. A total of 14 per cent of the sample was observed to be using microfinance services and 9 per cent were paying off their loan.[15] The striking feature in Table 10.6 is the high use of MFI services in Kariobangi Market and their low use among respondents in the Light Industries (which instead had the highest percentage of loans from commercial banks). However, explaining these results only in terms of a 'sector preference' for MFIs would not be adequate without taking into consideration the gender differences between the two clusters. As mentioned earlier, two-thirds of business owners in Kariobangi Market are women, whereas the Light Industry businesses have

[15] Some respondents had accounts with microfinance institutions because they were interested in savings products rather than loans.

Table 10.6 Use of MFI accounts and loans, by research location

	Account in an MFI (per cent)				Business loan from an MFI (per cent)			
	Korogocho	Kariobangi Market	Light Industries	Total	Korogocho	Kariobangi Market	Light Industries	Total
Currently have	9	28	5	14	5	18	4	9
Used to have	30	22	14	22	29	16	12	19
Never had	61	50	81	64	66	66	84	72
Total	100	100	100	100	100	100	100	100

Source: Author's fieldwork.

a large majority of men. Even though many MFIs have recently increased their services to men, the majority of their clients traditionally have been women. In fact, women constituted 78 per cent of the respondents currently servicing an MFI loan.

The other interesting result in Table 10.6 is the high percentage of respondents (30 per cent) in Korogocho who reported using MFIs in the past but eventually stopped using them. This confirms a growing hostility towards MFIs that was noticed also during qualitative interviews, focus groups, and informal conversations with entrepreneurs. Respondents reported problems with excessively high interest rates and the general terms and conditions attached to MFI loans. Moreover, entrepreneurs complained that MFIs' lending rates, combined with strong inflationary pressures,[16] were eroding the small profits they had made in the market. Numerous respondents said they had therefore decided to return to informal financial arrangements.

10.4 Conclusions

The empirical investigation discussed in the second part of this chapter supports many of the arguments presented in the theoretical part. This concluding section reports four main 'indications' emerging from the case study in Kariobangi that can be useful for future work.

First, far from operating in an institutional vacuum or suffering from a lack of options, SMEs in Nairobi are likely to use a mix of financial instruments and, surprisingly, are actively connected with both informal social networks

[16] Kenya registered a peak inflation of 19.72 per cent in November 2011.

and formal financial institutions. The focus of most literature on the limited access (or exclusion) of SMEs to formal finance is not useful because it overlooks the complex dynamics within the context of informality and the potential for informal finance to promote the survival and growth of SMEs.

Second, although the majority of entrepreneurs use a combination of formal and informal financial instruments, there are differences between the three degrees of informality (i.e. high, intermediate, and low). In particular, the empirical analysis supports Portes' argument (1994) that the more businesses operate in a context of informality and outside the reach of formal institutions, the more they rely on social networks. Even though Portes refers to the issue of regulation and contract enforcement in this regard, the argument is valid also at the financial level. The result is presented graphically in Figure 10.1 and is consistent for nearly all types of financial networks. Except for welfare groups and investment clubs, informal businesses in Korogocho tend to be more involved in informal networks than businesses located in Kariobangi Market and the Light Industries, which are characterized by higher degrees of formality. As shown in Table 10.3, gender plays a relevant role as well.

The third indication is that informal financial networks tend to play less of a role in the start-up phase of a business. Figure 10.2, on how entrepreneurs accumulated their start-up capital, shows that the majority used their own savings from previous jobs and loans (or grants) from family or friends. The contribution of financial social networks was significant but limited, especially for men. This finding seems to indicate that personal ties such as friends or family are more important than informal financial groups for new entrepreneurs, whereas more complex organizational forms such as ASCAs and ROSCAs become important when the business is established and functioning. However, further analysis is needed to test the hypotheses emerging from the field research.

Finally, the empirical analysis has shown that use of formal banking services is high, with 77 per cent of the sample having access to an active bank account, and the proportion being even higher among women (Table 10.3).[17] Respondents valued bank services either because they reduced transaction costs and simplified operations with suppliers and customers, or because they provided a safe place to keep savings earned in the entrepreneurial activity. Inclusion in the banking system was therefore seen both as a potential contributor to the growth of the business and as an instrument of protection in case of emergencies and financial shocks. Access to credit was lower (18 per cent reported either having or had access to a bank loan), but entrepreneurs increasingly considered this a viable option. This is occurring in parallel with a declining popularity of microfinance services. There was still

[17] The proportion is substantially higher than that found by Johnson et al. (2012) reported in Table 10.1, where only 36 per cent of the sample had an active bank account.

a high percentage of active MFI accounts in the sample (especially in the tailoring cluster), and MFI services appeared to be highly valued by numerous entrepreneurs. But a staggering 23 per cent of the total sample decided to quit MFIs, while in Korogocho this figure was even higher, at 30 per cent. The reason is probably that MFIs are receiving pressure from both formal and informal institutions.

On the formal side, there are banks in Kenya, such as Equity Bank, Cooperative Bank, and Family Bank, which are aggressively targeting the low-income population and are increasingly competing to provide microfinance services, to the point that many respondents reported that they no longer saw a clear distinction between microfinance institutions and commercial banks. At the same time, MFIs also have to compete with a variety of informal financial networks that remain popular, especially among the most informal participants in the local economy. This is confirmed by the high reliance on ROSCAs and ASCAs in Korogocho, and in particular among women. When entrepreneurs were asked the reasons why they preferred informal financial instruments to MFIs, the answers were mostly related to the greater flexibility of the former, lower transaction costs and interest rates, as well as the capacity of the informal financial instruments to provide support during periods of difficulty. However, due to the evolving financial landscape in Kenya as well as the exploratory nature of this study, many questions remain unanswered and require substantial further empirical investigation.

References

Abuodha, C. and R. Bowles (2000). 'Business Licence Reform in Kenya and Its Impact on Small Enterprises'. *Small Enterprise Development*, 11(3): 16–24.

Atieno, R. (2001). 'Formal and Informal Institutions' Lending Policies and Access to Credit by Small-Scale Enterprises in Kenya: An Empirical Assessment'. Nairobi, Kenya. African Economic Research Consortium.

Barr, A. (1998). *'Enterprise performance and the functional diversity of social capital'*. Oxford: Centre for the Study of African Economies, Institute of Economics and Statistics, University of Oxford.

Bhattamishra, R. and C. B. Barrett (2010). 'Community-Based Risk Management Arrangements: A Review'. *World Development*, 38(7): 923–32.

Carr, M. and M. A. Chen (2002). *Globalization and the Informal Economy: How Global Trade and Investment Impact on the Working Poor.* Cambridge, MA: WIEGO, Women in Informal Employment Globalizing and Organizing, Working Paper.

Castells, M. and A. Portes (1989). 'World Underneath: The Origins, Dynamics, and Effects of the Informal Economy', in A. Portes, M. Castells, and L. A. Benton (eds.), *The Informal Economy: Studies in Advanced and Less Developed Countries*. Baltimore: Johns Hopkins University Press: 11–37.

Central Bank of Kenya (2012). Bank Supervision Annual Report 2012. Central Bank of Kenya, Bank Supervision Department, Nairobi, Kenya. Available at <http://www.centralbank.go.ke/images/docs/Bank%20Supervision%20Reports/Annual%20Reports/bsd2012-r.pdf> (accessed 15 June 2013).

Chen, M. A. (2006). 'Rethinking the Informal Economy: Linkages with the Formal Economy and the Formal Regulatory Environment', in B. Guha-Khasnobis, R. Khambur, and E. Ostrom (eds.), *Linking the Formal and Informal Economy: Concepts and Policies*. Oxford: Oxford University Press: 58–74.

Collins, D., J. Murdoch, S. Rutherford, and O. Ruthven (2009). *Portfolios of the Poor: How the World's Poor Live on $2 a Day*. Princeton, NJ: Princeton University Press.

De Soto, H. (1989). *The Other Path*. New York: Harper & Row.

—— (2000). *The Mystery Of Capital: Why Capitalism Triumphs in the West and Fails Everywhere Else*. New York: Basic Civitas Books.

Dessy, S. and S. Pallage (2003). 'Taxes, Inequality and the Size of the Informal Sector'. *Journal of Development Economics*, 70(1): 225–33.

Devas, N. and R. Kelly (2001). 'Regulation or Revenues? An Analysis of Local Business Licences, with a Case Study of the Single Business Permit Reform in Kenya'. *Public Administration and Development*, 21(5): 381–91.

Dixit, A. K. (2004). *Lawlessness and Economics: Alternative Modes of Governance*. Princeton, NJ: Princeton University Press.

Djankov, S., I. Lieberman, J. Mukherjee, and T. Nenova (2003), 'Going Informal: Benefits and Costs', in B. Belev (ed.), *The Informal Economy in the EU Accession Countries: Size, Scope, Trends and Challenges to the Process of EU Enlargement*. Sofia: CSD, 63–80.

Djankov, S., R. La Porta, F. Lopez-de-Silanes and A. Shleifer (2002). 'The Regulation of Entry'. *Quarterly Journal of Economics*, 117(1): 1–37.

Fafchamps, M. (2004). *Market Institutions in Sub-Saharan Africa: Theory and Evidence*. Cambridge, MA: MIT Press.

Feige, E. L. (1990). 'Defining and Estimating Underground and Informal Economies: The New Institutional Economics Approach'. *World Development*, 18(7): 989–1002.

Gugerty, M.K. (2007). 'You Can't Save Alone: Commitment in Rotating Savings and Credit Associations in Kenya'. *Economic Development and Cultural Change*, 55(2): 251–82.

Guha-Khasnobis, B., R. Khambur, and E. Ostrom (2006). 'Beyond Formality and Informality', in B. Guha-Khasnobis, R. Khambur, and E. Ostrom (eds.), *Linking the Formal and Informal Economy: Concepts and Policies*. Oxford: Oxford University Press: 1–18.

Harriss-White, B. (2010). 'Work and Wellbeing in Informal Economies: The Regulative Roles of Institutions of Identity and the State'. *World Development*, 38(2):170–183.

Hart, K. (2006). 'Formal Bureaucracy and the Emergent Forms of the Informal Economy', in B. Guha-Khasnobis, R. Khambur, and E. Ostrom (eds.), *Linking the Formal and Informal Economy: Concepts and Policies*. Oxford: Oxford University Press: 21–35.

Hodgson, G. M. (2006). 'What are Institutions?' *Journal of Economic Issues*, 40(1): 1–25.

ILO (2002). *Women and Men in the Informal Economy: A Statistical Picture*. Geneva: ILO Employment Sector.

Jack, W. and T. Suri (2011). 'Mobile Money: The Economics of M-PESA'. National Bureau of Economic Research Working Paper Series, No. 16721. Available at <http://www.nber.org/papers/w16721> (accessed 9 December 2011).

Johnson, S. (2004). '"Milking the Elephant": Financial Markets as Real Markets in Kenya'. *Development and Change*, 35(2): 247–74.

Johnson, S., G. K. Brown and C. Fouillet (2012). 'The Search for Inclusion in Kenya's Financial Landscape: The Rift Revealed'. Report prepared for Financial Sector Deepening (FSD)—Kenya, Nairobi, March.

Kenyon, T. (2007). 'A Framework For Thinking About Enterprise Formalization Policies in Developing Countries'. World Bank Policy Research Working Paper No. 4235. Washington DC: World Bank.

Kinyanjui, M. N. (2010). 'Social Relations and Associations in the Informal Sector in Kenya'. *United Nations Research for Social Development, Research Paper* No. 43.

—— (2012). *Institutions of Hope: Ordinary People's Market Coordination and Society Organisation Alternatives*. Ontario, Canada: Nsemia Inc. Publishers.

Loayza, N. V. (1994). 'Labor Regulations and the Informal Economy'. World Bank, *Policy Research Working Paper No. 1335*. Washington DC.

—— A. M. Oviedo, and L. Servén (2006). 'The Impact of Regulation on Growth and Informality: Cross-Country Evidence', in B. Guha-Khasnobis, R. Khambur, and E. Ostrom (eds.), *Linking the Formal and Informal Economy: Concepts and Policies*. Oxford, Oxford University Press: 121–44.

Lourenço-Lindell, I. (2002). 'Walking the Tight Rope: Informal Livelihoods and Social Networks in a West African City'. Stockholm Studies in Human Geography. Stockholm: Almqvist & Wiksell.

Malkamäki M., S. Johnson, and M. Nino-Zarazua (2009). 'The Role of Informal Financial Groups in Extending Access in Kenya'. Results of the Finaccess Survey, Financial Sector Deepening (FSD)—Kenya. Nairobi.

Meagher, K. (2005). 'Social Capital or Analytical Liability? Social Networks and African Informal Economies'. *Global Networks*, 5(3): 217–38.

—— (2006). 'Social Capital, Social Liabilities, and Political Capital: Social Networks and Informal Manufacturing in Nigeria'. *African Affairs*, 105(421): 553–82.

—— (2007). 'Manufacturing Disorder: Liberalization, Informal Enterprise and Economic 'Ungovernance' in African Small Firm Clusters'. *Development and Change*, 38(3): 473–503.

—— (2010). *Identity Economics: Social Networks and the Informal Economy in Nigeria*. Suffolk: James Currey.

North, D. C. (1990). *Institutions, Institutional Change, and Economic Performance*. Cambridge: Cambridge University Press.

—— (2005). *Understanding the Process of Economic Change*. Princeton, NJ: Princeton University Press.

Portes, A. (1994). 'Paradoxes of the Informal Economy: The Social Basis of Unregulated Entrepreneurship', in J. S. Neil, R. Swedberg (eds.), *The Handbook of Economic Sociology*, Princeton, NJ: Princeton University Press: 426–49.

Roitman, J. L. (2005). *Fiscal Disobedience: An Anthropology of Economic Regulation in Central Africa*. Princeton, NJ: Princeton University Press.

Sindzingre, A. (2006). 'The Relevance of the Concepts of Formality and Informality: A Theoretical Appraisal', in B. Guha-Khasnobis, R. Khambur, and E. Ostrom (eds.), *Linking the Formal and Informal Economy: Concepts and Policies*. Oxford: Oxford University Press: 58–74.

Sonobe, T., J. E. Akoten, and K. Otsuka (2011). 'The Growth Process of Informal Enterprises in Sub-Saharan Africa: A Case Study of a Metalworking Cluster in Nairobi'. *Small Business Economics*, 35(3): 323–35.

Tripp, A. M. (2001). 'Non-Formal Institutions, Informal Economies, and the Politics of Inclusion'. Research Discussion Paper 2001/108, UNU/WIDER, Helsinki, Finland.

Yenkey, C. B. (2010). 'The Social Structure of Speculation: Investor Attributes and Short Term Share Ownership in Kenya's Emerging Stock Market'. *SSRN eLibrary*. Available at <http://ssrn.com/abstract=1597326> (accessed 15 June 2013).

Part III

Formalizing the Informal? A Critical Assessment

11

Determinants of Earnings in Informal Self-Employment: The Case of Ghana

James Heintz and Lynda Pickbourn

11.1 Introduction

Informal employment, defined by the International Conference of Labour Statisticians (ICLS) as employment that is not subject to labour legislation, income taxation, social protection, and entitlement to employment benefits remains a persistent feature of most developing economies, and continues to account for a significant proportion of new jobs created in many developing countries.[1] Women are more reliant on non-agricultural informal employment than men, and in sub-Saharan Africa much of this employment is self-employment in very small household enterprises (ILO, 2002). However, the factors which influence earnings in informal self-employment in sub-Saharan Africa and the barriers to improving the quality of such employment are not fully understood. This chapter examines the determinants of earnings in non-agricultural self-employment in Ghana with the objective of identifying strategies for improving employment outcomes.

Given the importance of informal employment in developing countries' economies, a substantial body of work has focused on the reasons for the existence of informal employment and the impact of informality on workers' earnings. Central to this is the debate over whether informal employment is

[1] The ICLS has proposed recommendations for the definition of the concepts 'informal sector and 'informal employment'. The 15th ICLS proposed a definition of the informal sector based on enterprise characteristics, according to which informal enterprises are unincorporated enterprises not subject to formal regulation or recognition and whose financial accounts are not separable from those of the household. The 17th ICLS extended this definition with its recommendations for defining 'informal employment' as a jobs-based or employment-based concept, in contrast to an enterprise-based definition, defining informal employment as employment not subject to social or legal protections or formal regulations.

freely chosen, or whether it results from structural factors in the labour market that force workers into informal employment. Neoclassical models of labour market dualism posit that informal employment exists because of distortions in formal labour markets that inflate labour costs and limit the supply of formal jobs. According to this view, differences in earnings among individuals in developing countries, controlling for individual productive characteristics, are primarily due to differences in the sectors of employment. The rationing of job opportunities in the formal economy shifts labour supply to informal activities, placing downward pressure on wages in those activities. As a result workers in informal employment earn less than their counterparts in formal employment (Fields, 1975).

An alternative perspective treats the decision to work in the informal sector as being voluntary, with workers weighing the benefits of working formally against those of working informally and choosing the form of employment with the greatest net benefits (Maloney, 2004; Loayza and Rigolini, 2006; Levy, 2008). Viewed from this perspective, differences in earnings among individuals arise from observable as well as unobservable differences among workers that sort workers into different sectors and different types of employment (Fajnzylber, Maloney, and Rojas, 2006). Both approaches assume that there is free entry into informal employment.

A better understanding of the determinants of earnings in informal employment would provide a basis for identifying possible constraints that limit choices and lead to inequalities in employment outcomes. There are only a limited number of studies of the determinants of earnings in self-employment in Ghana, and these tend to emphasize individual or enterprise productivity. Sandefur, Serneels, and Teal (2007) present estimates of earnings functions for self-employed individuals in Ghana using labour market survey data collected for selected urban areas. Their analysis of earnings in self-employment is limited to human capital variables (age, earnings, and job tenure) and firm size (to capture economies of scale). A recent effort to model the income-generating process in informal self-employment in Ghana estimates a production function for household enterprises using panel data from selected urban areas in order to attribute the value-added generated in the enterprises to specific factors of production, such as capital and labour (Falco, 2011). The analysis provides useful insights into the productivity of household enterprises based on the traditional factors of production. However, approaches that focus only on the productivity of individuals or enterprises often fail to take into account factors operating at the household level which also affect earnings. For example, the presence of unpaid family workers at the household level and their contributions to enterprise earnings are not acknowledged.

Although observable and unobservable worker characteristics play an important role in determining workers' earnings, institutional factors such as social norms and structural constraints are also important. These institutional factors govern the distribution of assets such as money, land, credit, education, and skill. They may determine the sectors within which individuals can operate informal enterprises, as well as the type of capital to which individual operators have access. In addition, perfect mobility may not exist within informal employment. Informal employment, including self-employment, is a heterogeneous category, and barriers to mobility can create structural differences in earnings. Such constraints represent important determinants of earnings from informal self-employment. However, they are often not recognized in studies which primarily attempt to control for individual productivity.

Using nationally representative survey data obtained from GLSS 5, we analyse the determinants of earnings of non-agricultural self-employed workers using a combination of individual, household, enterprise, and location variables. The GLSS survey is a multipurpose household survey which collects data on a large number of variables, including demographics, education, health, detailed information about the labour force, household expenditures, agricultural activities, unincorporated household enterprises, remittances, migration, and housing, among other areas. The survey was administered by the Ghana Statistical Service (GSS) from September 2005 to September 2006, and holds detailed information on 8,687 households and on individual household members. The household enterprises module contains detailed information on all household enterprises operated by members of the household. Combining the household enterprises module with data from the other modules of the GLSS survey makes it possible to consider a broad range of factors which influence the earnings of these workers, beyond simply focusing on why their earnings differ from those of workers in the formal sector.

The chapter is structured as follows. Section 11.2 describes the labour market and institutional context in Ghana. Section 11.3 presents the data used for our analysis, and discusses some important issues relating to the measurement of earnings from self-employment. Section 11.4 presents our econometric model, the variables that are used in our analysis, and a discussion of the results. Finally, the conclusion discusses the implications of our findings for future research and policy.

11.2 Ghana: The Economic and Labour Market Context

Ghana is a predominantly rural, low-income country with a population of 24.3 million. In 2010, the country's per capita gross national income (GNI) was $1,240. The economy relies heavily on the export of cocoa, gold, and timber, and agriculture accounts for 58.8 per cent of total employment. Informal employment outside agriculture constitutes a substantial proportion of total employment.

Table 11.1 summarizes the distribution of employment across categories which reflect employment status (e.g. employee, own-account worker, employer, and contributing family worker), informality status (formal versus informal employment), and sector (agricultural and non-agricultural), based on data from the most recent round of GLSS 5. Employment categories are based on an individual's primary occupation. Agricultural employment dominates the structure of employment in Ghana, accounting for 59.5 per cent of men's employment and 53.5 per cent of women's employment. In agriculture, women are more likely than men to be reported as working as contributing family workers. Outside agriculture, total informal employment is estimated to be about 24.2 per cent of all employment, while formal employment constitutes just 17 per cent. Formal employment accounts for a larger share of men's employment (20.9 per cent) than women's employment (13.4 per cent).

Women's labour force participation rates are high and rates of open unemployment are relatively low. This reflects the critical importance of paid employment as a source of household income. Men have greater access to wage employment as paid employees than women. Women are more likely than men to be employed in the non-agricultural informal sector: 25.4 per cent of women are informal, own-account workers, compared with only 6.8 per cent of men (Table 11.1). For both men and women, self-employment, both formal and informal, accounts for a larger share of total employment outside agriculture than wage employment.

Given the importance of non-agricultural self-employment in Ghana, it is useful to look at the characteristics of the individuals operating non-agricultural household enterprises (Table 11.2). The majority of operators of household enterprises have some primary education, although this is higher among male operators (80.9 per cent) than female operators (63.5 per cent). Secondary education is far less common among operators of household enterprises. Nearly 60 per cent of men who operate household enterprises are English-language literate compared with only about 31 per cent of women. Fewer than one in five operators of household enterprises have registered their enterprises. Thus, by this criterion the vast majority of these enterprises are informal.

The majority of operators of non-agricultural household enterprises identify their primary form of employment as non-agricultural self-employment (70.8 per cent, Table 11.2). However, a significant number identify their primary occupation as something other than non-agricultural self-employment. Most of the individuals in this second group identify their primary employment activity as agricultural (26 per cent), although a much smaller number identify their primary employment status as non-agricultural paid employees

Table 11.1 Structure of employment in Ghana, 2005–6 (per cent)

	Men	Women	Total
Share in formal non-agricultural employment			
Formal private employee	8.2	2.5	5.3
Formal public	7.7	2.9	5.2
Formal own-account	3.5	6.9	5.3
Formal employer	1.6	1.0	1.3
Share in informal non-agricultural employment			
Informal employee	8.3	2.5	5.3
Informal own-account	6.8	25.4	16.4
Informal employer	1.2	1.5	1.3
Contributing family worker	0.5	1.7	1.1
Agricultural employment			
Agricultural employee	2.9	0.9	1.8
Agricultural own-account	42.7	24.6	33.3
Agricultural employer	2.6	1.2	1.9
Contributing family worker	11.3	26.8	19.3
Other			
Other/unknown	2.8	2.1	2.5
TOTAL	**100**	**100**	**100**
Other indicators			
Labour force participation	74.6	71.2	72.8
Unemployment rate	4.5	4.8	4.6

Source: Authors' calculations based on GLSS 5.

Table 11.2 Characteristics of operators of non-agricultural household enterprises (per cent)

	Men	Women	Total
Some primary education	80.9	63.5	68.5
Some secondary education	19.0	7.2	10.6
English language literacy	59.7	30.9	39.1
Operate formal enterprise	27.9	15.1	18.8
Primary status: non-agricultural self-employed	62.3	74.3	70.8
Primary status: agricultural	31.6	23.7	26.0
Primary status of non-agricultural employee	5.7	1.5	2.7

Source: Authors' calculations based on GLSS 5.

(2.7 per cent). Therefore, we discern two patterns among operators of household enterprises. In the first group are those who specialize in non-agricultural self-employment and for whom the household enterprise is a primary source of income. The second group comprises people who operate a non-agricultural enterprise as a diversification strategy—primarily diversifying into secondary non-agricultural activities when the main activity is agricultural.

Table 11.3 Sources of start-up finance and sector of activity by enterprise, 2005–6 (per cent)

	Men	Women	Total
Sources of start-up finance			
Own savings	62.2	58.4	59.5
Bank credit	1.7	1.2	1.4
Remittances (from abroad)	0.5	0.5	0.5
Income from other business	11.1	9.0	9.5
NGO support	0.1	0.2	0.2
Local government programme	0.1	0.3	0.3
Money lender	1.7	1.3	1.4
Relative/friend	15.7	20.9	19.5
Unknown/not reported	7.0	8.1	7.8
Sectors of activity			
Manufacturing	33.6	33.1	33.2
Construction	8.8	0.1	2.5
Retail trade	27.0	42.9	38.4
Repair	6.0	0.2	1.8
Prepared food/restaurant	4.4	11.3	9.4
Transport	3.9	0.0	1.1
Other services	12.4	11.3	11.6
Other sector of activity/unknown	3.9	1.2	1.9

Source: Authors' calculations based on GLSS 5.

Table 11.3 presents summary information on the sources of start-up finance for non-agricultural enterprises and the sector of activity. The financial resources for starting most household enterprises were reported to come from individual savings or from relatives and/or friends. Very few enterprises seem to rely on bank credit or money lenders for their start-up capital. Retail trade and various small-scale manufacturing activities are the most important sectors of activity for non-agricultural household enterprises. Retail activities are particularly important for women operating enterprises. Food preparation also accounts for a larger share of women's employment than men's. However, the reverse is true for other sectors of activity. For example, construction, repair services, and transportation are male-dominated.

11.3 Earnings from Informal Self-Employment Outside Agriculture: The Institutional Context

In the standard neoclassical framework, differences in earnings are primarily due to differences in human capital as well as differences in unobserved individual productivity and motivation. Thus, one would expect factors such as age, education, and experience to be important determinants of the earnings of workers in Ghana's informal sector. Beyond these individual determinants of earnings, however, a variety of institutional factors external to the labour market, such as location, infrastructure, gender dynamics, social networks, and credit market imperfections may also shape labour market outcomes, either directly or indirectly. In this section, we expand on the institutional determinants of earnings in informal self-employment, with a specific focus on gender dynamics and norms, since the majority of individuals operating non-agricultural household enterprises in Ghana are women.

In Ghana, as elsewhere, education is an important determinant of people's earning potential. But, as one might expect, access to education remains out of reach for the majority, and inequality of access to good quality education remains pronounced. Under the current educational system, basic education consists of two years of pre-school, six years of primary school, and three years of junior high (i.e. post-primary) school. Post-basic education is defined as four years of senior high school, technical and vocational education and training (TVET), and/or tertiary education in universities and polytechnics. Access to tertiary education is largely determined by the quality of basic and secondary education, and research suggests that only 10 per cent of the population achieves an education level of senior high school or higher, while the poorest 45 per cent of Ghana's population have no access to tertiary education (Palmer, 2005). The poor, who cannot afford good quality basic education of the sort offered by private schools, have limited access to formal post-basic education because of the disadvantages they face at the basic level (Palmer, 2005 and 2007). Only 59 per cent of women have ever attended school, compared with 79 per cent of men, and only 6 per cent of girls attain senior secondary education or higher, compared with 16 per cent of boys (Palmer, 2005).

Such significant inequality in the distribution of education opportunities has important implications for earnings differentials in the informal sector. Education is important, not only because of its contribution to human capital, but because it determines the segment of the informal sector within which an individual can operate a household enterprise. Generally, higher income segments of the informal sector are likely to be open only to those with higher levels of education, while those less educated are likely to be concentrated in lower income segments of the sector. Thus women, because of their lower levels of education, are more likely to be concentrated in lower income segments of the informal sector. But this is not the only way in which education impacts earnings. There is a large body of work that documents the importance of social networks in shaping labour market outcomes, as well as the role of education in determining the quality of the social networks that individuals can access (see, for example, Granovetter, 1973; Campbell, Marsden, and Hurlbert, 1986). Education can impact earnings from informal self-employment indirectly via the social networks to which the operators of household enterprises have access. Social networks provide a pool from which potential clients of a household enterprise can be drawn. In the absence of institutions to protect consumers, social networks may provide a valuable source of information to potential clients about the quality of services offered by household enterprises and the reliability of the proprietor. Education provides access to social networks based on a shared educational background, such as having attended the same high school or university; having a higher level of education increases the likelihood that one's social networks will comprise higher income individuals who may be potential clients or whose references can be valuable to a new enterprise.

As with education, gender inequality can play a role in determining access to social networks. Sociologists have noted that social networks can operate in gendered ways to produce systematic and persistent differences in labour market outcomes for women and men (Portes and Jensen, 1989; Zhou and Logan, 1989; Gilbertson, 1995; Hagan, 1998). Social networks in Ghana are typically structured along gendered lines, with women accessing networks that consist primarily of other women. For example, Goldstein (2000) shows that women in Ghanaian villages are more likely to engage in risk-pooling strategies with other women in the village than they are with their husbands or other male relatives, while men were more likely to share risk with male relatives. If women rely on women-centred networks to gain access to informal employment, then these networks are likely to provide access primarily to areas of economic activity dominated by women, such as retailing and food preparation.

Access to affordable credit can exert a positive impact on the earnings of household enterprises by facilitating investment in productive capital, by facilitating the expansion of existing enterprises, and by providing working capital when needed. For example, women engaged in rice processing in northern Ghana may not always have cash to purchase rice when the price is low and therefore must pay more for inputs. Access to credit would allow such women to purchase raw materials on more favourable terms. However, formal financial institutions are notoriously unwilling to lend to small household enterprises (Epstein and Heintz, 2006). In the absence of credit from the formal financial sector, people may have to rely on relatives and friends for loans or gifts. Others may have to rely on high-cost credit from informal financial sources. These credit market imperfections can act as a constraint on the earnings of operators of household enterprises in Ghana. Again, there is evidence of significant gender bias in terms of access to credit, both because of the high rates of interest resulting from credit rationing, and because women lack the collateral that formal financial institutions require (Baden et al., 1994; Schindler, 2010). Even in informal credit markets, there is evidence that Ghanaian women are more credit-constrained than men (Udry and Conley, 2004).

Norms of household provisioning, together with norms that limit women's access to productive resources such as land, create an incentive for women to generate an independent income through informal employment. The ethnographic literature on norms of household provisioning in Ghana and in other parts of Africa has extensively documented the absence of household pooling of income by married couples (Goldstein, 2000; Whitehead, 1981; Ekejiuba, 1995; Bruce and Dwyer, 1988). Instead, each spouse has specific responsibilities: wives are responsible for supplementing household food supplies as well as feeding and clothing children, while husbands are required to provide staple food and shelter. In most households, a woman receives a regular, fixed amount from her husband in the form of either cash or staple food. Regardless of the amount she receives from her husband, it is ultimately the woman's responsibility to provide meals for the household (Goldstein, 2000; Warner, Alhassan, and Kydd, 1997). Often, women may have to supplement the daily stipend they receive from their husbands and, when stocks of the staple food run out, or when their husbands do not have any money, women may even become the main providers of food.

This obligation to make up for household food shortfalls and care for children constitutes an important motivation for women to engage in various remunerative activities independently of unpaid household responsibilities. Such employment is often concentrated in activities such as petty trading, small-scale manufacturing, and food preparation—activities that require little start-up capital and have low returns despite the high turnover. Many of these activities are simply an extension of the unpaid labour that women perform at home, such as cooking meals and burning firewood to make charcoal. The fact that most of these activities can be carried out at home, or in close proximity to the home, means that women can continue to perform their domestic chores while at the same time meeting their needs for cash to meet their financial obligations. But there may also be another explanation: by making small and frequent sales, women can ensure that they will have cash on hand to meet their various obligations to the household. Activities that generate large sums of cash on an irregular basis may be unappealing to women, not only because they lack the requisite skills, but also because the irregularity of income from these activities makes it difficult for women to meet their daily financial obligations to the household.

There is also abundant evidence that gender norms and ideologies may be responsible for maintaining the gender division of labour by restricting the economic activities that women may perform (Obbo, 1976; Roberts, 1988; Kevane, 2000). In Ghana, for example, certain activities, such as construction and transportation, are not considered appropriate for women. Even when women manage to break into areas previously considered the domain of men, they are restricted in the ways in which they may perform those activities. A good example of this relates to human transportation involving men and women transporting goods from one part of an open-air market to another: while men working in teams make use of wheelbarrows and carts to transport large volumes of goods and thus increase their earnings, women work individually and carry the loads on their heads; thus their earnings are limited by how much they can physically carry.

Clearly, the earnings of self-employed operators of household enterprises are shaped by a variety of factors related to the labour market as well as external to the labour market. The self-employed are not an undifferentiated group of workers: they differ in their access to the resources that are important in shaping labour market outcomes, as well as in the segments of the informal sector in which they operate.

11.4 Measuring Earnings of Non-Agricultural Household Enterprises

Income from self-employment is notoriously difficult to capture in household surveys, particularly when most self-employment is informal, and the enterprise's finances are not separate from the other financial transactions of the household. Misreporting is commonplace, and different approaches for capturing income from self-employment may yield widely divergent results. The GLSS provides three ways of calculating earnings from non-agricultural household enterprises:

(i) Cash earnings from self-employment, as reported in the labour force module of the survey;

(ii) Net profits of the enterprise, as reported in the household enterprise module of the survey; and

(iii) Profits calculated based on reported revenues and expenses, as reported in the household enterprise module of the survey.

In this study we focus on the first two sources of information on earnings from self-employment. According to Coulombe and McKay (2008), calculating net earnings of household enterprises based on the revenue and expenditure data collected by the GLSS produces a large number of negative earnings estimates which cannot be considered reliable. Therefore, we focus on the direct reporting of income from self-employment, rather than trying to derive enterprise earnings from reported revenues and expenditures. Problems of misreporting, erroneous recall, and confusion over what is being measured (e.g. revenues or profits) are also relevant for these indicators of earnings from self-employment. Therefore, we consider multiple measurements of earnings to ascertain the degree to which our results are sensitive to the way in which earnings are reported.

We consider two closely related measurements. The first is simply the aggregate reported cash earnings from self-employment. This measurement may underestimate earnings, since goods and services produced for own-use are excluded. Therefore, we consider a modified measurement which adds the estimated value of production for own use to the reported earnings from self-employment.

We also consider direct estimates of enterprise profits collected in the household enterprise module of the GLSS. The estimates are organized in terms of the reported use of the profits from the enterprise: for personal use, household expenditures, transfers to other households, savings, or for other purposes. We calculate total reported profit by summing across these categories. In a significant number of cases, the reported amount of profits that is directed towards savings is significantly greater than the amount reported for any other use. This raises the possibility that respondents are reporting the total stock of savings attributable to the enterprise, rather than the flow of savings out of profits over a given time period. Given this possibility, we also calculate total reported profits excluding savings.

Therefore, we consider four possible measurements of earnings from non-agricultural household enterprises: (i) reported self-employment cash earnings (from the labour force module), (ii) reported self-employment earnings plus the value of production for own use, (iii) total reported profits of the enterprise (from the household enterprise module), and (iv) total reported profits less savings out of profits. Earnings are expressed on a monthly basis.

Table 11.4 summarizes median monthly earnings across the four measurements of enterprise income expressed in thousands of cedis.[2] The table also includes the median value of enterprise assets (valued at original purchase price). Medians are used to reduce any distortions in the mean caused by significant outliers. In cases where one individual operates more than one enterprise, we add up the reported earnings and assets from all the enterprises to get total earnings and assets. Median earnings are highest for total reported enterprise profits (including reported savings) and lowest for reported earnings from self-employment, excluding production for own use. The two earnings variables with the most comparable medians are the total reported income from self-employment plus the value of production for own use (403,000 cedis across all observations) and total reported enterprise profits excluding savings (413,000 cedis). These two earnings variables are also positively

[2] In 2007, Ghana undertook a currency reform in which 1 new Ghana cedi (1 GHC) was set equal to 10,000 cedis (¢10,000) under the previous currency system. Given the timing of the GLSS 5, the values in Table 11.4 are reported in terms of the older cedi, not the new Ghana cedi.

Table 11.4 Median monthly earnings and assets of non-agricultural household enterprises, 2005–6 (thousands of cedis)

	Men	Women	Total
Reported cash earnings, labour force module	584	299	380
Reported earnings + production, own use	600	334	403
Reported enterprise profits, all uses	700	430	494
Reported enterprise profits, excluding savings	611	345	413
Reported assets of non-agricultural enterprises	100	15	30

Source: Authors' calculations based on GLSS 5.

correlated with a correlation coefficient of 0.44. This correlation coefficient, while not close to one, is significantly stronger than the correlation between the first two earnings variables (the highest and lowest values), which is just 0.23. In the subsequent analysis, therefore, we focus on these two measurements of enterprise earnings.

Women who operate household enterprises have lower monthly earnings than men across all four earnings variables in Table 11.4. It is also worth noting that the median reported value of enterprise assets is very low, particularly for women. If the magnitude of these reported asset holdings are even roughly correct, it suggests that very little capital is invested in the majority of non-agricultural household enterprises in Ghana.

11.4.1 Estimation of Earnings Functions: Variables

We estimate a Mincerian earnings function for individuals who specialize in operating household enterprises (i.e. those who identify the household enterprise as their primary source of income). The regression equation for this function takes the following form:

$$\ln y_i = f(s_i, x_i, z_i) + u_i i = 1, \ldots, n$$

where the dependent variable is the log of hourly earnings. In the above expression, s_i, x_i and z_i represent individual, household, and enterprises level sets of variables, respectively.

We use the two earnings measurements discussed in the previous section in our analysis: (i) the sum of total reported self-employment income, and (ii) the value of production for own use and total reported enterprise profits excluding savings. These variables are measured as estimated monthly earnings. For individuals with two non-agricultural household enterprises, the earnings are summed across both activities. We take two approaches to controlling for hours of work. First, we express each of the two earnings variables in terms of average hourly earnings. Second, we keep the variables as monthly earnings, but include estimated monthly hours of work of the operator, unpaid contributing family members, and paid employees as explanatory variables.

Earnings of household enterprises are attributed to the operator of the enterprise. This poses a problem in that the labour supplied by unpaid contributing family workers increases the earnings of the enterprise. A measurement of hourly earnings which divides total earnings by the hours worked by the operator of that enterprise will overstate hourly earnings when other family members have contributed their labour time. To correct for this potential bias, we divide enterprise earnings by the total hours worked by the operator of the enterprise and any reported hours of contributing family workers when computing average hourly earnings. When one household has two or more members who each operate a distinct household enterprise, the work time of unpaid contributing family workers is divided between the household enterprises based on the number of contributing family workers reported working in each of the enterprises.[3]

Table 11.5 summarizes the definitions of the explanatory variables used in the OLS regressions. The definitions are mostly self-explanatory. However, in a few cases, additional explanation is warranted. The education variables are mutually exclusive dummy variables which indicate the maximum level of education attained. If all educational dummies have a value of zero, then the individual has no formal schooling. The 'water tap' variable takes on a value of one if the household has access to water through a tap (either in the house, at a neighbouring house, or through a public or private external tap). Finally, the 'credit' variable takes on a value of one if there is evidence that individuals have access to credit from any source (i.e. formal credit, informal credit, or credit from family or friends). In the GLSS 5 data, evidence of credit is defined as having a current loan outstanding or having repaid an earlier loan over the past year. Information on credit history prior to the past year is not available.

11.4.2 Estimation of Earnings Functions: Results from OLS Regressions

The estimates presented in this section are conditional on individuals operating a household enterprise and specializing in non-agricultural self-employment The results from the basic specification are presented in the first two columns of Table 11.6. We use two measures of hourly earnings: the total reported profits of household enterprises less savings (*ln earn1*), and total reported cash income from non-farm self-employment plus the value of

[3] Note that since the earnings variables are presumed to represent net earnings rather than revenues, a similar adjustment for paid employees is not necessary, since the earnings variables would have already taken into account the amount paid to these workers for their labour.

Table 11.5 Definitions of independent variables used

Variable	Description
Age	Age in years
Age^2	Age in years squared (divided by 100 to adjust the scale)
Female	1 = female, 0 = male
Married	1 = married, 0 = not currently married
Urban	1 = urban residence, 0 = rural residence
Primary	1 = max. education attainment—some primary school, 0 = otherwise
Post-primary	1 = max. education attainment—some post-primary (middle) school, 0 = otherwise
Secondary	1 = max. education attainment—some secondary school, 0 = otherwise
Vocational	1 = max. education attainment—vocational school, 0 = otherwise
Tertiary	1 = max. education attainment—tertiary, 0 = otherwise
Electricity	1 = Household has electricity, 0 = otherwise
Water tap	1 = Household has access to water tap (either internal or external to residence), 0 = otherwise
Adult-mig	1 = adult migrant to current location within past 5 years, 0 = otherwise
Eng-lit	1 = English language literate (both reading and writing), 0 = otherwise
Credit	1 = Evidence that household has access to credit from some source (formal, informal, or from relatives), 0 = otherwise
Assets	Value of assets owned by the enterprise
Years	Number of years of operation
Formal	1 = enterprise is registered; 0 = otherwise
Hrs-Proprietor	Number of hours worked by the proprietor
Hrs-Family worker	Number of hours worked by contributing family workers (unpaid)
Hrs-Employees	Number of hours worked by paid employees

Source: Estimates based on GLSS 5.

production for own use (*ln earn2*). The coefficients of the standard explanatory variables typically included in Mincerian equations—age, and age-squared, as well as the education variables, all have the expected signs and statistical significance. Returns to education beyond primary education are positive but increase only slightly for post-primary and secondary education; the largest returns to education accrue to tertiary education. This provides an interesting non-linear shape to the returns to education curve: strong returns to primary education, then flat returns through secondary education, and another jump for tertiary education.

Somewhat surprisingly, the returns to English literacy are negative. This may indicate that the variable is capturing some other unobserved individual characteristic. A study of opting for self-employment in Ghana found that English language literacy was associated with a lower probability of being self-employed for Ghanaian women (Heintz and Pickbourn, 2012). Therefore, individuals who are both literate and self-employed may share some unobserved characteristics which affect self-employment earnings.

Access to electricity has a positive and significant impact on earnings, as does access to credit, suggesting that labour market outcomes are affected by non-labour market factors, such as credit market imperfections and infrastructure. There is some ambiguity in interpreting the direction of causality of these findings. For example, households whose members have higher earnings may also be more likely to have access to basic infrastructure and credit. However, basic water and power infrastructure is not provided exclusively at the individual household level, and access to such infrastructure varies from one district to another. Therefore, any correlation between incomes and infrastructure would be due to the impact of infrastructure on individual earnings. In addition, by defining the credit variable broadly to include forms of credit which low-income households typically access (e.g. through kinship networks), we attempt to reduce the influence of income determining access to credit from formal financial institutions.

Earnings are also positively impacted by the value of assets held by the enterprise and by the number of years that the enterprise has been in operation: earnings rise with the value of assets owned and the age of the enterprise. Whether or not the business is registered does not seem to have a strong impact on earnings—the variable is only slightly significant in the first specification, and its significance disappears in alternative specifications.

The estimations do show that women have significantly lower earnings than men, even after controlling for human capital, infrastructure, access to credit, business assets, and years of operation. This could be because women are concentrated in low-earning segments of the household enterprise sector, as suggested earlier.

The strong, negative coefficient on the female dummy variable raises questions about whether the earnings functions of men who operate household enterprises are different from those of women who operate household enterprises. We therefore estimated separate earnings functions for men and women. These results are presented in columns 3–6 of Table 11.6. Almost all the variables have similar effects on earnings for both men and women. However, access to credit has a strong, positive effect on earnings for women, but no such effect on men's earnings, suggesting that credit market imperfections, and in particular discrimination in access to credit, have a particularly strong impact on the earnings of women who operate household enterprises. An urban location also appears to reduce women's cash income from household enterprises, but has no significant effect on men's earnings. This could be due to market saturation in urban locations, or to women in urban areas operating mostly low-income household enterprises. Having migrated in the last five years also appears to significantly increase the cash income of men and to lower the cash income of women, although this effect is not significant. The difference in signs could be due to gendered differences in the

Table 11.6 Determinants of hourly earnings

	ln earn1	ln earn2	ln earn1	ln earn2	ln earn1	ln earn2
	All	All	Men	Men	Women	Women
Age	0.0363***	0.0493***	0.0125	0.0361*	0.0420***	0.0494***
	(0.00976)	(0.0107)	(0.0196)	(0.0198)	(0.0114)	(0.0129)
Age²/100	−0.0396***	−0.0579***	−0.0162	−0.0507**	−0.0452***	−0.0558***
	(0.0110)	(0.0122)	(0.0212)	(0.0216)	(0.0130)	(0.0148)
Female	−0.185***	−0.272***				
	(0.0530)	(0.0576)				
Married	−0.0315	0.0579	0.0445	0.132	−0.0343	0.0655
	(0.0469)	(0.0507)	(0.0982)	(0.0983)	(0.0551)	(0.0613)
Urban	0.0501	−0.107*	0.108	0.0160	0.0446	−0.152**
	(0.0581)	(0.0627)	(0.113)	(0.113)	(0.0681)	(0.0754)
Primary	0.255***	0.333***	0.339*	0.247	0.253***	0.349***
	(0.0691)	(0.0751)	(0.174)	(0.175)	(0.0757)	(0.0845)
Post-primary	0.309***	0.380***	0.532***	0.319**	0.261***	0.411***
	(0.0706)	(0.0763)	(0.159)	(0.159)	(0.0802)	(0.0890)
Secondary	0.300**	0.488***	0.457**	0.348*	0.280*	0.549***
	(0.118)	(0.128)	(0.209)	(0.209)	(0.152)	(0.170)
Vocational	0.238*	0.377***	0.593**	0.427*	0.0779	0.325*
	(0.130)	(0.142)	(0.229)	(0.231)	(0.165)	(0.184)
Tertiary	0.654***	0.942***	0.874***	0.955***	0.620**	0.928***
	(0.184)	(0.200)	(0.285)	(0.286)	(0.256)	(0.285)
Electricity	0.291***	0.250***	0.339***	0.267**	0.287***	0.248***
	(0.0529)	(0.0574)	(0.105)	(0.105)	(0.0616)	(0.0685)
Water tap	0.0130	0.0149	0.143	−0.0714	−0.0507	0.0445
	(0.0554)	(0.0598)	(0.102)	(0.102)	(0.0662)	(0.0733)
Adult migrant	0.0344	0.0337	0.214**	0.0323	−0.0262	0.0454
	(0.0531)	(0.0576)	(0.104)	(0.103)	(0.0622)	(0.0694)
English literate	−0.138**	−0.169**	−0.184	−0.106	−0.117	−0.192**
	(0.0645)	(0.0696)	(0.121)	(0.121)	(0.0768)	(0.0851)
Credit	0.180***	0.163***	0.0553	0.0282	0.223***	0.212***
	(0.0579)	(0.0625)	(0.105)	(0.105)	(0.0698)	(0.0774)
Assets	0.0147**	0.0252***	0.0227*	0.0312**	0.0106	0.0224**
	(0.00718)	(0.00778)	(0.0122)	(0.0122)	(0.00888)	(0.00988)
Years	0.00747***	0.00875***	0.00402	0.00894**	0.00880***	0.00872***
	(0.00214)	(0.00234)	(0.00401)	(0.00404)	(0.00254)	(0.00284)
Formal	0.0975*	0.0908	0.131	0.0227	0.0642	0.127
	(0.0589)	(0.0634)	(0.0975)	(0.0976)	(0.0739)	(0.0814)
Constant	6.678***	6.387***	6.858***	6.715***	6.435***	6.067***
	(0.204)	(0.223)	(0.405)	(0.408)	(0.232)	(0.260)
N	2,786	2,798	717	719	2,069	2,079
Adj. R-sq	0.064	0.069	0.083	0.059	0.046	0.047

Statistical significance: * 10%, ** 5%, *** 1%.

Dependent variable: natural logarithm of estimated hourly earnings (standard errors in parentheses).

Source: Estimates based on GLSS 5.

operation of social networks of migrants: male migrants may have access to wider, better connected networks than female migrants.

The magnitudes of the effects of other variables vary between women and men. For example, secondary education appears to have a larger marginal impact on women's earnings than men's, although the size of this difference is sensitive to how income is defined and measured.

In an alternative set of specifications, we used total monthly income as the dependent variable. We did this for two reasons. First, the possibility of measurement error in both the numerator and denominator of the dependent variable may be contributing to spurious results in the preceding analysis which looks at the determinants of hourly earnings. Second, the disaggregation of hours worked into the hourly contributions of the proprietor, unpaid family workers, and paid employees may provide interesting insights into the impacts of each of these variables on earnings. The results from this set of specifications are presented in Table 11.7.

There are some differences in the results from this specification. Whereas an urban location does not have a significant impact on hourly earnings, it does appear to have a positive impact on total reported profits of household enterprises less savings for both men and women. Access to a water tap has a positive impact on women's monthly income, defined as total reported cash income from non-farm self-employment plus value of production for own use, while having migrated in the last five years increases men's monthly incomes.

The most interesting results are in the impacts of hours worked on monthly income. The hours worked by the proprietor have a positive impact on monthly income using either definition for both men and women. Hours of paid employees also have a positive impact on monthly income using either definition, even though payments to employees are netted out in the calculation of profits. This result may be capturing the effects of a scale factor that is not captured in the assets variable: for example, larger enterprises may have more paid employees and thus higher earnings, although they may not necessarily have high-value assets.

The hours contributed by unpaid family workers have a positive and significant impact only when monthly income is defined as total reported profits less savings, suggesting perhaps that proprietors may take into account some kind of transfer to unpaid family workers when they report their personal income from self-employment. Unfortunately, there is no way to ascertain whether this is indeed the case from the data available. It is also interesting that the total number of hours of unpaid family workers has a greater impact on men's earnings than it does on women's earnings, suggesting that male proprietors are able to capture a greater surplus from unpaid workers than are female proprietors.

Table 11.7 Determinants of monthly income from non-agricultural household enterprises

	Men	Men	Women	Women
	ln inc1	ln inc2	ln inc1	ln inc2
Age	0.0292*	0.0412**	0.0721***	0.0756***
	(0.0168)	(0.0179)	(0.00957)	(0.0113)
Age²/100	−0.0336*	−0.0540***	−0.0781***	−0.0833***
	(0.0181)	(0.0194)	(0.0109)	(0.0128)
Married	0.0490	0.146	−0.0686	0.0342
	(0.0849)	(0.0893)	(0.0460)	(0.0536)
Primary	0.374**	0.288*	0.253***	0.323***
	(0.150)	(0.160)	(0.0634)	(0.0742)
Post-primary	0.593***	0.405***	0.315***	0.485***
	(0.139)	(0.147)	(0.0671)	(0.0780)
Secondary	0.482***	0.400**	0.314**	0.577***
	(0.183)	(0.193)	(0.129)	(0.151)
Vocational	0.570***	0.365*	0.136	0.373**
	(0.202)	(0.213)	(0.142)	(0.164)
Tertiary	0.905***	0.975***	0.560***	0.962***
	(0.243)	(0.261)	(0.216)	(0.248)
Urban	0.189*	0.0802	0.176***	−0.0244
	(0.0993)	(0.105)	(0.0570)	(0.0662)
Electricity	0.386***	0.294***	0.333***	0.280***
	(0.0920)	(0.0972)	(0.0515)	(0.0601)
Water tap	0.112	−0.0966	0.0626	0.139**
	(0.0890)	(0.0938)	(0.0555)	(0.0645)
Adult migrant	0.249***	0.0388	−0.0775	0.00844
	(0.0910)	(0.0957)	(0.0514)	(0.0602)
English literate	−0.150	−0.0927	−0.0804	−0.169**
	(0.105)	(0.110)	(0.0644)	(0.0748)
Credit	0.0676	0.0304	0.186***	0.153**
	(0.0918)	(0.0967)	(0.0576)	(0.0672)
Assets	0.0174	0.0285**	0.0165**	0.0304***
	(0.0107)	(0.0113)	(0.00747)	(0.00868)
Years	0.00433	0.00827**	0.00868***	0.00840***
	(0.00334)	(0.00355)	(0.00213)	(0.00250)
Formal	0.249***	0.182**	0.0919	0.150**
	(0.0863)	(0.0906)	(0.0624)	(0.0720)
Hrs—proprietor	0.000836**	0.00182***	0.000722***	0.00102***
	(0.000342)	(0.000364)	(0.000148)	(0.000174)
Hrs—family wrk	0.00136**	−0.000644	0.000923	−0.0000182
	(0.000651)	(0.000686)	(0.000568)	(0.000655)
Hrs—employees	0.000169***	0.000115***	0.000309***	0.000190**
	(0.0000414)	(0.0000437)	(0.0000709)	(0.0000829)
Constant	11.41***	11.31***	10.57***	10.24***
	(0.355)	(0.376)	(0.195)	(0.229)
N	759	759	2252	2250
Adj. R-sq	0.204	0.153	0.159	0.123

Statistical significance: * 10%, ** 5%, *** 1%.

Dependent variable: natural logarithm of estimated monthly earnings (standard errors in parentheses).

Source: Estimates based on GLSS 5.

11.4.3 Issues Related to Selection

The earnings regressions presented in the previous section are conditional on individuals reporting earnings from non-agricultural household enterprises. This may pose a problem if we want to generalize the results and apply them to the entire population. For example, individuals who operate household enterprises may share common unobserved attributes that lead them to choose self-employment, and that may also affect earnings. When these kinds of selection dynamics exist, the estimated relationships may be biased.

One common method for addressing selection bias is to use a two-step estimator, such as that developed by Heckman (1979), in which a selection equation (e.g. a probit model) is estimated in the first step and an adjustment for selection is introduced to the earnings regression. The challenge in developing a selection model is to identify exclusion restrictions: variables which influence the decision to take on self-employment but which do not affect earnings. Here we examine three variables which could serve as exclusion restrictions: the ratio of children under five years to working-age adults in the household, non-employment household income (divided by number of people in the household), and whether the individual is a native-born Ghanaian. These variables have been shown to be important influences on the decision to take on self-employment in Ghana (Heintz and Pickbourn, 2012). We assume that these variables affect the choice of self-employment without directly affecting earnings in non-agricultural self-employment.

There is an added difficulty in applying the Heckman procedure. Several of the explanatory variables in the earnings equations measure characteristics of the enterprise, and are therefore observed only when individuals operate household enterprises. In the hourly earnings estimations, these variables are enterprise assets, years of operation, and registration status. Wooldridge (2010) outlines an estimation procedure under these conditions, using a two-stage least squares instrumental variable (IV) estimation technique in the second part of the Heckman two-step estimation. In this procedure, the variables used to introduce exclusion restrictions are also used as instruments in the IV regression.[4] We apply these procedures to the hourly earnings equations (Table 11.6). The selection equation consists of all the variables in the earnings equations plus the three variables discussed above as exclusion restrictions. We are interested in testing whether the selection adjustment (i.e. the inverse Mills ratio) is statistically significant in the earnings equations. A lack of statistical significance suggests that the selection process is

[4] The total number of potentially endogenous variables should not be equal to or greater than the number of variables used as exclusion restrictions. In our case, this poses a problem. Therefore, we drop the registration status variable in the IV regressions, since this variable was not statistically significant in most of the OLS hourly earnings equations.

Table 11.8 Estimated coefficients and standard errors for the inverse Mills ratio, Heckman two-step selection models (standard errors in parentheses)

	(1)	(2)	(3)	(4)
	Male	Male	Female	Female
	Earn1	Earn2	Earn1	Earn2
Standard Heckman Two-Step Model	−0.445 (0.647)	−0.008 (0.616)	−0.389 (0.494)	−0.234 (0.490)
IV Two-Step Selection model	−0.472 (0.772)	−0.003 (0.740)	−1.120 (3.315)	−0.478 (1.143)

Note: Equations 1, 2, 3, and 4 in Table 11.8 correspond to equations 3, 4, 5, and 6 in Table 11.6, respectively.
Source: Estimates based on GLSS 5.

independent of the determination of earnings, and no adjustment to correct for selection bias is needed. Table 11.8 presents the coefficients and standard errors for the selection adjustment (inverse Mills) for the standard Heckman two-step procedure and the IV procedure.

We find no statistically significant selection adjustment. We therefore conclude that the OLS results presented in the previous section represent reliable estimates of the determinants of earnings for individuals operating non-agricultural household enterprises. Given our specification of the selection equation and the limitations of the data set used, we found no evidence of a meaningful selection problem. Our findings provide further support for having confidence in the OLS estimates having taken into consideration variables shown to be important determinants of selecting into self-employment in Ghana.

11.5 Conclusions

The focus on individual and enterprise productivity as the primary determinant of workers' earnings in the literature on the determinants of earnings in self-employment and informal employment overlooks the fact that informal employment is not a homogeneous employment category. Like other forms of employment, a variety of structural and institutional constraints acts as barriers to mobility within the sector, leading to significant differences in earnings among informally employed workers. Our analysis suggests individual endowments of human capital and productive assets matter for determining earnings in self-employment. However, these variables are complemented by other factors which operate at the household or institutional level, such as access to electricity and credit, as well as gender differences.

Our analysis suggests that standard recommendations for improving earnings for informal workers may be limited. For example, returns to schooling are non-linear for the self-employed. Returns to primary education are large and significant. However, incremental gains from further schooling (e.g. secondary education) appear to be small, although the marginal returns to secondary education may be larger for women than for men. Vocational training has a significant impact on earnings, but only for men. Since more women specialize in non-agricultural self-employment, additional vocational training within the existing education system may not lead to real benefits. Educational reform—rather than simply more education—may be important for improving earnings outcomes for the self-employed.

It is not clear that 'formalization'—that is, requiring enterprises to register with government authorities—leads to better outcomes, particularly in terms of hourly earnings. Instead, improving access to credit and infrastructure appears to be a more promising policy area. Finally, our analysis suggests that there are significant differences in gender dynamics within informal self-employment which affect individual welfare, but these may be difficult to transform through policy alone. Nevertheless, social norms that limit women to low-income forms of self-employment, while more resistant to change, can still be modified over time through the introduction of legislation to reduce gender inequalities in access to financial and productive resources.

This research represents an initial step towards a better understanding of the determinants of labour market outcomes in what is commonly called the informal sector. Although the empirical results presented here are specific to Ghana, the approach taken and the issues raised would be important and relevant for a wide range of countries. However, the analysis has limitations. Earnings are not determined solely by individual, household, enterprise, and institutional variables: demand-side factors may also play a role in determining the earnings of self-employed operators of household enterprises. In addition, the lack of panel data on household enterprises makes it difficult to control for unobserved individual characteristics that may be affecting earnings. Findings from ethnographic and qualitative research suggest that the results we present here are credible, but many questions remain unresolved in the quantitative analysis with regard to causality and unobserved individual characteristics. As more and better data become available on labour market dynamics in Ghana, such estimates will improve, as will our understanding of the determinants of earnings for those individuals who rely on informal self-employment as their primary source of income.

References

Baden, S., C. Green, N. Otoo-Oyortey, and T. Peasgood (1994). 'Background Paper on Gender Issues in Ghana'. Report prepared for the West and North Africa Department, Department for Overseas Development (DFID), UK.

Bruce, J. and D. Dwyer (1988). *A Home Divided: Women and Income in the Third World.* Palo Alto, CA: Stanford University Press.

Campbell, K., P. Marsden, and J. Hurlbert (1986). 'Social Resources and Socioeconomic Status', *Social Networks*, 8(1): 97–117.

Coulombe, H. and A. McKay (2008). *The Estimation of Components of Household Income and Expenditures: A Methodological Guide Based on the Last Three Rounds of the Ghana Living Standards Survey, 1991/1992, 1998/1999 and 2005/2006*. Accra: Ghana Statistical Service.

Ekejiuba, F. (1995). 'Down to Fundamentals: Women-centered Hearthholds in Rural West Africa', in D. F. Bryceson (ed.), *Women Wielding the Hoe: Lessons from Rural Africa for Feminist Theory and Development Practice.* Oxford: Berg Publishers: 47–62.

Epstein, G. and J. Heintz (2006). 'Monetary Policy and Financial Sector Reform for Employment Creation and Poverty Reduction in Ghana'. *PERI Working Paper* No. 113. Amherst, MA: Political Economy Research Institute.

Fajnzylber, P., W. Maloney, and G. Rojas (2006). 'Microenterprise Dynamics in Developing Countries: How Similar are They to Those in the Industrialized World?' Evidence from Mexico'. *World Bank Economic Review*, 20: 389–419.

Falco, P. (2011). *'Determinants of Income in Informal Self-Employment: New Evidence from a Long African Panel'*. Oxford: Centre for the Study of African Economies, University of Oxford.

Fields, G. (1975). 'Rural-Urban Migration, Urban Unemployment and Underemployment, and Job-search Activity in LDCs'. *Journal of Development Economics*, 2(2): 165–87.

Gilbertson, G. (1995). 'Women's Labor and Enclave Employment: The Case of Dominican and Colombian Women in New York City'. *International Migration Review*, 29(3): 657–70.

Goldstein, M. (2000). 'Intrahousehold Allocation and Farming in Southern Ghana'. Doctoral dissertation, University of California, Berkeley, CA.

Granovetter, M. (1973). 'Strength of Weak Ties'. *American Journal of Sociology*, 78(6): 1360–80.

Hagan, M. (1998). 'Social Networks, Gender and Immigrant Incorporation: Resources and Constraints'. *American Sociological Review*, 63(1): 55–67.

Heckman, J. (1979). 'Sample Selection Bias as a Specification Error'. *Econometrica*, 47(1): 153–60.

Heintz, J. and L. Pickbourn (2012). 'The Determinants of Selection into Non-Agricultural Self-Employment in Ghana'. *Margins: The Journal of Applied Economic Research*, 6(2):181–209.

ILO (2002). *Women and Men in the Informal Economy: A Statistical Picture.* Geneva: International Labor Office.

Kevane, M. (2000). 'Extrahousehold Norms and Intrahousehold Bargaining: Gender in Sudan and Burkina Faso', in A. Spring (ed.), *Women Farmers and Commercial Ventures: Increasing Food Security in Developing Countries*. Boulder, CO: Lynne Rienner Publishers.

Levy, S. (2008). *Good Intentions, Bad Outcomes: Social Policy, Informality, and Economic Growth in Mexico*. Washington, DC: Brookings Institution.

Loayza, N. and Rigolini, J. (2006). 'Informality Trends and Cycles'. *World Bank Policy Research Working Paper No. 4078*. Washington, DC: World Bank.

Maloney, W. (2004). 'Informality Revisited'. *World Development*, 32(7): 1159–78.

Obbo, C. (1976). 'Dominant Male Ideology and Female Options: Three East African Case Studies', *Africa*, 46(4): 371–89.

Palmer, R. (2005). 'Beyond the Basics: Post-Basic Education and Training and Poverty Reduction in Ghana'. *Post-Basic Education and Training Working Paper Series* No. 4. Centre of African Studies, University of Edinburgh. Available at <www.cas.ed.ac.uk/__data/assets/pdf_file/0017/28322/Palmer_Ghana_PBET_WP4.pdf> (accessed 15 June 2013).

—— (2007). 'Education, Training and Labor Market Outcomes in Ghana: A Review of the Evidence'. *Research Consortium on Educational Outcomes and Poverty Working Paper* No. 9. Cambridge: RECOUP.

Portes, A. and L. Jensen (1989). 'The Enclave and the Entrants: Patterns of Ethnic Enterprise in Miami before and after Mariel'. *American Sociological Review*, 54(6): 929–49.

Roberts, P. (1988). 'Rural Women's Access to Labor in West Africa', in S. Stichter and J. Parpart (eds.), *Patriarchy and Class: African Women in the Home and the Workforce*. Boulder: Westview Press: 97–114.

Sandefur, J., P. Serneels, and F. Teal (2007). 'Poverty and Earnings Mobility in Three African Countries', in P. Paci and P. M. Serneels (eds.), *Employment and Shared Growth: Rethinking the Role of Labor Mobility for Development*. Washington, DC: World Bank: 69–89.

Schindler, K. (2010). 'Credit for What? Informal Credit as a Coping Strategy of Market Women in Northern Ghana'. *Journal of Development Studies*, 46(2): 234–53.

Udry, C. and T. Conley (2004). 'Social Networks in Ghana'. Working Paper No. 888. Economic Growth Center, Yale University, New Haven, CT. Available at <http://www.econ.yale.edu/~cru2/pdf/endognetworks.pdf> (accessed 20 May 2013).

Warner, M., R. Alhassan, and J. Kydd (1997). 'Beyond Gender Roles? Conceptualizing the Social and Economic Lives of Rural Peoples in sub-Saharan Africa'. *Development and Change*, 28(1): 143–68.

Whitehead, A. (1981). 'I'm Hungry, Mum: The Politics of Domestic Budgeting', in K. Young et al. (eds.), *Of Marriage and the Market: Women's Subordination in International Perspective*. London: CSE Books.

Wooldridge, J. M. (2010). *Econometric Analysis of Cross Section and Panel Data*, Second edition. Cambridge, MA: MIT Press.

Zhou, M. and J. Logan (1989). 'Returns on Human Capital in Ethnic Enclaves: New York City's Chinatown'. *American Sociological Review*, 54(5): 809–20.

12

From the Street to the Store: The Formalization of Street Vendors in Quito, Ecuador

Sergio Ferragut and Georgina M. Gómez

12.1 Introduction

The presence of informal street vendors on the sidewalks, squares, and streets of the historic centre of Quito in Ecuador increased dramatically during the period 1950 to 2003. In the context of a process of development, the local government, the municipality of Quito (Municipio del Distrito Metropolitano de Quito—MDMQ), initiated a formalization process that affected almost 6,500 informal street vendors. Under different arrangements, the municipality built and refurbished eleven popular commercial centres (Centros Comerciales Populares—CCPs) where the formalized street vendors have been relocated since 2003. In addition to facilitating access to physical infrastructure, the municipality provided them with training and support with their management.

Formalization is conceptualized as an intervention aimed at bringing into the formal economy those wage-earning and self-employed workers who have been earning an income in the informal economy. In this chapter, we argue that not all those who have undergone the process of formalization have benefited equally, since individuals have different characteristics and therefore achieve different results in terms of their living and working conditions.

Before undertaking this research, different approaches for understanding the impact of formalization on the working and living conditions of vendors were considered; however, the one provided by decent work deficits, developed by the International Labour Organization (ILO), was identified as the most appropriate. While formalization targets the individuals and their business units, it also concerns the household. The decent work deficits' approach enables a broad understanding of people's working conditions that goes beyond a study of income levels. Given that very few studies have examined decent work at the micro level, one of the challenges, and contribution, of this study was to operationalize the concept and redefine the indicators so that they could be used for measuring the particular deficits experienced by vendors before and after formalization.

This research relied on both primary and secondary sources. Documents produced by different branches of the local government, international organizations, and other institutions were used to frame the case and understand the actors involved. Six weeks of fieldwork were conducted during August and September of 2009, and included first-hand observations, pictures, a survey, and interviews. The survey questionnaire was finalized after having visited the market and spoken informally with some of the vendors in order to develop indicators that were the most relevant to their situation. The questionnaire was employed with fourteen vendors working at one of the allocated commercial centres. Other actors interviewed included five representatives of the organizations involved in the negotiations (i.e. municipality of Quito, the Inter-American Development Bank (IDB), the company for the development of the historic centre (ECH), the company for the urban development of Quito (Innovar), the unit responsible for implementing the modernization of informal street vending (UECM), and the administration of the commercial centre Ipiales Mires), as well as nine vendors who were relocated from the streets. Three of the vendors were interviewed as part of a focus group, while the rest were interviewed individually. Unfortunately, the sample is not large enough for the conclusions to be considered representative of the entire population of street vendors; nevertheless, it serves the purpose of gaining an insight into the changes in the vendors' lives after formalization.

12.2 Informal Economy and Formalization

The ILO defines the informal economy as 'all economic activities that are in law or in practice not covered or insufficiently covered by formal arrangements' (ILO, 2007a: 1). The change of terminology from the informal sector to informal economy 'takes account of the considerable diversity of workers and economic units, in different sectors of the economy and across rural and urban contexts that are particularly vulnerable and insecure, that experience severe decent work deficits and often remain trapped in poverty and low productivity' (ILO, 2007a: 1). This definition is far from being unchallenged, but serves the purposes of this chapter.

A parallel dilemma at the policy level is 'whether the ILO and its constituents should promote the informal sector as a provider of employment and incomes or seek to extend regulation and social protection to it and thereby possibly reduce its capacity to provide jobs and incomes for an ever increasing labour force' (ILO, 2002: 1). This links to the discussion on whether informal jobs are, per se, low-income jobs. Portes and Schauffler (1993: 45) found that 'owners of micro enterprises and some of the self-employed earn significantly more than salaried workers in the formal sector'. In turn, Teltscher (1994) and Perry et al. (2007) established that during the 1990s some people resorted to becoming informal street vendors in order to survive while others did so by choice, thus disproving some of the assumptions that characterized those working in the informal sector as 'survivalists'. As noted by Cross and Karides (2007: 29) in a more recent study, 'Vendors can maintain an economic existence that ranges from basic survival to middle class existence.'

In the view of the ILO, workers and enterprises at the bottom of the labour pyramid experience a series of disadvantages or 'decent work deficits', which are most prevalent in the informal economy because the working conditions in informality are for the most part precarious and vulnerable (ILO, 2007a: 3). Other authors have argued that in most developing countries poverty results more from the inability of workers to obtain secure and decent incomes than from unemployment (Ocampo and Jomo, 2007: 13). Consequently, the ILO advises policy-makers to concentrate efforts on addressing salient decent work deficits for workers and entrepreneurs in the informal economy while at the same time bringing them into the mainstream economy (ILO, 2007b: 2).

The general guidelines for decent work keep evolving as the discussion on this concept gains momentum. The aim is to set goals that would assist policy-makers at the country level. Decent work requires 'making interventions in enabling dimensions of living that affect the circumstances in which a working person, given [his or] her labour and personal characteristics, starts out to achieve a decent life' (Majid, 2001: 1). Four pillars or dimensions have been identified by the ILO as the most relevant for the achievement of decent work: (1) employment, (2) social security, (3) fundamental rights, and (4) social dialogue (see Figure 12.1). According to Ghai (2002: 2), 'While the first two components of decent work refer to opportunities, remuneration, security and conditions of work, the last two emphasize the "social relations" of workers.' In other words, the first two components of decent work are concerned with material needs while the last two are concerned with values and legislation.

The ILO has extended the concept of decent work to the micro level by identifying a set of seven securities, in addition to basic security, that capture all the different aspects that make work decent, and which the organization refers to as labour, employment, job, work, skill reproduction, income, and representation. These constitute the main *dimensions* through which decent work deficits can be analysed comparing existing conditions with what may be considered 'ideal' ones. In order to assess deficits in these areas, the ILO has created the People's Security Surveys (PSSs), which track seven forms of work-related security comprising decent work (Standing, 2002: 443). They are the following ones:

1. *Labour market security* relates to the ability of the economically active population to obtain and maintain income-generating work (Kantor, Rani, and Unni, 2006: 2091).
2. *Employment security* relates to 'the ability to keep one's work' (Kantor, Rani, and Unni, 2006: 2092) and 'protection against arbitrary dismissal, and employment stability compatible with economic dynamism' (Standing, 2002: 442). It captures the overall vulnerability of workers to loss of jobs over time due to circumstances beyond their control.
3. *Job security* 'relates to having an occupational niche and is measured by the reason why the respondents entered their line of work, the perceived ease with which others can learn their skills and self-classification by relative skill levels' (Kantor, Rani, and Unni, 2006: 2093).
4. *Work security* 'relates to the physical conditions of work' (Kantor, Rani, and Unni, 2006: 2094), such as 'protection against accidents and illness at work, through safety and health regulation, [and] limits on working time, on unsociable hours, and on night work for women' (Standing, 2002: 442).
5. *Skill reproduction* 'assesses how well workers can gain and maintain skills' (Kantor, Rani, and Unni, 2006: 2095).
6. *Income security* relates to having an income that is adequate, reasonably good relative to others, regular and assured, access to non-wage benefits and income-supplementing (or replacement) entitlements (Standing, 2002: 445).
7. *Representation* implies the 'protection of [a] collective voice in the labour market, through independent trade unions and employers' associations and other bodies able to represent the interests of workers and working communities' (Standing, 2002: 442).

One of the few studies that evaluated decent work deficits among workers in the informal economy at the micro level was carried out in Surat, India (Kantor et al., 2006). In comparison with the present research, the one in Surat covered both wage-earners and self-employed workers. In addition, it was conducted through the households, whereas the approach used for this research was through the workplace. Table 12.1 summarizes the dimensions of the decent work deficits and how they were interpreted for this study.

Table 12.1 The dimensions of security and indicators used

Labour market	Employment	Job	Work	Skill reproduction	Income	Representation
Operationalizing and assessing the seven dimensions of work-related securities relevant to the self-employed						
Having access to an income-generating job	Having protection against fluctuations and changes in the market due to reasons or circumstances beyond the control of the worker	Having the skills and an occupational niche that would allow a person to keep a job over time with opportunities for advancement and improvement	Having a safe and secure working environment (in accordance with local regulations)	Having the chance to use previously learnt skills while gaining new ones at work	Having an income that is adequate, reasonably good relative to others', regular and assured, and access to non-wage benefits and income-supplementing entitlements	Having the right to form and participate in associations or organizations of workers recognized by the existing authorities Having associations and organizations that represent the interest of the workers
Indicators used for this research aimed at exploring and evaluating working conditions for vendors:						
• irregular/seasonal work. • hours and days of work per week. • would like to work more hours/days. • work excessive hours. • work excessive hours but want to work more. • mean hours in paid work. • working more or less hours/days a week after formalization.	• owns or rents store. • having a fixed location before formalization. • stability as informal. • years working as vendor. • believes will continue working as vendor in one year. • have the store insured against robbery and/or fire. • have access to social security benefits (medical care, pension, work insurance).	• income fluctuations after formalization. • expected income fluctuations during the next year.	• feels secure in the market against robberies, accidents, and harassment. • feels safe in the market in terms of health threats. • overall perception of safety and security before and after formalization.	• feels that is using all its potential and capabilities at work. • received training as part of formalization. • access to certified formal training.	• perception of average income relative to other vendors working in the same type of market. • fluctuations of average income since formalization (seasonality of increases and decreases). • sources of income other than the store. • income during the last month. • expenditures during the last month.	• membership and participation in associations or organizations of vendors before and after formalization. • knowledge about other existing associations or organizations currently at the market. • actor approached when there is problem in the market.

Source: Authors.

12.3 The Path to Formalization in Quito

In 1978, the historic centre of Quito was the first place in the world to be declared a Cultural World Heritage site by the United Nations Educational, Scientific and Cultural Organization (UNESCO). During the 1980s, debt and financial crises directly contributed to a continuing deterioration of the historic centre. In 1987, this was exacerbated by an earthquake which damaged infrastructure, houses, buildings, and monuments in the historic centre. In response, and in order to capitalize from UNESCO's declaration of 1978, in 1988 the Municipality of Quito decided to formulate a plan for rehabilitating the area. As this process unfolded, space in the historic centre became a scarce and valuable resource.

The municipal intervention had different dimensions: (a) designing a master plan to develop the area, (b) designing the appropriate financing mechanisms, (c) building institutions that would coordinate the development of the area, and (d) developing specific projects that included the relocation and reorganization of ambulatory commerce and street vending (Carrion, 2006: 2). One of the first problems identified in the process was that many of the historic spaces were used by informal street vendors, which by the mid-1990s were perceived to be an obstacle to the overall development of the area. A census by the Municipality of Quito in 1991 found that 10,000 informal street vendors worked in the historic centre (Carrion, 2006: 2). These findings revealed to policy-makers the size and significance of the informal sector in the city centre.

Throughout the 1990s, the concept of the informal economy changed, and its potential contributions to economic growth was first reassessed and later recognized, at least in Quito. In 1996, the Municipality of Quito conducted a study of the vendors which concluded that 'informal commerce constituted a popular solution in the face of the shortage of formal employment opportunities and it satisfied the consumer demand of the low-income sector of the population of the city' (Middleton, 2003: 84).

In 1996, the Municipality of Quito created a public–private enterprise for the development of the historic centre, the company for the development of the historic centre (Empresa Para el Desarrollo del Centro Historico—ECH) which was responsible for implementing the Master Plan for the Renovation and Development of the Historic Centre that had been approved in 1992. The ECH served as a platform to attract funding at the local, national, and international levels. The biggest portion of the financing was a loan from the IDB, which contributed $41 million, out of the total planned investment of $51 million (Carrion, 2006: 6). The IDB's contribution aimed at supporting the integral rehabilitation of the historic centre. The functions of the

ECH progressively grew to encompass many areas of responsibility beyond its original mandate, and in 2005 it became the company for the urban development of Quito (Empresa Para el Desarrollo Urbano de Quito—Innovar).

The new approach to the rehabilitation of the historic centre not only recognized the cultural and historic value of the area, but also placed special importance on its residents and those who earned a living in it. An important step in the formalization process was the vendors' registration, which started in 1991 but was only completed during the final stages of the negotiations around the formalization process around 2003. Only vendors who were registered with the municipality were later entitled to obtain a store in the popular shopping centres.

The local government recognized the street vendors' right to be included in the development and rehabilitation of the historic centre, which encouraged them to negotiate with the local authorities a public space where they would be able to sell their goods. The associations acted as the interlocutors of the vendors with the Municipality of Quito, monopolizing, to some extent, the main channels of communication and information in their favour. As noted by Middleton, 'there was clearly discomfort with having to deal with the leaders of the organisations, many of whom were said to be "mafiosos" who were exploiting the traders in their own interests' (Middleton, 2003: 96). In order to address this issue, the municipality organized several open meetings to inform and discuss with all vendors directly. A total of ninety-six trader associations, formed on the basis of their geographical location long before the formalization process, decided to accept the invitation and participate in the negotiations. Together, they represented a total of 5,600 traders (Middleton, 2003: 96).

Construction of the popular shopping centres to relocate the vendors within the historic centre of Quito began in 1998. In 2000, a new unit in the local government for implementing the modernization of informal street vending was created. By June 2003, all the 'formalized' street vendors had moved into the shopping centres. It was agreed that the popular shopping centres would first be managed by the UECM, which would support the vendors in their transition 'from the stall to the store', and eventually, responsibility would be transferred to a body representing the vendors (Middleton, 2003). The future of the UECM is uncertain at present, as its mandate has been extended a number of times. Seven years since the inception of the popular shopping centres, it is evident that vendors cannot afford the cost of running the centres without the support of the UECM (e.g. administration, security, cleaning, maintenance of infrastructure).

In the popular shopping centres listed in Table 12.2 (ordered by number of stalls), it is mandatory for the vendors to open their stores from Monday to Saturday. Although the vendors own the stores that were awarded to them

Table 12.2 Popular shopping centres in Quito after formalization (as of August 2009)

Name	Location (streets)	Capacity (number of stores)
1) Centro Comercial El Tejar	HCQ—Lopez between Hermano Miguel and Mejia	1,200
2) Centro Comercial Hermano Miguel	HCQ—Imbabura between Hermando Miguel and Mejia	1,600
3) Centro Comercial Granada	HCQ—Corner of Chile and Cuenca, La Merced Square	430
4) Centro Comercial Montufar	HCQ—Montufar between Olmedo and Mejia	397
5) Centro Comercial La Merced	HCQ—Cuenca between Mejia and Olmedo	208
6) Centro Comercial Ipiales Mires	HCQ—Corner of Mejia and Mires	209
7) Centro Comercial San Martin	HCQ—Avenue Pichinca and Inclana	429
8) Centro Comercial Nuevo Amanecer	HCQ—Lopez between Hermano Miguel and Mejia	250
9) Centro Ipiales del Norte	NORTH—Gonzalo Gallo and Jorge Piedra	n/a
10) Centro Comercial Ipiales del Sur	SOUTH—Avenue Mariscal Sucre and Moran Valverde	350
11) Centro Comercial Chiriyacu	SOUTH—Gualberto Perez	500
12) Centro Comercial CABLEC ('Feriantes de Martes y Sabados')	SOUTH	2,100
Total number of stores available as of August 2009:		**7,673**

Note: HCQ = Historic Centre of Quito.

as part of the formalization process, one of the clauses of the contract establishes that they are not allowed to rent out or sell the store for a period of seven years. On completion of that period, property titles are issued to them, after which they are free to dispose of the store as they wish. This policy is complemented by deploying large numbers of police officers throughout the historic centre to ensure that neither old nor new informal vendors sell on the streets. As a result, the vendors who remain informal have moved to the periphery of Quito.

12.4 The Ipiales Mires Popular Commercial Centre

This study chose the Ipiales Mires popular commercial centre because of its relatively small size, and its location on the site where the informal street vendors used to ply their trade in the 1950s. It was built between 1998 and 2003, with financial support from local and international organizations. It has four levels, each with approximately the same number of stores, and the capacity to accommodate 209 vendors. All the stores are more or less the same size and have storage space, electricity, and a metallic roll-up door that can easily be closed and locked when the vendor is out of the store. One set of stairs connects each of the levels but there is no elevator, making access to the top floors difficult for people with disabilities or for vendors who need to carry large volumes of merchandise into the stores. Although the centre does not have its own parking, customers and vendors are allowed to use the shopping centre car park located across the street. A bus stop across the street connects the market with the main points in the city. All levels have toilets and security cameras. There is good ventilation and a central patio with a glass roof that provides natural light for most stores in the market, complementing the artificial light provided in the corridors and stores. The third level has a food court with eight small restaurants that share a common space with tables, and the second level has seven telephone booths and an ATM machine. The office of the UECM, responsible for the administration of the Ipiales Mires centre, has three full-time employees and is located on the fourth floor, where there is also a meeting area for both the UECM staff and the vendors. Also located on the fourth floor, there is a day-care centre that operates at full capacity.

All merchandise offered in the stores is new, but of medium to low quality, and most of it is from Ecuador (77 per cent). Almost all vendors sell only one type of product in their stores. In most cases, prices are not displayed and are settled after bargaining with the vendor and in cash only. Even when prices are displayed, they are usually not final but only serve as the starting point of negotiation for a final price. The vendors reported selling the majority of their products to low- and middle-income Ecuadorians. In addition, 30 per cent reported tourists as the second most important group of customers. Finally, none of them reported selling to *'pelucones'* (upper income Ecuadorians). Although vendors generally sell most of their products by unit, some of them have become suppliers to new street vendors who usually buy from them the quantity of products they expect to sell each day. It is important to highlight the fact that while the Municipality of Quito has managed to reduce the number of informal street vendors in the historic centre, informal street vending in general remains a common phenomenon on the periphery of Quito and in other provinces throughout Ecuador.

A number of stores are vacant, and most economic activity takes place on the first and second levels and next to the food court on the third level of the centre. When asked why so many stores at the centre were closed, one of the vendors interviewed explained that some families who used to run a single stall on the streets, got more than one store at the popular centres because at the time of the registration each family member registered as an individual vendor. They were motivated mainly by speculation—the owners were not operating the store, but simply waiting for the process of formalization to be completed in order to be able to sell the store and make a profit. In addition, some vendors worked some days of the week in this particular market, and some other days elsewhere. Most vendors are the second and third generation descendants of the original vendors who started working at La Ipiales around the 1950s.

12.5 A Closer Look at Formalized Vendors

Three main topics guided the interviews: (1) the circumstances that led the person to engage in informal street vending, (2) the profile of a typical day in the life of a street vendor, and (3) as vendors in Ipiales Mires. At the end of the interview, vendors were also asked to reflect about what had 'improved' and what had 'gotten worse' since formalization. The real names of the vendors interviewed have been changed in order to protect their anonymity (see Appendix).

The average age of those surveyed was 51. The large majority of them were married and the average size of their household was 3.64 persons. Seventy one per cent of them were born in rural areas and had moved to Quito when they were young in order to find jobs. On average, vendors had completed 12.2 years of formal education, which is well above the average level of education for Ecuadorians living in Quito, at 11.1 years. Among the surveyed vendors, the women had higher levels of education than the men. In the past, most vendors had very low levels of education and training, but they began to perceive it as a means of eventually climbing the social ladder. As a result, they attached great importance to educating their children, but on completing their education, they encountered barriers to accessing certain segments of the labour market, which ultimately forced many of them also to become vendors—the trade they had learnt while growing up.

Most of the vendors (92 per cent) did not hire employees either permanently or seasonally; however, many of them reported receiving help from family members and friends during peak periods such as Christmas. The majority of those interviewed (57 per cent) had worked for a wage before becoming informal street vendors: of these, 71 per cent were men compared with 42 per cent of women. Of those interviewed, 78 per cent had been selling the same type of products since they began. Some of them reported managing to build networks, which, over time, had allowed them to move upwards in the value chains of the products they sold, by incorporating other activities. For instance, a vendor explained that once she noted that the box in which her merchandise was packed had come from Colon. A few days later she went to a travel agency to find out where Colon was, and a few months later, having got a loan from an aunt, she was on her way to Colon, Panamá, to buy the merchandise directly from the producers. This allowed her to increase her profit margins over time, but at great personal risk.

The vendors produced 35 per cent of the products they sold, and of the remaining products 80 per cent were acquired through retailers and the remaining 20 per cent were purchased directly from the producers. Sixty-four per cent of vendors bought their merchandise by cash and only 35 per cent used credit. Informal street vendors in the historic centre have had access to credit for a long time, and owning their stores has not changed the way they operate. Their main source of credit since the 1990s has been the suppliers (retailers) of merchandise. Before that time, their main source of credit was family and friends (Teltscher, 1994). This type of credit entailed no cost for the vendors, and, for the suppliers, it was essential in order to keep selling and attracting new customers. Vendors' most important collateral for credit is not property titles but '*la palabra*' (their word or promise). The rules for maintaining the supply of credit are very straightforward: if a vendor fails to pay off his or her credit, suppliers will not grant further credit and the vendor will not be able to operate any more. Since there are few suppliers, information on a bad payer circulates fast among them.

12.6 Decent Work after Formalization

Table 12.3 summarizes the findings on how formalization has affected the decent work deficit of vendors in the seven dimensions explained. The first dimension, labour market security, discusses the ways in which formalization affected the access of vendors to an income-generating job. On average, vendors reported that they worked 51 hours a week, which is well above the average for workers in Quito and other urban areas throughout Ecuador, which is 45.2 hours. On average, at the Ipiales Mires centre, men reported working 58 hours a week, while women reported working 43 hours. Despite the fact that most vendors were already working long hours, 66 per cent of them reported that they would like to work even more hours—more men (83 per cent) expressed this than women (50 per cent). This may be motivated not so much out of 'entrepreneurial drive' but by the need to secure a livelihood. The larger number of men than women wanting to work more hours may be due to the fact that women engage in more childcare than men do, and they simply would not have the time to work more, even if they wanted to. Of the vendors interviewed, 50 per cent reported working more hours and days before formalization, while 21 per cent reported working less. As noted by one of the vendors describing his routine before formalization, 'we would start working at 4 or 5 am and by noon we would be out of merchandise. We would then travel to Guayaquil to get more merchandise and come back at

Table 12.3 Analysis of dimensions of decent work before and after formalization

Analysis of the seven dimensions of decent work		
Assessment of the seven dimensions of decent work before and after formalization		Analysis through the indicators of decent work
1) Labour	Improved but still presents deficits.	• vendors have a regular job but are usually exposed to fluctuations in the market that are beyond their control. • vendors work excess hours. • vendors are working less hours now than before formalization.
2) Employment	Improved but still presents deficits.	• vendors own their stores. • most vendors have been working as vendors for most of their lives. • most vendors remain without any type of social security coverage. • associations, which provided the equivalent to social security for many vendors, have lost relevance. • most vendors had a fixed location before formalization, which provided them with a sense of stability.
3) Job	Deteriorated.	• most vendors reported a decrease in income and fluctuations depending on season (only 28 per cent believe their incomes will increase during the next year). • as vendors transition from 'the stall to the store', they remain vulnerable and incapable of securing a niche in the market.
4) Work	Improved.	• overall levels of safety (health) and security (robberies, fire, etc.) improved for most vendors, especially safety.
5) Skill reproduction	Improved.	• most vendors have received formal training after formalization. • although most vendors reported benefiting from the training, also most of them reported currently not using what they learnt at work. • as some of the vendors have high levels of education, there is still a mismatching of capabilities and work among many of them.
6) Income	Deteriorated.	• most vendors reported reduced sales and income. • most vendors reported fluctuations in sales and income. • some vendors reported having a second source of income besides the store.
7) Representation	Deteriorated.	• before formalization, associations formed based on the particular reality and needs of vendors. • although some associations took advantage of vendors, many of them fulfilled very important functions (e.g. security, health, mediation among vendors). • working on the CCPs presents a radical change of that reality. • most vendors remain dubious and sceptic about the actual importance of having representation.

night, so we would be ready to sell the next day. Sometimes, we would have to do it three or four times in the same week.' Having their own store with a roll-up lockable metallic door and storage space, gives vendors more flexibility in deciding their opening and closing hours and allows them to spend less time transporting merchandise and setting up the stall. It has also allowed them to leave the store in case of emergencies without having to worry about being burgled. In the past, once the stall was set up early in the morning, the vendor would have to spend most of his or her time in the stall waiting for customers and protecting the merchandise.

The second dimension of security of employment refers to stability against external shocks and sudden loss of income. Almost 80 per cent of the vendors owned the store where they worked. As many as 64 per cent of the respondents reported having a fixed place from where they would sell their products before formalization, and 66 per cent reported paying a regular fee, often to their associations, for the use of public space. Some vendors who registered with the municipality were also required to pay a monthly fee for the use of space, but no vendor reported having to pay the police. Although the payments were not high, vendors who did not pay faced eviction and maybe even violence. As explained by one of the vendors, 'if you did not pay, the associations would get you out. Since we always needed to work, we always paid.' The majority of those who paid worked at the same fixed space for many years. The concepts of 'ownership' and 'property', and the resultant stability also prevailed among most informal street vendors in the past. Most vendors surveyed reported working at the same location for most of their life. Associations used to paint the streets, indicating where each vendor who was a member could install and sell his or her products. Many of the vendors described the stalls where they used to work as their second home. As stated by one of the vendors, 'when in school they asked me for my address, I would say Cuenca and Sucre, that was the corner where my parents had their stall ever since I can remember; basically, we (the children of vendors) grew up in those streets'. After years at the same location, and with the consent of the association, vendors who wished to move to a new location could sell their space to other vendors, provided the association that controlled that block accepted the new vendors as members. In sum, street stalls could be sold, bought, and even inherited.

After formalization, all vendors surveyed believed that they would continue to work at the same store during the following year, although none of them had insurance against either fire or robbery, for example. The expectation of continuing to work at the same location might not be reassuring to the vendors but a mark of resignation, as most of them did not expect to be able to find a different type of job. It emerged from the survey that the majority of vendors were not covered by any type of social security (i.e. health, pensions, retirement)—a reality faced by many Quiteños. As one vendor put it, 'vendors in general, treat themselves every time they are sick'.

The third dimension is job security. The comparative advantage of many of the informal street vendors had not been based on their entrepreneurial skills, but rather on their low costs of operation and location in terms of convenient access for their customers. After formalization, their costs of operation increased due to taxes and other overhead expenses. Only 7 per cent of vendors reported increases in income after formalization; whereas 85 per cent reported a decrease in income. Only 28 per cent of vendors expected their income to increase over the coming year. If these results are combined with the information on sales obtained by the Municipality of Quito through the raffles, it can be inferred that only a small group of vendors accounts for most of the increases in sales. Street and store vending belong to different occupational niches and require different types of skills and capabilities to succeed.

The fourth dimension, personal security at work, has improved with formalization. At the time of the survey, 85 per cent of the vendors believed that the Ipiales Mires centre was secure (against, for example robbers, fire, and harassment), while 50 per cent believed that it presented safety issues (e.g. physical health). The main reasons given for this perception of insecurity were stress due to the small amount of business activity, exposure to cold, and excessive noise. At the same time, many of them recognized that the working environment had improved considerably. Some of the vendors pointed out that when they were selling on the streets, they did not have easy access to toilets. Long and irregular working hours and eating on the streets every day had caused many of them to develop gastric, digestive, and respiratory conditions. Having toilets available on each floor of the Ipiales Mires centre contributed to the overall hygiene of the workplace and added a certain level of comfort for the vendors. Overall, 71 per cent of vendors at the Ipiales Mires centre felt safer and more secure there than on the streets, while none of them felt less safe and secure.

Fifth, the dimension of skill reproduction covers the extent to which workers are utilizing the skills they already have while gaining new ones at work. Of the vendors surveyed, 35 per cent believed that their skills were not being fully utilized at work. This relates to the fact that many of them became vendors not by choice but out of need. As noted earlier, some of the vendors had high levels of education, but had not been able to find jobs in their areas of expertise. As a result, they had had to resort to informal street vending in order to survive. Most vendors reported having family members or friends who helped them learn how to become vendors. One of the vendors interviewed said, 'Growing up as the child of a vendor exposes you to a totally different reality than the one experienced by a regular child. The child of a vendor is "street smart". For instance, by the age of three, the child of a vendor already knows the value of money; if you ask any other children, they would not even know what money is.' The children of vendors usually help their parents at work, and some of them eventually become vendors themselves.

After formalization, 92 per cent of the vendors received training related to their business. All training was provided by the Municipality of Quito through the UECM, and almost 70 per cent received certification upon completion, but most of them said they had not been able to apply what they had learnt to their daily work. The main areas covered by the training provided were accounting, customer services, and business planning. The majority of vendors interviewed reported that they had never kept separate accounting for their business and household—not even after formalization. As one vendor put it, 'The flow of sales was so big and prices changed so much that we did not have time to write down anything.' Most of them used what we term 'single pocket accounting', which is basically keeping all money and receipts in one pocket and memorizing important expenditures both for the business and the household combined.

The sixth dimension is security of income and refers to keeping income flows adequate for the livelihoods of vendors. More than half of the vendors (52 per cent) believed that they earned more or less the same as other vendors in the other popular shopping centres. The majority of them (71 per cent) reported fluctuating sales throughout the year, especially during peak periods, such as Christmas and Mother's Day. Such fluctuations are common to commerce in general. Most vendors highlighted a reduction in sales and income since they had moved to the popular shopping centres. Of those interviewed, 35 per cent reported having another source of income during the previous month. The most common sources of extra income were other business (37 per cent), pensions (37 per cent), remittances (12 per cent), and gifts (12 per cent).

Income and sales have a direct impact on family life. As reported by one of the vendors, 'When sales are good, I buy a chicken to share with my family. I arrive home happy and we all cook together—everyone is happy to see me home. When I do not sell, I arrive home with little food and even though they do not say anything, I know it is my responsibility to provide for them, so I feel depressed.' Head of households, both men and women, are usually also heads of businesses, and just as they do not separate their accounts, they do not separate their frustrations, with one area spilling over to the other. As a result, family life follows the business cycles for most of the vendors.

In terms of the seventh dimension, security of representation, formalization seems to have reduced the appeal of the associations. At the time of the fieldwork, only 21 per cent of the vendors surveyed reported being part of an association or organization of vendors, while 51 per cent reported being part of an association or organization of vendors before formalization. When asked which institution they approached when facing a problem at work, 91 per cent reported approaching the UECM office. Less than half of the vendors (42 per cent) reported knowing about the existence of associations or organizations of vendors operating in the Ipiales Mires centre at the time of the survey. Before formalization, associations formed and grew over time based on geographical location and common interests and needs. Their main responsibilities were to protect and organize the use of space among the vendors, act as interlocutors between the vendors and the authorities, and provide a socio-economic safety net in times of emergency. In addition, many associations provided vendors with security, electricity, and cleaning services. Most vendors interviewed reported participating in the meetings of their associations back then. When the vendors started to move into the newly constructed commercial centres, efforts were made to assign them stores following more or less the same grouping patterns they had had in the streets; however, this was not accomplished, and as a result, organizations lost touch with their original base of members. In addition, many of the responsibilities assumed by the associations in the past were taken over by the UECM, such as organizing the use of common space and administering the rules for the market. Furthermore, many vendors expressed anger and frustration over the alleged corruption that took place among the leaders of the associations, who were accused, not only of taking 'the best' stores in the new centres, but also of owning more than one store. As a result, many of the vendors no longer felt represented by their associations and believed they no longer served a useful purpose.

12.7 Conclusion: Spaces Lost, Spaces Gained

Over the past sixty years, the informal economy has played a crucial role in the overall economy of Ecuador, both in terms of job creation and its contribution to GDP. The rapid population growth concentrated in Quito and Guayaquil, compounded by rural–urban migration, accelerated the process of urbanization that resulted in an excess supply of labour. As both the government and the market failed to create a sustained demand for labour, the informal economy emerged as an alternative means of income generation, especially for the most vulnerable groups within societies. Over the years, some governments have shifted their policy stance, from efforts to reduce and control the informal economy to efforts to support its potential.

The declaration of the historic centre of Quito as Cultural Patrimony of Humanity by UNESCO in 1978 placed added pressure and responsibility on the Municipality of Quito to organize and administer the use of public space in the area. Informal street vendors were perceived as the main obstacle. The Plan for the Modernization and Reorganization of Informal Street Vendors approved in 1998 not only recognized the right of vendors to participate and benefit from the process, but also aimed at supporting their reorganization and relocation within the historic centre.

The reorganization of street vending meant significant changes in the way vendors lived their lives. Many informal street vendors did not manage to participate in the process, and thus remained excluded, both from the benefits of formalization and their main source of income, which was the commercial activity that used to take place at La Ipiales. Although the exact number of vendors in this situation is unknown, it is estimated that about 3,000 vendors were not members of any associations at the time of formalization. As associations were based on location, and ambulant vendors usually moved throughout the streets, most of them were not members of any vendors' association. As a result, most of them did not manage to register, to obtain a store at one of the centres, or access training and support from the UECM. Further research about the consequences of formalization for this group is needed.

The analysis of the working and living conditions of vendors before and after formalization provided mixed results. While some dimensions of their working conditions have improved (i.e. labour, employment, work, and skills use and upgrading), others have worsened (i.e. jobs, income, and representation). Among the formalized vendors, two groups can be distinguished: a smaller group who fully benefited from the process and are better off now than they were before formalization, and a larger group of vendors who have accessed only some of the benefits of formalization. The first group is composed of growth-oriented vendors who had entrepreneurial capabilities before formalization and have seized on formalization as a unique opportunity. The second group comprises vendors who entered the informal economy in order to survive. They usually live on a day-to-day basis, earning incomes only a little above the poverty level, which sometimes are not enough to cover all their basic needs. Prior to formalization, one of the pillars of their survival strategy was diversification of sources of income. After being moved to the popular commercial centres, they have had to work every day at the same location, which has limited their capacity for diversifying their sources of income and adjusting to changes in demand. For them, the loss of mobility and sales shows mixed results in terms of vulnerability.

Hence, this study highlights two important aspects of the formalization process. The first relates to coverage: not all of the street vendors were included in the formalization process, although it affected all of them in their working and living conditions. The second point relates to the impact of having a formalized business. It is not obvious that the working and living conditions will automatically improve with formalization. While growth-oriented vendors have good chances of benefiting from formalization policies even though these do not provide much support through the transition from the stall to the store, survival vendors might be better off with policies that aim at supporting them in the long term.

Figure 12.1 illustrates the process of formalization. The two triangles in the figure represent the existing jobs in the formal and informal economies. In the informal economy, most workers are located at the bottom, while in the formal economy most workers are at the middle of the triangle. Moving towards the top of the triangles, average earnings tend to increase and the opposite occurs towards the bottom. There tend to be more women towards the bottom of the triangles.

Both markets are segmented horizontally and vertically. Based on a distinction made by Rodgers (1989: 8), horizontal segmentation 'denotes the separation of complete production systems, in which all labour has some common characteristics' (e.g. distinction between formal and informal sectors), while vertical segmentation 'involves the use of labour from different segments in a single production process' (e.g. large enterprise with both regular and casual labour). Both sectors of the economy are interdependent and interlinked, symbolized in the figure by the arrows connecting the

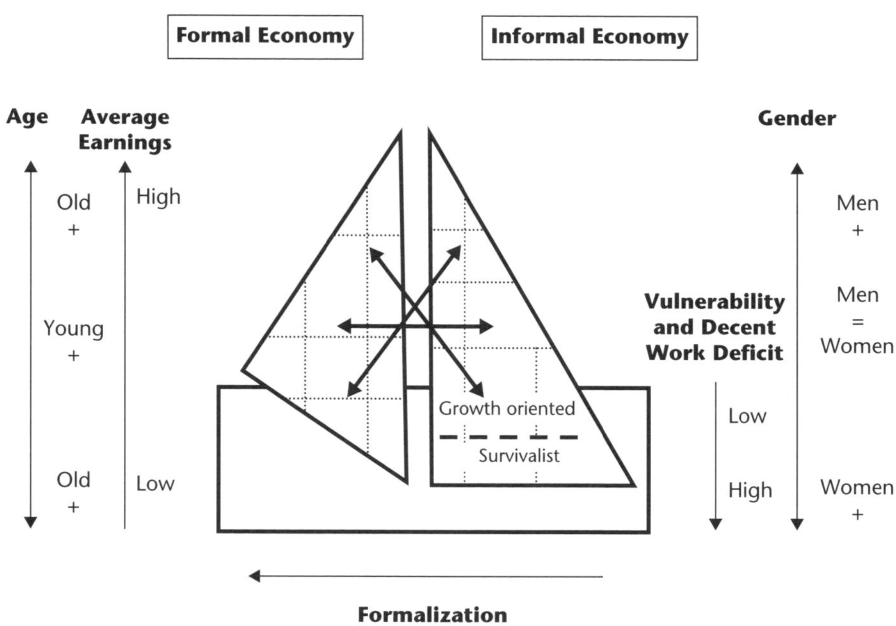

Figure 12.1 The formalization process

Source: Authors, based on literature on the informal economy and observations from fieldwork in Quito.

segments of the two triangles. As explained by Chen (2006: 77), 'Economic relations of production, distribution, and employment tend to fall at some point on a continuum between pure "formal" relations (i.e. regulated and protected) at one pole and pure "informal" relations (i.e. unregulated and unprotected) at the other, with many categories in between.' The rectangle at the bottom of the figure represents the area of the labour market where workers suffer greater vulnerability risks and decent work deficits. Workers in the formal economy tend to experience better working conditions; however, flexibilization, globalization, and macroeconomic policies implemented during the last few decades have exposed them to vulnerability and decent work deficits. Many among the 'working poor' have a formal job and still earn less than is required to be above the poverty line, and thus, the rectangle also represents the risk of falling into poverty. As stated by the ILO (2002: 4), 'It is useful to adopt the view that formal and informal workers coexist along a continuum, with decent work deficits most serious at the bottom end, but also existing in some formal jobs as well, and with increasingly decent conditions of work moving up the formal end.' The figure therefore shows that formalization does not necessarily mean a reduction in vulnerability and decent work deficits; indeed, some workers at the bottom of the formal economy might experience similar decent work deficits and vulnerability to those experienced in the informal economy.

Appendix

List of interviews for this research conducted in August 2009, in chronological order.
Researcher for the interviews: Sergio Ferragut

Alfredo Santillan, Coordinator of City Studies at the Facultad Latino Americana DeCienciasSociales (FLACSO)
Luis Gonzales, Manager, PCC Ipiales Mires
Gonzalo Ortiz-Crespo, Sociologist and former City Councillor of Quito
Colonel Luis Montalvo, Director, Unidad Ejecutora del Comercio Minorista (UECM)
Alejandro Lopez-Lamia, IDB
Rocio Estrella, ECH-INNOVAR
Jorge, 40 years old, taxi driver, former customer at La Ipiales
Edgard, 37 years old, taxi driver, former customer at La Ipiales

Vendors (real names of vendors have been changed to protect their identity)

Facundo (man, 35 years old), formalized vendor, PCC Ipiales Mires
Santiago (man, 65 years old), formalized vendor, PCC Ipiales Mires

Celeste (woman, 65 years old) and Francisco (man, 75 years old), formalized vendors, PCC Ipiales Mires
Magdalena (woman, 60 years old), formalized vendor, PCC Ipiales Mires
Granddaughter (woman, 28 years old) of formalized vendor, vendor, PCC Ipiales Mires
Group of ladies (3 women between 65 and 75 years old), formalized vendors, PCC Ipiales Mires

References

Carrion, F. (2006). *'Balance del Proyecto de Sostenibilidad Social del Centro Historico de Quito'*. Quito: FLACSO.

Chen, M.A. (2006). 'Rethinking the Informal Economy: Linkages with the Formal Economy and the Formal Regulatory Environment', in B. Guha-Khasnobis et al. (eds), *Linking the Formal and Informal Economy: Concepts and Policies*. Oxford: Oxford University Press: 75–92.

Cross, J. and M. Karides (2007). 'Capitalism, Modernity, and the "Appropriate" use of Space', in J. Cross et al. (eds.), *Street Entrepreneurs—People, Place and Politics in Local and Global Perspective*. Oxford: Routledge: 19–36.

Ghai, D. (2002). *'Decent Work: Concepts, Models and Indicators'*. Working paper. Geneva: ILO/ILS.

ILO (2002). *'The Informal Economy and Decent Work'*. Geneva: International Labour Office. Please refer to <http://www.ilo.org> (last accessed June 2013).

—— (2007a) *The Informal Economy*. Geneva: ILO.

—— (2007b). 'The Informal Economy: Enabling Transition to Formalization'. Paper presented at the Tripartite Interregional Symposium on the Informal Economy: Enabling Transition to Formalization'. ISIE/2007/1, Geneva. Please refer to <http://www.ilo.org> (last accessed June 2013).

Kantor, P., U. Rani, and J. Unni (2006). 'Decent Work Deficits in Informal Economy: Case of Surat'. *Economic and Political Weekly*, 41(21): 2089–97.

Majid, N. (2001). *'Economic Growth, Social Policy and Decent Work'*. Geneva: ILO, Geneva. Available at <http://ilo-mirror.library.cornell.edu/public/english/employment/strat/download/ep19.pdf> (last accessed June 2012).

Middleton, A. (2003). 'Informal Traders and Planners in the Regeneration of Historic City Centres: The Case of Quito, Ecuador'. *Progress in Planning*, 59(2): 71–123.

Ocampo, J. A. and K. S. Jomo (2007). *Towards Full and Decent Employment*. Hyderabad: United Nations.

Perry, G., W. Maloney, O. Arias, P. Fajnzylber, A. Mason, and J. Saavedra-Chanduvi (2007). *Informality: Exit and Exclusion*. Washington, DC: World Bank.

Portes, A. and R. Schauffler (1993). 'Competing Perspectives on the Latin American Informal Sector'. *Population and Development Review*, 19(1): 33–60.

Rodgers, G. (1989) 'Trends in Urban Poverty and Labour Market Access', in G. Rodgers (ed.), *Urban Poverty and the Labour Market: Access to Jobs and Incomes in Asian and Latin American Cities*. Geneva: ILO: 1–33.

Standing, G. (2002). 'From People's Security Surveys to a Decent Work Index'. *International Labour Review*, 141(4): 441–54.

Teltscher, S. (1994). 'Small Trade and the World Economy: Informal Vendors in Quito, Ecuador'. *Economic Geography*, 70(2): 167–87.

13

Formalizing the Informal in Rwanda: From Artisanal to Modern Brick and Tile Ovens

An Ansoms and Jude Murison[1]

13.1 Introduction

After a devastating period of civil war (1990–3) and genocide (1994), the overall picture of Rwanda's post-conflict reconstruction process seems ambiguous. On the one hand, the country is characterized by an authoritarian governance structure that aims to 'engineer' the social life of its citizens. There is very little room for dissent by a struggling civil society, and a lack of press freedom (Longman, 2011; Reyntjens, 2011). On the other hand, efforts at economic reconstruction have shown impressive results. In terms of macroeconomic stability, Rwanda has performed extremely well. Indeed, as noted by the International Monetary Fund (IMF), 'growth has averaged about 8 per cent a year' over the last decade (IMF, 2011: 5). There have been considerable achievements in education and health over the past decade (UNDP, 2007), and whereas improvements in political governance have been poor, international donors have applauded the government of Rwanda (GoR) for its technocratic abilities, and Aid is considered to be efficiently allocated. In the World Bank's Governance Indicators, Rwanda figures among the top 30 per cent of best performing countries in terms of 'control of corruption', and more than 50 per cent of all countries were considered to perform worse than Rwanda in terms of 'government effectiveness', which measures the competence of public-service delivery and state bureaucracy. Moreover, Rwanda's

[1] The authors would like to thank Nilgün Gökgür for her in-depth comments and suggestions. They also acknowledge the input received from Danielle De Lame, Filip Reyntjens, and Susan Thomson.

performance in terms of both these indicators has improved considerably since 2005 (World Bank, 2011).

This positive image has been essential for attracting new foreign and domestic investors. Between 2006 and 2011, private investment grew to over 12 per cent of GDP, a six-fold rise compared to the previous decade (IMF, 2011). This seems promising, given that one of *Vision 2020*'s pillars[2] focuses on the importance of private-sector-led development, and more specifically, the emergence of domestic business owners and operators (GoR, 2000). The major aim is to closely involve the private sector in the growth process, and assign it a key role in the poverty reduction policy framework.

In this chapter, we identify how the Rwandan government's policies have indeed attracted capital by facilitating the operation of large-scale, capital-intensive projects. However, the policies promoting a formalized business sector have discouraged small-scale investment initiatives at the local level. In particular, we discuss the case of traditional brick and tile making, which used to be one of the most important labour-absorbing off-farm income-generating activities in rural Rwanda. Environmental regulations now prohibit traditional kilns owned and operated by local businessmen. As a result, these kilns have been replaced by modern kilns operated by officially registered business people (or cooperatives) who pay taxes, unlike those operating informally. We study the impact of this transition upon employment creation and local domestic livelihoods.

The case study material used in this chapter is based on research carried out in two phases: Ansoms conducted research on rural livelihoods in 2007 in six different settings in the southern province of rural Rwanda (for more information on methods, see Ansoms, 2010). In two of them, one relatively close to Kigali (referred to as 'setting A') and the other relatively close to Gitarama (referred to as 'setting B'), brick and tile making was, or had been until recently, a major livelihood activity that involved a large proportion of the local population. In 2011, both authors (Ansoms and Murison) returned to these settings for follow-up research that assessed the impact of the Rwandan government's rural policies on the ground. During both research phases, between fourteen and twenty focus group interviews per setting (of 4–7 people) were conducted with village leaders and with diverse socio-economic categories (see Table 13.2).

[2] Vision 2020 was developed in 2000, and outlines the main plans of the Rwandan government and the strategic pillars for achieving specific developmental objectives by the year 2020.

13.2 Doing Business in Rwanda

As mentioned above, Rwanda is increasingly attracting private investment. Indeed, the Rwandan government has enhanced its efforts to create an investment-friendly environment. Over the past couple of years, its ranking in international business 'hotlists' has drastically improved. 'Regulatory quality' which measures the presence and impact of market-friendly policies has improved steadily since 2007 (World Bank, 2011). Even more spectacular has been the rise in its ranking in the World Bank's *Doing Business* 2010 report, from the 143rd place (2009) to the 67th place (2010). Indeed, Rwanda featured as the world's 'top reformer'. The World Bank's report also praised the Rwandan reforms in commercial law, improvements in regulations to ease access to credit, and the measures taken to accelerate trade and property registration (World Bank, 2010). Since then, progress has continued: in 2012 Rwanda ranked among the forty-five top performers worldwide. According to the World Bank *Doing Business* report for 2012, Rwanda even outperforms standards of the Organization for Economic Co-operation and Development (OECD) in terms of the procedural process to start up a formally registered business: in Rwanda, this takes barely two procedures, three days, and involves costs equivalent to 4.5 per cent of per capita income (World Bank, 2012a).

However, a recent consultant's report, analysing the impediments to sustainable and broad-based private-sector development, concludes that despite the apparent openness to business initiatives, there is a high economic concentration of large and medium-sized enterprises in the formal sector. A considerable proportion of the formal sector is dominated by partially privatized enterprises, together with resurging new state-owned enterprises. These operate alone or in joint-venture arrangements with large domestic private investors who have close ties to the ruling party (Gökgür, 2011). More importantly, employment creation by formally registered companies was apparently only about 8,810 jobs per year between 2006 and 2010, far less than the 120,000 to 125,000 jobs that the World Bank had estimated as being crucial to absorb the large and growing labour force (Gökgür, 2011: 9).

At the same time, growing population pressure and land scarcity increasingly deprive the youth of a viable future as farmers. Yet one of the fundamental issues for Rwanda's future is how to create sufficient jobs that will allow the low-skilled youth to participate in Rwanda's 'economic success' (Ansoms and Rostagno, 2012). According to Gökgür (2011: 9), the only alternative is therefore for 'the bulk of new entrants [to] be absorbed into the informal sector—non-farm micro and household enterprises'.

There is already a highly fragmented and strongly competitive informal sector in which 115,279 informal micro enterprises and 615,108 non-farm household enterprises thrive (Gökgür, 2011). Whereas until the recent past, government regulations interfered little with these informal activities, small-scale actors operating in the informal sector are now increasingly confronted with new sets of regulations, increased taxation, and formal requirements for business registration. In terms of taxation, 'any person who undertakes to carry out commercial activities has to pay a business licence tax...determined according to type of business and the location' (Bumbakare, 2009: 5–6). Many of these taxes are relatively less burdensome for businesses operating on a larger scale, whereas they are a considerable or even insurmountable obstacle for small-scale entrepreneurs. But even more important are the regulations that attempt to formalize the informal sector. The formal requirements discourage local-level small-scale investment initiatives, and sometimes oblige informal entrepreneurs to eventually give up their activities.

There are several illustrations of this. Sommers (2012), for example, points out how prohibiting street vending, defined as 'unorganized commerce', impacts negatively on the economic livelihoods of Kigali youth. He notes, 'What has ensued is a kind of economic cat and mouse involving people trying to hawk goods without getting caught and government officials on the lookout for precisely this sort of economic behavior' (Sommers, 2012: 36). Likewise, petty trade in Kigali city is prohibited. Petty trade markets in the city centre have been closed and are now located at a significant distance from the centre. There is also increasing regulation of rural markets that aims to push all economic activity into government-sponsored spaces. Petty traders in these markets need an official licence in order to operate, and attempts by farmers to 'sell on the road' are discouraged by a system of fines (setting A, 2011). Equally worrisome is the recent generalized prohibition of riding a bicycle on tarmac roads (Syfia Grands Lacs, 2011). This decision is explained as a precautionary measure, since most bicycle accidents apparently take place on asphalt roads. Yet it also deters local small-scale farmers and traders from reaching the market if they do not operate at a scale that allows them to buy or rent a truck for transport. Given the limited number of traders who operate at such a scale, it also negatively affects the bargaining power of local farmers to negotiate a good price for their produce. Other regulations, such as the obligation for people to wear shoes when entering markets, increasingly complicate local life.

Another argument used by the government of Rwanda to defend its prohibition of particular informal activities relates to protection of the environment. Since 2006, Rwanda has banned the use of plastic bags. Although pollution caused by plastic is a genuine concern in Africa, the ban has had negative consequences for small-scale traders. The environmental argument was also used to discredit traditional brick and tile kilns. There was a legitimate anxiety that the wood consumed in the firing process would contribute to deforestation. Since 2003, the firing of traditional kilns has been prohibited during certain periods, although it has been unofficially tolerated at other times. People have lived in constant insecurity about whether their investment in a traditional kiln would pay off, or whether their kilns would be destroyed and their products confiscated before they could benefit from their investment. However, since 2010, the ban has been formally enforced and all traditional kilns have been destroyed. People now face large fines and prison sentences if they continue to bake bricks or tiles in traditional kilns (see also section 13.3).

We acknowledge that Rwanda has indeed made spectacular progress in the facilitation of business initiatives that operate on a large scale within the formal sector. New business owners and operators can apply for permission to operate through the Internet; they conduct business in an environment in which corruption is low and property rights are secured; and they are not (or are rarely) confronted with embezzlement, which is often presented as 'typical' in the African context. Yet these policy initiatives, tailor-made for large-scale operations, seriously harm the operations of small-scale initiatives embedded in Rwanda's large informal economy. Measures to protect the environment, promote security, and reinforce the formal economy increasingly marginalize informal entrepreneurs, and, in some cases, even oblige them to stop their activity from one day to the next. In section 13.3, we discuss how this can affect employment creation and local livelihoods.

13.3 Evolution of the Brick and Tile Business in Rwanda

There is little information on the brick and tile business in Rwanda apart from that provided by Jefremovas (2002). Yet it used to be 'one of the most important sources of rural nonfarm employment in the country' (Jefremovas, 2002: 21). Jefremovas' research was carried out between 1984 and 1989, and is much more in-depth than our own data. Brick and tile making was only one of the livelihood activities we studied. Moreover, the activity had already been officially stopped approximately two years before our field work in 2007, forcing us to rely mainly on recall data. Nonetheless, the information we collected on the way in which artisanal brick and tile making was organized in the 2000s is very much in line with Jefremovas' analysis of how this activity was done in the 1980s. At the same time, the similarities between pre-war and post-war traditional brick and tile making are in sharp contrast to the current situation. Locally owned traditional kilns have disappeared and have, in some cases, been replaced by modern kilns that operate very differently.

13.3.1 Traditional Brick and Tile Making: Labour, Capital Investment and Clay Land

In the brick and tile business, there are different types of traditional kilns (described in depth by Jefremovas, 2002). The most common types, both before and after 1994, were clamp kilns for brick production, and more permanent adobe brick kilns for tile production. Clamp kilns were temporary structures that were made out of the bricks due to be fired, and were entirely disassembled after the firing process. On the one hand, the quality of the bricks varied depending on how close the bricks were to the firing holes, and clamp kilns consumed a lot of fuel, generally wood. On the other hand, as observed by Jefremovas (2002: 22), 'clamp kilns require little or no investment and have complete flexibility of size'. The average capacity in the 1980s was approximately 60,000 to 75,000 bricks per oven per baking cycle, and our own data does not indicate drastic changes in post-1994 operations.[3] The adobe tile kilns were more permanent structures, built with adobe bricks. The average capacity in the 1980s was 3,000 to 5,000 tiles.[4] Adobe tile kilns also consumed a lot of wood, and produced tiles of variable quality in comparison with the improved kilns (Jefremovas, 2002).

Jefremovas differentiates between three types of labour organization in the brick and tile business: small-scale peasant production, large capitalist enterprises, and cooperatives. Small businesses used to thrive in areas where access to marshland for clay extraction was relatively open. The labour employed in these small-scale businesses could be organized in different ways. Entrepreneurs, active in this business, would either (i) work on their own; (ii) hire a labour force and work together with it; or (iii) work in a group with other investors (usually a group of between two and five friends, each bringing and leaving with their own lot of bricks, but firing them collectively). Interestingly, one person could also combine all three forms within a period of one year. In our own research on post-1994 brick and tile production, we came across similar modes of organization. In setting B, some people had their own kiln space and kilns, while others rented space on which they built their own temporary kilns. The advantage of firing the bricks together was that a larger kiln could be built, which reduced losses in the number of bricks not well fired on the outer side of the kiln.

Large-scale enterprises emerged in areas where access to clay soil (marshland) was controlled by a few individuals and/or where kiln investors were able to secure access to large urban markets. The bricks and tiles produced

[3] The larger the kiln capacity, the smaller the percentage of bricks lost during the firing process (Jefremovas, 2002).

[4] There were not sufficient data to estimate this for the post-1994 period in our two settings.

were often sold on a contract basis. In nearly all cases, investors had other occupations, and thus seldom performed the physical work themselves; instead, they hired labour on a piecework basis. This was confirmed in our own research. In setting A, the largest area of the marshland had been confiscated by the State in 1997, and has been provided on concession to Madhivani business group for sugar cane production.[5] As a result, access to clay land has become much more restricted. One of our interviewees observed, 'the fact that Madhivani occupied the marshland meant that a lot of people lost their clay fields where they made bricks' (setting A, 2011). Another highlighted the fact that 'people no longer had a place to work because everything was taken by Madhivani' (setting A, 2011). Only plots in the immediate surroundings of the marshland still had the necessary clay deposits. These areas were increasingly controlled (already owned or bought) by better-off people, who had invested in large-scale brick and tile enterprises.

A third mode of labour organization is the grouping of entrepreneurs into cooperative structures. Indeed, as early as the 1980s, the authorities had tried to strengthen their control over brick and tile businesses by occasionally requiring entrepreneurs to group themselves into cooperative structures. In cases where cooperatives already existed in areas where access to clay was relatively open, their functioning was limited. The rationale for their existence was mostly to comply with government regulations. During her research, Jefremovas observed that 'most men stated that they were "temporarily" working for themselves, while still being cooperative members so as to avoid potential trouble with local authorities' (2002: 52). When operating in settings where access to clay soil was limited, cooperative structures were mainly set up for the purpose of securing access to clay. Jefremovas describes how a group of men presented themselves as a cooperative, since they 'would have found it difficult to get access to land without calling themselves a "cooperative"' (2002: 54). However, in reality, they each worked for themselves.

Next to the entrepreneurs, there were also labourers working in the brick and tile business. They were employed by both large-scale enterprises and small-scale entrepreneurs (although not all small-scale producers hired labour). Jefremovas (2002) differentiates between four categories of labour: (i) skilled labour, responsible for extracting the clay, and forming and drying the bricks or tiles; (ii) unskilled labour, responsible for transporting the bricks or tiles to the kilns; (iii) skilled labour (*maçons*), experienced in building, firing, and supervising the kiln; and (iv) unskilled labour (*aide-maçon*), performing the manual work of firing and drawing the kiln.

[5] The total concession was about 3,000 hectares. On the impact of this large-scale land acquisition on local livelihoods, see Ansoms (2009).

Our own data confirms that these four categories of labour continued to exist in the post-1994 traditional brick and tile business. Table 13.1 gives an approximate overview of salaries in all four labour categories, both during the 1980s and circa 2005, when traditional brick and tile making was still

Table 13.1 Comparative analysis of wage rates for different categories of labour in the brick and tile business

Labour category	1980s	After 1994 in the 'traditional' system(around 2005)	In the 'modern' system(2011)
Consumer price index	1985 100	2005 587	2010 909
Price per dried brick	• 0.5 Rwf per brick—capacity of 700 to 750 bricks per day • 1 Rwf per tile—capacity of 400 tiles per day	• 2-3 Rwf per brick in setting A, with a capacity of 500–800 bricks per day • 2 Rwf per brick in setting B	• 2-3 Rwf per brick in setting A • 2 Rwf per brick in setting B • 10 Rwf per tile in setting B
Transportation of bricks to kiln	• 100 Rwf per 1,000 bricks	• 800 Rwf per 1,000 bricks in setting A • no data on setting B	• 600–1000 Rwf for 1,000 bricks (2,000 Rwf if the distance is far) in setting A • 1 Rwf per brick—capacity of 100 bricks per hour in setting B
Wage of skilled labourer (*maçon*)—responsible for building the kiln	250 Rwf—350 Rwf per day	Very diverse: from 600 to 2,500 Rwf per day, but mostly around 2,000 Rwf	*Maçons* to 'build' kilns are no longer needed. However, stacking the bricks into the modern kiln requires specific skills, for which the pay is 2,500 Rwf per day in setting A
Wage of unskilled labourer (*aide-maçon*)	100 Rwf per day	Very diverse: from 300 to 1,200 Rwf per day, but mostly around 1,000 Rwf	1,000–1,200 Rwf per day (setting A)
Wage of unskilled agricultural labourer		• Setting A: 300–500 Rwf per day (2007) • Setting B: 300–400 Rwf per day (2007)	• Setting A: 700-800 Rwf per day • Setting B: 500 Rwf per day
Exchange rate • Rwf per US$ • Rwf per PPP US$	 101 175	 558 1,671	 583 1,281

Note: Rwf = Rwandan francs.

Sources: Jefremovas, 2002 (for data on the 1980s); the data in the other two columns were gathered during own field research in 2007 and 2011. The consumer price index has been calculated based on the World Bank's *World Bank Development Indicators* with 1985 as the base year (World Bank, 2012b).

permitted. The salaries are indicative, and may vary considerably depending on the physical capacity of the labourer, the season in which the labour is performed, and the location of the brick and tile business. To put prices and salaries in context, we have added the consumer price index (with 1985 as a base year).

Overall, in the twenty-year period between 1985 and 2005, the increase in salaries for all four labour categories was more or less in line with the increase in the consumer price index. Salaries earned in the brick and tile business were significantly higher than what people could earn as agricultural wage labourers. Besides higher salaries, the people interviewed also mentioned that being able to obtain a loan from the brick investor was an important advantage of being engaged in the brick- and tile-making business.

13.3.2 Formalizing the Informal: From Traditional Kilns to Modern Enterprises

Traditional brick and tile baking was banned around 2006 in setting A, and around 2007 in setting B. After a temporary reprieve, the activity was banned again in both settings around August 2010. Interviewees in both settings reported a strong deterioration of overall living conditions when this livelihood option disappeared. People who were active in brick and tile firing lost an alternative source of revenue to their agricultural activities, and this affected a large proportion of the population. As one person explained, 'the whole *umudugudu* [village] would work there; it allowed us to work in a way not bound by seasons' (setting A, 2007). In setting B, interviewees estimated that 'around 80 percent of the *umudugudu* was active in this activity; even people from [another location] came over to our *umudugudu* to work in the kilns'. One of the respondents remarked that 'when the activity became prohibited, we died a little bit' (setting B, 2011).

When the activity was banned, the local population initially resisted. The authorities used force to confiscate bricks and they put several people in prison. One of our interviewees reported being imprisoned for thirteen days because he had produced bricks to build his own house. After the local defence forces caught him, he was detained by the executive secretary of the *cellule*[6] (setting B, 2007). In 2011, interviewees indicated that there were several types of fines for those caught participating in traditional brick or tile firing. One person reported that his kiln was found and destroyed by the police just after the ban (2006–7). He then fled to avoid having to pay a fine that he could not afford, and stayed away for a prolonged period. At the time

[6] The *cellule* refers to the administrative unit equivalent to a group of hills. It gathers several *imidugudu* or 'villages'.

of our research in 2011, people were too cautious and fearful to build a large traditional kiln as the sentence—according to our research respondents—was estimated to be two to five years' imprisonment, along with a fine of 500,000 Rwf. Nonetheless, some people did dare to build small kilns within their compounds (see also section 13.3.3), risking fines of 50,000 Rwf. Another fine, estimated at 50,000 Rwf, was imposed if people were caught cutting and transporting wood without permission (setting B, 2011). Through this system of fines and threats of imprisonment, the authorities were effectively able to abolish a livelihood activity that had been one of the most important off-farm employment opportunities in the rural areas.

It was envisaged that traditional brick and tile firing would be replaced by more modern systems embedded in the formal economy. However, at the time of our research in 2007, people had very little information on how the brick and tile business would be organized in the near future. Some mentioned that traditional kilns would still be allowed, but only if people obtained prior permission from the Ministry of Environment and from all relevant local authorities. Others thought that it was a matter of 'working together' in associations or cooperative structures. In setting A, some people were better informed and were setting up a cooperative that would be allowed to reactivate the brick and tile business. One interviewee mentioned that each member had to contribute a membership fee of 450,000 Rwf.[7] At that time, the total working fund of the cooperative was around 5,000,000 Rwf, but this would further increase when additional members joined. It was not yet clear to them whether they would be allowed to work with traditional kilns or whether they would have to use modern kilns in the future. As mentioned by an interviewee, 'We are obliged to follow the laws and directives of the State on the protection of the environment. But the State did not stop our activity because we used traditional kilns; they stopped it because we used wood for the heating' (setting A, 2007). Another added that they would probably be allowed to use traditional kilns if they used coffee husks or sawdust from carpenters instead of wood.

By the time of our research in 2011, the situation had become slightly clearer. In setting B, external entrepreneurs had started up brick and tile businesses using modern and improved kilns. Our interviewees estimated the cost of such a kiln at 3,000,000 Rwf, stating that 'we are not capable to come up with such a sum'. These entrepreneurs are mostly business people from Gitarama, operating with formally recognized permissions (setting B, 2011). In setting A, the cooperative mentioned above had become a legal entity with formal permission to operate, and had used its working fund to build

[7] This amount represents five times the annual consumption level of someone living at the poverty line (90,000 Rwf per adult equivalent per year in 2006).

a modern kiln. Improved kilns already existed before 1994, but were relatively unpopular because of the high investment needed to build them, and the specialized knowledge needed for operating them. Jefremovas observed that in the 1980s, 'a number of owners had gone to see new styles of kilns being promoted by the government, but none were interested. They were just too expensive and not very productive, despite small savings in fuel and big increases in quality... Owners were not willing to invest more than they could recoup in a single firing' (2002: 44). Now, however, improved kilns are officially the only type of kiln allowed. The fact that the cooperative obtained permission to fire bricks and tiles was partly based on its investment in a modern kiln. It was not entirely clear to us whether the local authorities were still tolerating the cooperative's use of traditional kilns. We have indications that this was the case, although no one was willing to openly confirm it. It was clear, however, that the cooperative paid taxes to the Rwandan government in return for formal permission to operate.

The cooperative first functioned during the 2010 brick season (June to September). At that time, it consisted of approximately fourteen members, several of whom were not local. The local members were mostly those who had access to clay land. One person described how they had consolidated the available clay land and brought it into the cooperative. Outsiders also joined the cooperative, as pointed out by one of our interviewees who said, 'There are even those who come from Ruhengeri' (setting A, 2011). A cooperative member explained that it provided employment for brick transporters and chargers. In addition, the cooperative bought bricks from brick makers for 3 Rwf each. None of the investors engaged in physical work themselves, though 'they follow all the activities taking place and do other things such as buying wood'.

The way in which these modern enterprises function is quite different from the traditional system. First, as mentioned above, investors have to pay a high fee to join the cooperative. This makes access to the modern kiln very exclusive: by no means can local entrepreneurs 'rent' the kiln to fire their own bricks. According to one interviewee, 'the building of traditional kilns was our business, whereas the construction of a modern kiln requires the involvement of a technician'. Another added that 'before, we baked the bricks ourselves, but now we have to work for the profit of others' (setting B, 2011).

Second, modern kilns require far fewer labourers than traditional kilns, thus providing only limited job opportunities. Moreover, the wages are relatively lower compared to those earned by working in traditional brick and tile making. Despite the formalization of the sector, labour is still hired on a temporary basis, and without formal contracts or social security provisions. Table 13.1 shows the wages of the four labour categories in the modern brick- and tile-making business, in comparison to those wages earned in traditional brick and tile making. The salaries of all labour categories remained constant or barely increased between 2005 and 2011, despite a 55 per cent increase in the consumer price index (see Table 13.1).

Third, the links between external investors and the local society are limited, which often results in the labour force being hired externally from the same area as the investor. One of our interviewees observed that, 'In the past, we were paid daily. Now, people have spent two years without working. It is really a big loss. And when an investor comes, he brings his own labour force to produce the bricks. We, the locals, become poorer and poorer. Before, we were accompanied by experts and produced bricks. People could buy cattle. But now, there is a cooperative that has a permanent labour force in the brick season' (setting A, 2011). In setting A, many of these migrant labourers come from Ruhengeri, and stay for the duration of the brick-making season.

13.3.3 Bricks and Tiles as Glue for Socio-Economic Interdependencies and New Families

The consequences of the traditional brick and tile sector collapse go beyond the immediate impact on local employment opportunities. It has led to the deconstruction of a complex system of socio-economic interdependencies that had provided opportunities for social mobility from the lower socio-economic layers. Table 13.2 presents the characteristics of six different socio-economic categories that can be found in rural settings. Each of these categories played a specific role in the brick and tile business. Entrepreneurs were most often found among the *abakungu* (who took up the role of large-scale investors), and the *abakene bifashije* (who invested at a smaller scale). Whereas the *abakungu* rarely engaged in physical work themselves and depended mainly on hired labour, the *abakene bifashije* would work either in groups with friends or with a few labourers. Most often, *maçons* employed by the *abakungu* also belonged to the category of *abakene bifashije*. The *abakene* and the *abakene nyakujya* mostly worked as labourers, producing bricks, firing or dismantling the kilns, or transporting bricks (transportation is a job done mainly by the youth). The brick business provided people in these socio-economic categories with much needed off-farm jobs. Many *abakene* would concentrate on agricultural activities during the rainy season, and the brick business provided them with an alternative source of revenue during the dry season. The *abakene nyakujya*, however, generally own little or no cultivable land, and therefore would continue to work in the brick business well into the rainy season (e.g. drawing fired kilns or loading trucks with bricks). The brick business also provided them with an alternative source of employment to the bleaker option of working as badly paid agricultural labour or being unemployed in the absence of any on-farm employment opportunities.

Table 13.2 Roles of various socio-economic categories in the brick and tile business

Category	Characteristics	Role
Abakire Very wealthy	Rich in terms of revenue, land, animals, monetary revenue (from paid employment as civil servants or in trades); savings at official banks; their prosperity often pushes them to migrate to urban centres	The only ones with the financial capacity to buy their participation in the cooperative that operates the modern kiln
Abakungu Wealthy	Rich in terms of food security, large farms (often with banana or coffee groves and/or forest) with rich soils, some animals, enough food; employ others on own farms; at times have access to paid employment (higher skilled jobs); have savings	Used to be large-scale investors in the brick and tile business—often controlled access to clay land in setting A. Often had the role of pure investor, and did not work together with their hired labour
Abakene bifashije Non-poor	Doing OK, with a bit more land than average, few animals; besides subsistence production they have a small income to satisfy a few other needs (e.g. children's school fees)	Used to be small-scale investors in the brick and tile business, often helped by a few labourers. Most *maçons* (skilled 'kiln builders' employed by *abakungu*) belonged to this category
Abakene Poor	Poor, with land to produce food for their own family but no surplus for sale in the market, often work for others; have no savings	Used to work in brick- and tile-making as labourers (or as *aide maçon*). Some rented kilns with a couple of friends to work 'for themselves'
Abakene nyakujya/ abatindi Vulnerable	Very poor, live on working on other people's lands, very little land with low harvests, no animals, no access to health care or schooling	Used to be able to make a decent living in the brick business, worked as unskilled labourers, transporters (mostly youth) or brick makers, and earned salaries twice as high as they would have as agricultural labourers
Abatindi nyakujya Very vulnerable	Destitute, beg for their livelihood, no land, no animals, live by working on other people's lands, but not very capable in terms of labour; ignorant, not respected, discriminated against	Rarely physically capable of working in the brick sector

Sources: Government of Rwanda 2001, for the first two columns; authors' own research for the last column.

The extra incomes derived from the brick and tile business also had a positive impact on the employment opportunities in other sectors. First, the competition for finding suitable labour not only led to higher salaries within the brick and tile business; it also improved salaries in other off-farm activities. Agricultural labour, for example, was better paid in both settings than in areas that did not have a thriving brick and tile business. Moreover, those active in the brick and tile business often had the means to employ additional labour to help them in their fields during the rainy season, further increasing employment opportunities and improving salaries for agricultural labourers. Second, the money generated by the brick business was generally spent locally, thereby helping to boost growth in other sectors. Local businesses, such as small bars and shops, began to thrive as people had additional income to spend on 'luxury' items. People were also able to invest in better housing, which provided income-generating opportunities to carpenters and other craftsmen (Ansoms and Murison, 2011).

After the ban on the traditional brick and tile business, people reported the complete implosion of the local economy. One interviewee in setting A, previously a small investor in the brick business, described how he had tried to maintain his carpentry business after the ban. He noted: 'I had lost all clientele. All activities have stopped, or we work less now that brick making has stopped. In the past, everyone had money, but now everyone is unemployed. This is why you see a lot of people sitting outside waiting for who knows what. Really, since our childhood, it was the brick-making activity that we knew. After this stopped, a lot stopped. There are also cabarets [bars] and boutiques [shops] that stopped' (setting A, 2007). On another occasion, people talked nostalgically about the past, when their village had a centre full of bars and life. One person said that 'shop owners sold a lot back then [when the brick and tile business was still allowed], now it is cold in the evening'. Another added, 'You could find brochettes and banana beer easily back then, and all would be sold that same evening.' Indeed, at the end of a full day of interviews in setting B, the centre with all its closed shops and bars gave the impression of a small ghost town (setting B, 2011).

Finally, the collapse of the traditional brick- and tile-making business has also led to an increase in the price of tiles. Fluctuations in brick prices have had less of an impact on local livelihoods in the rural setting since most houses are made of adobe bricks that can be produced and dried locally. Only a few people (such as the *abakungu* or the *abakire*) are capable of building houses with fired bricks. However, the higher price of tiles is more problematic. At the time of our research in 2011, tiles cost 40 Rwf each. Although we have no prices for previous years, interviewees agreed that the price of tiles had increased drastically in just a few years. Sommers and Uvin (2011) report a similar development during their 2006–7 fieldwork. People have few options for the types of roofing used on their houses. In the past, very poor people (including the *abatindi* and the *abatindi nyakujya*) covered their roofs with banana leaves. However, the Rwandan government no longer permits this since it conflicts with the image it wants to project of a modern Rwanda. In the past few years, roofs made with banana leaves have either been replaced through communal work coordinated by local authorities, or they have been destroyed. Apart from tiles, the only other option available is corrugated iron, which is not always readily available locally. Moreover, it has to be bought as a single piece, which means that the expenditure has to be made at once. In comparison, when people use tiles for roofing, they can buy the tiles over a longer period of time, adding to the roof section by section. Tiles therefore remain the main roofing used in both of the research settings. However, the higher price of tiles still makes it more unlikely that young men will be able to build and roof a house of their own.

This objective is even further complicated by the Rwandan government's *imidugudu* ('villagization') policy. The 'villagization' approach was originally introduced immediately after the war to resettle refugee households. Later, it was extended to regroup the existing population, and was more intensely implemented in the eastern part of the country. People were obliged to burn their existing houses and move, often to houses or shelters of poorer quality which were in the area demarcated as the *umudugudu* (the village). Several authors have analysed the adverse impact of this policy on livelihoods and social relations at the local level (Newbury, 2011; Leegwater, 2011; Human Rights Watch, 2001; Van Hoyweghen, 1999). The two settings studied in this paper were not directly affected by the first wave of the 'villagization' policy. More recently, however, the centralization policy continues in a somewhat less drastic way, but nevertheless affects the two settings. Newly established households—new households or newly married couples—are obliged to install themselves in grouped settlements at specifically designated sites in each *cellule*. However, a large proportion of the rural youth cannot create their own households in the *umudugudu* since they cannot afford the cost of land in these specific areas or the cost of constructing a house.

Sommers and Uvin (2011: 3) noted that: 'Regulating the standard size of an *umudugudu* house helps make the quest towards completing a house virtually impossible for nearly all poor male youth in rural Rwanda.' The authors recount how young people try to save as much as possible to buy roof tiles, before adding that 'what was striking about this situation was how many male youth in rural Rwanda stated that they know they might never complete a roof for their house in their lifetime. It can take 600 to 800 tiles to make one house roof. Given their current age and rates of accumulation, many youth who were interviewed might not gather much more than half of the required roof tiles in their entire working life' (Sommers and Uvin, 2011: 4).

Our own research revealed similar accounts of the desperate situation faced by young people. Many young men are obliged to stay with their parents, and cannot live independently as adults because they cannot find productive employment or generate the required income in order to afford a house. Those with some means can rent a house, although the monthly rent for a two-room house can easily amount to 7,000 Rwf (setting A, 2011). Some get married in a 'clandestine' way: for example, a young couple may occupy the kitchen of the boy's parental house (usually a separate building, as is required by the current housing policy) without asking the parents' permission. Young men whose girlfriends became pregnant, have been known to have moved to other regions because of the shame in not being able to provide a house for their family. This problem closely relates to an increasing phenomenon of unmarried young girls with children (settings A and B, 2011; Sommers, 2012). The youth feel increasingly frustrated by the contrast between their self-perceived personal failure and the government-promoted image of Rwanda as a development success story.

This frustration has made some people so desperate that they have started to produce bricks and tiles at home, as was revealed in several interviews in setting B. It emerged that some people had developed a system whereby a very small-scale kiln would be hidden within the compound, and in some cases within the house itself. Interviewees disclosed that some people even fired tiles next to their beds. Besides the risk of fire, there are other hazards associated with this practice. The first problem is getting the unfired bricks home. Those who risk doing so are called *abanyagisasu*, meaning those carrying grenades on their back. There is the problem of having to fire the bricks in secret, particularly since at the beginning of the firing process there is a lot of smoke. In order to prevent the authorities from detecting the smoke, firing has to be done at night. People also have to avoid 'smelling like kilns' in the morning because that would expose their activity. Some people try to sell the bricks or tiles produced, but this has to be done at night, with drivers coming in after sunset to pick up the products. At each of these stages, there is the very obvious risk of being caught. Obviously, it is very difficult to hide this activity from immediate neighbours and the *umudugudu* head, with smoke emanating from the house and cars driving around at night. One of our interviewees who was the village head of setting B until 2008, admitted that he often knew who baked bricks at home. People would pay him 1,000 Rwf as a bribe to avoid being reported. He explained, 'I would just tell him to stop this activity—how could I denounce a brother?' Most cases of people being caught involved the police or local defence forces. Even then, there seemed to be room for negotiation and bribing. The fine was reported to be about 5,000 Rwf, 'if you want to avoid being reported to the official juridical instances' (setting B, 2011). In some cases, people described being imprisoned, but it was clear that villagers were less and less inclined to risk undertaking this illegal activity as the chances of being caught had increased over time. One interviewee mentioned: 'If you engage clandestinely in the kiln business now, you will be caught by the authorities because you live together with your neighbours. And then you will be imprisoned, your children will lack schooling and food. We prefer to not take the risk.' Another person added that those who were still engaged in this activity did it out of desperation to 'not have to become a thief' (setting B, 2011).

The sudden and radical disappearance of the traditional brick and tile business has definitely had adverse consequences in terms of local livelihoods. Access to off-farm employment has decreased, not only in the brick and tile business, but in other sectors that previously flourished because of the higher living standards it generated. Socio-economic interdependencies have subsequently broken down, removing opportunities for social mobility from the poorer socio-economic layers. In addition, people felt that local social cohesion had eroded. The fact that new investors often come from outside the area and are rarely involved in local village life, makes them less sensitive to the immediate local living conditions. Finally, and perhaps more problematically, prospects for young people have become bleaker since the loss of the traditional brick and tile business. In a context of increasing landlessness, they are often aware that they will not be able to obtain sufficient land to raise a family. At the same time, there are very few employment options outside the agricultural sector, and they are confronted with strict housing regulations that complicate their transition to adulthood and their ability to establish their own family. As a result, they are increasingly frustrated, angry, and desperate.

13.4 Conclusion

The government of Rwanda's single-minded focus on a growth model based on large-scale investments is accompanied by an undermining of local level and mostly informal entrepreneurial activities. The government's traditional neoliberal policy agenda aims for maximum overall macroeconomic growth, with very little attention given to how this growth is redistributed and even shared by its poor.

The deficiencies of the current growth model are worrisome. The already bleak prospects, imposed by increasing land scarcity and greater concentration in the agricultural sector, are aggravated by declining employment opportunities in the informal off-farm sector. At the same time, employment opportunities in the formal sector remain limited, and the sector is not capable of properly absorbing the excess labour force in rural areas. Poor youth, without access to advanced education or land, feel increasingly marginalized and cut off from the opportunity of social mobility. Moreover, the constant dichotomy between the hopelessness and reality experienced by these groups on the ground, and the stories of national prosperity, only serve to enhance social-economic tensions. Rwanda's stability and future as a country will depend not only upon the continued success of its economic growth, but also on the need to ensure economic opportunities for its youth. The informal off-farm sector could and should play a crucial role in this regard. The government of Rwanda needs to devise strategies to embrace and support this micro and household sector instead of undermining it in the name of economic growth. International development partners need to take note of these issues and advise those in power accordingly. After all, presumably these organizations are working in Rwanda, not only for its government, but for all Rwandans alike, including the poor and very poor.

References

Ansoms, A. (2009). 'Privatisation's bitter fruit: The case of Kabuye Sugar Works in Rwanda', in S. Marysse, F. Reyntjens, and S. Vandeginste (eds.), *L'Afrique des Grands Lacs: Annuaire 2008–2009*. Paris: L'Harmattan: 55–71.

—— (2010). 'Views from Below on the Pro-Poor Growth Challenge: The Case of Rural Rwanda'. *African Studies Review*, 53(2): 97–123.

—— and D. Rostagno (2012). 'Rwanda's Vision 2020 Halfway Through: What the Eye Does Not See'. *Review of African Political Economy*, 39(133): 427–50.

Bumbakare, C. (2009). *Local Taxes as Impediment for SME Formalization: What is Being Done*. Report written by the Commissioner for Domestic Taxes of the Rwanda Revenue Authority.

Gökgür, N. (2011). *Formulating a Broad-Based Private Sector Development Strategy for the Ministry of Trade and Industry*. Rwanda. Inception Report.

GoR (2000). *Rwanda Vision 2020*. Kigali: Ministry of Finance and Economic Planning.

Human Rights Watch (2001). *Uprooting the Rural Poor in Rwanda*. New York: Human Rights Watch.

IMF (2011). *2010 Article IV Consultation and First Review under the Policy Support Instrument*. IMF Country Report No. 11/19, Washington: International Monetary Fund.

Jefremovas, V. (2002). *Brickyards to Graveyards: From Production to Genocide in Rwanda*. New York: State University of New York Press.

Leegwater, M. (2011). 'Sharing Scarcity: Issues of Land Tenure in South-east Rwanda', in A. Ansoms and S. Marysse (eds.), *Natural Resources and Local Livelihoods in the Great Lakes Region: A Political Economy Perspective*. Basingstoke: Palgrave McMillan: 104–22.

Longman, T. (2011). 'Limitations to Political Reform: The Undemocratic Nature of Transition in Rwanda', in S. Straus and L. Waldorf (eds.), *Remaking Rwanda: State Building and Human Rights after Mass Violence*. Wisconsin: Wisconsin University Press: 25–47.

Newbury, C. (2011). 'High Modernism and the Ground Level: The Imidugudu Policy in Rwanda', in S. Straus and L. Waldorf (eds.), *Remaking Rwanda: State Building and Human Rights after Mass Violence*. Wisconsin: Wisconsin University Press: 223–39.

Reyntjens, F. (2011). 'Constructing the Truth, Dealing with Dissent, Domesticating the World: Governance in Post-Genocide Rwanda'. *African Affairs*, 110(438): 1–34.

Sommers, M. (2012). *Stuck: Rwandan Youth and the Struggle for Adulthood*. Georgia: The University of Georgia Press.

—— and P. Uvin (2011). *Youth in Rwanda and Burundi: Contrasting Visions. Special Report*. Washington, DC: United States Institute of Peace.

Syfia Grands Lacs (2011). 'Rwanda: Le vélo interdit en ville sur les grands axes' (online journal), www.syfia-grands-lacs.info (accessed 12 December 2011).

UNDP (2007). 'Turning Vision 2020 into Reality: From Recovery to Sustainable Human Development', in *National Human Development Report Rwanda 2007*. Rwanda: United Nations Development Programme.

Van Hoyweghen, S. (1999). 'The Urgency of Land and Agrarian Reform in Rwanda'. *African Affairs*, 98(392): 353–72.

World Bank (2012a). *Doing Business 2012: Doing Business in a More Transparent World*. Washington: World Bank.

—— (2012b). *World Development Indicators*. CD-ROM.

—— (2011). *World Bank Governance Indicators* (online report), http://info.worldbank.org/governance/wgi/index.asp (accessed 20 December 2011).

—— (2010). *Doing Business 2010: Reforming through Difficult Times*. Washington: World Bank.

14

Neoliberal Reforms, Regulatory Change, and the Informal Economy: The Case of Turkey from a Comparative Perspective[1]

Basak Kus

14.1 Introduction

There is considerable evidence to show that during the past few decades the size of the informal economy in developing countries has grown considerably (Portes and Sassen, 1987; Johnson, Kaufmann, and Shleifer, 1997; Charmes, 2000; ILO, 2002; World Bank, 2004; Schneider, 2005; Palmade and Anayiotos, 2005; OECD, 2009). According to internationally comparable estimates, more than one third of the developing world's GDP and half of its labour force operates outside the purview of the State. Yet existing studies of the informal economy offer limited explanations for this development.

One popular assumption from the 1960s and 1970s held that informality was a characteristic of economic underdevelopment. On this premise, informality would disappear with increasing rates of capitalist growth. However, the recent increase in informalization throughout the developing world has occurred just as many of these economies have been achieving significant private-sector growth. Another popular assumption at the end of the 1980s held that informal economies develop in reaction to the constraints and costs placed on economic actors by government regulations (De Soto, 1989). However, as Heintz and Pollin (2003: 6) note, 'Government regulations in

[1] I thank the editors, Frédéric Lapeyre, Isabelle Hillenkamp, and Andreia Lemaître, for their thoughtful comments on the earlier versions of this chapter. I also thank my research assistant Dana Louie for making the final stylistic adjustments.

developing nations have been declining over the past two decades as informalization has risen.'

Here, drawing on an in-depth study of the Turkish case and using comparative data from transition countries we argue that the State's changing regulatory relationship with the private sector under neoliberal reforms has been an important factor in the expansion of informal economic activities.

In Turkey, neoliberal reforms brought about a double-edged transformation in the State's regulatory relationship with the private sector. On the one hand, deregulation resulted in a substantial reduction in the legal rules and requirements that had been constraining economic activities. On the other hand, the State's effectiveness in policing the activities of the private sector diminished. Although the Turkish government's regulatory easing was intended to promote private-sector growth, it also had the unintended effect of eroding the State's powers to oversee and regulate economic activities. In this context, as the regulatory barriers to private entrepreneurship fell, so did the regulatory barriers to informality. In Turkey, growth and informalization emerged as concomitant outcomes of the neoliberal regulatory transformation. Thus, rather than being a response to declining growth rates or increasing regulations, informalization in Turkey was a by-product of the specific deregulatory climate created by neoliberal reforms and an integral element of Turkey's transformation to a market economy.

To what extent can one generalize from the Turkish experience? Single-case studies, while they are helpful for developing theories, and for process tracing, rarely provide sufficient grounds to make a generalizable argument. How do we know then that this framework might validly account for the growth of the informal economy in other nations as well?

In their attempt to test the generalizability of an argument, comparative scholars examine whether similar factors lead to the same outcome in otherwise dissimilar contexts (most different cases/method of agreement), or whether different outcomes are observed in otherwise similar contexts due to absence of similar forces in place (most similar cases/method of disagreement). Available data from transition economies provide us with a rare opportunity to test our argument in both ways, in however a preliminary fashion. These countries are former socialist economies, and hence remain similar in terms of their political and economic histories, while they remain quite different from Turkey. Comparing their experiences vis-à-vis each other, the most similar cases, and to Turkey, a very different case, allows us to examine simultaneously whether similar regulatory trends (deregulation combined with ineffective enforcement) were associated with similar outcomes (informal growth pattern) across unalike contexts, but also to examine whether the diverging regulatory circumstances of these otherwise similar contexts over time have led to different outcomes in terms of informal economic growth pattern. We should note of course that, because of space limits, our comparative analysis is necessarily preliminary, and does not capture the nature of market transitions in these nations in all its complexity. Having said that, the trends that we observe in these contexts tend to support our thesis rather than challenge it. We find that in all of these nations, rising informality and private-sector growth went hand in hand during the initial stage of neoliberal reforms—a time of substantial deregulation in the economic sphere. In other words, economic informalization in these former socialist countries, like in Turkey, took place in the context of a neoliberal de-regulation process, and was not linked to over regulation. In the Central European countries—Poland, Czech Republic, and Hungary—the trend of increasing economic informalization came to a halt only when, in the second half of the 1990s, these countries had strengthened their regulatory focus on their way to membership of the European Union.

The chapter is organized as follows. Section 14.2 provides the theoretical background for this study. It is argued that informalization is a phenomenon that is inherently linked to the nature of the State's regulatory intervention in the economy. This leads to a discussion of the link between neoliberal reforms and the growth of the informal economy from a regulatory perspective. Section 14.3 focuses on the Turkish case, examining how the regulatory changes that took place as part of Turkey's neoliberal transformation influenced the growth of informal economic practices. Section 14.4 discusses the generalizability of the framework using comparative data from transition countries. The chapter then concludes, emphasizing the role of neoliberal transitions in promoting informal growth patterns. It also discusses the theoretical contributions and policy implications of the study.

14.2 Neoliberal Reforms and the Informal Economy: A Regulatory Perspective

The term 'informal' was originally used to describe the subsistence activities of the urban poor who were excluded from formal employment in labour surplus economies. However, it now applies to economic activities as diverse as street vending, tax evasion, unregistered employment, counterfeit production, and shuttle trade. These diverse activities have one thing in common: they all take place beyond the reach of the State. Informalization can thus be defined as a process characterized by an increase in the profit- and income-generating activities that take place outside the purview of the State (Castells and Portes, 1989; Hart, 2005).

A large amount of literature exists on the causes of informalization in an economy, but three strands of thought stand out. First, the view that emerged from the earliest wave of research characterized informalization as part of the larger context of underdevelopment. According to this perspective, sufficient development of the capitalist economy and industrialization would result increasingly in informal economic activities being formalized.[2]

A second line of thought rejects the association of informalization with a lack of capitalist development, and argues, instead, that the structural characteristics of advanced capitalism are not only compatible with informalization, but foster it (Portes and Sassen, 1987; Sassen, 1994 and 2002; Itzigsohn, 2000). From this perspective, by providing firms with an opportunity to achieve flexible production, profit generation, and cost reduction, informalization constitutes 'an integral feature of advanced capitalism' (Castells and Portes, 1989: 12).

Finally, a third perspective portrays informality as a rational response on the part of economic actors to the intrusive State. According to this view, economic actors resort to informality in contexts where the State imposes high costs of entering and remaining in the formal realm through burdensome regulations and requirements. De Soto (1989) offers a popular application of this view. He describes how small and medium-sized entrepreneurs in Peru who migrated to towns and cities from rural areas in the second half of the twentieth century rapidly became extralegal. This, he believes, was a result of the State's institutional arrangements, which inhibited entrepreneurial activity and made it costly for economic actors to enter and remain in the formal realm (De Soto, 1989: xvii).

While these views provide helpful insights into this multidimensional, multi-causal phenomenon, they offer limited help in explaining why the size of the informal economy increased in many developing countries during the 1980s and 1990s. For instance, regarding the argument that informality is related to levels of development, it is true that, on average, the size of the informal economy as a per cent of GDP is bigger in the less developed countries than in the developed ones. However, the fact that the size of the informal economy varies significantly across developing countries poses a challenge to this explanation. What is more, in many developed and developing countries alike the size of the informal economy has continued to expand during times of positive growth (Johnson, Kaufmann, and Shleifer, 1997; Charmes, 2000; Schneider, 2005; Palmade and Anayiotos, 2005; Kus, 2010).

Another argument, that informalization is integral to advanced capitalism as a profit-making and cost-reducing strategy, remains plausible. However, capitalist economies differ significantly in terms of the institutional structures

[2] Both the Marxist and neoclassical theories of development agreed on this view. For a short but interesting discussion of Marxist and neoclassical theories of industrial development, see Portes and Sassen (1987).

within which they operate, and it is partly due to these variations that the degree and style of informality varies among them. It is thus important to identify the kinds of institutional conditions within a State and how they foster informalization. This gives rise to the question of the State's involvement in the process of informalization. De Soto's (1989) argument that informalization results from the State's rigid regulatory arrangements can easily be challenged, both on empirical and theoretical grounds. To begin with, informalization in developing economies over the past few decades has taken place in a fundamentally deregulated context (Itzigsohn, 2000; Heintz and Pollin, 2003). This is hard for De Soto and his proponents to explain. From our perspective, however, this is not at all surprising. As various social scientists have noted, the State–informal economy relationship is more complicated than De Soto makes it out to be.

As Fernandez-Kelly and Garcia (1989) have shown, rather than simply being an outcome of a heavily regulating State, informalization often takes place under the auspices of the State. Through the actions of local and federal agencies, the State may tolerate, or even stimulate, informal economies so as to achieve certain economic and social outcomes. Portes and Centeno (2006) and Kus (2010) have also found that the capacity of the State to enforce regulations matters as much as, if not more than, the actual degree of regulation in an economy. Examining quantitative data at the macro level across a broad set of countries, Kus (2010) showed that, while the average size of the informal economy is indeed larger in countries with higher degrees of State regulations, a reduction of those regulations by no means leads automatically to greater formalization. In contexts where the State lacks the capacity or the political will to enforce those rules effectively, reducing the scope of regulations is likely to lead to more informality rather than less.

In a similar vein, the social and cultural characteristics of the society in which economic actors remain subject to rules and regulations also matters. Referring to the Latin American experience, Portes and Centeno (2006) argue that the attempt to foster a regime of minimal but dependable regulations that would lead to the growth of the private sector and promote formalization has backfired, because the underlying societal structures in Latin America are different from those of liberal, developed States. In those societies where poverty and inequality abound, they argue, neoliberal reforms, by means of weakening unions and government regulators, have ended up creating more opportunity for private firms to benefit from informal channels. The end result has been 'the decline of protected work, a significant rise in microenterprises and informal employment, and a sustained increase in economic inequality' (Portes and Centeno, 2006: 38). This argument is in line with the findings of earlier research by Itzigsohn (2000), and Olmeda and Murray (2002).

As noted before, although there is a vast body of literature on neoliberal reforms, only a few studies have sought to analyse the empirical link between the growth of those reforms and the expansion of the informal economy in developing countries (Itzigsohn 2000; Olmeda and Murray 2002; Pérez Sainz, 2005; Jonakin, 2006; Portes and Centeno, 2006). Focusing on informalization in the labour market, in particular, Pérez Sainz (2005) emphasizes three major channels through which neoliberal reforms have contributed to informalization: the decline of public-sector employment, deregulatory changes in social security laws, and the weakening of unions. Itzigsohn (2000) shows how deregulation of the labour market has blurred the distinction between formal and informal work. Similarly, Olmeda and Murray (2002), focusing on Argentina, suggest that the 1991 National Employment Law, one of the major legislative elements of Argentina's shift to neoliberalism, essentially institutionalized and legitimized what had hitherto been seen as defining features of informal labour markets, such as precariousness, lack of social protection, and limited rights to wage bargaining. More recently, Jonakin (2006) argues that the growth of informal activities in the 1980s and 1990s constituted a structural prerequisite of neoliberal export-promotion strategies.

In this chapter, building on Fernandez-Kelly and Garcia (1989), Itzigsohn (2000), Portes and Centeno (2006), and Kus (2010), we examine how the changing contours of the State's regulatory relationship under neoliberal reforms have fostered informalization in the Turkish economy. Using the case of Turkey, we show that two concurrent regulatory trends that underpinned neoliberal transformations, namely deregulation and the declining quality of legal enforcement in the economic sphere, played a major role in the development of an informal pattern of economic growth. Neoliberal reforms eliminated many of the regulatory constraints that had, until then, substantially limited the activities of the private sector. At the same time, however, they weakened the State's already limited capacity for law enforcement in the economic sphere. This double transformation led to a business environment that facilitated the starting and operating of a business, but also the operating of businesses through informal means.

14.3 Neoliberal Reforms and the Informal Economy: The Turkish Case

Turkey shifted to neoliberal policies at the end of the 1970s in the context of a severe economic crisis. Throughout the 1960s and 1970s, Turkey, like many other developing countries, had followed a State-led development strategy based on import-substituting industrialization and centrally administered plans. This development model was interrupted by the first oil crisis in 1974.

By the mid-1970s, the inflation rate had reached triple digits, unemployment had risen to 15 per cent, and the import-substitution growth strategy that had been in place for almost two decades left the country with foreign exchange shortages. It was at this time and in this context that Turkey, like many other countries facing similar economic challenges, embarked on a radical neoliberal reform package under the leadership of Turgut Özal.[3]

Transforming Turkey from an inward-oriented economy with a large public sector to a dynamic export-oriented market economy was the central tenet of the reform programme. This required a substantial reorientation in the nature of the State's regulatory intervention in the economy. Starting from the early 1980s, successive governments undertook a wide array of deregulatory policies so as to encourage the growth of an export-oriented private sector. Regulatory restrictions on market entry, access to finance, and international trade were largely removed; taxes were reduced, and labour laws were modified so as to create a more flexible labour market. Along the way, however, the State's effectiveness in policing the economic sphere severely diminished (Buğra, 1994).

14.3.1 Deregulatory Changes in the Economic Sphere

The deregulatory changes that were put in place to liberalize the Turkish economy were most visible in the area of trade. As Togan and Balasubramanyam (1996) show, protection rates for different sectors of the economy were reduced significantly. The share of restricted imports in total imports, which was 25 per cent in 1975, was reduced to less than 2 per cent by 1984 (Togan and Balasubramanyam, 1996). In addition, the government embarked on an export-promotion policy that encouraged exports through tariff exemptions on imported inputs, foreign exchange allocations, tax rebates, and exemptions from various taxes.[4]

Tax policies were also altered to promote growth of the private sector. The government reduced the effective rate of corporate tax and included many tax breaks and exceptions in the tax code. The share of corporate tax revenues in total tax revenues dropped from 12 per cent in 1988 to 5.9 per cent in 1993, despite the fact that the number of corporate taxpayers more than

[3] Before he became Prime Minister in 1983, an office he would hold until 1989, Turgut Özal was in charge of the economy as Head of the State Planning Organization and Undersecretary of the Prime Ministry (1981–3). Prior to that, he was one of the executives of the MESS (Metal Industry Businessmen's Association)—a leading vocal group of the time that promoted business interests.

[4] The share of customs tax in the total tax revenue, which was about 10 per cent in the 1960s dropped to less than 2 per cent at the end of the 1980s.

doubled in that period (Yilmaz, 1996).[5] Taxes on wealth (including property tax, capital transfer tax, endowment tax, and capital gains taxes) were also substantially reduced.[6]

Moreover, significant changes also took place in the State's laws. New labour legislation restricted workers' right to unionize.[7] The number of registered unions fell from 781 in 1975 to 81 by the end of the 1980s (Önder, 2000). Limits were imposed on the amount of severance payments, annual vacations, and the financial liability of employers, and many of the legal obstacles to firing workers were removed (Önder, 2000; Gülmez, 2005).

In short, by the end of the 1980s, many of the regulations associated with the State-led and inward-looking development model of import substitution, which had hitherto constrained the growth of the informal economy in Turkey, had been eliminated. The various government leaders who held executive office in the 1990s[8] shared the ideological premises of the 1980s' reform process and pushed ahead with liberalization reforms, further diminishing the State's regulatory intervention in the economy.

14.3.2 Declining Quality of Policing in the Economic Sphere

The same period also saw a significant decline in the effectiveness of the State in 'policing' the economic sphere. There were both institutional and ideological factors underpinning this development. On the ideological front, seeing the State as a repressor of economic freedom and entrepreneurial spirit, political leaders regarded evasion of law by economic entrepreneurs in Turkey as 'justified' and proved reluctant to punish offenders under existing laws. It was believed that a punitive approach would prevent entrepreneurs from growing their businesses. The principle of 'economic punishment for economic crimes' was hailed by the administration in the 1980s as a substitute for penitentiary punishment, even in the most rampant cases of economic crimes, despite opposition from the judiciary and parliament (Öniş, 2004).

One of the most serious applications of this principle was the 'fictitious exports' episode during the early 1980s, when certain enterprises tried to take advantage of generous export subsidies and tax returns through a variety of mechanisms, notably over-invoicing. It soon became apparent that a large number of firms had violated the law, claiming large amounts of export

[5] In 1980s the share of corporate tax revenues in the total tax revenues was significantly higher than the OECD average (52 per cent compared with the OECD average of 38 per cent); by 1995 it was significantly lower (28 per cent compared with the OECD average of 35 per cent).

[6] The ratio of wealth tax revenue to gross national product (GNP), which was already lower than the OECD average as of 1980, had fallen still lower by 1995 (Yilmaz, 1996).

[7] Through Acts 2821 (Trade Unions Act) and 2822 (Collective Bargaining Strike and Lockout Act).

[8] Respectively, Akbulut, Yilmaz, Ciller, and finally Ciller-Erbakan governments.

subsidies and tax returns by reporting a larger amount of exports than they had actually exported. When the Prime Minister was confronted about his administration's treatment of this particular issue, he argued that in this specific case the State was to blame and that these entrepreneurs acted with the objective of making the economy work better (Çetin, 1988). The government went so far as to issue an official decree concerning exports, dated 29 December 1983 (887/7340), which stated that no official, in the performance of his duty, might prevent exporters from conducting their trade activities. It added that the transportation of goods by exporters should not be stopped. In the official Gazette issued on the same day, a decree concerning Law No. 1567 on Protecting the Value of the Turkish Currency declared: 'It is free to bring into Turkey foreign currency of all types by all means. It need not be registered; its origins cannot be investigated.'[9] As a result, such fictitious export activities continued until they reached levels that could no longer be ignored, and finally the offenders were indicted under existing laws and put in prison, but only for a limited period. However, with amendments made to the existing laws, they were soon bailed out.

The 'fictitious exports' practices and the government's handling of the issue reveals the lack of political will on the part of the government to enforce the laws in the economic sphere. It must be noted, however, that ideologically driven lack of political will was not the only reason for the State's deteriorating effectiveness in enforcing regulations pertaining to the economic sphere: there were also significant institutional changes in the structure of the State that undermined its capacity for law enforcement.

One such major change was the greater degree of centralization and insulation that had come to characterize the policy-making process. Policy-making became centralized within a small circle consisting of the Prime Minister and a select number of ministers and technocrats. The bureaucratic agencies that had played a key role during the State-led development era, such as the State Planning Organization, were deliberately side-tracked so as to reduce the amount of resistance to market reforms. While this provided the government with 'corporate coherence' and 'autonomy', to quote Evans (1995: 13), and proved instrumental in the speedy implementation of the reforms and the fast recovery from the crisis, it also cut off the institutionalized channels that bound the State to society. In other words, coherence and autonomy were achieved at the expense of embeddedness and accountability.

Another important institutional factor was the substantial empowerment of the executive branch vis-à-vis the legislative and judicial branches under the newly adopted 1982 constitution. The new constitution endowed

[9] Official Gazette dated 29 December 1983, number 18266.

the Prime Minister and the Council of Ministers with the power to change laws through extra-parliamentary means, even in very critical policy areas. Cabinet decrees and special laws emerged as tools of regulatory change in this context. To put things in perspective, while the total number of decrees that had the force of laws issued by ten successive governments in the 1970s was thirty-four, two successive governments in the 1980s issued 186 such decrees (Ünay, 2006: 123). Although this was instrumental in the quick implementation of reforms, along with centralization of policy-making it generated an institutional platform whereby the making and changing of laws remained solely at the discretion of a small group of people—the small number of ministers and technocrats close to the Prime Minister—and provided ample opportunity for legal manipulation. As Buğra (1994) notes, throughout the 1980s and 1990s, whenever there was even the slightest conflict between the existing legal provisions and policy objectives, governments either changed the rules or displayed a clear disregard for the existing ones. In other words, laws became disposable.

As Ünay (2006: 13) observes, the frequent breach and modification of established rules and practices, accompanied by a deliberate disregard for judicial and parliamentary opposition, served to increase the pace and scope of socio-economic change. However, it introduced into the legal system a great degree of ambiguity. In a speech delivered in 1985 at the Annual Meeting of the Turkey Bar Association, the President of the Association criticized the government for making the legal system unpredictable and confusing by frequently issuing ever-changing decrees that were difficult to understand (from *Cumhuriyet,* 1985; author's translation). He stressed that some of those decrees included elements that impaired the independence of the judiciary and as such undermined the State's legal capacity. In short, as Buğra (1994: 232) states, 'as the Turkish State, represented by a very narrow group of people, acted as the main agency for the neoliberal restructuring, it had simultaneously dismantled some of the basis of its own power that would permit its much-needed intervention as a regulator'.

14.3.3 Growth and Informality—Two Faces of Turkey's Neoliberal Transformation

Throughout the 1960s and 1970s, within the framework of an import-substituting, State-led development model, the Turkish economy remained highly concentrated, with the State and a few large conglomerates located in and around Istanbul producing much of the output and employing the majority of the active workforce. Barriers to market entry, trade restrictions, and difficulty of access to finance provided limited room for the growth of small and medium-sized enterprises (SMEs) across the country. At the end of the 1970s, the State employed 40 per cent of the manufacturing sector's labour force and generated 30 per cent of its value added. The 500 largest industrial firms in the country accounted for more than half of all sales of manufactures, and more than half of these firms were located in Istanbul and its environs (Barkey, 1990: 63).

The regulatory transformation that took place with neoliberal reforms remained quite successful in promoting the growth of the private sector and export activity in Turkey. Within a period of less than two decades, from being a heavily regulated, import-substituting economy, dominated by massive public enterprises and large, private conglomerates clustered in a limited geographical area, Turkey turned into an export-oriented market economy with a substantial number of SMEs spread across the country. Between 1980 and 1996, the share of the private sector in total employment increased from 64 per cent to 85 per cent,[10] and its share in total value added increased from 60 per cent to 77 per cent. A significant amount of this new private economic activity was based in the new industrial centres across Anatolia. From 1980 to the mid-1990s, Istanbul's share in total value added declined from 28 per cent to 15 per cent, and its share in total employment fell from 45 per cent to 34 per cent, as Anatolia began to claim a larger share. Most of the new entrants to the economy across Anatolia were SMEs. The share of SMEs in total employment rose from 37 to 46 per cent.

However, during the same period, evasion of the State's rules became not only feasible but also a fairly acceptable business practice across different sectors, and in a variety of degrees and forms. There exists compelling evidence that a substantial part of the new wave of entrepreneurship in Turkey, particularly in mainland Anatolia during the 1980s and 1990s, remained informal. Enterprises in these emerging centres started mostly as small to medium-sized family firms with limited capital in labour-intensive industries, such as textiles, clothing, and food processing. They employed workers with little or no social security or health benefits, evaded taxes, and even failed to register as legal entities (Pamuk, 2008).

Thus the Turkish economy was characterized by the concurring trends of growth of the private sector, export orientation, the rising prominence of SMEs, and a growing informality in the economy (Figure 14.1). Between 1980 and 1995, the share of unregistered labour in total employment increased from 32 per cent to 37 per cent. The two aggregate estimates of the informal economy, which are presented in Figure 14.1, also point to the informalization of the Turkish economy under neoliberal reforms. In interpreting these aggregate measures, it is important to note that the actual measurement of the size of

[10] The figures on Turkish economy provided here are from the Turkish Statistics Institute, unless otherwise noted.

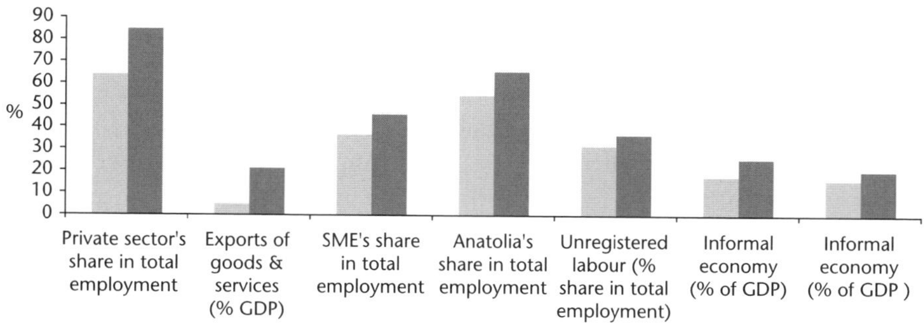

Figure 14.1 Informality in the Turkish economy (1980–95)

Source: Turkish Statistics Institute's *TURKSTAT*, as provided in Yeldan, Boratav, and Kose (2000); Öğünç and Yilmaz (2000).

the informal economy varies depending on the specific indirect measurement technique used.[11] However, what is evident in the case of Turkey is a growth trend in the size of the informal economy regardless of the measurement methods used (see Kasnakoglu, 1993; and Temel, Simsek, and Yazici, 1994).

The findings of a recent survey conducted by a research institute among the members of the Union of Chambers and Commodity Exchanges of Turkey (TOBB)[12] support these conclusions. According to this survey, the sectors where informality levels seem to be higher are the ones where the highest rates of economic growth and export activity were observed in the 1980s and 1990s, namely textiles and apparel, food, and retail and wholesale businesses. Thus, 79 per cent of the enterprises operating in the textile and apparel sector, 66 per cent in the food sector, and 68 per cent in retail and wholesale businesses reported facing informal competition, compared with an economy-wide average of 64 per cent.

14.4 Neoliberal Reforms, Regulatory Change and Informalization: Beyond the Turkish Case

This chapter considered the link between the ascendency of neoliberal reforms and the expansion of the informal economy from a regulatory

[11] The aggregate size of the informal economy as a percentage of GDP can be measured by using a variety of indirect measurement techniques. In Figure 14.1, the first aggregate figure on the size of the informal economy was calculated using a simple currency method, which measures the informal economy in terms of the increase in monetary notes in circulation. The second aggregate figure was measured using a currency demand method, which tracks the rise in demand for currency.

[12] TOBB is the largest non-profit business organization in Turkey, covering *365 chambers and commodity exchanges*. The survey was conducted by the Economic Policy Research Foundation of Turkey, TEPAV, in 2006.

perspective, taking the case of Turkey as a point of reference. Specifically, we argued (1) that the growth of the informal economy is inherently linked to the state's regulatory intervention in the economy, (2) that neoliberal reforms brought about a double-edged regulatory transformation, which included, on the one hand, deregulatory policies aimed at promoting the growth of the private sector, and on the other hand, decreasing enforcement efforts in the economic sphere, and (3) that this led not only to an expansion in private economic activities but also in informal practices in the Turkish economy during the 1980s and 1990s.

How can we know that the validity of this argument extends beyond the Turkish case? Available data from transition economies provide us with a glimpse of insight into the generalizability of these trends. These nations are quite similar to each other and quite different from Turkey in terms of their political and economic histories and structures. Comparing their experiences vis-à-vis each other, the most similar cases, and to Turkey, a very different case, allows us to examine simultaneously whether similar regulatory trends (deregulation combined with ineffective legal enforcement) were associated with similar outcomes (informal growth pattern) across unalike contexts (Turkey and post-socialist countries). It also allows us to examine whether the diverging regulatory circumstances of these otherwise similar nations over time have led to different outcomes in terms of patterns of informal economic growth.

14.4.1 Double-Edged Regulatory Transformation in Transition Economies

Most commentators divide the neoliberal transition process into two stages in terms of the nature of the regulatory environment of business, and the kinds of entrepreneurship that flourished (Estrin et al., 2006). The first stage in the late 1980s and early 1990s was characterized by a double-edged regulatory transformation similar to that observed in Turkey. This was a period of substantial deregulation, as well as a time of uncertainty. These nations dismantled a wide range of legal restrictions on private economic activities, and opened their borders to free trade so as to realize their transition from centrally planned economies to market-economies (Kornai, 1997; Clement and Murrell, 2001; Szelenyi, 2008).

By 1995, most had become substantially liberalized.[13] Table 14.1, which presents data from the *World Economic Outlook,* captures this change. The

[13] Indeed, as Szelenyi argues, in terms of per capita FDI, privatization, and liberalization of markets for foreign goods, among other things, the Central European countries had become even more neoliberal in the 1990s than England under Thatcher or the US under Reagan, where the governments initiated these policies in the first place (see Szelenyi, 2008: 10).

Table 14.1 Economic liberalization in transition economies (1989–97)

	Deregulation Index		Private sector's share in GDP		
	1989	1997	1991	1995	2002
Hungary	0.34	0.93	33	60	80
Poland	0.24	0.89	45	60	75
Czech	0	0.93	17	70	80
Georgia	0.04	0.72	27	30	65
Azerbaijan	0.04	0.62	–	25	60
Kazakhstan	0.04	0.86	12	25	65
Russia	0.04	0.83	10	55	70

Source: IMF 2000, *World Economic Outlook: Focus on Transition Economies.*

index, which represents a weighted average of three components: domestic market liberalization, foreign trade liberalization, and enterprise privatization and banking reform, with the highest possible score of 1, reflects the degree to which the regulatory environment of these economies became private sector-friendly in a matter of only a few years.

At the same time, the early transition period involved limited legal and institutional structures to provide the basis for an entrepreneurial market economy (Chilosi, 2001; Verheul et al., 2002; Estrin et al., 2006). The importance of the rule of law to the functioning of a market economy remained underestimated, or deliberately ignored, forsaken in favour of the objective of moving fast forward with reforms in the early transition stage. Similar to the Turkish case, market reforms in these nations were initiated and implemented by a narrow circle of policymakers who held much discretionary power in their hands. As Clement and Murrell (2001: 3) note, the objective of creating institutions that would effectively uphold the law in the economic sphere receded into the background, 'as an unfashionable policy move', in many of these transition economies, 'less newsworthy and more difficult to execute than simply lifting regulations'.

The growth patterns displayed by the private sector and the informal economy in transition economies during the initial phase of neoliberal reforms remain similar to the Turkish experience. As in Turkey, the initial stage of neoliberal reforms, which remained characterized by deregulation and opening of the markets, saw a swift increase in the size of the private sector. At the start of the transition process in the late 1980s these economies contained very few private firms. For instance, there were only 19,000 firms in Hungary, compared with 200,000 in neighbouring and comparable Austria (Estrin et al., 2006). Just like the case in Turkey, most of the existing firms were very large, and there were almost no small enterprises outside agriculture or local crafts. According to Acs and Audretsch (1993), the percentage of workers employed in small enterprises in the late 1980s was less than 2 per cent. As seen in Table 14.1, however, the share of private-sector output in GDP rose dramatically in a matter of a few years. Firm numbers increased more than tenfold in parts of Central and Eastern Europe by 1994, with 167,000 firms registered in the Czech Republic, 101,000 in Hungary, and 95,000 in Poland (Estrin et al., 2006). It is important to note that only a small part of the rise of private-sector employment and output has stemmed from the direct privatization of public enterprises. A far more important role has been played by the newly established small and medium-sized enterprises—the 'privatization from below' (Borish and Noel, 1996; Surdej, 2000).

Again similar to the Turkish case, the 'privatization from below' took place, to a considerable degree, on informal grounds. The combination of market opening that came with deregulatory policies combined with ineffective legal enforcement in the economic sphere gave way to widespread informality. As seen in Figure 14.2, this was virtually the case in all transition economies.

Soon after the start of the neoliberal transition process, however, regulatory trends began to diverge across transition economies. The Central European countries Poland, Hungary, and Czech Republic came under pressure to improve the rule of law to meet EU membership expectations. They began to undertake essential steps to harmonize their legal frameworks with that of the EU's in various fields including customs law, competition law, company law, public procurement, and regulation of financial and assurance institutions. The legal harmonization process also involved commitments and assurances of their implementation. By the mid-1990s, as the data in Table 14.2 from the World Economic Outlook show, the legal effectiveness in these countries had come significantly close to that of Western European countries. This was not the case in other transition economies,

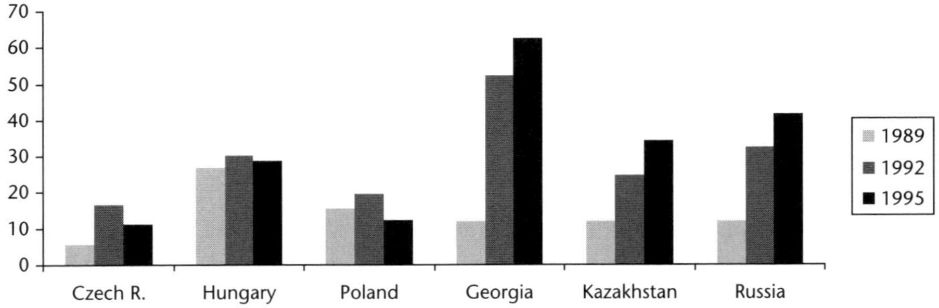

Figure 14.2 Economic informality in transition economies as a per cent of GDP
Source: Johnson et al. (1997).

Table 14.2 Legal effectiveness in transition economies

	Legal Effectiveness circa mid-1990s
Hungary	8.7
Poland	7
Czech Republic	6.8
Georgia	−6.1
Azerbaijan	−7.8
Kazakhstan	−5.3
Russia	−5.4

Source: IMF, 2000, *World Economic Outlook: Focus on Transition Economies.*

however. In Russia, Kazakhstan, and Georgia, the State's legal effectiveness in the economic sphere fared weaker and weaker as market reforms ensued in the absence of external exigencies, such as the prospect of EU membership. As our framework would have us predict, the Czech Republic, Hungary, and Poland began to reverse the tide of informality starting from the mid-1990s, as seen in Figure 14.2. In post-Soviet countries on the other hand, the private sector continued to have a significant and expanding informal dimension in the context of economic liberalization combined with ineffective policing.

These trends provide further proof that deregulation on its own does not bring about formalization, as De Soto (1989), or other neoliberal accounts of the informal economy predicted. Indeed, combined with ineffective policing in the economic sphere, deregulation might well lead to a pattern of private-sector growth that embodies informality as an integral element. The case of Turkey, which we discuss in depth here, provides important insight as to why this is the case, and how the specific institutional and ideological mechanisms produced that outcome.

14.5 Conclusions

The informal economy, which exists and operates outside the State's 'bureaucratic gaze' (Hart, 2005), accounts for a significant proportion of economic activity in the developing world. This chapter has attempted to provide insights into the proliferation of informal economic activities over the past few decades. While the existing literature offers several perspectives on the growth of the informal economy, each fails to adequately account for the most recent period of growing economic informalization in the developing world, which took place during an era of increasing private-sector growth and decreasing regulation.

This chapter offers a new take on the growth of informalization in the developing world by examining the link between the ascendency of neoliberal reforms and the expansion of the informal economy from a regulatory perspective. Drawing on an in-depth study of the Turkish case, and using comparative data from transition countries, it showed that two concurrent regulatory trends that underpinned neoliberal transformations—namely deregulation and the declining quality of legal enforcement in the economic sphere—played a major role in promoting an informal pattern of economic growth.

In linking State regulation to informality, it is important to bear in mind that the impact of regulations might vary across regions and within the same country, as well as across different sectors of the economy. State agents might be more effective, or more willing to enforce regulations, in some localities and realms than in others. Although our analysis here has focused on the macro level, taking the Turkish State and the Turkish economy as the main reference points, we must nevertheless acknowledge that there is much variation within those categories themselves.

In looking at the linkages between neoliberal reforms, regulatory change, and the informal economy, this chapter also discredits the idea that deregulation is conducive to formalization. Proponents of neoliberalism and its tenets argue that informalization results from the costs placed on economic actors by rigid State regulations. Thus they assert that the best way for States to entice actors to the formal system is to deregulate. Yet the Turkish case disproves this hypothesis.

The chapter also contributes to the now vast literature on the nature and implications of neoliberal reforms. While the effects of neoliberal reforms on economic processes have been widely studied, only a handful of studies have explored their implications for the informal economy (Standing, 1989; Itzigsohn, 2000; Heintz and Pollin, 2003; Portes and Centeno, 2006; Olmedo and Murray, 2002; Pérez Sainz, 2005). This chapter shows that the decreasing effectiveness of the State in policing the economic sphere was a key factor in both the State's neoliberal transformation and the growth of its informal economy. Existing analyses have almost entirely ignored this factor and its underlying causes. In a time when corporate and other economic scandals have rocked both developed and developing countries, it is critical that we understand how both the structures and the actors within the system can affect the State's ability, or its willingness, to enforce the rules and regulations of the economic system. We suggest that more research needs to be done to understand these matters.

Finally, and on a related point, we should note that the general assumption surrounding neoliberal reforms places the private sector at the fulcrum of the transformation of a State-run economy to a market economy. Yet the increasing number of economic actors that remain outside the purview of the

State during this transformation are often ignored. Although formal private entrepreneurship is an undeniably important part of the system of neoliberal reform, it is also important not to underestimate the role of informalization in this process.

References

Acs, Z. and Audretsch, D. (eds.) (1993). *Small Firms and Entrepreneurship: An East-West Perspective*. Cambridge: Cambridge University Press.

Barkey, H. (1990). *The State and the Industrialization Crisis in Turkey*. Boulder: Westview Press.

Borish, M. and M. Noel (1996). 'Private Sector Development during Transition: The Visegrad Countries'. Washington: The World Bank. Discussion Paper No. 318

Buğra, A. (1994). *State and Business in Modern Turkey: A Comparative Study*. Albany, NY: SUNY Press.

Castells, M. and A. Portes (1989). 'World Underneath: The Origins, Dynamics and Effects of the Informal Economy', in A. Portes, M. Castells, and L. A. Benton (eds.), *The Informal Economy: Studies in Advanced and Less Developed Countries*. Baltimore: The Johns Hopkins University Press: 11–41.

Çetin, B. (1988). *Soygun: Hayali Ihracatin Boyutlari*. Bilgi Yayinlari.

Charmes, J. (2000). 'Informal Sector, Poverty, and Gender: A Review of Empirical Evidence'. Background paper for the 2001 *World Development Report*. Washington, DC: World Bank.

Chilosi, A. (2001). 'Entrepreneurship and Transition'. *MOCT-MOST: Economic Policy in Economic Transition*, 11: 327–57.

Clement, C and Peter Murrell (2001). 'Assessing the Value of Law in the Economic Transition from Socialism: An Introduction', in Peter Murrell (ed.), *Assessing the Value of Law in Transition Countries*. Ann Arbor: University of Michigan Press.

De Soto, Hernando (1989). *The Other Path*. New York: Harper and Row.

Estrin, Saul, K. Meyer, and M. Bytchkova (2006). 'Entrepreneurship in Transition Economies', in M. Casson, B. Yeung, A. Basu, and N. Wadeson (eds.), *The Oxford Handbook of Entrepreneurship*. Oxford, UK: Oxford University Press: 693–725.

Evans, P. (1995). *Embedded Autonomy: States and Industrial Transformation*. Princeton, NJ: Princeton University Press.

Fernandez-Kelly, Patricia, and Anna M. Garcia (1989). 'Informalization at the Core: Hispanic Women, Homework, and the Advanced Capitalist State', in Alejandro Portes, Manuel Castells, and Lauren A. Benton (eds.), *The Informal Economy: Studies in Advanced and Less Developed Countries*. Baltimore: The Johns Hopkins University Press: 247–64.

Gulmez, M. (2005). *Sendikal Haklarda Uluslararasi Hukuka ve Avrupa Birligine Uyum Sorunu*. Belediye-Is Yayinlari.

Hart, K. (2005). 'Formal Bureaucracy and the Emergent Forms of the Informal Economy'. *WIDER Research Paper*, 11. Helsinki: UNU-WIDER.

Heintz, J. and R. Pollin. (2003). 'Informalization, Economic Growth and the Challenge of Creating Viable Labor Standards in Developing Countries'. *PERI Working Papers*, No. 60, Political Economy Research Institute, University of Massachusetts at Amherst, MA.

ILO (International Labor Office) (2002). *Key Indicators of the Labour Market.* Geneva: ILO.

IMF (International Monetary Fund) (2000). *World Economic Outlook—October 2000: Focus on Transition Economies,* Washington, DC: IMF.

Itzigsohn, J. (2000). *Developing Poverty: The State, Labor Market Deregulation, and the Informal Sector in Costa Rica and the Dominican Republic.* University Park, PA: The Penn State University Press.

Johnson, S., D. Kaufman, and A. Shleifer (1997). 'The Unofficial Economy in Transition'. *Brookings Papers on Economic Activity*, 28(2): 159–240, Washington, DC.

Jonakin, J. (2006). 'Vice and Virtue: Assessing the Informal Sector's Awkward Role under Neoliberal Reform'. *Review of International Economy*, 13(2): 290–312.

Kasnakoglu, Z. (1993). 'Monetary Approach to the Measurement of Unrecorded Economy in Turkey'. *METU Studies in Development*, 20(1–2): 87–111.

Kornai, János. (1997). 'Eliminating the Shortage Economy', in Janos Kornai (ed). *The Struggle and Hope: Essays on Stabilization and Reform in a Post-Socialist Economy.* Northampton, MA: Edgar Elgar.

Kus, Basak. (2010). 'Regulatory Governance and the Informal Economy: Cross-national. Comparisons.' *Socio-Economic Review*, 8: 487–510.

OECD (Organization for Economic Co-operation and Development) (2009). *'Informal is Normal? Towards More and Better Jobs in Developing Countries'.* Paris: OECD.

Öğünç, F. and G. Yilmaz. (2000). 'Estimating the Underground Economy in Turkey'. Discussion paper, The Central Bank of the Republic of Turkey Research Department, September.

Olmedo, C. and M. J. Murray (2002) 'The Formalization of Informal/Precarious Labor in Contemporary Argentina'. *International Sociology*, 17(3): 421–43.

Önder, N. (2000). 'The Political Economy of the State and Social Forces: Changing Forms of State–Labour Relations in Turkey'. PhD thesis, York University, York (Canada).

Öniş, Ziya (2004). 'Turgut Özal and his Economic Legacy: Turkish Neo-liberalism in Critical Perspective.' *Middle Eastern Studies*, 40(4): 113–34.

Palmade, V. and Andrea Anayiotos (2005). 'Rising Informality: Reversing the Tide'. *Viewpoint series*, Note 298. World Bank Group.

Pamuk, Sevket. (2008). 'The New Industrial Districts and the Rise to Power of AKP in Turkey'. London School of Economics and Political Science, public speech.

Pérez, Sainz and J. Pablo (2005). 'Labor Exclusion in Latin America: Old and New Tendencies', in N. Kudva and L. Beneria (eds.), *Rethinking Informalization.* Ithaca, NY: Cornell University Open Access Repository.

Portes, A. and M. A. Centeno (2006). 'The Informal Economy in the Shadow of the State', in P. Fernández-Kelly and J. Sheffner (eds.), *Out of the Shadows: The Informal Economy and Political Movements in Latin America.* Princeton, NJ: Princeton University Press: 23–49.

Portes, A. and S. Sassen (1987). 'Making It Underground: Comparative Materials on the Informal Sector in Western Market Economies'. *American Journal of Sociology*, 93(1): 30–61.

Sassen, S. (1994). 'The Informal Economy: Between New Developments and Old Regulations'. *Yale Law Journal*, 103(2289–304) (Symposium on The Informal Economy).

—— (2002). 'Informalization in Advanced Market Economies'. *Issues in Development, Discussion Paper*, 20. Urban Planning Programme, International Labour Office, Geneva.

Schneider, F. (2005). 'Shadow Economies around the World: What Do We Really Know?' *European Journal of Political Economy*, 21(3): 598–642.

Standing, Guy (1989). 'The British Experiment: Structural Adjustment or Accelerated 'Decline', in Alejandro Portes, Manuel Castells, and Lauren A. Benton (eds.), *The Informal Economy: Studies in Advanced and Less Developed Countries*. Baltimore: Johns Hopkins University Press: 279–97.

Surdej, Aleksander (2000). 'Small and Medium Sized Enterprise Development in Poland After 1990'. *World Institute for Development Economics Research*, Working Paper 216.

Szelenyi, I. (2008). 'From Socialist Workfare to Capitalist Welfare State: Competing Strategies and Outcomes of Transformation of Social Institutions in European Neo-Patrimonial and Neo-Liberal Post-Communist Regimes During the Second Phase of Reforms'. Working paper, in preparation for *The Oxford Handbook of Comparative Institutional Analysis*.

Temel, A., A. Simsek, A. and K. Yazıcı (1994). 'Kayıtdısı Ekonomi Tanımı, Tespit Yöntemleri ve Türk Ekonomisindeki Büyüklüðü', State Planning Organization.

Togan, S. and V. N. Balasubramanyam (1996). *The Economy of Turkey Since Liberalization*. London and New York: St Martin's Press.

Ünay, S. (2006). *Neoliberal Globalization and Institutional Reform: The Political Economy of Development and Planning in Turkey*. Hauppauge, NY: Nova Publishers.

Verheul, I., S. Wennekers, D. Audretsch, and A. Thurik (2002). 'An Eclectic Theory of Entrepreneurship: Policies, Institutions and Culture', in D. Audretsch, A. Thurik, I. Verheul, and A. Wennekers (eds.), *Entrepreneurship: Determinants and Policy in a European-US Comparison*. Boston/Dordrecht: Kluwer Academic Publishers.

World Bank (2004). *Doing Business in 2005: Removing Obstacles to Growth*. New York: Oxford University Press.

Yeldan, E., K. Boratav, and A. H. Kose (2000). 'Globalization, Distribution, and Social Policy in Turkey'. Working paper, Schwartz Center for Economic Policy Analysis.

Yilmaz, H. (1996). *Türkiye'de vergi yapısı ve 1980'den sonra sektörel vergi yuklerin gelisimi*. Ankara: Devlet Planlama Teşkilatı. İktisadi Sektörler ve Koordinasyon Genel Mudurlugu. Proje Yatirimlari Degerlendirme ve Analiz Dairesi.

Postface: Another Look at the Informal Sector, its Many Stakes and Challenges

Jean-Philippe Peemans

A postface aims to highlight the convergence of interests, concerns, or opinions between its writer and the book presented. It can also underline the original contribution of the book to a certain domain of studies. The reflections that follow are largely inspired by the introduction to this book by Hillenkamp, Lapeyre, and Lemaître, which provides a broad outline of the various contributions. It also presents the general theoretical framework for examining the informal economy from a broader perspective than those provided by strictly quantitative or functionalist approaches. These conventional approaches focus narrowly on the issue of how to formalize the informal sector to prevent it from deterring growth, or how to use it in one way or another to support growth. The informal sector as well as poverty are thus seen as a kind of 'new frontier' for the economy as potential sources of growth, provided they are managed by well-targeted programmes of support for training, microcredit, and micro-entrepreneurship, preferably with a clearly affirmed gender component.

As Hillenkamp, Lapeyre, and Lemaître rightly put it, the 'mainstream' view of the informal sector since the introduction of this concept in the 1970s, has been shaped mainly by the modernization paradigm which has dominated development studies since the Second World War. The versions of the theory of modernization during the period 1950–60 have focused on 'traditional rural society' as the major locus of poverty and underdevelopment, and the subsequent posterior 'discovery' of the urban informal sector opened up a new discursive field of study along the same lines.

Through that construction of the rural and urban popular layers defined solely in terms of monetary poverty, modernization discourses succeeded in a double dispossession of the popular identity. On the one hand, all the realities of this segment of society were reduced to a monetary indicator, which, by its very nature, refuses the status of actors to those who are wrapped in it. On the other hand, all popular initiatives were disregarded if they did not correspond to the performance criteria of the modernization discourse. The only project in which they could participate related to allowing them gradually to have activities that would contribute to overall economic growth. Despite their claim to originality, the discourses on poverty of the 1990s and 2000s have been a continuation of that recurring approach. More than ever, this approach espouses the cause of freeing the poor from their 'culture of dependency', including dependence on the State, and by promoting 'a new economic mentality' among them, in order to transform them into entrepreneurs and consumers who support growth (Salmen,1992).

The different variants of the modernization paradigm have therefore played, and continue to play, a major ideological role in the implementation and legitimization of what Harvey has called 'accumulation by dispossession' (Harvey, 2003). At the heart of the apparent success of the historic expansion of the logic of capital accumulation on a global scale, there is the constantly renewed ability of the players who control the accumulation process to deprive the popular actors of access to material resources on the grounds of their supposed inability to manage them rationally. This reasoning has underpinned the different waves of enclosures over many centuries, including the current wave of land grabbing in the South. The cultural aspect has also played an important role in the dispossession strategy by refusing to ascribe to 'popular knowledge' the status of partner in the development discourse. The relatively recent label of 'informal' has been adopted as a new component in that history of the process of dispossession. It emphasizes the characteristic of a chaotic phenomenon without a historical basis, for which the only future lies in formalization as defined by the criteria of modernization.

Hillenkamp, Lapeyre, and Lemaître highlight the contribution of Polanyi in presenting an alternative image of the non-capitalist and pre-capitalist societies than that of societies without history, frozen into immobility. The concepts of household management, reciprocity, and redistribution observed in those societies give them a rationality that is by no means inferior, but simply differs from the market-based one. That rationality is centred on the conditions necessary for the reproduction of a given societal set.

Initially, the Polanyian approach, being the opposite of the Rostovian approach to development, was not perceived as such. Suffice it to recall that in the 1960s some influential anthropologists considered Polanyi's distinction between 'marketplace' and 'market system' as a simple variant of the modernization theories, with the traditional 'marketplace' progressing inevitably towards the modern 'market system'. As observed by Bohannan and Dalton (1965: 32): '...the market principle has affected more and more institutions and has outgrown the marketplace because the essential ingredients of production—labor, land, machines—cannot be transacted in a marketplace... The marketplace and its institutional arrangement has undergone other, non economic changes. Just as its economic importance lapses with the "development of the national economy", and it becomes merely a place of final sale, so its political importance lapses with the development of the polity, its religious significance with the acceptance of world religions, and its social significance with the adoption of the guitar, the radio... and high life.'

The role of what has been called the 'Scandinavian school' in development studies has been a pioneering one to recognize the originality of Polanyi's approach. That school has been seen as contributing to the elaboration of another approach to development, by providing an alternative paradigm to modernization. During the period 1970–80, the Scandinavian school was one of the first to seek to identify other development actors than those recognized by the modernization approach. It did not directly refer to popular actors because it focused on the role of 'ordinary citizens' to advance a rationale other than that of the 'prince' and the 'merchant' (Hettne, 1990). However, it provided an important contribution to the recognition of other views and perspectives of development than those offered by the hegemonic paradigm.

Since the 1980s, several new research orientations have taken another look at the practices of local communities forgotten or ignored by the modernization approach. This has paved the way to alternative views about these actors and the informal sector. Initially, many of these studies were stimulated by an examination of their common practices of survival, in the face of the devastating impact of neoliberal adjustment policies in various countries of Latin America, sub-Saharan Africa, and Asia.

They highlighted the practices of urban popular classes, which included a blossoming of associative initiatives that enabled their members to self-organize, not only for the purpose of survival, but also for responding to their individual and collective needs that were excluded from the realm of public policies. This signalled a shift in the perception of the underclass that extended beyond informality and poverty. Their lives were seen as combining production activities with the creation of networks of reciprocity, redistribution, and collective security, and the management of 'territories of life', despite the crushing weight of the constraints they suffered.

In addition, the enhancement of the role of women was seen as central to the progressive recognition of the reality of popular actors. This was the result of a long conceptual and empirical journey. In the original versions of the theory of modernization, rural women were presented as being at the heart of traditional behaviour that blocked any progress towards change and rational individualism. At the end of the 1960s, a current of thought inspired by the work of Boserup (1970) sought to show that rural women were, instead, capable of initiatives to bring about change, and were therefore potential agents of modernization. The 1970s thus saw intense debates on the role of women in development. Liberal feminist discourses stressed the importance of the 'advancement of women' to integrate them into the modernization process. Radical feminists sought to show that in the process of modernization family relations as well as work relations often reformulated the role of women through a reinvention of the old forms of the patriarchal system (Boserup,1970; Visvanathian et al.,1997; Bisilliat and Verschuur, 2000).

While these debates resulted in the formal institutionalization of gender studies, it was only from the 1980s onwards that the role of women in the lower strata of society came to be highlighted in the South. It was revealed through the informal associative practices of solidarity adopted in low-income urban neighbourhoods and villages to deal with the devastating consequences of governments' structural adjustment policies, and the disintegration of the redistributive functions of the State, particularly in Latin America. During the past twenty years, the role of women and the nature of the popular economies have appeared more and more as interdependent and interrelated realities. In Africa, as in Asia and Latin America, women are at the heart of the functioning of the 'marketplace', interacting with popular social networks that embody the Polanyian household management and reciprocity principles (Basu, 1995).

This is not the place to recall in detail the major contributions made by various schools of the new anthropology of development to the discovery of the realities of popular economies (see, for example, Anderson, 1994; Brokensha et al., 1980; de Villers, 1992; Kearney, 1996; Olivier de Sardan, 1995; Richards, 1985; Scott, 1990). Their views have been based on their field observations of peasant economies and urban popular economies. And, increasingly, they have played an important role in revealing the limits of the neo-functionalist institutionalism of the time, and in enabling a rediscovery of the importance of Polanyi's 'substantive' approach and its relevance for grasping the complexity of the strategies of popular actors.

Another breakthrough was the establishment of a long historical perspective on the presence of popular actors and popular economies in both rural and urban areas. A recent school of thought that did much to promote a new narrative of the history of resistance of local communities, particularly the peasantry, was presented by the so-called Subaltern Studies Group. Established in the 1980s in India, this school of thought called into question the elitist and modernization theories of colonial and post-colonial Indian historiography. It sought to define what constituted the cultural basis of peasant resistance and insurgency movements. It insisted on the 'irredentist' character of peasant culture, its non-submission to the values imposed by colonial and post-colonial elites, and on the cultural autonomy of the dominated actors, despite the hegemony of the economically and politically dominant actors. The peasant world was recognized as a world of players capable of initiative and resistance, despite being integrated into the modern world in a 'subordinate' position. The influence of the Subaltern Studies Group has extended far beyond India, leading to similar approaches in other countries of Asia, Latin America, and Africa (Guha and Spivak, 1988).

However, it was the meeting between Braudel and Wallerstein, publicized particularly through the work of the Fernand Braudel Center, which helped to stress the importance of the historical approach in identifying the role of 'forgotten' actors and territories neglected by the modernization views of the past and present. It contributed to the rediscovery of the role of the underprivileged actors in the long history of development. Indeed, Braudel helped to give new dimensions to Wallerstein's 'world systems' theory, other than those of capital accumulation and the history of the nation State since the sixteenth century. Braudel pushed back the history of development beyond that founding century of modernity. He did this by emphasizing the role of those he called the 'actors from the bottom' in the construction of the bases of material and spiritual civilization in the countryside and in the cities of the world.

According to Braudel, the first level of human development in the long run is the history of the construction of material life whereby all peoples have gradually mastered their natural environment and have mobilized resources to ensure sustainable living conditions. Above this historic basement, a second level has progressively been built, which he calls the level of exchange. This is where the market appears, which constitutes the meeting place for peasants, artisans, and small shopkeepers and merchants. These 'actors of the bottom' are very different from the so-called traditional 'poor masses' in the language of modernization. This Braudelian 'second level' clearly equates with the Polanyian 'marketplace'. Capitalism, characterized as the rise to power of coalitions of actors seeking to establish monopolies, is the economy of the third level. The third level becomes dominant, and it imposes its laws gradually on the other two levels. However, its ability to transform the whole of society radically varies, depending on the history of relationships between actors of the three levels in the different national development processes in the North and South (Braudel, 1985).

These three levels of a long-term analysis constitute permanent areas of conflict between dominant and dominated actors at local, regional, and national levels. The axis of these conflicts is the opposition between two antagonistic vectors: on one hand, that of the dominant players of the third level in Braudel, driven by the combined logic of accumulation–centralization–differentiation; and on the other hand, resistance of the dominated actors—not only the working class of the capitalist sector, but also the actors of the resilient first level. These are driven by the needs of collective security for maintaining the conditions for their sustainable reproduction. In this regard, the urban or rural local levels, particularly in the South today, are permanent areas of struggle around the mobilization of human and material resources along one or the other of these logics. For centuries, and even until today, the fate of the local level is a major visible issue experienced by the populations: being incorporated into the logic of capital accumulation or maintaining the functioning of the 'Polanyian market' embedded in the social fabric through the implementation of what one may call 'historical governance'.

Although Braudel had never studied the realities of the contemporary 'popular economy' in the South, his approach was essential for an understanding of the latter in terms of development issues. First, it brought the 'informal sector' and its popular practices out of an approach based solely upon twentieth-century phenomena, related to the limitations or the failures of the State's modernization policies. The rural and urban masses have developed their own conditions of local development over centuries, long before the emergence of capitalism in Western Europe. There have always been conflicts among actors, and the territorial dimension is central to these conflicts. They are related to the three levels—local, regional, and national—and to their still problematic interactions. In that sense, the Braudelian vision complements the Polanyian vision in understanding the complexity of development processes. Finally, around the world, the first and second levels, the so-called 'traditional sectors' in modernization theory, are not doomed to disappear because of the expansion of the 'modern sector'. They are dominated by the third level, but they survive or can even resist that domination and maintain a distinct identity. In other words, the linear vision of universal development proposed by modernization theorists is full of contradictions. The resulting real development processes are largely dependent on conflicts in specific places and spaces, between dominant players seeking to impose the logic of accumulation, and the dominated actors who deploy various strategies of resistance in order to secure their living conditions.

A critical update of the long-term perspective, in line with the approach of this book, also helps to avoid the pitfalls resulting from idealized interpretations of the popular economy. These 'idealized templates' highlight only trust and solidarity, and the defence of the common interest as a kind of ethical alternative to the cynical amorality of those actors of accumulation. The most interesting observations of the 'real' popular economy, particularly in sub-Saharan African countries, have shown that they are characterized by numerous contradictions: between a tendency to assert individual interests, on the one hand, and the concern to maintain a social link where the logic of reciprocity and redistribution have a place. But the latter can be maintained only at the price of very restrictive rules of access to resources, and of very coded standards of behaviour that are at the heart of the historical governance of the communities involved. Transgression of these often unwritten rules and standards risks stringent penalties for the offenders, including social ostracism or even death. Moreover, the world of the popular economy has nothing to do with the codes of civil and social equality inspired by the normative imaginary of modernization.

Horizontal practices for securing the weaker players often depend on vertical circuits of clientele, in which protection and redistribution are managed by a minority of relatively powerful actors (the big men). Recognizing the conflicts amidst actors within the popular economy itself, is therefore necessary to avoid the deadlock of an idealistic approach to the latter. The harsh realities and the asymmetry of power relations in historical governance should not be underestimated.

The contribution of Hillenkamp, Lapeyre, and Lemaître clearly highlights the fact that the accelerated pace of globalization, far from reducing the proportion of the informal sector in the economies of the South, has instead increased it in many countries. Increased globalization of the accumulation strategies of the dominant players has been accompanied by the greater internationalization of popular actors' networks, creating thereby a sort of new world map of informality. For generations, peasants and the urban popular masses were connected by myriads of networks of human and material exchange, most of the time invisible to elites and foreign observers. Today, these networks have become transnational, through human, economic, and monetary flows that connect even remote villages to various urban centres, both at the national and global levels.

In many respects, not elaborated in this short postface, the past three decades, from 1980 to 2010, could be labelled 'the infamous thirties'. They have called into question the foundations of the relationship between growth, accumulation, and development which had marked the 'glorious thirties'—1950–80. Over the past three decades, the new 'great transformation' in the Polanyian sense of the term, has set the parameters of what could be called 'the global political economy of inequality'. Extrapolating Braudel's approach to the present time, it may be said that it is through this process, that 'the fourth level' of the long history of development has emerged: the level of the globalized players of accumulation, whose international networks of power define, both in the North and the South, the conditions of 'real development'. These 'fourth level networks' include big business leaders in all industrial, financial, and service activities, who have the 'world market' as a strategic space reference for making profit. But they also encompass a wide array of other actors in international organizations, national political systems, media empires, and academic circles, who ensure, at different levels, that reference to 'the global' supersedes all other references in the fields of politics, economics, and even culture and ethics.

For observers who focus solely on growth, that 'fourth level' is linked with new opportunities in terms of poverty reduction and employment, at least in the countries which have been able to participate in the fourth level networks. But those who have a more comprehensive view of human development are very concerned by the increasing social and environmental externalities associated with that new phase of capitalist modernization. In particular, they point to the deepening agrarian and urban crisis in most countries of the South. For the popular masses, urban and rural, who for centuries have been accustomed to bearing the human and social costs of every new phase of the 'sphere of accumulation', it is simply yet another shock that confronts them. For these classes, the dominance of State power or market power are not antagonistic, but are experienced as interchangeable tools of power used by different layers of the ruling elites to constantly build and rebuild the frameworks of the 'political economy of inequality'. Abandoned to their own lot by the elites of global accumulation, they have been adopting new initiatives to survive, to organize, and to find new forms of 'coded solidarity', in order to face the structural social crisis, and fulfil their basic needs, such as food, water, health, hygiene, and shelter. A central dimension of these popular practices is that they are rooted in 'places of life': urban neighbourhoods, small rural towns, and hundreds of thousands of villages around the world. In these places, neglected or abandoned by the 'sphere of accumulation', or threatened by that sphere's appetite for material resources (e.g. land, water, forests, and other natural resources), can be found a myriad of initiatives representing new ways of seeking to achieve human and sustainable development.

However, it is important to emphasize the contradictory aspects of the evolution of the popular economies in the global world as imposed by the actors of the Braudelian 'fourth level'. These aspects are rendering those popular economies much more complex than in earlier historical periods. Numerous forms of 'new infamous informalities' have emerged corresponding to those of the 'infamous thirties' in the sphere of global accumulation. The devastating logic of the 'sphere of accumulation' left to its sole propensity of profit for profit's sake, carries with it a form of systemic entropy whose moral and social components are too often overlooked compared with the environmental entropy theorized by Georgescu-Roegen (1971).

Deregulation of the 'sphere of accumulation' has allowed the thriving of 'infamous informalities' at the core of the business sector, evidenced, for example, by the wide range of recent scandals in banking practices. Systemic deregulation, begun in the early 1980s, has combined with a dynamic and exponential increase of international financial flows facilitated by restructuring, concentrations, and relocations of the old 'centres of accumulation' of the North, and by the rise of new 'emerging centres of accumulation' in the South and in the former 'Eastern bloc'. Most of these streams relate to commercial and financial transactions, a considerable proportion of which are undertaken beyond the reaches of national jurisdictions that are often ill-adapted to the new context of globalization. It has allowed the amassing of huge profits that escape both national tax frameworks and regulatory control of their potentially fraudulent, or even criminal, nature. This has fuelled a virtual 'black hole' of world accumulation, made possible by so-called tax havens and offshore financial centres. According to the Boston Consulting Group, offshore centres were repositories of fortunes amounting to $7,800 billion in 2011.

At the heart of these informal centres of global accumulation, various dominant financial actors are present in diverse sophisticated guises. They provide shelter for super profits generated by specialists in tax evasion, and for masses of profits made through fraudulent trade in raw materials (diamonds and timber being the most notorious cases), manufacturing of counterfeit products, contraband of all sorts, drugs, weapons, and human trafficking, to name a few. These 'black flows' intersect and mingle in the 'black hole' which constitutes the interface between the informal periphery and the informal centre of global accumulation. Indeed the 'black hole' feeds itself through a perpetually increasing stream of financial resources that seek to hide their origins and recycle or 'launder' their ill-gotten gains. According to the United Nations Office on Drugs and Crimes (UNODOC), global crime generates $2,100 billion annually—fifteen times the amount of global development aid (UNODOC, 2012). It is also estimated that every year, United States banks recycle hundreds of billions of dollars that originate from Latin American drugs cartels (Walker, 2011).

The diversity of these activities cannot be discussed here. However, to illustrate, extraordinary organization is required upstream in the production, transport, and marketing circuits of drugs and the securing of their earnings, and downstream in the recycling of these profits, particularly in large real estate transactions of all types, including massive investments in the land grab operations that often require the use of violent force. What is important to emphasize is that these activities have resulted in the proliferation, diversification, or even professionalization of extensive networks of producers, intermediaries, and henchmen, as well as millions of voluntary or forced workers and petty producers, who are involved in all relevant flows and trafficking (Nicaso and Lamothe, 2006). The case of the El Salvador M-13 gang, with its motto 'Mata, roba, viola, controla', or 'kill, steal, rape, control', and with around 30,000 members across the United States, Canada, Mexico, and Central America, is a recently well-documented example, among many, of the multiple forms of moral and physical violence which pervades most of these activities.

Therefore, it can be said that the dramatic evolution of the new central informal sector has promoted, or even caused, a no less spectacular emergence of new peripheral informal sectors, which have a high ability to parasitize, racketeer, or even destroy the historical popular economies. These peripheral informal sectors have fuelled the diversification and multiplication of new mafia-style networks based on trafficking of all kinds and financial circuits, whose opacity is at the nexus between the centre and the periphery of the 'infamous informalities'. Theoretically, this criminal informal economy has nothing to do with the popular economy, but in reality it often uses the most brutal forms of violence to impose its control over local resources and territories, with a very heavy impact on the historical popular economies. These networks often share the same territory, and they can recruit some young people from the popular economy who are attracted by their prestige and wealth. Over time, they gradually impose new codes of conduct that redefine reciprocity and redistribution according to the logic of gangs and armed bands capable of controlling a territory through violence and terror.

At the same time, several decades of erosion and degradation of the public sector and radical restructuring of the private sector in many countries have led to swelling numbers of people who are trying to survive through all kinds of informal practices, which have nothing to do with the practices of the traditional popular economies. But gradually new types of interaction are formed between the two, often entailing a weakening of the old practices of reciprocity and redistribution. Among these new social elements, often living as parasites of the popular economy, there are, in many countries, an increasing proportion of unemployed graduates. They are both a product of the policies of modernization and bear witness to their failures.

Many of them have joined the world of NGOs, which have proliferated in parallel with the downsizing of the State. Forty years ago, NGOs were often a source of aid and support for popular resistance in the face of brutal dictatorships, a role which a minority of them still assume in some countries. But in the wake of structural adjustment, and especially the so-called pro-poor and pro-democracy neoliberal policies, many new NGOs have been created by educated people as means of employment, even though this makes them subservient to the goals and projects of international donors promoting these policies. In this context, some of these groups are at the heart of self-proclaimed civil societies, though without real popular support. And many of them campaign for more civil and democratic liberties based on Western criteria of modernization.

Other groups of educated people, on the other hand, are playing a major role in attempts to rebuild a social order based upon one or another form of religious fundamentalism, around which they are trying to redefine the principles of reciprocity and redistribution. These attempts are present in many sectarian orientations, inspired by different kinds of fundamentalism. Christian, Jewish, Hindu, and Muslim sects and currents are involved, at different levels of intensity, depending on specific contexts. In some contexts, their ability to mobilize the popular economy actors in mass protest movements is not negligible, as attested by recent events, such as the so-called 'Arab Spring' (Beck and Hüser, 2012).

Events like this show that such mobilizations can quickly lead to a manipulation of popular actors in support of demands which are quite alien to their historical practices. Historically, actors of the traditional popular economies generally stayed away from the tribulations of various kinds of modernizing elites, and more or less authoritarian nation States. Besides some fake mobilization in flag-waving spectacular official demonstrations, they stayed deliberately 'elsewhere', being affected only by events threatening the vertical networks of clientele contributing to their security. In the case of the Arab world, analysts concerned by the revolutionary potential of the masses have sometimes attributed an apparently low key deliberate politicization to an indelible 'bazaar economy' tare (Amin, 2012). In counterpoint to that pessimistic judgement, it has been shown that in cases where popular economies have had long-lasting historical roots of resistance, especially in some Latin American countries, it has led to rather strong political mobilization in support of revolutionary movements aimed at regime change at the national level (Petras and Veltmeyer, 2011).

Recent experiences tend to show that in many cases where there has been a low degree of politicization, the revitalization of the religious link has often worked as a substitute for politics in the popular economies, especially if it is accompanied by an offer of social security by its promoters. Radicalization has been accompanied by a transformation of religion into a political project, with the emergence of networks of activists having a forceful social and cultural influence, or even advocating the conquest of power by all means, including armed violence. This postface is clearly not the place to analyse the complexity of that evolution, but it can be said that the latter has contributed to today's panoply of 'infamous informalities'. This has mainly resulted in conflicts where sectarianism and neo-tribalism are inextricably intermingled and are manipulated by various kinds of new quasi-elites operating in international networks, and often supported by foreign interests pursuing particular geostrategic goals. These situations are full of puzzling paradoxes. In some cases the popular economies, which were often a place of stubborn resistance to colonial occupations (as in Libya and Syria), are now being mobilized by groups proclaiming the need for 'liberation against oppression', but who do not hesitate to call on military intervention by former colonial powers to help them take over power. Moreover, recent events show that such forms of mobilization with a religious base do not attempt to jeopardize, or even challenge, the principles of economic neoliberal modernization as the only practical basis for development policies.

The dramatic changes evoked here are an additional element of the weakening, or even destruction, of large segments of existing popular economies. These new realities, which seriously affect the popular economy in many countries of the South, reduce the space for resistance that their will to survive has opposed, for centuries, to the inexorable trend to entropy carried by the logic of accumulation. This book's authors are very well aware of the contradictions that run through the popular economy today. They allude to the phenomena of social disintegration and the new forms of violence exemplified by the development of aggressive ethnic movements and sectarian communities, and suggest that such economies could therefore take very different paths in the future. Many could lead to new cul-de-sacs, far removed from the kinds of sustainable development that could improve the living conditions of the populations concerned.

One has to recognize that involution and decay are affecting a fair number of traditional popular economies today. That regressive evolution is the product of the various impacts of the new modalities of operation by the 'sphere of accumulation'. The central and peripheral spaces of that sphere have nurtured the proliferation of multiple 'infamous informalities' already discussed. At the same time, multifaceted assaults by the neo-modernization ideology have also played a role in that debilitating process. The following lucid reflection of Polanyi is worth quoting in connection with that process: '...it is not economic exploitation, as it is often assumed, but the disintegration of the cultural environment of the victim which is the cause of degradation. The economic process can provide the vehicle of destruction and, almost invariably, the economic inferiority will make the weak give up, but the immediate cause of its loss is not mainly economic; it is rooted in the deadly wound inflicted on the institutions in which his social life is incarnated' (Polanyi,1983: 88).

The traditional autonomy of the popular economy is threatened today by both religious messianic entrepreneurs and by neoliberal entrepreneurs who propose or impose from the outside. The first group tries to take power through the manipulation of religion, while the second tries to capture the principles of the popular 'marketplace' to make it serve the interests of the 'market system'. The political manipulation of religion is parallel to the economic manipulation of 'trust'. The religious dimension has historically been one component of people's identity, among other socio-economic material and cultural practices, but not the sole reference to secure individual and collective life. 'Trust' has been at the root of the market embedded in social reciprocity (as in the African 'tontines'), and not only a tool to secure an individual's integration into the 'market system' (as in most microcredit projects).

The authors of this book also show, through several case studies, that the realities of today's popular economy cannot be reduced solely to pessimistic opinions. The few paragraphs that follow aim to show that, in fact, other realities lead to believe that the popular economies will retain a central place in the global development of the twenty-first century.

Today, it appears still more clearly than in the observations made during the period 1980–90, that the practices of groups of peasants and popular urban classes in thousands of villages and boroughs in Africa, Latin America, and Asia are aimed at securing and improving their daily living conditions. These informal groups can invent other ways of managing their space or even create new social links in areas abandoned by the weakened nation State. Local development is then based on 'horizontal networks' of popular sociability, and informal relations of cooperation have an important place in the ongoing reinvention of the social links that enabled participants to live in the village or in the urban area. These realities have reactivated a consideration of what some have called the 'organizational heritage': 'ethical and moral values, the consensus in work exchanges, transmission systems of knowledge, mutual assistance and defense reflexes, shared arts and religious beliefs, social rules ensuring the fundamental stability of society. Such an heritage has been constituted with a lot of effort and time' (Mignot-Lefèbvre and Lefevbre, 1995).

Popular economies maintain their vitality and display a practical capacity for renovation, even in countries that have been experiencing a strong expansion of the 'sphere of accumulation'. This reality which, at first glance, appears to be paradoxical, is visible in a number of Asian countries. In these countries, inclusion in income-earning opportunities offered by the 'sphere of accumulation', through more or less stable wage employment, allows monetary transfers to complement incomes generated in the popular economy without abandoning it as a means of security. The extent of possible transfers naturally depends on the economic level of the 'accumulation sphere', and the employment and wage conditions prevailing there. From that point of view, opportunities in China and several countries in South East Asia are very important.

And it is in Asia that we can see the emergence of a hybrid popular class—half peasants-half wage workers—with no reason to believe that this ongoing semi-proletarization could cause the disappearance of the peasantry in the foreseeable future. This is an important finding for the study of development: the trend toward the 'depeasantization' of the peasantry is no longer as inexorable as was predicted, even recently, by modernization theorists, liberals, or Marxists, who always maintained the view of a 'pure traditional' peasantry. The emergence of this new hybrid popular class, between the countryside and the city, challenges one of the postulates of the different variants of the modernization theory. For the popular classes, the vision of space—rural and urban—has never corresponded to the imagined space of modernization, which is sharply divided between the 'traditional countryside' and the 'modern city'. Hybrid popular players move easily between the 'accumulation sphere' and the 'popular marketplace'.

Chatterjee (2008) recently analysed these new realities in Asia, speaking of the popular economy—urban and rural—as being one of the actors of 'non-corporate capital', combining the profit logic and the logic of redistribution. In this sense, they differ from the dominant players of 'corporate capital' who are driven only by the profit-seeking motive. He insists on the ever more confrontational nature of the relationship between these two categories of actors, as much within urban and rural areas as in the urban–rural relationships. This approach reinforces the idea that in the diverse South, including in China today, the 'sphere of accumulation' has not been able to 'eat' all the society, and impose its rules and standards everywhere, despite the explosion of the accumulation dynamics over the past thirty years.

Another important trend, highlighted in the introduction to this book and in various chapters, is the vitality of the associative and redistributive aspects in present-day popular economies. Between the rural and urban popular economies' micro units, a logic of formal and informal networks is permanently reinventing itself with regulatory mechanisms based on a hybrid mix of competition and cooperation. Small rural and urban producers cooperate with other producers, who are also neighbours and share the many vagaries of daily life and survival in the same living environment. For example, urban women's workshops are often also initiatives of women's associations, which have other activities in common. The urban borough is a place to live and a mini-territory with multifaceted practices of informal cooperation, reciprocity, and solidarity. It has the capacity for reinvention of active forms of sociability, in changing contexts, in the wake of a centuries-old historical trajectory.

Countless experiments, revealed by the practices of local people in the past thirty years, rely on complementarities between different types of informal associative initiatives. They show that the creation of a cultural identity can be viable only where material security is assured. Basic needs (habitation, transport, food, education, health, the natural and symbolic environment) are necessary components for the creation of a territory that provides its inhabitants with an identity and viable social bonds.

In most micro-regions, urban neighbourhoods and villages in the South, there is a need for the consolidation of an associative economic sector. This is not the place to discuss the most appropriate definition of this reality, sometimes corresponding to what was historically called 'social economy' in the North and, more recently in Latin America, 'solidarity economy', while some organizations such as the United Nations Research Institute for Social Development (UNRISD) prefer to talk about 'social and solidarity economy'. Beyond the semantics, what matters is the reality of networks of cooperatives and mutual funds for health care, which consolidate informal associative initiatives in accordance with their spirit, and the nature of their practices. This may be achieved by expanding their scope of action and ensuring complementarities between their various activities, such as agricultural, non-agricultural and craft-making activities, commercial activities and services, savings and credit unions, mutual funds, and producers' and consumers' cooperatives (Peemans and Laurent, 1998).

A 'social economy' has by definition a strong component of economic and social democracy, since the assemblies of its members constitute its power base. Basically, what distinguishes an associative economy from a capitalist economy is not the existence of a market or non-market activity; rather it stems from the fact that associate members exercise power through their direct participation (whether as producer, member, or volunteer) with the objective of fulfilling the goals of the association, and not as holders of varying proportions of capital as shareholders. The social economy sector can participate quite actively in commercial activities and produce goods and services for the market. However, its institutional framework, by definition, can frame and control the functioning of the 'marketplace', and prevent it from being transformed into a mere instrument of a 'market system' type of accumulation for the benefit of a minority. An associative and cooperative economy is thus totally alien to the so-called 'third sector' of neoliberal inspiration.

That is why considerations of the role of an associative and cooperative economic sector must be viewed from a comprehensive perspective of development, including the links between production and exchange practices, cultural identity, and the construction of 'territories of life'. An important issue is the reaffirmation of the other dimensions of development corresponding to popular aspirations. The consolidation of an associative economy, rooted in the principles founded on 'historical governance' for the construction of a 'territory of life', can contribute to escaping the ongoing development impasse.

Therefore, another major development issue is the relationship between popular economy practices and 'local governance' in the South. It is important for local governance to rely on the legacy of 'historical governance' built over centuries by the people to ensure their security related to the 'construction of a territory'. In that sense, the principles of 'historical governance' are at total odds with the principles of 'neoliberal governance' imposed by Western donors over the past quarter of a century. Neoliberal governance is an obstacle to an articulation between the construction of 'territories for sustainable development' and a State capable of supporting and protecting that construction. Neo-liberal governance proposes limiting the role of the State to one of establishing a limited number of individual rights and guarantees: it is a democracy of procedure, or what Gathii calls 'market constitutionalism' (Gathii, 2000).

More than ever, the importance of articulating local governance with the reconstruction of the State is primordial. Given the threats facing their future, popular economies can no longer stay away from State politics as they have done in the past. A substantive democracy, in the Polanyian sense, is based on a collective and united will to expand the bundle of collective freedoms of citizens and their collective, economic, and social rights, instead of an individualistic definition of freedom and rights. The territorial dimension is important for rebuilding a 'substantive democracy' against the vagaries of a 'formal democracy', which has become, most of the time, an appendage of global market rhetoric and a smoke screen for global market failures. The importance given to local territories refers to the problem of constructing new balances of power between actors for whom the territory's resources have to help build a place to live, and the ones in the 'sphere of accumulation' for whom those resources have to be mobilized for the sake of profit.

In a large majority of countries in the South, the legitimization—or re-legitimization—of the State will depend on its ability to establish institutions that enable the largest possible number of civic associations and local communities to expand the sphere of their economic and social rights through the construction of an associative economy. This would provide a counterweight to the monopoly of the private sector in the 'sphere of accumulation', and help realize the full potential of the rationality of a reinvented Polanyian 'marketplace', in symbiosis with a redefinition of the socio-economic stakes of State sovereignty.

Such a perspective could change the course of 'real development' in the global world of the future, giving to the 'popular economies' a major role in the construction of a sustainable type of development. This is not to be confused with the discourses about global growth and global modernization. The merit and profound originality of the present book is that it sets various topics about the so called 'informal sector' in that broad perspective. It is a perspective that takes account of all the complexities of the 'popular economies' of today, showing, among other aspects, the manifold initiatives of diverse local communities, and the challenges they have to face, not only to survive, but also to build a better future. In that sense this book is not only an important scientific contribution to the knowledge of development realities, it also opens up new theoretical avenues to support meaningful strategies of sustainable development with a popular base involving local actors.

References

Amin, S. (2012). 'Les révolutions arabes, un an après'. Bruxelles, EPO: Etudes Marxistes, 98. Available online at <http://pambazuka.org/en/category/features/80745> (accessed 15 June 2013).

Anderson, L. E. (1994). *The Political Ecology of the Modern Peasant: Calculation and Community.* Baltimore, MD: Johns Hopkins University Press.

Basu, A. (1995). *The Challenge of Local Feminisms: Women's Movements in Global Perspective.* Boulder, CO, Westview Press.

Beck, M. and S. Hüser (2012). *Political Change in the Middle East: An Attempt to Analyze the 'Arab Spring'.* GIGA Working Paper No. 203. Institute of Middle East Studies, German Institute of Global and Area Studies, Hamburg.

Bisilliat, J. and C. Verschuur (2000). Le genre: Un outil nécessaire. Introduction à une problématique. Les Cahiers Genre et Développement, No. 1. Paris and Geneva : L'Harmattan.

Bohannan, P. and G. Dalton (1965). *Markets in Africa.* New York. Anchor Books.

Boserup, E. (1970). *La Femme Face au Développement Economique.* Coll. Sociologie d'aujourd'hui. Paris: Presses Universitaires de France.

Braudel, F. (1985). *La Dynamique du Capitalisme.* Paris: Arthaud.

Brokensha, D., M. Warren, and O. Werner (eds.) (1980). *Indigenous Knowledge Systems and Development.* Washington, DC: University Press of America.

Chatterjee, P. (2008). 'Peasant Cultures of the Twenty-First Century'. *Inter-Asia Cultural Studies,* 9(1): 116–26.

De Villers, G. (ed.) (1992). 'Economie populaire et phénomènes informels au Zaïre et en Afrique'. Les Cahiers du CEDAF, 3-4. Paris: L'Harmattan.

Gathii, J. T. (2000). 'Representations of Africa in Good Governance Discourse: Policing and Containing Dissidence to Neo-Liberalism'. *Third World Legal Studies,* 1998–99, Postcolonialism, Globalization and Law. International,Third World Legal Studies Association: 65–108.

Georgescu-Roegen, N. (1971). *The Entropy Law and the Economic Process.* Cambridge MA: Harvard University Press.

Guha, R. and G. C. Spivak (1988). *Selected Subaltern Studies.* Oxford: Oxford University Press.

Harvey, D. (2003). *The New Imperialism.* Oxford: Oxford University Press.

Hettne, B. (1990). *Development Theory and the Three Worlds.* Harlow: Longman Scientific and Technical.

Kearney, M. (1996). *Reconceptualizing the Peasantry: Anthropology in Global Perspective.* Boulder, CO: Westview Press.

Mignot-Lefebvre, Y. and M. Lefebvre (1995). *Les Patrimoines du Futur: Les Sociétés aux Prises avec la Mondialisation.* Paris: L'Harmattan.

Nicaso, A. and L. Lamothe (2006). *Angels, Mobsters and Narco-Terrorists: The Rising Menace of Global Criminal Empires.* Toronto: John Wiley and Sons.

Olivier de Sardan, J. P. (1995). *Anthropologie et Développement.* Paris: Karthala.

Peemans, J. P. H. and P. J. Laurent (1998). Les enjeux d'une reconnaissance de la nature des pratiques d'économie sociale en Afrique. Louvain-la-Neuve: Institut d'Etudes du Développement.

Petras, J. and H. Veltmeyer (2011). *Social Movements in Latin America, Neoliberalism and Popular Resistance*. Basingstoke: Palgrave-Macmillan,.

Polanyi, K. (1983). *La Grande Transformation*. Paris: Gallimard.

Richards, P. (1985). *Indigenous Agricultural Revolution: Ecology and Food Production in West Africa*. London: Hutchinson.

Salmen, L. (1992). *Reducing Poverty: An Institutional Perspective. Poverty and Social Policy Series*, 23(1). Washington, DC: World Bank.

Scott, J. C. (1990). *Domination and the Arts of Resistance: Hidden Transcripts*. New Haven, CT: Yale University Press.

UNODOC (2012). *World Drug Report 2012*,New York: United Nations.

Visvanathian, N., L. Duggan, N. Wiegersma, and L. Nisonoff (eds.) (1997). *The Women, Gender and Development Reader*. London: Zed Books.

Walker, C. (2011). 'American Banks 'High' on Drug Money: How a Whistleblower Blew the Lid off Wachovia-Drug Cartel Money Laundering Scheme'. Alternet.org, 10 June; available at <http://www.encod.org/info/AMERICAN-BANKS-HIGH-ON-DRUG-MONEY.html> (accessed 22 May 2013).

Index

Adaptability 14
Africa v, 4n1, 10, 11, 16, 80, 84–6, 135, 147, 150n3, 164, 168, 169, 171–3, 191, 199, 238, 239, 276–9, 285, 286
Agricultural employment 194, 195
Alternative(s) 6, 14, 29, 32, 34, 40, 64, 68, 70, 72n8, 124, 127, 168, 171, 172, 229, 243, 246, 275, 276, 279
Argentina 12, 16, 48, 64–6, 66n4, 71, 71n6, 72n8, 99, 100, 100n2, 101–3, 108, 259
Asia v, 10, 16, 84, 85, 172, 276–8, 286, 287
Assistance 51, 52, 84, 86, 93, 102–4, 286
Association(s) 12, 14, 17, 29n4, 54, 57, 58, 59, 73, 76, 85, 86, 88, 107, 123, 124, 125, 128, 133, 140n13, 144, 151, 170, 173, 174, 217, 218, 220, 225, 226, 228, 229, 230, 244, 260n3, 263, 287, 288, 289
Aymara 54, 57

Bolivia 7, 12, 16, 47–54, 54n7, 58, 59, 59n13, 60
Bosnia Herzegovina 7
Bourdieu P. 107, 134, 139, 139n9
Braudel F. 3, 93, 278–281
Brazil 12, 16, 17, 25, 31–4, 34n9, 35, 36, 38, 41, 43, 115–17, 117n1, 118–24, 124n5, 125–9
Buenos Aires 16, 65, 66, 100n2, 105n12
Burkina Faso 17, 147, 149

Capabilities 14, 15, 35, 73, 218, 225, 227, 230
Capital accumulation 5, 6, 10, 25, 64, 74, 127, 275, 278, 279
Capitalism 34, 51, 257, 278, 279
Capitalist enterprise 4n1, 5, 64, 240
Castells, M. 13, 168, 256, 257
Centrality 5, 64
Chen M. 13, 47, 48, 50, 167, 232
Childcare 34, 224
Church(es) 32, 54
Citizenship v, 28, 29, 35, 40, 51
Colombia 48
Community development 16, 64, 65, 67, 129
Community development banks (or community banks) 17, 67, 115, 116, 118, 120, 121, 123, 124, 126
Complementarity 5, 57, 90–2, 94
Conjunto Palmeiras 125
Contract(s) 3, 8, 26, 27, 37, 56, 69, 75n9, 87, 104n8, 107, 139, 148, 168, 170, 172, 176, 184, 221, 241, 245
Cooperative(s) 16, 25, 30–44, 53, 54, 57, 59, 64–76, 87, 93, 117, 151, 153, 154n7, 155, 156, 158, 159, 161, 162, 163, 163n11, 164, 173, 181, 185, 236, 240, 241, 244–7, 288
Coping (strategies) 6, 16, 70, 78–82, 84, 87, 90, 93
Coraggio J. L. 12, 29, 32, 53n4, 64, 66, 74
Costa Rica 52
Crisis v, vi, 7, 10, 11, 14, 32, 51, 66, 68, 74, 94, 108, 133, 144–5, 219, 259, 262, 281

Decent work 2, 9n6, 17, 29, 40, 49, 53, 65, 71n5, 214–17, 224, 225, 231, 232
Democracy 12, 29, 41, 43, 44, 85, 121, 283, 288, 289
Democratic Republic of the Congo 16, 78, 80
Dependence 12, 58, 61, 79, 102n5, 170, 171, 275
De Soto H. 167, 171, 254, 257, 258, 269
Domination 57, 58, 196, 278, 279
Dominican Republic 48

Economic growth 2, 5, 13, 14, 18, 25, 172, 219, 251, 255, 259, 265, 266, 270, 275
Economic integration (Karl Polanyi) 4, 5, 13, 26, 30, 48, 53, 55, 56, 58, 60, 79, 99, 107
Ecuador 12, 17, 214, 222–4, 229
Education 17, 34, 35, 36, 41, 50, 56, 59, 67, 73, 80–2, 104, 125, 128, 132, 139, 150, 157, 158, 177, 193–8, 203, 204, 207, 211, 219, 223, 225, 227, 235, 251, 287
El Alto (El Alto) 16, 48, 54, 55–7, 55n8, 59, 59n12, 60
Embeddedness 3, 7, 8, 9, 28, 29, 30, 31, 37, 37n11, 40, 84, 88–90, 92, 94, 107, 108, 110, 134, 239, 244, 262, 279, 285

Entitlements vi, 35, 36, 40, 191, 217, 218
Entrepreneurship 50, 126, 167, 171, 255, 264, 266, 271, 274
Environment (natural) vi, 16, 26, 28, 29, 31, 36, 37, 38, 40, 41, 43, 44, 73, 238, 244, 278, 281
Ethnicity 11, 150, 157, 168, 170
Exploitation vi, 57, 61, 91, 285
Eymard-Duvernay F. 26, 27

Fafchamps M. 78, 94, 169, 172
Fair trade 29, 54, 57, 58
Family network 54, 56, 84, 178
Family workers 10, 48, 49, 192, 194, 203, 204, 207
Farming 55, 82, 139, 142, 143, 144
Food 34, 52, 55, 56, 60, 67, 81, 102, 104–6, 110, 150, 196, 198, 199, 222, 228, 247, 250, 264, 265, 281, 287
Formalization 1, 3, 14, 17, 32, 53, 65, 126, 167, 169, 211, 214–16, 218–32, 245, 258, 269, 270, 275
Foundation(s) 58, 124, 135, 170
Fourier C. 31
Fraser N. 44

Gender vi, 17, 28, 35, 56, 57, 109n16, 150, 157, 158, 168, 177, 181, 182, 184, 197–9, 205, 211, 231, 274, 277
Ghana 17, 191–9, 201n2, 202, 204, 209–11
Global economy 10, 13
Globalization v, 13, 232, 280, 282
Governance (of organizations) 27, 28, 29, 33, 43, 66, 87, 133, 168, 169, 279, 280, 288, 289
Granovetter M. 3, 27, 37, 197
Guha-Khasnobis B. 3, 167, 168

Harriss-White B. 13, 172
Hart K. 3, 4, 50, 168, 256, 269
Health 47, 51, 52, 61, 67, 71, 71n6, 72, 73, 76, 80, 81, 86, 87, 91, 92, 102, 103, 109, 132, 140, 193, 217, 218, 225, 226, 227, 235, 247, 264, 281, 287, 288
Household 4, 16, 17, 30, 37n11, 52, 57, 59, 78–83, 87, 89, 90, 93, 94, 99, 100, 102–12, 128, 132–4, 136, 138–40, 142–5, 150, 150n3, 151, 172–4, 179, 191, 191n1, 192–205, 207–11, 215, 217, 223, 228, 237, 238, 249, 251, 275, 277
Householding v, 4, 4n1, 5, 6, 7, 8, 12, 16, 26, 28, 30, 37, 37n11, 38, 41, 42, 53, 55, 56, 60, 61, 64, 75, 76, 79, 87, 88, 94, 100, 107
Hugon P. 3
Identity 11, 14, 28, 34, 75, 89, 232, 274, 279, 285, 287, 288
ILO (International Labour Organization) 9, 9n6, 10, 11, 47, 49, 49n1, 50, 51, 65, 71n5, 168, 191, 214–17, 232, 254
Income (or earnings) level 6, 10, 17, 32, 34, 37n11, 39, 43, 47, 50, 52, 59, 60, 66, 67, 71n7, 74, 75, 78, 82, 83, 99, 100, 102–4, 104n7, 106, 107, 111, 112, 115–18, 121, 122, 126–8, 140, 148–50, 157, 158, 160, 161, 164, 168, 173, 175, 178, 179n9, 181, 185, 191–211, 215–19, 222, 225–8, 230, 277
Income generation or income-generating activities 3, 11, 12, 32, 35, 56, 57, 65, 81, 83, 86, 88, 90, 102, 105, 108, 109, 116, 141, 191, 217, 208, 224, 229, 236, 248, 256
India 7, 84, 138n3, 172, 217, 277, 278
Inequality 28, 54, 101, 197, 198, 211, 258, 280, 281
Informal employment 9–11, 101, 102, 111, 191, 191n1, 192–4, 198, 199, 210, 258
Informalization 10, 13, 18, 254–9, 264, 265, 269, 270, 271
Initial or start-up capital 173, 177, 179, 180, 184, 196, 199
Innovation (social) 14, 65, 70, 118, 124, 125, 172
Institutionalization 36, 44, 73, 277
Investment 13, 52n3, 120, 123, 132, 134, 135, 143, 145, 173, 174, 177–9, 179n10, 180, 184, 198, 219, 236–40, 245, 251, 282

Kenya 17, 79, 138n3, 167, 168, 172, 173, 173n2, 174–6, 179n9, 181, 181n13, 183n16, 185
Kinship 84, 88, 93, 99, 107, 109, 110, 168, 205

Labour market(s) 10, 48, 49, 52, 57, 60, 101, 101n4, 107, 112, 115, 145, 192, 193, 197, 198, 200, 205, 211, 217, 218, 223, 224, 232, 259, 260
Latin America v, 10–12, 16, 32, 48, 51, 52, 53, 53n4, 55n8, 57n9, 72n8, 85, 103, 118, 124n5, 258, 276–8, 282, 284, 286, 288
Laville J.-L. 4, 26, 30, 32, 36, 64, 66, 74
Livelihood security v, 2, 3, 4, 5, 6, 7, 8, 9, 10, 11, 13, 15, 16, 56, 65, 224, 228
Local development 16, 25, 27, 28, 33, 36, 40, 43, 44, 279, 286

Market v, 2–4, 5, 7–10, 12, 14, 17, 26–8, 30, 33, 37, 37n11, 38, 39–43, 44, 52, 54n6, 56–8, 60, 61, 64, 67, 69, 70, 72, 73, 75, 76, 78, 79, 80, 88, 91–4, 100, 102, 107, 112, 120–2, 125, 127–9, 133, 142–5, 147–55, 163, 164, 168, 169, 171–3, 173n2, 175,

175n4, 176, 176n6, 177–9, 182–4, 197, 198, 200, 205, 215, 218, 222, 225, 229, 231, 237, 238, 240, 247, 255, 256, 260, 262–4, 266, 266n13, 267–9, 275, 278–81, 286, 288, 289
Marketplace 93, 275–8, 285, 287–9
Marx K. 55, 257n2, 286
Micro and small enterprises 3, 11, 12, 17, 48, 49, 50, 116, 126, 167, 175, 258, 267, 268
Microcredit 7, 17, 67, 104n9, 108, 109, 111, 115–23, 126–9, 132–5, 138, 140, 141, 143–5, 151, 158, 274, 286
Micro-entrepreneur(s) 17, 118, 147, 149–56, 158–65, 274
Microfinance 6, 7, 16, 17, 54n7, 81, 86, 87, 104, 104n10, 115, 116, 118–23, 132, 133, 138, 141, 145, 147, 151, 154, 154n7, 155, 156, 159, 161, 163, 164, 173, 175, 182, 182n15, 184, 185
Migrants 31, 54, 59, 140n14, 171, 204, 206, 208, 246
Migration 11, 54, 57, 59, 142, 144, 193, 229
Modernization 1, 2, 3, 4, 6, 7, 11, 14, 215, 220, 230, 274–81, 283, 285–7, 289
Money 11, 31, 68, 72, 85, 86, 90, 91, 100, 102, 103, 106, 109, 109n16, 110, 117, 132, 134, 139, 148, 152, 161n10, 178, 179, 193, 199, 228, 248
Money collectors 151
Money lender(s) 84, 93, 196
Morduch J. 78, 84, 147
Morocco 7, 17, 132–5, 138–40, 140n13
Multiscalar policies 15
Mutual funds 288

Nairobi 17, 167, 168, 175, 179n9, 183
Neo-institutionalism 8, 26
NGOs 30, 31, 32, 33, 35, 37n11, 38, 43, 44, 58, 67, 70n1, 90–2, 94, 104, 122, 124, 129, 196, 283
Nicaragua 7
Non monetary resources or economy 8, 27, 28, 30, 37, 37n11, 38, 43
North D. 3, 169, 170

Obligation (social) 5, 6, 53, 83, 85, 88, 89, 91, 94, 110, 199, 238
Ouagadougou 17, 147, 149, 152, 158n9, 164
Outsourcing v, 13
Own account worker(s) 10, 48, 49, 194, 195

Peasants 2, 11, 93, 240, 277, 278, 280, 286, 287
Pensions 51, 61, 71, 227, 228
Petty commodity production or trade 10, 13, 56, 57, 60, 199, 238, 282
Piecework 13, 241
Plural economy 4, 8, 9, 16, 25–7, 43–4, 64, 65, 74
Polanyi K. v, 4, 4n2, 5, 7–9, 12, 13, 16, 23, 25–7, 30, 31, 31n6, 33, 43, 48, 53, 54, 60, 64, 66, 74, 79, 80, 87–91, 93, 94, 99, 107, 122, 275–80, 285, 289
Political economy vi, 7, 8, 9, 12, 280, 281
Popular economy v, 10–12, 14, 16, 47, 48, 53, 54, 54n6, 56, 57, 60, 61, 279, 280, 283–8
Populism 12, 31
Portes A. 13, 64, 168, 171, 176, 184, 198, 216, 254, 256, 257, 257n2, 258, 259, 270
Poverty reduction 1, 2, 7, 14, 36, 51, 115, 116, 119, 121, 236, 281
Profit 201
Proletariat 11, 39, 41
Protection 5, 6, 13, 16, 18, 47, 48, 51–5, 58, 60, 61, 72, 73, 76, 78, 79, 99, 100, 102, 103, 107–9, 111, 112, 184, 191n1, 217, 218, 238, 244, 260, 280
Public policies vi, 1, 2, 6, 7, 10, 12–15, 17, 32, 36, 43, 48, 49, 51–4, 58, 60, 61, 65, 67, 72n8, 74, 91, 115–29, 148n1, 172, 231, 232, 236, 237, 259, 260, 266, 266n13, 268, 276, 277, 279, 283, 285

Quito 17, 214, 215, 219–24, 227–9, 231, 232

Rationality 27, 75, 275, 289
Reciprocity v, 4, 5, 6, 7, 8, 10, 11, 12, 16, 26, 28, 30, 31, 31n6, 37, 37n11, 38, 39, 41, 42, 53, 54, 56, 58, 60, 61, 64, 75, 76, 79, 80, 88–94, 99, 107, 275–7, 280, 283–5, 287
Recovered enterprise(s) 16, 65, 66, 66n4, 72, 73, 76
Redistribution v, 4, 5, 6, 7, 8, 11, 26, 28, 30, 31, 31n6, 37, 38, 39, 41, 42, 47, 51–3, 56, 58, 60, 61, 64, 75, 76, 79, 80, 91, 92, 94, 100, 107, 275, 276, 280, 283, 284, 287
Resilience v, 10, 11, 164, 279
Resistance 14, 68, 139, 262, 277–9, 283–5, 291
Rights 3, 15, 35, 51, 68, 73, 126, 216, 239, 259, 289
Rio de Janeiro (State of) 16, 25, 31, 33, 44, 126
Risk management 15, 75, 79, 80, 82, 87, 138
Risk minimization (or reduction or mitigation) 2, 7, 172
Risk pooling (or sharing) 82, 84, 87, 92, 198
Rosario (Argentina) 16, 99, 100, 100n2, 101–4, 106, 110–12
Rwanda 17, 80, 235–9, 242, 245, 247–52

Savings and credit (associations, cooperatives or unions) 85–7, 92, 107, 140n13, 151, 170, 173, 288
Segmentation (of labour markets) 48, 231

Self-employment 10, 11, 17, 33, 50, 68, 71, 102, 120, 143, 173, 191–8, 200–4, 206, 207, 209–11, 214, 216–18
Self-managed workers 16, 64, 65, 71, 73, 76
Self-management 12, 34, 36, 40, 42, 43, 58, 76
SENAES (Brazilian State Secretariat for Solidarity Economics) 125, 126, 129
Singer P. 12, 53n4
Social insurance or security 3, 14, 16, 50, 51, 57n10, 65, 71, 71n5, 72, 75, 76, 85, 101, 170, 216, 218, 225, 226, 245, 259, 264, 284
Social justice 44, 56
Social movement 32, 34, 35, 36, 39, 40, 72n8
Social networks 3, 17, 44, 54, 90, 167, 168, 170–3, 183, 184, 197, 198, 207, 277
Social protection 2, 9, 14, 16, 32, 47–53, 60, 61, 64, 70, 71, 76, 78, 87, 99, 100, 100n3, 102, 102n6, 103, 111, 191, 216, 259
Social reproduction 9, 12, 29, 32, 55, 140, 275, 279
Social ties or bonds v, 2, 10, 30, 31, 37n11, 79, 128, 161, 164, 168, 170, 171, 176, 287
Solidarity v, 6, 9, 11, 12, 13, 14, 16, 17, 30, 31, 32, 34, 37, 47, 53–61, 72, 75, 84, 85, 87–90, 99, 100, 102, 103, 107, 109–12, 115, 120, 122, 123, 135, 277, 279, 281, 287
Solidarity economics 123–6, 128
Solidarity economy 12, 33, 35, 39, 40, 54, 54n7, 57–9, 59n13, 60, 66, 73n8, 115, 124n8, 288
Solidarity finance 17, 121–3, 125–7, 129
South Africa 4n1, 172
South Kivu 16, 78–82, 85n5, 86, 87, 91, 93
Stiglitz J. 132, 147, 148
Street vendors 59, 106, 214–30
Structural adjustment 10, 32, 51, 52, 277, 283
Substantive economy 2, 4, 5, 16, 25, 27, 30, 31, 37, 43, 44, 64–6, 74–6, 79, 277
Surplus (economic) 7, 28–30, 69, 70, 75, 207, 247, 256
Sustainability 14, 28, 29, 36, 40, 44, 66, 68, 76, 120, 123, 143, 237, 278, 279, 281, 285, 289
Symmetry 31, 64, 90–2, 94

Taxes 3, 47, 49, 50, 71, 71n6, 72, 103, 167, 176, 191, 227, 236, 238, 245, 256, 260, 260n4, 261, 261n5, 261n6, 262, 264, 282
Technology 7, 26, 125, 173n2
Territory 26, 44, 67, 123, 283, 287–9
Théret B. 99n1, 102n6, 111
Trust 29, 55, 67, 86, 89, 94, 101, 104, 106, 120, 122, 124, 177, 178, 279, 285
Turkey 18, 254–6, 259–64, 264n10, 265, 265n12, 266–70

Unions of workers 12, 30, 39, 54, 73n8, 76, 123, 217, 258, 259, 261, 261n7
Universities 39, 69, 197
Urban plots 55, 60

Venezuela 12
Violence 1, 14, 33–5, 226, 282–5
Vulnerability v, 9n6, 13, 14, 15, 16, 17, 44, 47–51, 53, 54, 56, 58, 60, 61, 65, 70, 71, 78, 91–3, 99, 103, 108, 111, 123, 126, 132, 142, 144, 215–17, 225, 229, 230, 231, 232, 247

Wage employment 10, 194, 286
War 1, 235, 239, 249, 274
Welfare regime 16, 47, 51, 52, 53
Williamson O. 3
Working conditions 2, 28, 29, 40, 50, 126, 214–16, 218, 230, 232